"This expanded and compelling edition of *Islamophobia and the Politics of Empire* is one of the most important books in the war on terror era. It is comprehensive, informative, and well researched, and written in clear and accessible language. This brilliant author offers an accurate understanding of the 'matrix of anti-racism,' which is sorely needed to push back against structural racism ... This remarkable book packs a wealth of information and has a sharp and perceptive analysis. Its straightforward style of writing makes it mandatory reading for a global audience."

Peter Hervik, Aalborg University, author of
The Annoying Difference

"Twenty years after 9/11, Kumar sheds new light on empire, anti-Muslim racism, and the toll of the war on terror, a war that has permeated every aspect of life from securitization to surveillance technologies to our understandings of terrorism ... The analysis of how Muslims have been racialized in different ways in the context of empire from the early modern era to the present is a major contribution to critical race studies. This book is comprehensive, illuminating, and inspiring—a tour de force!"

Jasbir K. Puar, Rutgers University,
author of *Terrorist Assemblages*

"A very impressive book that traces the historical legacy of Islamophobia and anti-Muslim racism to the politics of European and American empires in the so-called Muslim world. Kumar insightfully argues that Muslims had been racialized long before Islamophobia grew in the US ... a must-read for anybody interested in understanding the persistence of Islamophobia in the West."

Amaney A. Jamal, Princeton University,
author of *Of Empires and Citizens*

"This important and prescient book well deserves a second edition. It has gotten so much more than a postscript or update as Kumar writes in new and extended ways about US militarism and imperial thinking and action around Islam and the Middle East. She shows how they continue to flourish through the putative end of the US war in Afghanistan and the end of the Trump presidency."

Catherine Lutz, Brown University,
author of *Homefront*

"Kumar interrogates the relationship between Islamophobia, colonialism, and imperialism in this timely and important new edition. Using a multifocal approach to race and racism, Kumar deconstructs the reduction of Islamophobia to religious intolerance and offers a critical perspective on the multiple intersecting discourses and practices of anti-Muslim racism. A must-read for both academics and non-academics, the book also sheds light on the media-state-empire nexus in the operation of current racial regimes."

Minoo Moallem, University of California, Berkeley, author of *Between Warrior Brother and Veiled Sister*

"Islamophobia is the new anti-Semitism of our time and the Muslim has now replaced the Jew in the racialized imagination of the Euro-American West. Deepa Kumar, an erudite scholar-activist, traces the rise of Islamophobia back to its roots in earliest days of Europe's colonization and racialization of the world ... A superb, necessary book, written with careful research, wisdom, and passion."

Aijaz Ahmed, University of California, Irvine, author of *In Theory*

"Kumar has written a conceptually sophisticated and historically rich book. This second edition is strengthened by her deeper analysis of the matrix of anti-Muslim racism, the political economy of empire, and of imperialist feminism. A must-read for all who want to understand Islamophobia and anti-Muslim racism."

Fawaz A. Gerges, London School of Economics, author of *The Hundred Years' War for Control of the Middle East*

"Kumar's clear-eyed, methodical mapping of what she names the matrix of anti-Muslim racism spans countries and centuries but remains laser-focused on a set of specific imperial forces that shape the racialization of Muslims. The expanded edition more fully fleshes out the continuities and contradictions of Western discourses about Islam and Muslim Others. It also offers an updated, highly readable synthesis of academic debates within a growing number of fields devoted to the critical study of Islamophobia. A must-read!"

Zareena Grewal, Yale University, author of *Islam Is a Foreign Country*

"Kumar provides a complex and comprehensive analysis of how the imperialist and Orientalist ideologies of Western nations have underpinned actions and attitudes towards Muslims and Muslim-majority countries, in the interests of empire-building, from the colonial to contemporary period. Updated to incorporate the Trump administration, this book is an urgent addition to scholarship seeking to debunk a simplistic 'clash of civilizations' narrative and expose the conditions and infrastructure that supports Islamophobic policies such as the 'war on terror'. Kumar writes with her characteristic force and passion, providing substantial evidence to support her arguments while remaining open to contradictions that make for a nuanced approach. A must for scholars of Islamic studies, social and political science, international relations, and related fields."

Elizabeth Poole, Keele University,
author of *Reporting Islam*

"Deepa Kumar's important book, *Islamophobia and the Politics of Empire*, is intellectually challenging, rich in detail, and supremely accessible. Moving deftly from narrative to fact, Kumar reveals the whole spectrum of anti-Muslim racism in the context of imperial power politics, especially in America. The second edition is a major revision of the 2012 classic, covering more recent events and substantial new developments in scholarship."

Ivan Kalmar, University of Toronto,
author of *Early Orientalism*

"This well-researched book offers an original, comprehensive, and clear analysis of how the race concept has been applied to Muslims. Ambitious in scope, it goes from the early modern era to the war on terror in order to situate anti-Muslim racism within the context of empire … It is an important contribution to critical race studies, a motley field that could engage more with anti-Muslim racism given its ubiquitous presence in the war on terror era. Whether you are a specialist, a novice, or a lay reader, you will come away having learned something valuable."

Arun Kundnani, author of
The Muslims Are Coming

"A foundational study of the imperial dimensions of the global war on terror that convincingly demonstrates how Islamophobia became a lexicon of modern state racism."

Nikhil Pal Singh, New York University, author of
Race and America's Long War

"Ranging across history, cultural analysis, and global politics, Deepa Kumar uncovers the deep roots of anti-Muslim racism. The result is a hugely illuminating reading of race and empire after 9/11. *Islamophobia and the Politics of Empire* is a vital resource for all anti-racist scholars and activists."

David McNally, University of Houston,
author of Blood and Money

"Of the ideologies that inspired colonialism and imperialism in history, anti-Muslim racism did the most in recent times in fulfilling a dual function: justifying post–Cold War imperialist wars abroad and scapegoating migrant communities to deflect social anger at home. In this impassioned book, Deepa Kumar thoroughly examines the genealogy of Islamophobia, its Orientalist antecedents, and its present-day functions – for the benefit of students as well as ant-iracist activists."

Gilbert Achcar, SOAS, author of Marxism,
Orientalism, Cosmopolitanism

"If you find yourself trying to understand not just what twenty years of fighting a 'war on terror' has wrought but also why it even exists in the first place, Deepa Kumar's second edition of *Islamophobia and the Politics of Empire* is an excellent place to start. This is a bold and ambitious inquiry into the long history and enduring present of anti-Muslim racism in our world."

Moustafa Bayoumi, Brooklyn College, CUNY,
author of This Muslim American Life

"Deepa Kumar's newly revised text is a handbook for the twenty-first century. It demonstrates that to fight and win against racism, we have to fight and win against imperial war and violence. It shows us that the global war on terror weaponized anti-Muslim racism as an everyday and banal act around the world, and that to change this we have nothing less to do than change the world itself."

Junaid Rana, University of Illinois at Urbana-Champaign,
author of Terrifying Muslims

Islamophobia and the Politics of Empire

Twenty Years after 9/11

Deepa Kumar

SECOND EDITION

With a Foreword by Nadine Naber

VERSO

London • New York

This revised second edition first published by Verso 2021
First edition published by Haymarket Books 2012
© Deepa Kumar 2012, 2021
Foreword © Nadine Naber 2021

1 3 5 7 9 10 8 6 4 2

Verso
UK: 6 Meard Street, London W1F 0EG
US: 20 Jay Street, Suite 1010, Brooklyn, NY 11201
versobooks.com

Verso is the imprint of New Left Books

ISBN-13: 978-1-78873-721-0
ISBN-13: 978-1-78873-723-4 (US EBK)
ISBN-13: 978-1-78873-722-7 (UK EBK)

British Library Cataloguing in Publication Data
A catalogue record for this book is available from the British Library

Library of Congress Cataloging-in-Publication Data

Names: Kumar, Deepa, 1968– author.
Title: Islamophobia and the politics of empire : twenty years after 9/11 / Deepa Kumar.
Description: Second edition. | Brooklyn : Verso Books, 2022. | "This revised second edition first
    published by Verso 2021 First edition published by Haymarket Books 2012, Deepa Kumar
    2012, 2021." | Includes bibliographical references and index. | Summary: "In this incisive
    account, award-winning scholar and activist Deepa Kumar traces the history of anti-Muslim
    racism from the era of mercantile imperialism to the war on terror"— Provided by publisher.
Identifiers: LCCN 2021020066 (print) | LCCN 2021020067 (ebook) | ISBN 9781788737210 |
    ISBN 9781788737234 (US ebk) | ISBN 9781788737227 (US ebk)
Subjects: LCSH: Islam—Public opinion. | Muslims—Public opinion. | Islamophobia. |
    War on Terrorism, 2001–2009. | Islam in mass media.
Classification: LCC BP52 .I8543 2022 (print) | LCC BP52 (ebook) | DDC 305.6/97—dc23
LC record available at https://lccn.loc.gov/2021020066
LC ebook record available at https://lccn.loc.gov/2021020067

Typeset in Minion by Biblichor Ltd, Edinburgh
Printed and bound by CPI Group (UK) Ltd, Croydon, CR0 4YY

Contents

Foreword

As I write, liberals and progressives across the world are celebrating the end of the Trump presidency. However, those of us concerned about the many forms of US-led violence across the globe that have been justified under the guise of the war on terror have likely come to the conclusion that not much is about to change. In November 2020, the authoritarian Egyptian regime placed nearly thirty people on a terrorism watch list. This list includes renowned pro-democracy activist Alaa Abdelfattah, who was a leading activist in the Arab Spring revolution for bread, dignity, and social justice. Perhaps the strategy here is to ensure that even if President Joe Biden or any international body pressures the Egyptian regime to release detained human rights activists, Abdelfattah and others who have also been labeled "terrorists" will never see justice.

The case of Abdelfattah reveals the significance of the discourse of the "Muslim terrorist." In Egypt, this discourse, produced and promoted by US Democrats and Republicans alike, serves as a cover for continuing the punishment, containment, and isolation of anyone who stands in the way of US empire. Thus, every US administration since 1979 (when Egypt and Israel signed the Camp David Accords) has provided Egypt with military, political, and economic support to repress Egyptian people while sustaining Egypt's status as a partner in advancing US agendas, including Israeli settler colonialism in the region. The United States frames its relationship with Egyptian dictators as an alliance in the "war on terrorism," a stance that helps rationalize policies such as extraordinary rendition, which outsource the torture as well as the execution of Muslims to places with more lenient torture laws than the United States. At the same time, the United States uses Egypt and other countries as evidence of the need to intervene to "promote democracy."

These contradictions—US alliances with nondemocratic regimes coexisting with the professed goal of promoting democracy—are also apparent in many US leaders' stances on Israel on the one hand and ending Islamophobia on the other. In early December 2020, UNICEF announced that the Israel Defense Forces killed one Palestinian child and injured four others over a two-week period by shooting them in the chest, eye, and head and that at least 232 children had been injured between January and September 2020.[1] Around the same time, Palestinians, Arabs, and US allies around the world heard Kamala Harris's campaign commitment to unconditionally support Israel, an anti-Arab/anti-Muslim settler colonialist regime, a position that contradicts her own stated condemnation of anti-Muslim domestic policies such as the Muslim ban as racist and discriminatory. While professing to condemn anti-Muslim racism, many Democrats, including Biden and Harris, have supported the Department of Homeland Security's Countering Violent Extremism program, which funds local community institutions to turn their members into spies. Community members are trained to rely upon racial profiling to report anyone perceived to be a practicing Muslim as a potential terrorist.[2]

Indeed, Harris's close alliance with the US military and Biden's capitulation to those who support the silencing, killing, and surveillance of Muslims—from Republican Michael Bloomberg who oversaw New York's racist surveillance of Muslim communities to elected officials who smear critics of Israel as anti-Semitic[3]—remind us that if we really want to end anti-Muslim racism, we need to be willing to dismantle US-led militarism, warmongering, and empire building. We should therefore be wary of empty rhetoric about ending stereotypes and individual acts of anti-Muslim hatred such as hate crimes and bigotry in the discourse on "tolerance, inclusion, and diversity," which does nothing to address structural racism.

This is why *Islamophobia and the Politics of Empire* is more urgent than ever. Kumar brilliantly analyzes the root causes of anti-Muslim racism, situating its many formations within the multiple, contradictory histories and material realities out of which it emerges, most importantly empire. Mapping what Kumar calls the "matrix of anti-Muslim racism," this book helps readers recognize how anti-Muslim racism has been fostered through European histories from the religiously inflected proto-racism in early modern imperial Spain, nineteenth- and twentieth-century scientific racism at the high point of European colonialism, to the war on terror. Readers will gain an understanding of how the logics of anti-Muslim racism were transferred from European to US empire and the complex ways in which anti-Muslim racism in the United States has evolved and been used.

Islamophobia and the Politics of Empire overcomes ongoing problems in the study of anti-Muslim racism including (a) the lopsided focus on domestic US politics that leaves US militarism and the global scope of US empire off the hook; (b) the generalized focus on a universal "Muslim" that obscures the diverse Muslim and non-Muslim communities that have been roped into the discourse of Islamophobia, including Arab Christians and Sikhs; and (c) the separation of the domain of "culture" from "politics" which belies how the stories that predominate any society can become institutionalized forces of power and control. As Kumar elucidates, the "matrix of anti-Muslim racism" entails global infrastructures taking on local form through institutions like the FBI, National Security Agency, and the Department of Justice as well as the corporate media and far beyond.

Everyone interested in global politics, social justice, racial justice, and ending war and empire should read this book. By reading *Islamophobia and the Politics of Empire,* my hope is that more and more people will establish a common framework for resisting the local and global forces of anti-Muslim racism including neoliberal economics, divide and conquer strategies, overt militarism such as bombing and killing, and covert militarism such as surveillance and support for dictators. I also hope this resistance will involve envisioning and practicing the world we want to live in, perhaps a world built upon the values of collective care, love, and dignity not only for people from the Middle East and South Asia, for all Muslims, or for anyone perceived to be Muslim but for all of us—and for our planet and for our collective futures.

Nadine Naber
December 23, 2020

Preface to the Revised Second Edition

Twenty years since the launch of the global war on terror, the human toll has been nothing short of devastating. The Cost of War project at Brown University estimated in 2020 that between 37 and 59 million people were displaced as a result of US wars in eight countries and that about 800,000 have been killed due to direct war violence in Afghanistan, Pakistan, Iraq, Syria, and Yemen.[1] Other reports that factor in deaths due to the consequences of war such as the loss of infrastructure, food and water, war-related disease, and other accompanying issues arrive at higher figures.

Life for ordinary people in the Muslim-majority countries that the United States has been waging war on has been traumatic. If you were killed accidentally in a drone strike, as has happened on numerous occasions, it was written off as "collateral damage." In fact, to avoid backlash around the number of civilians killed by drones, the United States simply decided to designate all military age men in countries being struck as combatants.[2] Thus, you didn't even count as a civilian, a statistic, much less as a human being who deserved life. Inside the United States, tens of thousands of Muslims were put through a registry, arbitrarily arrested, detained or deported, and forced to leave family members behind.

The war on terror rages on, exposing millions more to what prison abolitionist scholar Ruth Wilson Gilmore has called a "vulnerability to premature death."[3] While Gilmore is referring to the black and brown people ravaged by the carceral state, we might fruitfully extend this aspect of racism to the ways in which Muslims, Arabs, and South Asians have been targeted by the national security state and turned into a dangerous "race." The brown terrorist menace has furnished the grounds on which to expand US global hegemony at the cost of attending to catastrophes such as the Covid-19 pandemic, which has claimed far more lives than were lost on 9/11 or even during World War II. Just between 2018 and 2020, the United States conducted counterterrorism operations in eighty-five countries and expanded to 800 its military bases around the world.[4] All this has cost trillions.[5]

The first edition of this book, published in 2012, came out of my involvement in the anti-war movement. As a scholar-activist, I set myself the task of trying to explain how Islamophobia enabled the war on terror. Since the fateful events of 9/11, many scholars turned their attention to the new process by which a "racial Muslim" was created. Muslims and those who "look Muslim" were amalgamated and turned into a homogeneous threat. The study of Islamophobia, which was at best modest before 9/11, spiked in the second half of that decade, growing dramatically between the years 2010 and 2012.[6] A new field of Islamophobia studies came into being. This is not to say that scholars in numerous fields had not already studied anti-Muslim racism before Islamophobia studies emerged, as I note in the introduction.

In this revised edition, I have incorporated some of the work produced since 2012 as well as scholarship I hadn't yet come across back then, including the work on the black Muslim experience. I also brought the book through the Trump administration. Every chapter has been revised to include new material and new arguments. Some chapters were incorporated into existing chapters, others were shelved and replaced by new ones. I have also deepened the analysis of imperialist feminism, the political economy of empire, and the matrix of anti-Muslim racism. All in all, I added about 45,000 new words, which is about 50 percent of the book. Every sentence has been edited. If you liked the first edition, I don't think you will regret reading this revised version.

I must confess that when I wrote the first edition, I hadn't imagined that this book would be so well received. It has been translated into five languages and has been read by tens of thousands of people around the world. It never occurred to me that I would have the honor of being listed alongside scholars I admire like Angela Davis and Hannah Arendt in *GQ*'s list of twenty must-read books in the early twenty-first century. To be honest, well-dressed gentlemen were not the audience I had in mind. That said, I am glad that they found the book useful, particularly in these pernicious times when right-wing racism is spreading around the world.

I hope the book continues to make a difference in the struggle against racism and for a just and equitable world.

Deepa Kumar
December 2020

Introduction:
Islamophobia Is Anti-Muslim Racism

On September 11, 2001, I watched the televised spectacle of the Twin Towers crashing down with a sense of horror. I was saddened over the deaths that occurred that day and worried that friends or relatives might be in the towers. Those who were killed that day included a multiracial assemblage of people from the United States as well as around the world. Even as I was processing the attack, I started to feel a sense of dread over what was to come: What would the United States do in response? I wondered, with a deep sense of apprehension, how many more people would be killed around the world in the years to follow.

When I went to school that day to teach my classes, one of the first people I encountered was a colleague who jeered, "Are you happy?" Momentarily stunned, I could only stutter that I was not and that I had just learned that some people I know might have been in the Twin Towers. I wondered if he asked me this question because of my politics and criticism of US foreign policy or because I am a brown-skinned person. Later that day, I stopped by the local Winn-Dixie grocery store, where the checkout clerk could barely conceal his contempt for me. Eventually he flat-out asked me to apologize for what had happened that day. Again, I was taken aback; I didn't know how to reply. As a normally outspoken teacher, scholar, and activist, I wasn't used to this sense of muteness. I just stood there and looked at him, temporarily dumbfounded. At this checkout counter, I learned something new: I "look Muslim." As I pondered this, placing my groceries on the conveyor belt, the only thing I knew beyond a shadow of a doubt was that my response, when it did come out of my mouth, would *not* reveal that I was neither

Muslim nor Arab. To me this is a basic principle of solidarity. To deny another's humanity is to deny one's own. When I regained my composure, I asked him if he had heard of Timothy McVeigh and Christian fundamentalists who had similarly murdered numerous people. I asked him if he thought that all Christians were responsible for these acts. He didn't reply.

What was at work was the phenomenon that the French-Tunisian writer Albert Memmi has called the "mark of the plural."[1] This racist logic denies individuality to those seen as part of a colonized collective. All Muslims and those who "look Muslim" were produced as a "race" of people who were collectively to blame for the actions of the few. Since then, Muslims have had to apologize not once but repeatedly for every attack perpetrated by Muslims on Western targets. White people are never asked to do the same, much less atone for the violence of people like Anders Breivik, Wade Michael Page, Dylann Roof, or other neo-Nazis and white supremacists.

Within a week of the grocery store incident, I heard that a young Arab student had been beaten up at a neighboring university and that the campus police had simply looked the other way. I was invited by the student chapter of Amnesty International at this university to be part of a panel titled "Why Islam Is not the Enemy." Notices were posted in my apartment complex asking people to report "suspicious" behavior and people. A Sikh Indian man wearing a turban was killed in Arizona. In the months that followed, tens of thousands of Muslims were "interviewed" and registered, and thousands were either imprisoned or deported as the policing powers of the national security state were strengthened. With wide public support, the military machine was deployed to rain death on Afghans. Islamophobia, or anti-Muslim racism, was enabling empire in new and old ways.

I have since been involved in organizing, teaching, and writing about this injustice. This book is the product of such engagement with activists in the anti-war movement, students and colleagues who have attended my lectures at universities across the world, and feedback from various editors and reviewers of my articles about Islamophobia both in independent media and in scholarly journals. It is a collective product, in this sense—driven by the need to produce knowledge that can effectively push back against racism. Just as the war on terror prompted state-funded and sponsored research to aid projects of war and incarceration, anti-racists took up the call to produce work that could play a part in resisting the death and destruction that was to follow. The skeptical reader should not assume that what follows in this book is a bending of reality to suit a particular perspective. Far from it. To change the world, one must have an accurate understanding of how it works. Moreover, no scholarly work is ever neutral. The intellectually honest among us admit where we stand even while we stay open to data and evidence that contradict our theories.

Even before I began my study of the history of Islam, of Muslim-majority countries, colonialism and imperialism, theories of race, and other related areas, I knew instinctively that the Islamophobic rhetoric that passed as common sense in the United States was dead wrong. I grew up in India in a Hindu home where the neighbors on both sides were Muslims, and the *azan* (the Islamic call to prayer) was an everyday sound. India is home to close to 200 million Muslims—more than any Arab nation—and, knowing from experience that Muslims are just as complex as any other group of people, I reacted viscerally to the stereotypes that passed as credible knowledge in the United States, the country where I have spent my entire adult life. Audiences at my lectures have occasionally asked if I was Muslim, and since I don't provide that information out of solidarity, I have found myself in the awkward position of having to assure them that Muslims are people "just like us." That my Muslim neighbors were warm and generous people, that we celebrated Muslim and Hindu religious days and festivals together, even if some of us were atheists. The labor I have found myself performing was to humanize South-Asian Muslims, which involved cutting against deeply held perceptions of the homogeneous or essentialized Muslim, the mark of the plural. I tried, however, not to fall into the opposite trap of Islamophilia, which might mean papering over or becoming an apologist for atrocities instigated and committed by Muslim political leaders, as occurred in the early era of conquest.[2] This is a tricky balance given the distortions of Muslim rule in India by Hindu fundamentalists.

I am grateful to the scores of scholars in the fields of history, political science, Arab American studies, international relations, women's studies, Islamic studies, religious studies, Middle East studies, African American studies, anthropology, sociology, media studies, postcolonial studies, American studies, and other related fields who have studied empire and the "Muslim world" for advancing my knowledge of this subject. I put Muslim world in quotation marks for obvious reasons—there is no singular Muslim world, just as there is no singular Christian world. To understand the complexity of life in the Middle East and North Africa (MENA) or South Asia through religion is reductionist and absurd. Yet, it is a mode of thinking called *Orientalism*, developed in the nineteenth century, that persists to this day. In fact, even the idea of a region known as the Middle East, as historian Osamah Khalil argues, is "the product of imperial interests and competition."[3] During the era of British imperial hegemony, it stretched all the way from North Africa to India. By the mid-twentieth century the "region's boundaries aligned with America's Cold War goals and stretched from Morocco to Pakistan."[4] The ensuing homogenized Muslim that inhabits this region includes people from North Africa to West Asia. Arabs, Iranians, Turks, Afghans, and South Asians became part of an essentialized race within the context of imperialism. To be sure, there is a recognition of difference between these ethno-national groups; however, as anthropologist Junaid Rana argues, the "process of merging them into a racialized figure of 'the Muslim' is far more prevalent."[5]

I have benefited, more recently, from the work of scholars in the field of Arab American studies who have analyzed the racialization of Arab Americans within larger geopolitical contexts. The field emerged in the 1960s and has produced a rich body of work on anti-Arab and anti-Muslim racism in the context of US global political, economic, and military agendas, including its support for Israeli settler colonialism. Before there was a subfield called Islamophobia studies, scholars in this area had already laid the intellectual groundwork for what was to come after 9/11.[6]

Liberalism and Islamophobia

As a scholar-activist I was alarmed to find that anti-Muslim racism had to be fought not just among conservatives but among liberals and leftists as well. Activists needed to be educated on why Afghan women were not to going be "liberated" by the US/NATO war. We had to turn to the valuable work of scholars like Leila Ahmed and her pioneering book *Women and Gender in Islam* and Fatima Mernissi and her classic book *Beyond the Veil*.[7] In the lead-up to the Iraq war of 2003, I was part of a large and vibrant anti-war group that opposed the war and stood firm against George W. Bush's imperial agenda. Somewhere between 6 and 11 million people in hundreds of cities around the world protested against the impending war, in what was considered the largest global protest on a single day in human history.[8] Yet, immediately after the war had started, the group began to shrink. The explanation on offer by those drifting away was that now that the United States had intervened, it was perhaps best to give it a chance to "bring democracy" to Iraq. It surprised me to hear this "white man's burden" argument parading as common sense in the twenty-first century.

We turned to all the excellent arguments against this racist logic put forward by postcolonial studies scholars such as Edward Said's *Orientalism*.[9] We also drew from the work of Middle East scholars such as Rashid Khalidi and Gilbert Achcar to articulate the actual role the United States has played in the Middle East and North Africa (MENA), which shows that it has propped up dictators and pushed back against democratic movements.[10] Those advancing the proposition that the United States should "bring democracy" were committed activists who didn't understand that they were using colonial and Eurocentric (or US-centric) frameworks, which work by naturalizing power dynamics and concealing imperial prerogatives. Ella Shohat and Robert Stam in their book *Unthinking Eurocentrism* teach us that Eurocentrism "envisions the world from a single privileged point" and creates racialized others of colonized people. Moreover, Eurocentric racism is not always obvious but manifests, they note, in "abstract, indirect, submerged, even 'democratic' forms."[11]

My first article on Islamophobia, titled "Danish Cartoons: Racism Has No Place on the Left," was about this problem among people who think of themselves as anti-racist.[12] Many on the left defended the caricatures of the Prophet Mohammad published in the Danish *Jyllands-Posten* on the grounds of "free speech," extolling the virtues of liberal democracy. The French satirical magazine *Charlie Hebdo* followed suit with its own racist caricatures of Mohammad. They then republished these cartoons in 2020. Whereas French political leaders had expressed reservations or denounced the cartoons when they were first published, in 2020 the cartoons were embraced across the political spectrum, with the French government taking a stand in support of free speech and French republican values.[13]

When racism is framed in terms of "free speech" and democratic rights, it becomes a covert liberal form of racism, which erases the humanity of those being subjected to what is in reality hate speech. Few, if any, compared the *Jyllands-Posten* and *Charlie Hebdo* cartoons to the racist caricatures of Jews in Germany in the lead-up to the Nazi genocide. Dehumanizing speech, I argued, has real consequences for oppressed groups. Another argument I took up was that in the supposedly "postracial" world, "equal opportunity" humor was acceptable. It is assumed that all groups can be subjected to ridicule in the name of comedy because racism doesn't exist in any real way in our "postracial" world;

thus, poking fun at all implies neutrality. As I wrote back then, "there is no neutral point in a world characterized by racism, wars, and imperialism—you are either on the side of the oppressed or the oppressor."[14] I was articulating what I think many people felt and knew, which was that the left didn't understand anti-Muslim racism and in fact held Eurocentric/colonialist assumptions about the MENA region and South/Central Asia. I was not the first to make this argument, nor was it necessarily the best articulation of the argument, but the piece struck a chord and within a few days of its posting received more than 10,000 unique hits.

Liberalism in service to empire became a shield behind which racism was hidden. The Bush administration was using liberal rights-oriented discourse—women's rights, human rights, democracy—to shore up its imperial ambitions and many committed to these rights failed to understand the pernicious nature of liberal Islamophobia, that is, racism that deploys liberal tropes. This was certainly not the first instance in which liberalism had become a pillar of racism. Political scientist Uday Singh Mehta's analysis of British colonialism on the Indian subcontinent shows that liberalism served to justify empire built on domination and the denial of liberal rights to the colonized.[15] Jasbir Puar, a scholar of women, gender, and sexuality studies, has articulated how gay rights became part of this liberal offensive in the twenty-first century. Gay liberation had been co-opted to cast the United States as an exceptional state—a bastion of democracy and human rights—as a way to win over US and global gay rights organizations to the project of the war on terror.[16] Activists were confronting these arguments in our day-to-day organizing. My involvement in the anti-war movement forced me to understand anti-Muslim racism in its myriad forms—overt, covert, liberal, conservative, and reactionary.

Empire and the Racial Muslim

Arab American studies scholar Nadine Naber, author of some of the first round of essays and books that set out to explain anti-Arab and anti-Muslim racism in the post-9/11 era, argued that the association of

> a wide range of signifiers such as particular names (e.g. Mohammed), dark skin, particular forms of dress (e.g. a headscarf or a beard) and particular nations of origin (e.g. Iraq or Pakistan) became part of an imagined "Arab/Middle Eastern/Muslim" enemy.[17]

Those perceived as such were "targeted by harassment or violence on the assumption that 'they' embody a potential for terrorism and [were] thus threats to U.S. national security," and therefore "deserving of discipline and punishment."[18] Scholar and public intellectual Moustafa Bayoumi argued that what was happening was a process of "racing religion." He analyzed the special registration program launched in the aftermath of 9/11 to argue that the program was "not necessarily a nefarious plot to racialize Islam" but a "bureaucratic and cultural response to political turmoil."[19] While it may not have been a self-conscious attempt to discriminate against Muslims, in practice it was a color-blind security measure that had the effect of turning Muslims into a race. As race scholar Arun Kundnani and I have argued, surveillance is a mechanism of racialization that turns the target group into a suspicious "race."[20]

A group of people viewed as a threat by the state and by lay people who subject Muslims and those who "look Muslim" to hate speech and hate crimes and call the authorities to report "terrorism tips" are part of a systemic project that race scholars Barbara and Karen Fields call *racecraft* and what sociologists Michael Omi and Howard Winant call *racial formation*.[21] To be sure, the racial Muslim was not a new project of racialization, but one that was expanded and amplified in the aftermath of 9/11. What needs to be emphasized is that races are produced by racism.[22] There is no biological basis for race. Races are made and produced through practices of exploitation, expropriation, and exclusion.[23] Race is therefore understood in this book as both ideology and practice rooted in the political economy of empire. Empire creates the condition for anti-Muslim racism, and Islamophobia sustains empire.

A note is in order about the term *Islamophobia* in the title of the book. I retain the term not only because it was the title of the 2012 book but because it is the widely used term today to describe discrimination against Muslims. Back in 2012 I defined *Islamophobia* as anti-Muslim racism and used the two terms interchangeably, as I have done in this second edition. However, doing so entails a risk because many people understand Islamophobia as religious intolerance or discrimination of an interpersonal nature rather than as racism rooted in institutional structures. As various scholars have argued, to reduce anti-Muslim racism to "religious animus" or a fear of Muslims as the term *Islamophobia* implies misses the larger picture of structural racism.[24] The term was popularized after a 1991 report released by a UK think tank, the Runnymede Trust, which reported on "unfounded hostility towards Islam," which had practical consequences in the form of "unfair discrimination against Muslim individuals and communities" and "the exclusion of Muslims from mainstream political and social affairs."[25] Hostility directed at individuals in the form of hate speech as well as hate crimes, discrimination, and exclusion are certainly dimensions of anti-Muslim racism. But such acts do not exist in a vacuum driven by some sort of inherent proclivity to hate those who aren't like "us" or even simply by cultural misunderstandings or ethnocentrism.

Moreover, while racism is experienced at the individual level, to limit our understanding of anti-Muslim racism to hate crimes and/or microaggressions, daily acts of humiliation, or exclusion from social life is to miss its structural roots. These are manifestations of a system that produces and is sustained by racism. It is this system we must name and understand if we are to get to the roots of anti-Muslim racism. This is why the book is titled *Islamophobia and the Politics of Empire*. Moreover, if Islamophobia is understood primarily as prejudice, exclusion, or discrimination, then the remedy is to bring Muslims into the mainstream and to educate against prejudice. These are worthwhile goals, but I argue that they are insufficient. As we will see, liberal Islamophobia is happy to designate Muslims as "good" if they consent to the war on terror and aid empire. Such a politics of inclusion does little to dismantle the fundamental source of anti-Muslim racism—empire. The central argument of this book is that anti-Muslim racism is best understood, in its myriad and ever-changing manifestations, as rooted in empire. Thus, Muslim inclusion within an imperial system that presides over war, genocide, and torture does little to dent racism.

My focus is on Western imperial powers, particularly the United States. This is not to say that anti-Muslim racism does not exist in other societies. Israel and India are clear examples of subimperial powers that deploy anti-Arab and anti-Muslim racism to shore up both national and geopolitical interests. For Israel the settler colonial project and its geopolitical position within the MENA region, particularly its rivalry with Iran after 1979, play a critical role. For India, its identity as a Hindu majority nation and its use of anti-Islam rhetoric to advance its regional ambitions in relation to its rival Pakistan, not to mention the use of communalism by Hindu elites to advance domestic ambitions, has led to various forms of Islamophobia, from the extreme Hindu nationalist kind to liberal variations. Even weaker states have weaponized Islamophobia as part of various political projects. Perhaps the most disturbing example has been Nobel Peace Prize winner Aung San Suu Kyi's Myanmar, which has used

Islamophobia to legitimate its ethnic cleansing of the country's Rohingya predominantly Muslim minority. Higher up the hierarchy of international state power, China and Russia have turned to Islamophobia to justify their national and imperial projects. China has deployed classic racist tropes about Muslims, Islam, and terrorism as part of its repression of the Uighur population in Xinjiang. Russia has done the same as part of its brutal war in Chechnya as well as in its projection of power in Central Asia and Eastern Europe. Right-wing parties in Denmark, Germany, Sweden, and Holland have made gains through anti-immigrant and anti-Islam rhetoric. The key turning point was 2010, when Far Right parties across Europe using Islamophobia made unprecedented electoral gains both domestically and in European Parliament elections. Political, economic, and social conditions—both domestic and international— inform projects of racialization. Significantly, as the global hegemon, the United States plays a central role in setting the terms of global discourse and politics.

Finally, one could legitimately ask: Shouldn't the United States continue to prosecute the war on terror in order to prevent another 9/11? This question is taken up in several chapters. The CIA uses the term "blowback" to describe such attacks as examples of the unintended consequences of US foreign policy.[26] The book also lays out how the "Islamic threat" was produced to justify imperial ambitions. To be sure, while groups such as al-Qaeda and ISIS are responsible for devastating attacks, the threat posed by "Jihadi terrorism," as it is called, is quite small. A number of scholars, including former counterterrorism specialists, have debunked the state's overinflated projection of the Jihadist threat.[27] Using US government data on attacks and plots, former CIA operations officer Marc Sageman has estimated that over a ten-year period only a small fraction of Muslims in the West turned to political violence—less than one in a million per year.[28] Moreover, the number of deaths in the United States due to Jihadi terrorism from 2001 (after the 9/11 attacks) to 2020 is 107, a figure dwarfed by gun deaths during that same period or the hundreds of thousands killed in the US war on terror.[29] This is why several scholars have called the fear generated by the "Islamic terrorist threat" a moral panic.[30]

Stuart Hall et al., in their pioneering book *Policing the Crisis: Mugging, the State, and Law and Order*, analyzed the fear generated towards racialized subjects.[31] Methodologically, this book employs a similar approach. Using a historical materialist mode of analysis, Hall and his collaborators examined the legal arena, the police, and the media in the construction of a moral panic around the black "mugger" in early 1970s in the UK. They argued that the economic crisis of the time was solved by "law and order" solutions that were based on generating fear towards black criminals. The new project of racial formation involved a focus on the "mugger" coded as a security threat. Even though the crime known as mugging did not increase, a moral panic was generated to justify policing measures. I similarly argue that the economic, political, and social crises of the late 1960s and 1970s created the conditions for the production of the "Arab terrorist" threat, which later evolved into the "Islamic terrorist" threat.[32] The next moment of crisis, 9/11, was an opportunity to generate a moral panic around terrorism in order to bolster and strengthen the national security state. However, my argument goes beyond an analysis of moments of crisis in that I take a long historical view. I study anti-Muslim racism as a product of empire—not just empire in crisis but as a normal modality of imperial domination from the early modern era all the way up to the twenty-first century.

Overview of the Book

The book begins in the early modern era in Spain, when bodily or somatic notions of race were developed. Chapter 1 discusses how imperial Spain adopted blood purity laws that cast Jews and Muslims as permanent outsiders who could not be assimilated through earlier logics of Christian universalism. Race and racism in this period had some of the markers of modern racism, but because it was still conceived in a religious idiom and because Muslims or, to be precise, Muslim converts known as *moriscos,* occupied a liminal space between inferiority and superiority, I call this *protoracism*. While Spain was a dominant power in the era of mercantile imperialism, the Ottomans and various other Muslim empires were significant forces on the global stage. European powers in the early modern era were unable to challenge or defeat them. Thus, the Turks were seen as equal to if not superior to Europeans in countries like Britain. In this context, it was not possible to see Muslims as uniformly inferior, a hallmark of modern racism.

Various factors including the development of agrarian capitalism in England, colonial expansion in the New World, slavery and the plantation system, and the industrial revolution created the conditions for the rise of Britain. Britain led the way in the transition from mercantile imperialism to capitalist imperialism. This set the stage for various projects of racialization. Orientalism as a body of thought that enabled colonialism emerged in this period; France played no small role in its development. I read the scholarship critical of Orientalism within the framework of the political economy of empire to argue that Muslims were created as races as seen in the notion of *Homo islamicus*. This Latin term translates to "Islamic man," a type of man who was said to possess a cultural essence that emerges from his civilization. Further, when compared to the "normal man" or the "European man" the Muslim man was found to be inferior (and it is men they were talking about; the chapter also unpacks gendered constructions and the rise of colonial or imperial feminism).

This homogenized Muslim race was produced, in the British case, through its experience of domination not only in relation to Arabs, Turks, and Persians/Iranians but South Asians as well. Homogenizing tropes, such as the "Oriental," were used in various contexts. Projects of racial formation do not have tight borders; they are instead porous with mechanisms used in one context to racialize a particular group being used and deployed in others. Moreover, in England before Orientalism could be deployed against the foreign other, it was used to create internal others, those who did not sit well within the new postindustrial revolution capitalist ethic.[33] Thus, an argument I make throughout the book is that both internal and external, or domestic and international, factors play a role in projects of racialization. At any rate, full-blown scientific racism that built on Enlightenment notions of race was birthed at this moment and at the high point of European colonialism. I argue that whereas Muslims occupied a liminal space in imperial Spain, the rise of capitalist imperialism and the ability of Britain to finally challenge the powerful Muslim empires with whom they earlier could only maintain cordial relations created the conditions for modern anti-Muslim racism. As various scholars have argued, it is only when societies came to accept individual freedom and equal rights that colonial conquest, slavery, and dispossession were explained in racial terms.[34] Drawing on this work, I argue that two conditions were needed for the production of modern anti-Muslim racism: colonial domination and "free" liberal societies.

In Chapter 2, I show how colonial America and the newly formed republic both borrowed from British racial language but also created unique modes of racializing Muslims. It outlines the work on West African Muslim slaves and how Native Americans and Turks were interchangeably described as "savages." While Orientalism as a complex, contradictory, and ever-shifting ideology has a long history in the United

States, it was only after the United States assumed its role as a preeminent imperial power in the MENA region and Asia that anti-Muslim racism was established as a global/domestic means of social control. While Arab and South Asian Americans faced racist discrimination prior to this period in the form of exclusionary naturalization laws that admitted only those perceived as white into citizenship, and while black Muslims were targeted by the FBI for practicing a form of Islam that gave voice to resistance against white supremacy and imperialism, these were part of earlier systems of white supremacy. Drawing on the work of scholars in Arab American studies, I outline my argument that the economic, political, and social crises of the late 1960s and early 1970s created the conditions for the "Arab terrorist" as a domestic and global formation, which would then evolve into the "Islamic terrorist" in later decades. I refer to this new process of terrorist racial formation as *terrorcraft*, which I explore in greater depth in a forthcoming book.[35] At any rate, US Orientalism and modernization theory in the postwar era served as the basis for the racialization of international and domestic threats.

Chapter 3 examines the persistence of Orientalism and its adaptations in the twenty-first century. It outlines six taken-for-granted ideological frames that are at the core of anti-Muslim racism today: Islam is a monolith; Islam is uniquely sexist and Muslim women need to be liberated by the West; Islam is anti-modern; the "Muslim mind" is incapable of science and rationality; Islam is inherently violent; the West spreads democracy because Muslims are incapable of democratic self-rule. These frames are part of an ideology that is so entrenched that those who offer a critical stance are given little credence. The primary definers of this ideology, which include politicians and other prominent public figures, set the terms of discussion, which are then reproduced in the news media as fact. The chapter focuses on unpacking and debunking these naturalized frames, drawing on the work of scholars in various disciplines.

In Chapters 4 and 5, I study the foreign policy establishment and its attitudes toward the "Islamic threat." Chapter 4 discusses the shifting, zigzagging attitudes toward "good" and "bad" Muslims, Arabs, Iranians, and Afghans. These constructions are the product of imperial ethnocentric racism because the good/bad designation flows from whether one supports or opposes US policy and empire. Moreover, one can easily go from "good" to "bad." The chapter also outlines the debate between the two main wings within the foreign policy establishment: the neoconservatives and the liberal interventionists. While the two disagree on whether to confront or accommodate the "Islamic threat," they are united

in their unreserved support for *Pax Americana*, a global system dominated by the United States. These two approaches within the political
class have led to two strands of Islamophobia: conservative and liberal.
The attacks of 9/11 produced a convergence and a commitment to take a
confrontationist approach, launching the war on terror as an endless and
boundless project of war making and race making. US imperialism was
greatly strengthened after 2001. In Chapter 5, I discuss the continuities
and discontinuities between the Bush, Obama, and Trump administrations. I analyze key policy documents as well as articles by policy makers
to outline how the foreign policy establishment, including various think
tanks, have prosecuted the war on terror. Significantly, while Trump
rejected the liberal consensus of the Bush and Obama administrations,
his "illiberal hegemony" continued some of the policies of his predecessors even while he instituted new approaches. Through all these
administrations, people in many Muslim-majority countries were subject
to racism in the form described by Ruth Wilson Gilmore as a "vulnerability to premature death" through conventional wars, sanctions, drone
warfare, and airstrikes.

Chapter 6 turns to the domestic context to outline how the security
and legal apparatus has terrorized Muslims. The chapter is titled "Terror-
izing Muslims" because it sets out to address both how the "racial
Muslim," a homogenizing category that sweeps up large swaths of people
from West Africa to Asia, has been produced as a terrorist threat in the
post-9/11 period and how policies designed to control this threat from
surveillance to preemptive prosecution have resulted in fear and terror
within targeted communities. The strengthening of empire after 9/11 not
only enabled US war making abroad, but also created new systems of
racial control inside the United States. Methods used during the Cold
War were adapted to the war on terror: the "red scare" became the "green
scare." (Green is the color of Islam.) The bulk of the chapter focuses on
the racializing practices of the domestic security apparatus, which
includes a number of institutions such as the Department of Homeland
Security, Federal Bureau of Investigation, the National Security Agency,
the Department of Justice, various city police departments, and the legal
system. To be sure, this separation of the domestic from the international
is artificial. Empire is at once national and international, and methods of
control developed domestically are applied abroad and vice versa. I
outline the systems of surveillance, arbitrary arrests, registration, indefinite detention, torture, and deportation deployed by the security
apparatus in a process that has been called the "securitization of Islam."

The key vehicle for this process of racial control has been the belief that "Islam" as ideology predisposes Muslims to violence.

Chapter 7 looks at the right-wing Islamophobic warriors (the "new McCarthyites") and their connections to the security establishment, the media, the academy, and the political class. I argue that the Islamophobia network, which consists of various groups including sections of the neocon camp, Zionists, the Christian Right, and various "ex-Muslims," are not a fringe minority as some have insisted, but rather part and parcel of the structures of US empire. Like Senator Joseph McCarthy before them, the new McCarthyites play a collective role in ramping up fear and hatred of Muslims, enabled by the liberal establishment. They are deeply invested in US imperialism and Israeli settler-colonialism and play a role similar to that of the Cold Warriors of yesteryear. I begin by studying the "Ground Zero Mosque" controversy of 2010, a key turning point in the rise of the network and the global counterjihad movement, to explain how liberal, conservative, and reactionary Islamophobia articulate together in the production of the racialized Muslim. While right-wing Islamophobia is about exclusion (the removal of symbols of Islam from public life, banning Muslims, and so on), liberal Islamophobia is about inclusion on imperial terms; both are forms of imperial racism. I then unpack the projects of the Islamophobia network from the 1990s on but particularly after 2001 and discuss the think tanks, foundations, and media outlets that support their work. Trump legitimated and elevated the new McCarthyites not only through his own suggestions that Obama is a "secret Muslim" but also by appointing right-wing Islamophobes to positions within his administration.[36] The end result was that the dog whistle racism of the post–civil rights era was overcome and blatant overt racism gained ascendance.

The conclusion brings together my arguments in the book through a map that I call the "matrix of anti-Muslim racism," which outlines how various spheres—the foreign policy establishment, the security appara-tus, think tanks, the academy—produce Islamophobia. Like *Policing the Crisis,* this book takes a multifocal approach to understanding race and racism. In addition to the legal, police, and media domains discussed in *Policing the Crisis,* I study knowledge production, particularly knowl-edge that informs policy, and the practices of the national security state. Dominant constructions of racialized others are best understood, I argue, as the product of multiple intersecting spheres and the complex ideologies and practices that emerge from them. I discuss how the main-stream media, as well as right-wing and progressive media, are the staging grounds on which various forms of Islamophobia—liberal, conservative, reactionary—are articulated and contested. Significantly, both right- and left-wing social movements vie for hegemony within the imperial matrix.

To summarize, this book is about anti-Muslim racism as an ideology and set of practices rooted within empire. First, I argue that Islamophobia is best understood as racism rather than religious intolerance. When Muslims and those who "look Muslim" in the United States as well as around the world are subject to systematic modes of oppression from surveillance, to detention, torture, and the denial of basic human rights, including the right to life, what is at work is not religious misunderstanding or intolerance but structural racism. These are racial regimes similar to others in US history from the time of settler colonialism on. For instance, the Iraq war of 1990, the genocidal sanctions regime, and the 2003 war and occupation are analogous to how Native Americans were treated. Second, Islamophobia isn't simply the product of fringe right-wing elements but exhibits in liberal and conservative forms. Right-wing Islamophobia exists on a continuum with liberal and conservative variants and adherents of all three sit comfortably within the infrastructure of empire. Third, systematic anti-Muslim racism emerges after World War II as new modes of controlling the MENA region, particularly modernization theory and American Orientalism, produce Arabs and Muslims as a race. Empire in crisis in the late 1960s and the strategic partnership with Israel gave rise to the global "Arab terrorist" as a threat to democracy. As various threats to empire emerge, the flexible category of "terrorist" incorporates these threats. Thus, methods of control devised to target the racialized terrorist have been used against white anti-war and Occupy Wall Street activists. Moreover, the Black Lives Matter movement has also been smeared as terrorist, and Native Americans protesting the Keystone Pipeline were targeted using counterterrorism tactics.

Fourth, "race" is not simply a category of classification or differentiation but rather a construct that emerges from practices of racism. Thus, while Orientalism has a long history in the United States and in European nations, it is a protean ideology that exhibits veneration as well as vilification. Significantly, Orientalism is not always tied to systems of oppression like colonialism or imperialism. What my analysis shows is that there is no straight line from the Spanish Inquisition to the torture regime of Abu Ghraib. Even while various projects of racialization draw on the past and attempt to fix "race" as existing across time, there are in fact no unbroken lines of continuity. Anti-racists should avoid falling into the trap of accepting the fictive concept of "race" and its transhistorical and essentializing modes of articulation. Thus, the book sets out to explain how historical context shapes various projects of racialization amidst variance and change. This variance is also explained by the fact there is no singular "West."[37] I have tried to avoid the trap of homogenizing the "West," a region whose boundaries also keep changing based on imperial power dynamics. Moreover, nations that get included in this category consist of populations that are both sympathetic to colonialism/imperialism and resistive as well.

Fifth, empire must constantly reconfigure strategy and battle to win hearts and minds both domestically and internationally. Empire is not a cemented structure but a process; it relies on racism to reproduce itself. Moreover, empire does not automatically produce or secure exploitative and exclusionary racial regimes. This is what explains in large part why "race" is constantly shifting and evolving; why there are projects of race making, unmaking, and remaking. It is not enough therefore to simply state that empire is the crucible of anti-Muslim racism; it is necessary to explain why, how, and when. The imperial terrain on which races are made and unmade is unstable, and our task as scholars is to make sense of how various contingent factors come together at certain moments to produce races but to also to undo particular racial configurations. As scholar-activist A. Sivanandan put it, racism "does not stay still; it changes shape, size, contours, purpose, function—with changes in the economy, the social structure, the system and, above all, the challenges, the resistances to that system."[38]

Sixth, resistance matters. Resistance in client states or countries headed by US-backed dictators can disrupt imperial aims and create the conditions for solidarity as well as resistance in imperial centers against what the Occupy Wall Street movement called the regime of the 1 percent. The matrix of anti-Muslim racism attempts to capture this fluidity and to explain the struggle for hegemony as a process, both ideological and material.

To point to changes, complications, and contradictions within anti-Muslim racism is not to erase its potency but to show that it is neither straightforward nor simple. It is a complex phenomenon that needs to be understood at many levels. It therefore requires us as scholars and activists to eschew a tendentious approach, one that seeks out the cases and examples that strengthen a particular argument while ignoring those that don't and to instead study the entire phenomenon with all its complications. Such intellectual and activist work involves an embrace of contradiction and a dialectical materialist mode of analysis. If I had put aside all the evidence that reveals countervailing tendencies, I could have produced an analysis free of contradiction, which might perhaps have been more straightforward and even emotionally satisfying. However, as I show in the conclusion, the imperial matrix of anti-Muslim racism is not a well-oiled machine where an input at one end, such as articulations by primary definers, produces an expected outcome at the other end.[39] Even while those with power exercise hegemony, because the imperial terrain on which races are made and unmade is unstable, not least due to resistance, it creates the conditions for unexpected outcomes.

Contradiction therefore is inherent to the system. Moreover, contradiction is also the basis of change. If anti-Muslim racism is not a permanent characteristic in the "West," encoded into the DNA of its people and its culture, then we can end it. This book is an offering and a call to action to end racism and empire. The words of the playwright Bertolt Brecht are an appropriate guide to all who take up this call:

It takes a lot of things to change the world: Anger and tenacity, science and indignation, the quick initiative, the long reflection, the cold patience and the infinite perseverance, the understanding of the particular case and the understanding of the ensemble. Only the lessons of reality can teach us to transform reality.[40]

1

Empire, Race, Orientalism:
The Case of Spain, Britain, and France

When the film *Sex and the City 2*, set in Abu Dhabi, was released in 2010, several reviewers rightly panned it for its racist stereotypes of Arabs and Muslims. It was as if the producers of the film had gone back to the 1920s, revived the Ali Baba film template, added a few iPhones and five-star hotels as a nod to the modernity of Abu Dhabi, and left everything else more or less intact. How do we understand this view of the Middle East and North Africa (MENA) as a region that does not change—a place where, despite high technology and consumer luxuries, the people remain static and essentially "Muslim"? This view of Islam emerges from a body of work known as Orientalism that came into being in the context of European colonization, which reached its peak in the nineteenth and twentieth centuries.

The late eighteenth century witnessed tumultuous changes. It was an era of revolution—the Industrial Revolution in Britain, the American and French revolutions, and the Haitian Revolution. These revolutions brought forth notions of human equality, secularism, anti-slavery, and democracy and ushered in a process where capitalism would shape global relations. While Spain had held sway during the era of mercantile imperialism, Britain would assume dominance in the nineteenth and early twentieth centuries, building a vast empire that spanned the globe. In this context, the once powerful Ottoman Empire would experience a decline relative to Europe. Other Muslim states seemed equally unable to prevent the onslaught. France invaded and occupied Algeria in 1830, and in 1881–83 seized Tunisia as well. In 1882 Britain colonized Egypt, and in 1898 it took over Sudan. Imperialism in this era, however, didn't always take the

form of direct colonization; indirect control was exercised through financial power. Between 1854 and 1879, the Ottomans borrowed heavily both
to finance the modernization of its army and to fund various reforms
designed to make it more competitive with Europe. However, the terms
of borrowing were unfavorable and it resulted in the establishment of
European economic control over Ottoman finances. A similar process was
at work in Egypt and Tunisia.[1] After World War I, the Ottoman Empire
finally collapsed.

There was nothing inevitable about this. Historian Albert Hourani notes
that from the eighth to the eighteenth centuries, powerful Muslim empires
stretched across the globe "from the Atlantic to the Pacific, with Arabic as
its lingua franca, the most universal language which had ever existed."[2] Up
until 1500 or so, Western Europe with its various feudal kingdoms was a
marginal player on the world stage relative to other great powers (such as
the Ottomans, Chinese, and Indians). In *Before European Hegemony,*
sociologist Janet Abu-Lughod demonstrated that their "relatively primitive
development" in the medieval era meant that Europeans were economi-
cally backward relative to Middle Eastern and Far Eastern systems of
production and exchange.[3] They overcame their backwardness in the
context of the rise of mercantile imperialism and capitalism. Abu-Lughod
argues that these factors explain European hegemony from the sixteenth
century on; it is not the case that "*only* the institutions and culture of the
West *could have succeeded*" [emphasis in original].[4] Yet, this is precisely
what Orientalism, as a body of thought and a practical means of colonial
domination, set out to establish. Building on late eighteenth and early nineteenth century European conceptions of history, Orientalists divided
human societies into civilizations that have a core set of values that drive
their progress (or lack thereof). The people who inhabit these civilizations
were said to have a cultural "essence" that explains who they are across
time. Essentialism of this sort is one of the pillars of race making.

This chapter begins with European ascendance in the early modern
era. It situates the rise of Spain in a period dominated by mercantile
imperialism. I argue that this was the context for the development of
nascent or protoracist notions about Muslims. Next, I turn to the rise of
Britain and the transition to capitalist imperialism. I place British Orientalism, a body of instrumental knowledge, within the political economy
of empire. Both Britain and France were central to the development of
Orientalism, which was not simply an ideology but a practical method of
colonial domination. Drawing on various scholars who have written critical appraisals of institutional Orientalism, I lay out its key characteristics

in order to unpack the notion of *Homo islamicus*, or Muslims as a subspecies of the genus Homo. Moreover, Orientalism had strong gendered dimensions, and the era also saw the development of colonial feminism, that is, feminism being weaponized to serve empire. The focus in this chapter is on Spanish, British, and French imperialism. Each of these powers had its own unique types of imperialism that informed different projects of racialization.

My key argument is that notions of race and of Muslims as inferior beings could come to the fore in a context where European nations were in a position to actually challenge and eventually dominate once-powerful Muslim empires. While Muslims occupied a liminal position between inferior and superior in imperial Spain in the early modern era, this would give way to outright inferiority in the nineteenth century. Thus, while protoracism existed before the nineteenth century, it is capitalist imperialism that sets the terrain on which Enlightenment notions of race were deployed. I argue that two conditions were needed for the production of Muslims as a race: colonial domination and "free" liberal societies.

The Early Modern Era

The period from the late Middle Ages to the post-Enlightenment era is a transitional one characterized by elements from both ages. Known as the early modern era, it runs roughly from 1500 to 1800 CE.[5] The period marked the arrival of several European imperial powers on the global stage and rivalry among them for domination over world trade. Mercantilism characterized the era's economic logic. The mercantilist system was based on a drive to establish lucrative trade and to ensure profits through a monopoly enforced by arms and military might. The profit generated through such trade was based on buying cheap and selling dear, where the centers of production and exchange were separated.[6] Portugal and Spain led the way and were followed by Holland, England, and France.

These empires were of a different kind than Rome, which was a tributary empire.[7] Historian Frederick Weaver characterizes the new European empires as mercantile empires because "monarchs were active partners with merchants" within a system of global trade and overseas expansion.[8] Merchants relied on trade privileges and protections offered by rulers to establish monopolies in specific trades. This was achieved through military means, which inevitably led to inter-European conflicts.[9] The Ottomans were a tributary empire with a primarily land-based system of trade; in contrast, the European intercontinental empires were mainly seaborne.[10]

In addition to profound economic and political changes, the early modern era also saw a shift in intellectual life. The Renaissance, a cultural movement that began in Italy in the fifteenth century and spread to the rest of Europe by the sixteenth, brought new ways of thinking. The sixteenth century saw the emergence of some of the first studies of Europe's Near East to adopt a more open-minded and disinterested tone. The study of Arabic in France, England, and the Netherlands and the scholarship from academics in these countries cast Islam and the Prophet in a more sympathetic light compared to what existed during the Crusades.[11]

Significantly, by the sixteenth and seventeenth centuries attitudes toward religion began to change. While Christianity was the key framework from which to make sense of the world in medieval Europe, now religion, Hourani explains, "came to mean any system of beliefs and practices constructed by human beings."[12] When thought of in this way, all religions were seen as worthy of rational study and analysis as human-made systems of thought. Further, Hourani notes that among the educated classes "travel, commerce, and literature brought some awareness of the phenomenon, majestic and puzzling, of Islamic civilization." The eighteenth-century English author Samuel Johnson noted: "There are two objects of curiosity—the Christian world, and the Mahometan world. All the rest may be considered barbarous."[13] The Mughal Empire, which ruled much of South Asia from the sixteenth to the mid-nineteenth century, was respected even if much was not known about it. Moreover, the Protestant Reformation of the early sixteenth century, which challenged the authority of the papacy and of Catholic doctrine, translated into an attitude toward Islam where it came to be seen as yet another schism, albeit a dangerous one. Thus, even while Martin Luther, who led the Protestant Reformation, had negative things to say about Islam, he viewed the Vatican as the greater enemy. For Luther, only after the defeat of Catholicism could Islam be beaten.[14]

Nabil Matar, who has written extensively on the relationship between Britain, Western Europe, and the Islamic Mediterranean, argues that English attitudes toward the Ottomans, whether as ally or enemy, always constructed the Muslim as equal. The Ottoman state was viewed as on par with England if not superior to it and other European states.[15] Orientalism based on a notion of a superior Europe and an inferior Orient had not yet emerged, not least because it made no sense given the grandeur and advances of Muslim empires both in the Near East and South Asia. If anything, the Muslim empires had superior accomplishments in comparison to their Western European counterparts both in this period and during the Middle Ages more generally, and many Muslim authors wrote of Europe's backwardness.[16] Matar shows that English travelers to the Mediterranean remarked that the Turks knew little of the Britons, and what they knew they found lacking.

This early modern view of the Ottomans reflected the fact that England was not in a position to challenge the Turks. Matar argues that the construction of Muslims in this period drew not from the actual encounter with Muslims but with the Native Americans. Whereas Britain had succeeded in dominating Native Americans, they were unable to do the same with Muslims. Thus, they "borrowed constructions of alterity and demonization from their encounter with the American Indians" and applied them to Muslims.[17] It was not, as Matar notes,

> England but the Ottoman Empire of the sixteenth and seventeenth centuries that was pushing into Europe, conquering Rhodes and Crete, attacking the Spanish, French, Dutch, English, and Scottish trading fleets . . . and enslaving thousands of men and women, many of whom converted to Islam.[18]

The attitude of Britons toward the Turks was one of "fear, anxiety, and awe."[19] Further, the idea of colonization was not applied to the Ottomans. Thus, Queen Elizabeth "cooperated commercially and diplomatically with both the Turks of the Ottoman Empire and the Moors of the Kingdom of Morocco, and never entertained or articulated—and nor did her subjects— projects for colonizing them."[20] In the seventeenth century, the British either embraced Ottoman civilization or vilified it. All along, however, there was a sense that the Turks were not outsiders. Certainly, they were not "outside the diplomatic scope of alliance and peace treaty, individual friendship and amicable correspondence—and even marriage."[21]

However, this was not the case in Spain and Portugal, the key mercantile empires of the early modern era. Whereas England was in no position to go up against the Ottomans, Spain and Portugal were able to rise as imperial powers of some standing by turning to the high seas. It is in this context that we see the rise of protoracism. For perhaps the first time in human history, bodily notions of difference, which were understood to be passed on from one generation to the next, made an entrance. The purity of one's blood or the color of one's skin meant that conversion to Christianity no longer guaranteed acceptance. Religion, however, was still the source of such protoracism. In this sense, it was not full-blown racism but a stage in the development of irredeemable otherness and inherent inferiority. Historian David Brion Davis argues that while we can find examples of xenophobia and prejudice that go all the way back to classical Greek society, "there is no evidence in antiquity or even in medieval and Renaissance Europe of the kind of fully developed racist society" that we witness in the post-Enlightenment period.[22] However, as a transitional period between the Middle Ages and modernity, the early modern era gave rise of transitional forms of racism that contained elements of the medieval othering and anticipated post-Enlightenment racism.

Protoracism in Spain

Spain and Portugal emerged as the first European empires to establish sea-borne trade, bypassing the land trade dominated by the Ottomans. Portugal started to trade extensively in African slaves and Spain followed suit. Spain also reached the New World and expanded its colonial acquisitions. Barely a few months after the capture of Granada, Isabella and Ferdinand had sponsored Columbus's voyage. The discovery and conquest of new regions, the trade in African slaves, and the difficulty of consolidating a united Spanish empire (which included various rival kingdoms) created the conditions for the rise of various forms of racism. In what follows, I focus on the racialization of Jews and Muslims, because similar mechanisms were used in both cases.

In the twelfth and thirteenth centuries, while Muslims and Jews occupied second-class status under Christian rule, they were nonetheless accepted as a part of Spanish society, and the Church tolerated their presence.[23] Conversion to Christianity was a means by which they could escape persecution; Christian universalism sought to include all non-Christians into its fold. This changed in the late fourteenth century when a wave of anti-Jewish pogroms swept through the kingdoms of Castile and Aragon.[24] Jews were given a choice between conversion or death and a large proportion of Sephardic Jews chose to convert. Faced with a similar choice or expulsion in 1492, many Jews again chose the path of conversion. However, this was no longer enough to protect them from discrimination.

The Spanish Empire was built on a Catholic Christian identity, which served as an ideological means to overcome regional differences. In 1483

Isabella and Ferdinand established the Inquisition under their control, with Rome's permission.[25] While the Catholic monarchs were undoubtedly devout Catholics, religious zeal alone does not explain their actions. Rather, as historian J. H. Elliot argues, the "establishment of the Inquisition throughout Spain had obvious political advantages, in that it helped to further the cause of Spanish unity by deepening the sense of common purpose."[26] For the monarchy, the Inquisition was a means to bring together the new empire of Spain consisting of a wide variety of people— Castilians, Aragonians, and others—in a collective mission under the banner of religion. Spanish nationhood was premised on a common Christian identity. In addition to this, the Inquisition became a means by which to regulate competition over jobs and resources between various ethnic groups in the name of religious orthodoxy.[27] The Inquisition was a product of political and economic interests couched in a religious idiom. In this context, Muslims and Jews became inassimilable others. Conversion was no longer available as a means to escape systematic discrimination.

In 1449, the city of Toledo instituted the first *limpieza de sangre* (purity of blood) statute, which prevented Jews who converted to Christianity from occupying official positions. This spread over the course of a few decades to all of Spain. At first, Muslims were not impacted by blood purity laws. However, they too were soon forced to convert. And like converted Jews, they were also required to provide proof of their ancestry if they were to advance socially. As historian Francisco Bethencourt argues,

> Under the conditions of Christian reconquest of Iberia, purity of blood was simultaneously a natural and cultural notion, used for a clear political project: first, to elevate the population of poor Old Christians; second, to deny converted Jews and Muslims access to public and ecclesiastical office; and third, to exclude them from economic, social, and political resources.[28]

The experience of Muslims in imperial Spain was both similar to and different from that of Jews. Unlike Jews, Muslims were not immediately forced to convert in 1492 or face expulsion. Indeed it was not until 1500 that they faced the same fate. A majority of Muslims were agricultural workers or skilled artisans in the textile and silk industries and as such were not in direct competition with the Old Christians who had aggressively pushed the blood purity laws.[29] The monarchy as well as feudal lords considered these Muslims to be a useful labor force and a source of fiscal revenue. Elite Muslims sold their lands and migrated to North Africa.[30] Those who remained converted and exercised a degree of power in delaying various discriminatory practices and laws, such as the banning of Arabic and Muslim customs, as well as outright mass expulsion, which did not occur till the early seventeenth century. Their power was tied to their relationships with various Muslim kingdoms in the Mediterranean and Near East. Iberian elites believed that the Moors were the domestic representatives of powerful Muslim Mediterranean kingdoms (as well as the Ottoman Empire) and therefore had to accord these heretics different treatment from that of the Jews who lacked this kind of protection.[31] Thus, geopolitical factors played a role in the differential treatment of Jews and Muslims.

Both groups, however, were turned into races both ideologically and in terms of practice. However, the idiom was still religious. This is therefore a form of protoracism rather than the full-blown racism of the secular and scientific kind seen in the nineteenth century. Moreover, as historian George Frederickson argues, what was believed to be inherited by blood was a "propensity to heresy or unbelief rather than intellectual or emotional inferiority."[32] *Moriscos* (the term given to converted Muslims) were not uniformly deemed as inferior, a hallmark of modern racism, even though there was a backlash and revulsion generated toward Moorish culture in the late medieval and early modern eras, as historian Olivia Constable has demonstrated.[33] Their contradictory position can be seen, for instance, in Cervantes' *Don Quixote* and its sympathetic portrayal of expelled *moriscos*. Published at the highpoint of *morisco* expulsion in the early seventeenth century, the novel features the *morisca* Ana Félix, a sympathetic character with whom we empathize in her quest to reclaim her family treasure in Spain. Ana passes as a male Turkish sea captain before being captured by the Spanish. She is set to be hanged but is given a chance to speak because a viceroy finds her, as a Turkish captain, to be "handsome," "gallant" and "humble."[34] Still dressed as a Turkish man, Ana reveals who she is and swears her loyalty to Christianity. She is believed, and her life is spared as those listening to her are moved to tears. In this character and her multiple personas, we see the complex and contradictory attitudes toward *moriscos* and Turks. While Ana calls Algiers "hell" and refers to the Turks as "barbarous," she herself is not cast as inferior or unworthy.[35] In fact, she and her father are invited to the home of the viceroy and the whole town visits with them, which is quite noteworthy in the context of mass expulsion.

More generally, the view of *moriscos* if seen as inferior sat uneasily with attitudes toward the powerful Muslim kingdoms in North Africa and the Near East. The association of *moriscos* with the Ottomans cast them as agents of a powerful empire and therefore worthy of a grudging form of respect. In the sixteenth and early to mid-seventeenth centuries, the Ottomans were respected and even feared in various parts of Europe. *Moriscos* therefore sat in a liminal space between inferiority and superiority. While some of the ingredients of modern racism existed at this point, the religious idiom and the lack of outright inferiority leads me to call this *protoracism*. As a transitional period, the early modern era contained aspects of the medieval period but also presaged what was to come in the centuries after. In particular, it was the intellectual and philosophical movement of the seventeenth and eighteenth centuries, known as the Enlightenment, that would lay the basis for modern notions of race.

Race and the Enlightenment

The Enlightenment, which built on the scientific thinking of the Renaissance, displaced religion and prioritized reason over Christian dogma. Many leading lights of the Enlightenment—such as Montesquieu, Kant, Hegel, and Hume—expressed what today would be considered shockingly racist views. However, as a whole, the Enlightenment was more contradictory than that. Philosopher Emmanuel Chukwudi Eze, in his anthology of race in Enlightenment philosophy, argues that while some thinkers were undoubtedly racist, others advanced theories of race that were neutral—and still others were anti-racist. Enlightenment thinkers classified human beings into races and in the process produced a schema in which whiteness came to be associated with cultural and racial superiority, while "unreason and savagery was conveniently located among the non-whites."[36]

The scientific thought of the Enlightenment created types of human beings that served as the framework from which modern racism, based on physical typology, could emerge.[37] The Swedish naturalist Carl Linnaeus is credited with first slotting people into different subspecies within the broader genus of human. He created a schema differentiating between Europeans, Africans, Asians, and American Indians. While this was an advance on medieval human typologies, monsters (a medieval preoccupation) were given credence in his work. It was for the German scholar Johann Friedrich Blumenbach to dispense with monsters as a human type and to produce a scientific means of classification. As historian Nell Painter notes, Blumenbach is not only significant for having used the term "Caucasian" to identify white people, but also for advancing notions of human difference based on skin color as well as other bodily measurements such as skull size and shape.[38] In his *On the Natural Varieties of Humankind*, he identified five categories of human beings— Caucasians, Ethiopians, Americans, Malays, and Mongolians.

Blumenbach echoed theories from antiquity about skin color and its relationship to the weather: dark skinned people lived in hot climates while light skinned in cold climates. However, he maintained that individual human bodies have lighter and darker parts and further that one could, even in colder climates, become dark after exposure to the sun. His views were more complex than previous iterations of weather-based theories and also more contradictory. Painter notes that while he argued that culture and climate played a determining role in human appearance, he also believed that certain groups maintained their distinctiveness over generations. Thus, the Swiss retained their "open countenance," and the Turkish their "manly and serious" demeanor; Jews, despite living alongside gentiles for long periods, were marked by inherent difference which in their "eyes alone" could be seen the "breathe of the East."[39] What we see therefore is that both bodily and cultural notions of race developed coterminously. Furthermore, Blumenbach believed that the "Caucasians" were the first human race from which all others either diverged or degenerated. Finally, the revival of classical scholarship from the Renaissance period on meant that features associated with Greek and Roman physiques were considered supreme and paleness was projected back onto antiquity as the beauty ideal.[40]

What is most significant about Blumenbach, Linnaeus, and other eighteenth century ethnologists' work is that, as Frederickson argues, it "opened the way to a secular or scientific racism by considering human beings part of the animal kingdom rather than viewing them in biblical terms as children of God endowed with spiritual capacities denied to other creatures."[41] This set the stage for modern scientific notions of race. The shift from religious to scientific modes of thought and analysis, while initiated in the Renaissance period, underwent a significant deepening in the eighteenth century; this informed the development of scientific racism as an ideology to justify slavery and conquest.[42]

The Enlightenment also saw the birth of scholarship on Islam that was both realistic and sympathetic.[43] For instance, several philosophers published tracts arguing that the Prophet Mohammad was not an imposter (a medieval argument). The French Enlightenment thinker Voltaire defended Mohammad as a great thinker and founder of a rational religion even as he (and other Enlightenment critics of organized religion) condemned Islam quite acerbically. Historian Norman Daniel explains Voltaire's contradictory stances in the following way:

> We must say that Voltaire first thought an attack on Islam useful for an attack on religion generally; and later saw the advantage of treating the facts less passionately, in order to recommend natural religion at the expense of Christian belief.[44]

To be sure, the Enlightenment produced contradictory views on Islam and Muslims. Enlightenment historian Edward Gibbon saw Mohammad as "an original and superior genius" but also as someone who lost his way as he grew more successful.[45]

Of note, Muslims in the eighteenth century were not uniformly seen as inferior to Europeans. While some Enlightenment scholars did hold such a view, Blumenbach didn't seem to have such an attitude toward the Turks, as noted above. To be "manly" and "serious" was virtuous in a sexist society where characteristics associated with femininity were considered inferior. At the most general level, Enlightenment thinkers sought to address humanity as a whole and saw in their own histories and social structures universal human traits. Christian universalism of the medieval period was replaced with a scientific or humanistic universalism. Historian Maxime Rodinson argues that this universalistic approach translated into a relativist position with regard to others: "In the eighteenth century, an unconscious sense of Eurocentrism was present but it was guided by the universalist ideology of the Enlightenment and therefore respected non-European civilizations and peoples."[46] However, as the nineteenth century progressed, Enlightenment universalism was replaced, in the context of colonialism, with an emphasis on difference between people and civilizations. Europe developed what race scholar Etienne Balibar calls an "imperialist superiority complex."[47] It is in this context that "race" as defined by inferiority would emerge in relation to Arabs, Muslims, and Asians.

Capitalist Imperialism and the British Empire

In the era of mercantile imperialism, Spain dominated the New World and built a vast empire. Spain's *Reconquista* (its conquest of Muslim Spain) and its spread into Africa and the Canary Islands provided a model for its colonization in the Americas. Thus, the *conquistadores* had a similar arrangement to the crown as those of military rulers in the *Reconquista,* where conditional rights were granted in exchange for military services.[48] The discovery and mining of precious metals, particularly silver and gold, generated vast wealth for the Spanish Crown. At the same time, however, shipments of these precious metals to Spain impacted its domestic economy, delaying the development of capitalism.

England was shut out of the most lucrative parts of the New World by Spain, but it did lay claim to some Caribbean islands. The development of agrarian capitalism in England set it on a trajectory toward new forms of colonialism and global dominance. Also, unlike Spain which was still tied to the papacy in the early modern era, England broke with Rome in the early sixteenth century. The Protestant Reformation enabled the Crown to declare supreme authority and to reject the power of the Catholic Church and its representative clergy in Britain. The Tudor monarchy (1485–1603) also curtailed the military and political power of the nobility. As economic historian David McNally notes, these and other measures put it on track to becoming an empire that would rise to prominence.[49]

Agrarian capitalism in England was based on a process of seizing land from the peasantry in order to make it productive of wealth for the upper classes; peasants were dispossessed through the enclosure of common lands. Enclosure gave rise to a privatized agricultural system where large-scale commercial farmers hired wage laborers to work on land to generate profit. This process, which began in the early modern era, went on into the eighteenth century, as McNally demonstrates.[50] The same logic was at work in the colonization of Ireland. As historian Ellen Wood argues, the distinguishing feature of British imperialism was that it was driven by the logic of capitalism.[51] When it began colonization of North America, Britain followed a similar path, appropriating Native American land.

While at first English trade was conducted in mercantilist terms, where commercial profits from buying cheap and selling dear trumped the nation's own imports and exports, this began to change, particularly after the Industrial Revolution. Capitalist or free trade imperialism was based on selling the products produced domestically and buying raw materials abroad.[52] Within this new system, and particularly after the Industrial Revolution, power shifted in England from merchants to the new industrial bourgeoisie. While a majority of this class were from the middle strata of English society, what was needed to succeed as an entrepreneur was not family name and social status, which were important markers of distinction in pre-industrial England, but the ability to deal with the vicissitudes of the market and to control the labor force.[53] This opened the door to those of humbler origins. The shift in power and the establishment of a new industrial form of capitalism precipitated new ideologies that sought to justify colonialism as well as the power of the new dominant classes domestically.

Saree Makdisi, a professor of comparative literature, argues that before Orientalism was directed at external targets, it was directed internally at the old ruling elite, the aristocracy, as well as the poor and working classes.[54] The ascendant middle classes were as quick if not quicker to orientalize their own ruling classes and the poor as they were to orientalize the East. Makdisi, like other scholars, argues that racist ideologies were not simply the product of empire in its encounter with the overseas "others" but with internal "others" as well, people who would later be considered white. Makdisi shows that through the course of the nineteenth century, a clearly polarized notion of what constituted the "normative self" was constructed in opposition to the "degenerate other." While the normative self was "productive, modern, sober, unadorned, disciplined, rational, frank, fair-minded, moderate, regulated, democratic, hardworking, honest, natural, scientific, virtuous, manly, masculine"—virtues I would argue that fit with an industrial capitalist ethic—the other was "vain, retrograde, obsessed with appearances, irrational, unproductive, undisciplined, lazy, unnatural, licentious, capricious, deceitful, emotional, fanatical, tyrannical, violent, indulgent, voluptuous, sensual, feminine, effeminate," and thus either a relic of a previous noncapitalist era or part of impoverished groups unsuitable as subjects of domestic capitalism.[55]

Beginning in the early nineteenth century, it became commonplace in London to talk about people who are today considered white as "racial and civilizational others."[56] It was not simply that these others were being compared to England's colonial populations or to slaves; they were "savages, pure and simple."[57] In a nutshell, Makdisi suggests that the moment of the creation of a distinctive white English occidental identity was also the moment when the othering of Arabs, Africans, Scots Highlanders, and the poor of London also took place.[58] It is therefore not possible to demarcate a racial or civilizational separation that falls neatly along national lines. Put another way, projects of racialization have both domestic and international contexts that shape them—a central argument in this book.

To be sure, as early as the seventeenth century stereotypes of the Turks and Moors can be found in literary works. Matar shows that in these works the

> "Turk" was cruel and tyrannical, deviant, and deceiving; the "Moor" was sexually overdriven and emotionally uncontrollable, vengeful, and religiously superstitious. The Muslim was all that an Englishman and a Christian was not: he was the Other with whom there could only be holy war.[59]

These tropes no doubt informed the orientalization of domestic populations in the late eighteenth and nineteenth centuries. However, in the seventeenth century this mode of representing Muslims existed primarily in literature and in theological works. Matar's analysis of government documents and commercial exchanges show that there was little of this racial or sexual stereotyping. This is in no small part because England in the seventeenth century was not yet capable of challenging the Ottomans. Thus, he cautions that to project a colonial framework back to the early modern period is a mistake.

Orientalism as a colonial discourse could reach maturity only after England had acquired the military and technological capacity to dominate the world. Its actual ability to build a vast empire that stretched the globe created the conditions for a form of racialization that had previously existed as stereotypes in the literary sphere to become a dominant ideology of colonization. This ideology, however, did not get reproduced exactly since it was shaped by the conditions of the post-Enlightenment period becoming more secular in orientation. While the "savage" Indian was interchangeable with the "savage" Muslim going back to the seventeenth century, as Matar argues, late eighteenth and nineteenth century racialization acquired a more capitalist gloss, with commercial needs eclipsing the drive to conversion, a hallmark of early modern imperialism. The eighteenth century English author, Daniel Defoe of *Robinson Crusoe* fame, captured this shift in his call for British domination of Muslim lands based not on Christian zeal but market needs.[60]

Britain invaded and occupied Egypt in 1882 not for religious reasons but in order to enforce debt repayment, as noted above, in this era of capitalist imperialism. British Orientalism fueled the project. Moreover, there were gendered dimensions to Orientalism and racialization. In her pioneering book *Women and Gender in Islam,* Leila Ahmed states that "the issue of women only emerged as the centerpiece of the Western narrative of Islam in the nineteenth century, and in particular the later nineteenth century, as Europeans established themselves as colonial powers in Muslim countries."[61] Lord Cromer was entrusted to oversee the occupation. Cromer positioned himself as an enlightened colonial over-lord committed to women's liberation. Cromer wrote:

> Islam as a social system has been a complete failure . . . The degrada-tion of women in the East is a canker that begins its destructive work early in childhood, and has eaten into the whole system of Islam.[62]

The solution for Cromer was that Muslims "be persuaded or forced into imbibing the true spirit of western civilization."[63]

Yet, at home, this "champion" of Egyptian women's rights worked feverishly to deny British women the right to vote as a founding member and president of the Men's League for Opposing Women's Suffrage. Even though the Victorian male establishment rejected feminism at home, it used the language developed in the domestic context in the service of colonialism. As Ahmed observes, the

> idea that Other men, men in colonized societies or societies beyond the borders of the civilized West, oppressed women was to be used, in the rhetoric of colonialism, to render morally justifiable its project of undermining or eradicating the cultures of colonized peoples.[64]

The oppression of women became another tool to demarcate the supposed inferiority not only of the colonized male but of the colonized society as a whole. Gendered Orientalism or imperial feminism emerged as a coherent ideology in this context. To be sure, despite claims to eman-cipate women, the conditions for Egyptian women under British colonial rule did not improve, and in certain areas such as education they saw a further curtailment, as Ahmed notes. This state of affairs continues in the twenty-first century when imperial feminism was deployed to justify the US/NATO invasion and occupation of Afghanistan in 2001, as described in Chapter 3.

Colonial overlords were not alone in developing this line of argumen-tation; they were aided by native collaborators. Qasim Amin, a

French-educated, upper-middle class lawyer penned *The Liberation of Women* in 1899, which reflected and reproduced colonial arguments. Amin argued that Muslim societies had to abandon their backward ways and follow the Western path to civilization and success. Egyptian women's liberation lay in following the "noble duty" that mothers in "advanced societies" assumed, which was to raise good sons. Liberation meant liberation from Islam, so that Muslim women could be turned into good, docile, Victorian mothers. Amin's book was not about the rights of Egyptian women or European women, but about making them better adjuncts and caregivers to men.[65]

In addition to men like Cromer and Amin, various women also participated in the project of imperialist feminism. Missionary women who traveled to Egypt and other parts of the world argued that only Christianity could save the poor downtrodden Muslim woman. British feminists, particularly upper- and middle-class white women who were active in the struggle for suffrage, also jumped on this bandwagon. As historian Antoinette Burton shows, suffragists argued that if Britain was to be a truly great civilization and great colonial power, it needed to give women equal rights.[66] Writing about British women supporters of empire, race and gender scholar Inderpal Grewal writes:

> As travelers, ethnologists, missionaries, and reformers, Englishwomen could show their equality with Englishmen by participating in the colonial project that was defined in purely heterosexual, masculinist terms as a "penetration" and "mastery" of "virgin" territory of feminine and weak cultures. By such participation, they could uphold their supposed racial and national superiority over Eastern women that, many Englishwomen felt, justified their possession of equal rights with men.[67]

British society and its colonial project were envisioned as benevolent and even enlightened. However, it was France that initiated this colonial mentality.

Napoleon and "Enlightened" Colonialism

France was an early pioneer of Orientalist thought. In 1795, the School of Living Oriental Languages was established in Paris. When Napoleon invaded Egypt a few years later, he was able to take with him Orientalists whose knowledge could be put to use for colonial purposes. Edward Said has argued that Napoleon's invasion of Egypt in 1798 stands out as the first instance when knowledge about the native people became central to the colonizing mission. It was a crucial moment in the emergence of Orientalism. While the occupation itself lasted barely three years and was something of a disaster, it provided an ideological model for future colonial conquests. Napoleon's invasion inaugurated the systematic use of scholarly knowledge to serve the needs of empire, both abroad and at home.[68]

This model of enlightened colonialism had three aspects. First, the colonizer must prepare thoroughly before launching the invasion so as to be well set up to handle obstacles. Second, it should enlist scholars to work alongside soldiers in the colonizing process. Napoleon took with him about 160 scholars to help with the day-to-day process of colonial administration and create a body of knowledge about Egypt for French use. Third, the colonizing nation must develop a justifying rationale. France, having just thrown off the yoke of its oppressive feudal monarchy, believed its mission to be one of restoring Egypt to its former greatness. We see here the precursors of what would come to be known as *mission civilisatrice*, or the "civilizing mission."

Napoleon was well prepared for this mission, as Said notes. Having been fascinated by the Orient from an early age, he had read European writings on the subject extensively, both recent and classical. Said focuses in particular on the French traveler Comte de Volney's two-volume exposition, *Voyage to Egypt and Syria*. Napoleon found Volney's assessment of the Near East as a locale for French colonialism particularly useful, as well as his list of obstacles that the colonial mission might encounter. One such obstacle was Egyptian distrust of Europeans. Napoleon went on to use *Voyage* as a colonizing manual.

In his manifesto, which was widely circulated in Egypt, Napoleon tried to win the hearts and minds of Egyptians:

> Peoples of Egypt, you will be told that I have come to destroy your religion. This is an obvious lie; do not believe it! Tell the slanderers that I have come to you to restore your rights from the hands of the oppressors and that I, more than the Mamluks [who ruled Egypt at the time], serve God ... and revere His Prophet Muhammad and the glorious Quran ... Formerly in the land of Egypt there were great cities, wide canals, and a prosperous trade [sic]. What has ruined all this, if not the greed and tyranny of the Mamluks? ... Tell your nation that the French

are also faithful Muslims. The truth is that they invaded Rome and have destroyed the throne of the Pope, who always incited Christians to make war on Muslims.[69]

Other than the obvious fabrications about the French being Muslims and destroying the papacy, what is noteworthy about this manifesto is its attempt to win over Egyptians through praise for Islam. Napoleon repeatedly insisted that he was fighting for Islam; the demonization of Islam was not yet part of the repertoire. Unlike Cromer, who stated one century later that the system of "Islam" was responsible for the supposed inferiority of the Egyptians, Napoleon would not disparage Islam. Instead, he harnessed his knowledge of the religion to aid the colonial mission. As Hourani observes, Napoleon had "an admiration for the achievements of Muhammad."[70] Napoleon invited sixty Muslim scholars from al-Azhar to his quarters and impressed them with his knowledge of and respect for the Quran. Everything that Napoleon said was translated for popular consumption into Quranic Arabic. This strategy worked, Said argues, and the people of Cairo lost their distrust of the French colonizers.[71]

When Napoleon left Egypt, he gave strict instructions to his deputy that Egypt was to be administered according to the model he had set: Orientalists were to be consulted before policies could be enacted, and the Muslim religious leaders he had won over also needed to be part of the arsenal of colonial rule. Napoleon charged his small army of scholars with the task of gathering vast amounts of firsthand information about Egypt. As Said writes, a team

> of chemists, historians, biologists, archaeologists, surgeons, and antiquarians [became] the learned division of the army. Its job was no less aggressive: to put Egypt into modern French . . . Almost from the first moments of occupation Napoleon saw to it that the Institut [the Egypt Institute set up by him] began its meetings, its experiments—its fact-finding mission, as we would call it today. Most important, everything said, seen, and studied was to be recorded.[72]

This work resulted in the publication of *Description of Egypt*, a compendium in twenty-three volumes published between 1809 and 1828. Its detailed information on every aspect of Egyptian society, from monuments to facial structures, was created for use not by Egyptians but by the French. While there is much accurate and valuable information in the *Description*, the important point that Said makes is that such vast knowledge was amassed without the input of the native people. This account of Egypt served to displace Egypt's own sense of itself and its place in the world in favor of a French colonial vision of the same. It was ultimately created to help the French dominate the Egyptians.

The French, naturally, did not present their conquest in such base terms as control and domination. Rather, as the quote from Napoleon's manifesto suggests, its goal was to restore Egypt to its glorious past of "great cities" and "wide canals." France would save a once-great country from ruin and show the natives what they could become under French tutelage. This paternalistic logic became more developed as the European colonial mission grew. The British developed their version, which the writer Rudyard Kipling immortalized in his 1899 poem "The White Man's Burden." The French variant, *mission civilisatrice*, was used to great success to win domestic consent for colonial conquests in a nation founded on the ideas of *liberté, égalité, fraternité* (liberty, equality, and fraternity). After all, if equality and liberty were available to all, how might one justify depriving the colonized of these basic rights? The civilizing mission offered a way out. It was also built on a framework of thought that was dominant in the nineteenth century.

The French occupied Egypt only until 1801. It was interimperialist rivalry with Britain that ultimately forced them to leave, but Egyptians also quickly realized that the French did not have their best interests at heart. Nevertheless, this method of colonization was seen as a model to be emulated. After Napoleon, Said writes, the "very language of Orientalism changed radically"; from then on, "the Orient was reconstructed, reassembled, crafted, in short, *born* out of Orientalists' efforts."[73] The Orient was no longer strange and exotic, but a region that could be understood and controlled. And Orientalist scholarship was the key that would unlock the secrets of the East. The study of the Orient developed in two phases. In the first wave, various Orientalist societies were created in France, the Netherlands, and England.[74] In the second phase, Orientalist congresses were held starting in Paris in 1873.[75] The field was dominated by Western scholars; at the seventeenth international congress held in Oxford in 1927, only about a dozen out of the 750 subscribing members were Muslim.[76]

To be sure, not all Orientalist scholarship was tied to the interests of empire. While Said acknowledges that fact, he also advances an analysis of Orientalism that has been criticized for its geographic essentialism, which is the notion all knowledge produced in the West about the East is necessarily ethnocentric.[77] One of the first critics of Orientalism, sociologist Anouar Abdel-Malek, notes that Orientalists produced valuable knowledge.[78] Some, however, advised governments and played an important role in enabling colonization—such as Silvestre de Sacy, an important Orientalist who influenced generations of scholars. Hourani observes that some Orientalists opposed the imperial policies of their countries; examples include E. G. Brown in England, who supported the constitutional revolution in Iran, and the French Louis Massignon, who supported the Algerian movement for independence.[79] Iranian studies professor Hamid Dabashi defends the work of Orientalist scholar Ignaz Goldziher and draws a distinction between Orientalists who "heavily invested in producing a particular knowledge of Islam and Muslims compatible with European colonial interests" and those like Goldziher, who was an anti-colonial activist in Egypt.[80] Orientalism is thus a complex and contradictory body of scholarly work and field of institutional knowledge. However, as Abdel-Malek also argued, the "dominant vision" of the East was one produced by "dons, military men, colonial officials, missionaries, publicists whose only objective was to gather intelligence information in the area to be occupied, to penetrate the consciousness of the people in order to better assure its enslavement to European powers."[81] It is to this body of institutional Orientalism that we turn next.

Institutional Orientalism and *Homo Islamicus*

Before outlining some of the key characteristics of the dominant and institutional forms of Orientalism, it is worth noting that there is considerable debate about what Orientalism is and how to understand it. Prior to the wave of decolonization struggles in the period after World War II, Orientalism was understood as the work done by an Orientalist or a scholar with knowledge of eastern languages and literature; as a style or quality of art associated with Eastern nations; or a "conservative and romantic" political approach to government problems.[82] In the two decades after World War II, several intellectuals launched searing critiques. The key figures were Abdel-Malek in his essay "Orientalism in Crisis" (1963), historian A. L. Tibawi in several essays, Edward Said in essays and in *Orientalism* (1978), and the sociologist Bryan Turner in *Marx and the End of Orientalism* (1978).[83] As a result of these interventions, Orientalism came to mean

> not only the work of the orientalist and a character, style or quality associated with Eastern nations, but also a corporate institution, designed

for dealing with the orient, a partial view of Islam, an instrument of
Western imperialism, a style of thought, based on an ontological and
epistemological distinction between orient and occident, and even an
ideology, justifying and accounting for the subjugation of blacks, Palestinian Arabs, women and many other other[s].[84]

When studied within culture and the arts, Orientalism is not monolithic,
as various scholars have argued. In her analysis of British and French
writing from the eighteenth to the twentieth century, American studies
scholar Lisa Lowe shows that not only are there differences between the
two imperial nation's literary works but that the "other" is represented
differently at different moments.[85] Historian John MacKenzie argues that
culture is extraordinarily heterogeneous and, like Makdisi, notes that
internal others played a role in the construction of external others.
Furthermore, various artistic forms relied on cultural borrowing. Writers
like Goethe drew from Persian and Arabic literary styles and European
architects similarly were influenced by ancient Egyptian aesthetics.[86]
MacKenzie argues therefore that Orientalism is a constantly changing,
versatile and protean form which is "as often consumed by admiration
and reverence as by denigration and deprecation."[87] Middle East historian Zachary Lockman notes that there was something of an obsession
among thinkers, writers, and artists who identified with the Romantic
movement in European art and literature about the region they called the
"Orient." The Romantic movement rejected the Enlightenment philosophers' emphasis on rationality and instead valorized emotion, intuition,
and imagination. For Romantic poets, philosophers, novelists, and painters, the East was a source of great wisdom and spiritual advancement.
They contrasted this image with their own societies, which had lost these
qualities in the mad rush to industrialization and capitalist modernity,
and they drew on Eastern styles of literary expression, architectures, and
other such creative arenas.[88] In what follows, I focus on institutional
Orientalism, or a system of ideas and practices that Abdel-Malek, Said,
Turner, and others have argued helped consolidate colonialism.
     We might identify four characteristic features of Orientalism. First, it
is based on a civilizational view of history—the idea that civilizations
come into being, prosper, and then go into decline. This view is inflected
by a teleological understanding of history, which sees various societies as
going through stages until they either stagnate or evolve to the highest
(and Western) state. Second, and this flows from the first characteristic, it
views Eastern societies as static and unchanging. Third, because so many

Orientalists drew on philology, the historical and comparative study of language, it assumes that everything one needs to know about a civilization can be found in its texts and languages. It sees Islam and its classical texts as key to understanding contemporary Muslims and their societies. And fourth, it built on Enlightenment theories of race and the notion that Muslims are a distinct race.

In the nineteenth century it was widely believed that human society was divided into different and distinct civilizations, each of which had a core set of values driving it. This theory held that the West, as a unique civilization with roots in ancient Greece, had certain qualities that differentiated it from all other civilizations. These included "freedom, law, rationality, science, progress, intellectual curiosity, and the spirit of invention, adventure and enterprise."[89] Every other civilization was then defined in relation to this notion of the "West." One of the first articulations of a general view of the history of humankind divided into different groups based on way of life, customs, and beliefs was advanced by J. G. von Herder in the eighteenth century. He argued that the basic units of humankind were groups of peoples or nations who shared a common language and customs that differentiated them from one another. Arabs were a simple people who were "for the most part solitary, romantic men."[90] While Islam had raised these people up from their simple and "savage" state to "a middle degree of civilization," they were unable to grow further, he asserted.[91] However, they left behind a legacy, the Arabic language, which allowed for communication between nations. (Arabic was still the lingua franca in many parts of the world.)

G. W. F. Hegel provided yet another grand theory of humankind. For Hegel, history is the process by which a universal Spirit is manifested in different ways at different moments. History consists therefore of phases that are the embodiment of a particular communal or national spirit or will. The history of humanity was for Hegel one in which each civilization contributed something to humanity as a whole based on their own unique spirit but then faded away. While Muslims and Arabs played an essential role in the evolution of human history, Hegel argued, they had ceased to be significant.[92] The Absolute Spirit traveled from the East to West, from its inception in the Orient through Greece and Rome to maturity with the rise of the Germanic people. Thus, "Islam has long vanished from the stage of history, and has retreated into oriental ease and repose," he argued.[93]

Such notions helped fuel the understanding that Oriental societies were stagnant. Each civilization, Orientalists argued, consists of people who have an "essence," which "constitutes the inalienable and common basis of the beings considered."[94] This essence defined them across time, Abdel-Malek observes. Such an essentialist understanding helped produce the notion that Muslim societies were locked within their sacred customs and a set of moral and religious codes that kept them static. Thus, regions ruled by Muslims were cast as premodern, backward, primitive, despotic, static, undemocratic, and rigid. In contrast, "Western" society was characterized as dynamic, innovative, and democratic.

The lack of evolution in Muslim lands was also attributed to "Oriental despotism." Enlightenment philosopher Montesquieu, writing in 1748, explained that Asia was destined to be despotic because of the way its hot climate affected the temperaments of its people. He argued that in cooler regions such as Europe, the people tended to be active and therefore braver, whereas in the warmer climates of Asia the people were inactive and therefore servile and effeminate.[95] It followed from this that democracy was more at home in the former, while the subservient people of the East were capable only of despotism. While Montesquieu's climate-based theory, which drew on precursors in the classical era, is long out of style, the notion of "Oriental despotism" and the belief that the people of the MENA region and South Asia are best suited to dictatorships has endured, as shown in Chapter 3. As political scientist Aslı Çırakman argues, Montesquieu's theory had a "long-term influence" on how the West viewed Turkey.[96]

Turner summarizes the Orientalist approach:

> Orientalism is based on an epistemology which is essentialist, empiricist and historicist. The essentialist assumption is present in the notion that "Islam" is a coherent, homogeneous, global entity, and also in the decline thesis where Islam is seen as declining because of some flaw in its essence. Social and political decline is a consequence of some historically ever-present element—authoritarianism, the lack of autonomous oppositional groups or laws, slavish adherence to formal custom or the failure of ruling institutions. This inner, flawed essence unfolds in history as a teleological process toward some final end-state which is the collapse of Islam and its civilization . . . The major problems of research for Orientalists are matters of philology, not epistemology.[97]

In other words, rather than examine how knowledge is produced and what methods are used to produce that knowledge (epistemology), Orientalists focused on explaining people through their languages and key texts (philology). Philologists like Sacy advocated the notion that the study of a society's written texts could yield insights into the timeless essence of a civilization. Orientalists therefore learned Arabic, Persian, Turkish, and Sanskrit and translated and analyzed the texts of the East. Rather than examine the historical context of Muslim and "Oriental" societies, philologists pursued textual analysis.

It followed from this that Islam, as defined by its classical texts, was the key lens through which Muslim-majority societies were understood. If women were oppressed, it was because of the teachings of the Quran; if Muslims supposedly lacked an entrepreneurial spirit, it was due to "Islamic tradition"; if modernization was rejected, again the Quran was to blame. In short, a whole host of characteristics associated with the "West" but allegedly absent in the "Muslim world" could be explained by recourse to religious texts and the mentalities they allegedly created. In this book, the term "Muslim world" has been put in quotation marks precisely to challenge the notion that Islam is the single most important factor in defining the people who live in the Middle East, North Africa, South Asia, and elsewhere or that there is a single undifferentiated entity called the "Muslim world." Instead, I try to show that like elsewhere in the world, religion is one factor among others that impact the lives of people who live in Muslim-majority societies (a term I prefer to *Muslim world*).

In addition to civilizational theories, the Orientalists drew on Enlightenment theories of race that placed European Caucasians at the top of a racial hierarchy. As Rodinson explains:

> The Oriental may always have been characterized as a savage enemy, but during the Middle Ages, he was at least considered on the same level as his European counterpart. And, to the men of the Enlightenment, the ideologies of the French revolution, the Oriental was, for all his foreignness in appearance and dress, above all a man like anyone else. In the nineteenth century, however, he became something quite separate, sealed off in his own specificity, yet worthy of a kind of grudging admiration. This is the origin of the *homo islamicus*, a notion widely accepted even today.[98]

The experience of colonial domination in Ottoman lands and over Persia and South Asia produced a sometimes separate and sometimes composite subspecies of human being containing Arabs, Turks, Iranians, and South Asians. As Abdel-Malek argues, *Homo islamicus* (Latin for "Islamic man") stood in contrast to the "normal man" or European man (and it was men that they wrote about, not women) defined by an essence that had shaped him from Greek antiquity to the present.[99] Muslims as a subspecies were fundamentally different from and opposed to the "western man." By reading the Quran and other religious, moral, or legal writings, Orientalists believed that they could determine how Muslims think and behave. Their essential character could be understood from the texts of their civilization.

The notion of *Homo islamicus* (as well as *Homo arabicus* and *Homo indicus*) comes out of the Enlightenment typologies discussed above. These typologies, however, were advanced at a moment when there was a move away from the Enlightenment universalism discussed above and an emphasis on irreconcilable differences among people and civilizations. By the end of the nineteenth century, not only was there a sense that the "West" represented the height of human accomplishment, but adaptations of Darwin's theory of the origin of species applied to infer the origin of races and notions of innate biological racial superiority were widespread. Francis Galton, Darwin's cousin, first coined the term *eugenics* in 1883, advancing the notion that human beings could improve their kind by selective mating between those with desirable traits. At the high point of European colonialism, it was believed that the "West" had triumphed because of innate qualities. Racist ideas about the superiority of "Aryans" or "Caucasians" were accepted by scientists and thinkers. Even those who rejected these notions of a superior Caucasian race held that "different ethnic groups, races, peoples and civilizations" had "more or less fixed cultural essences," Lockman argues.[100] Because race-based theories assume that the members of a race are all alike, scholars within this tradition could make sweeping generalizations about how the racialized Muslim thinks and behaves. Most of all, the "Muslim mind" was disparaged. Kipling wrote, "You'll never plumb the Oriental mind. And even if you do, it won't be worth the toil."[101] By "Oriental" Kipling, who was born in India, was referring to all Asians and not just those in the MENA region; thus, South Asian Muslims and Hindus were amalgamated into a composite racial category.

It followed from this logic of civilizational and racial superiority that the West had to lead lesser nations and peoples. In the late nineteenth century, when Kipling wrote "The White Man's Burden," he was simply reinforcing an idea that was by then widespread. He wrote of the inherent superiority of the "West" and its "burden" to civilize and tame the peoples of the "East." Characterized as "half devil, half child," the colonized were seen both as evil and barbaric, and as childlike and therefore in need of protection. When the poem was originally published, Kipling used the subtitle "The United States and the Philippine Islands" as a way to urge the Americans to take on the same responsibilities as the British.[102] And take them on they did. Woodrow Wilson, seen as visionary for championing self-determination, put it as follows:

> In order to trace the lineage of the European and American governments which have constituted the order of social life for those stronger and nobler races which have made the most notable progress in civilization, it is essential to know the political history of the Greeks, the Latins, the Teutons, and the Celts principally.[103]

In sum, the Orientalist view of the East as it emerged in the nineteenth century was based on a racial and civilizational characterization of Muslims. This is not, however, to suggest that Orientalist scholarship existed or was used in colonial contexts without contradiction or that British and French Orientalisms were monolithic or singular bodies of thought across time. There were Orientalists who rejected notions of racial superiority; at the same time, however, they agreed that race was a useful category of analysis. There were those who admired Islam and others who disparaged it; some actively aided the colonial mission while others fought colonialism. Orientalist ideas were used differently in various contexts. Put simply, the relationship between Orientalist thought and the project of empire-building is complex and historically specific.

However, it is undeniable that the aforementioned assumptions underlying institutional Orientalism made the theory useful for imperial domination and colonial conquest. The worldview proposed by the Orientalists is one in which the "West" is seen as a dynamic, complex, and ever-changing society that cannot be reduced to its key religion or any other single factor, while the "Orient" or the "world of Islam" is presented as unchanging, barbaric, misogynistic, uncivilized, and despotic. The only logical conclusion that flows from this is that it is the responsibility of the West to intervene in these static societies and bring about change. The West had acquired a superiority complex, and the rest of the world would have to submit to its dictates.

Conclusion

In the late eighteenth century, numerous revolutions brought forth notions of human equality, secularism, anti-slavery, and democracy and ushered in a process where capitalism would shape global relations. While Spain had held sway during the era of mercantile imperialism, Britain would lead the transition to capitalist imperialism and assume dominance in the imperial arena, building a vast empire in the nineteenth and early twentieth centuries that spanned the globe. It is in this context that Orientalism as a body of thought tied directly to the project of colonial control was elevated. While equality was enshrined as a principle fought for in various revolutions, the now "free" colonizing nations denied democratic rights to the people they subjugated. This was the context for the racialization of Muslims. It was built on the notion that civilizations had an "essence" that marked the evolution of people across time producing races of people with fixed and immutable characteristics. Their inability to grow beyond a certain point justified colonial intervention, which, it was claimed, would lead to upliftment. Moreover, capitalism set limits on the expansion of rights. As economist Samir Amin has observed, "Enlightenment thought offer[ed] us a concept of reason that is inextricably associated with that of emancipation. Yet, the emancipation in question is defined and limited by what capitalism requires and allows."[104]

South Asians were also part of this project of racialization, particularly since India was the "jewel" in Britain's crown. Kipling generated influential tropes about the East that applied not only to South Asians but Arabs as well. As Said has argued, the composite "Oriental" of the nineteenth century brought together people from North Africa to India into one homogeneous group.[105] In his analysis of the role of liberals in bolstering empire, Uday Singh Mehta observes that even though various thinkers did not use the term *race*, there was a process of racialization at work. He argues that the infantalization of Indian subjects played such a role. When Kipling wrote about the colonized as "half child" in his poem, he was simply popularizing dominant notions. Mehta writes:

> Childhood is the theme that runs through the writings of British liberals on India with unerring constancy. It is the fixed point underlying the various imperial imperatives of education, forms of governance, and the alignment with progress. James Mill's characterization of India

as being in the infancy of the "progress of civilization," Macaulay's characterization of the British, who in the context of the empire must be
like fathers who are "just and unjust, moderate and rapacious," Trevely-
an's comment that Indians would "grow to man's estate," J. S. Mill's view
of the British as forming a "government of leading strings" that would
help "as a means of gradually training the people to walk alone"; all are
claims that constitute a virtual genre in imperial discourse. They all
coalesce around the same general point: India is a child for which the
empire offers the prospect of legitimate and progressive parentage and
toward which Britain, as a parent, is similarly obligated and competent.
For both the Mills as for Macaulay this point is the basis for the justification of denying democratic rights and representative institutions to
Indians, along with various other imperial interdictions.[106]

The "white man's burden" applied to various colonized peoples; Orientalist modes of thought developed in the nineteenth century drew from
logics of empire in various contexts. Thus, the concomitant processes of
racialization involving South Asians, Arabs, and Muslims were intertwined from the start in the era of capitalist imperialism.

In early modern Spain, Muslims occupied a liminal space between
inferiority and superiority, the latter thanks in no small part to the power
of the Ottomans and various North African states. As these powers
declined, however, notions of inferiority could rise to the surface. In
short, it is actual systems of domination that engender racism as both
practice and ideology. Barbara and Karen Fields write:

> People are more readily perceived as inferior by nature when they are
> already seen as oppressed. Africans and their descendants might be, to
> the eye of the English, heathen in religion, outlandish in nationality,
> and weird in appearance. But that did not add up to an ideology of
> racial inferiority until a further historical ingredient got stirred into
> the mixture: the incorporation of Africans and their descendants into a
> polity and society in which they lacked rights that others not only took
> for granted, but claimed as a matter of self-evident natural law.[107]

Moreover, as historian Patrick Wolfe argues,

> European xenophobic traditions such as Judeophobia, Islamophobia
> or Negrophobia are considerably older than race. Though most if not
> all of its ingredients can be found in earlier classifications, race itself is

a distinctive configuration of ideological elements that we do not find configured in this way before the late eighteenth century, but that we do find so configured, and mutually reinforcing, from that time on.[108]

Building on these scholars, I offer that even while Muslims were viewed in hostile ways in previous centuries, two further ingredients were needed—societies based on equal rights and the political economic domination of Muslim lands in the era of capitalist imperialism—for an ideology of racial alterity and inferiority to develop. The ability to colonize Muslim lands and to deny rights to the colonized created the conditions for modern anti-Muslim racism. No doubt, as Wolfe argues, earlier tropes were drawn upon in this project of racialization. However, the necessary and sufficient conditions for the production of Muslims as a race in its modern form were present only in the nineteenth century in the era of capitalist modernity. To be sure, the racialization of Muslims was unstable and variable and took different forms at various moments in time. Even at a particular historical conjuncture, Orientalism was mediated in different ways in various spheres from politics to culture. This is because the "West" is not a monolith, there is therefore no singular production of those racialized by empire; anti-racism is also part of the mix.

Even today, and as I demonstrate in Chapter 3, variations of these notions abound. For instance, books like Raphael Patai's *The Arab Mind*,[109] which was used by the US military to devise the torture techniques used in Abu Ghraib and elsewhere, are a reassertion of *Homo arabicus*. It is based on the homogenization of Arabs, who are supposedly all of one mind. The practice of torture enacted at CIA "black sites" all over the world then instrumentalized this racist caricature to create regimes of oppression.[110] Arabs, South Asians, Afghans, and those perceived as racialized security threats were subject to a systematic denial of rights and a vulnerability to premature death. In the next chapter I turn to the United States and its systems of racialization.

2

The United States, Orientalism, and Modernization

The US/UN sanctions on Iraq in the 1990s resulted in the deaths of over a million Iraqis.[1] The 1990 war on Iraq had already devastated the country, destroying its modern infrastructure and denying Iraqis the right to security, access to water, health, shelter, and, more generally, the requirements for a decent life. Denis Halliday, an assistant secretary-general who was the United Nations Humanitarian Coordinator in Baghdad, resigned after a thirty-four-year career with the UN in protest of the sanctions regime. He stated: "I don't want to administer a programme that satisfies the definition of genocide."[2] Another UN humanitarian coordinator, Hans von Sponeck, also resigned in protest and penned a book that laid out the devastation caused by the US/UN sanctions.[3] Madeleine Albright, secretary of state during the Clinton administration, was asked by journalist Lesley Stahl on the show *60 Minutes* whether the price of sanctions in the form of half a million dead Iraqi children was worth it, and without hesitation Albright replied, "we think the price is worth it."[4] Iraqis were marked by a vulnerability to premature death, through a deeply racist logic. The draconian sanction regime was acceptable to the political elite because it advanced US imperial aims.

The complex and historically specific relationship between Orientalist thinking and race making, on the one hand, and the project of empire-building in the United States, on the other, is the subject of this chapter. The United States was itself a product of British imperialism, but it was also its heir, enthusiastically embracing such concepts as manifest destiny, which the British had developed long before it became a guiding principle for American expansion in the nineteenth century. The British believed in the right of conquest of "backward" peoples in the name of civilization (for example, the Irish and Native Americans), while the rapidly growing population of land-hungry settlers (the majority of whom had been dispossessed of land in England through enclosure) pushed for more expansion. The expansionist pressure accumulated so much momentum that by the middle of the eighteenth century, it drove the Anglo-American colonists to provoke the Seven Years' War and a little over a decade later to rebel against the British Empire. Rather than a rejection of empire, however, the American War of Independence was in many respects a dispute over the proper course of empire in North America. Indeed, through the mid-eighteenth century, the Anglo-Americans had been the most enthusiastic of British imperialists, fighting in four colonial wars.[5]

No longer impeded by the British Crown, the settler-colonial drive only accelerated following the American victory, eventually consuming much of the North American continent. Racialization was central to this process, as the acquisition of territory was made possible by the dispossession of Native Americans and Mexicans. But land was only valuable if there was a source of labor to work it, and here too, racialization was central. This is most obvious with respect to the use of slave labor, which expanded as the acquisition of territory opened up new lands for the cultivation of export crops, most importantly cotton. Cotton production developed in a symbiotic relationship with the English Industrial Revolution, the driving force of which was cotton textiles. As historian Sven Beckert notes, "the peculiar combination of expropriated lands, slave labor, and the domination of a state that gave enormous latitude to slave owners over their labor was fabulously profitable." Indeed,

> it was on the back of cotton, and thus on the backs of slaves, that the U.S. economy ascended in the world . . . American cotton farmers had succeeded in turning themselves into the world's most important growers of the industrial age's most important commodity.[6]

Settler colonialism and slavery were justified in the "land of the free" through recourse to racism, and racism enabled imperial expansion. In the early twentieth century, an American journalist re-articulated European notions of racial superiority as follows:

> Out of the prehistoric shadows the white races pressed to the front and proved in a myriad of ways their fitness for the hegemony of mankind. Gradually they forged a common civilization; then, when vouchsafed

their unique opportunity of oceanic mastery four centuries ago, they spread over the earth, filling its empty spaces with their superior breeds and assuring to themselves an unparalleled paramountcy of numbers and dominion . . . At last the planet was integrated under the hegemony of a single race with a common civilization.[7]

This was Orientalism repurposed for the US context. In this chapter, I outline the process by which Muslims were racialized. Drawing on various scholars, I discuss Orientalism in three periods: antebellum America, the postbellum era, and the period after World War II when the United States took over the reins of the Middle East and North Africa (MENA) from Britain and France. All these periods are marked by contradictory and changing attitudes toward Muslims. If the American nation was founded in opposition to "Oriental despotism," it is also the case that the United States was focused on the Western hemisphere and didn't enter the MENA region as an imperial hegemonic power until the postwar period. Thus, I argue that while the ideology of Orientalism has a long presence in the United States, it was not until the postwar era that instrumental knowledge was developed to aid imperialism and that Orientalism, but also modernization theory, became the basis for the racialization of Muslims. To be sure, in the first part of the twentieth century while Arab and South Asian Americans experienced racism through discriminatory citizenship laws, and black Muslims were racially targeted by the FBI, this was the product of previous systems of white supremacy. In the postwar era, a new process of racialization was born, tied to US imperial ambitions in the MENA region. Scholars in the field of Arab American studies have shown that starting in the late 1960s, Arab Americans were turned into a threatening race of people. Drawing on this work, I argue that terrorist racial formation is an evolving project that goes from a focus on Arabs to include Iranians and later South Asians. It was the crisis of empire and the use of counterinsurgency methods to handle threats abroad and at home that gave rise to the global "Arab terrorist," produced in conjunction with Israel.

Colonial and Antebellum America

Muslims first entered the United States with slavery. Kambiz GhaneaBassiri in *A History of Islam in America* suggests that even before the rise of Atlantic slavery, Muslims trickled in to the New World.[8] However, the first significant population of Muslims were enslaved West Africans. There is little consensus among scholars about the number of enslaved Muslims from West Africa in colonial America, not least because the religion of slaves was not well documented. In his pioneering book on black Muslims in the antebellum era, Afro-American studies scholar Allan Austin estimates that tens of thousands of black Muslims were among the enslaved population.[9] In the Americas as a whole there were more. Historian Sylviane A. Diouf acknowledges the absence of accurate data on the religion of slaves but nevertheless asserts that there were "hundreds of thousands of Muslims in the Americas."[10]

These enslaved people preserved their religion in the new hostile world they were forced into, even playing significant roles in the Haitian revolution and other revolts, as Diouf demonstrates. In the United States, however, black Muslims were less militant.[11] Austin's portrait of several dozen African Muslims shows that they continued to practice their religion, even in cases when they pretended to accept their master's religion. Over time, however, they converted to Christianity. This happened particularly after 1830, as scholar of religion Sherman Jackson argues, when Protestantism became the key vehicle to wage a campaign against American slavery.[12] He further notes that enslaved African Muslims were unable to sustain their religion and that it was only in the twentieth century that Islam could be associated with black Americans in any significant way.[13] From then on, and up until the 1970s, the majority of Muslims in the United States were black.[14]

Another way in which "Islam," that is, perceptions of the religion and its adherents, entered America was through British colonizers and their experiences with various Muslim kingdoms and empires. One source of contact was on the high seas. In the early decades of the seventeenth century, people from the North African Barbary States (Algiers, Tunis, Morocco, and Tripoli) had captured close to 500 English ships.[15] Soldier and colonial governor John Smith (of Pocahontas fame) blamed the Turks for some attacks. In fact, he cut his military teeth fighting the Ottomans in Europe. Smith prided himself on being a crusader against Muslims, and these attitudes toward the Turks shaped his view of Native Americans.[16] More generally, as noted in Chapter 1, the words *Turk* and *native* became interchangeable in English colonial vocabulary to mean *savage*. This is in no small part because England in the seventeenth century was not yet capable of challenging the Ottomans. Thus, from the earliest moments of colonization and slavery, "Islam" and Muslims had a presence in North America.

However, Islam was not the primary source of racialization in the colonial and antebellum period. Modes of racializing black slaves and indigenous people in policy and the law focused more on their labor (slaves) or land (Native Americans) rather than their religion. Black Muslims were not racialized in ways that differed from their non-Muslim sisters and brothers.[17] If anything, GhaneaBassiri argues, they were depicted as better than non-Muslim slaves. Enslaved African Muslims occupied a liminal space where they were made "exceptions to the prevailing negative stereotypes of blacks and Muslims" [the Ottomans], with "shifting communal boundaries defined by race and religion."[18] In seventeenth century Virginia in the context of the codification of chattel slavery, black slaves were turned into property. As a consequence, they were denied all rights including the right to practice religion. There is no evidence to suggest that during this period there was an attempt to criminalize Islam or to cast Islam as a security threat (see Chapter 6).[19] Where religion did feature in antebellum America, it was to keep black and native slaves in servitude despite conversion to Christianity.[20]

Like Muslims and Jews in Spain during the early modern era, black slaves and indigenous people were unable to escape persecution through conversion. Interestingly, in colonial America the law differentiated between black servants and Turks and Moors. An act passed in 1682 stated:

> all servants except Turks and Moores (sic) which shall be brought or imported into this country, either by sea or land; whether Negroes . . . Mullattoes or Indians, who and whose parentage and native country are not christian (sic) at the time of their first purchase of such servant by some christian, although afterwards, and before such their importation . . . they shall be converted to the christian faith . . . shall be judged, deemed and taken to be slaves.[21]

West African slaves and Indians became the irredeemable subjects of Christianity, exempt from its assimilationist and universalist ideology in the context of English colonialism. Turks and Moors, however, escaped this fate, very likely because England was not in a position to challenge the Ottoman Empire and various North African Muslim powers.

Perceptions of Islam from colonial America to the nineteenth century were shaped by European, and particularly British, thought, as Fuad Shaban, professor of English literature, points out.[22] At the same time, knowledge was produced inside the United States about the religion and its prophet. Shaban suggests that nineteenth century attitudes toward the Prophet Mohammad in literary circles were ambivalent and included both condemnation and admiration.[23] Additionally, attitudes toward the Ottomans, from the seventeenth century to the formation of the new republic, shaped public thinking.[24] In the American mindset, or at least that of the educated classes, the Ottomans were a major imperial power even if during this period they had lost some of their power. The political elite that founded and oversaw the American nation "after 1776 regarded the Muslim world, beset by oriental despotism, economic squalor, and intellectual stultification, as the antithesis of the republicanism to which they had pledged their sacred honor."[25]

American studies scholar Timothy Marr argues that the new republic valorized norms such as chastity, hard work, progressivism, and democracy (associated with the United States), which were counterposed to sensuality, indolence, irrational fatalism, and despotism (associated with the Ottomans). Just as leading lights of the French Enlightenment had denounced Oriental despotism in the lead-up to the French Revolution, the Americans too believed that their republic marked a departure from tradition with an insistence on democracy. Further, capitalist values and ethics (as in the British case discussed in Chapter 1) informed constructions of "us" and "them." Thus, even though the Ottomans were a distant empire, rhetorically the American nation was constructed in opposition to its despotism and, in this context, Islam was counterposed to Christianity.[26]

This construction was mediated differently in different spheres. In the late eighteenth century, hundreds of Oriental tales told the story of Easterners who were "incipient democrats" and could be "converted by free expression, honest love, and benevolent works."[27] In short, Orientals were not irredeemable. The underlying logic of these narratives was that American decency and democracy had the potential to change the world. This tone was also reflected in the work of American missionaries. Unlike English, Dutch, and Spanish missionaries who followed in the footsteps of soldiers, American missionaries were preceded by both soldiers and merchants.[28] Trade and capitalist imperatives were central to US imperialism just as much as they were central to the British Empire. In addition to various religious notions, Shaban argues that missionaries in the nineteenth century took with them the frontier mentality as well as the American notion of "manifest destiny" based on the idea that the United States had a mission to bring civilization to the world.[29]

US wars on the Barbary Coast in the early nineteenth century put a spotlight on Muslims in the Barbary States, which were nominally under the control of the Ottomans. When Tripoli declared war on the United States in 1801, President John Adams called for regime change. While this was a relatively minor incursion with barely a dozen or so marines, it is featured in the "Marines' Hymn," which begins with the words "From the halls of Montezuma to the shores of Tripoli," capturing the range of US imperial ambition. To be sure, at this stage, the United States was in no position to colonize North Africa or Ottoman territories, and they fell into the hands of the French and British over the course of the next century. It nevertheless produced imperial rhetoric about the Muslim other. Specifically, when US ships came under attack in the early 1800s, those on these ships were taken prisoner. This generated a national interest in captivity narratives.

The immense popularity of Barbary captivity narratives reflected not only an interest in the stories of the increasing number of American sailors captured by North Africans and held in bondage and slavery, but also a demand for captivity tales related to Native Americans.[30] These were stories about a "civilized" West and a "barbaric" North Africa.[31] They were tales of capture, imprisonment, slavery, and escape. While white slavery was clearly denounced, the stories either indirectly justified enslavement of Africans or denounced North Africans as subhuman. One popular narrative described the treatment of an American captive in Algiers at the hands of "merciless Mahomatans" as being so awful and so filled with "horror" that even their "tenderest mercies towards the Christian captives, are the most extreme cruelties."[32] His escape was presented as a triumph of a democratic nation that would not allow its sailors to languish under slavery. With no sense of irony, white slavery was denounced at the moment when US slavery was on the rise with West African captors having no hope of return. Few of these narratives questioned the hypocrisy at work.[33]

However, abolitionists capitalized on this opportunity to denounce American slavery, seeing in the attention received by white slavery a chance to discuss the enslavement of West Africans. Moreover, actual encounters with Muslims dissipated negative stereotypes. For instance, when Americans learned that Muslims treated their enslaved populations in more humane ways and that they had a long history of abstaining from alcohol, it was used in some quarters to advance anti-slavery and temperance arguments. The logic employed by advocates in these movements was that Americans could hardly claim the mantle of civilization if they practiced such immoral behaviors. Nor could they claim to be superior to the Turks in opposition to whom their national identity was constructed. This was still an Orientalist mode of representation, but one that used shaming tactics to force reforms. Interestingly, Benjamin Franklin writing under a pseudonym satirized American arguments in favor of slavery from the point of view of an Algerian named Sidi Mehemet Ibrahim.[34]

As more travelers visited the lands ruled by Muslims, they found even more evidence to show that enslaved people there were not treated as poorly as they were in the US South. Thus, if abolitionist arguments began by comparing American slaveholders to the "tyrants" of Turkey, they shifted their tone when they encountered evidence of its relatively benign nature in Muslim ruled regions.[35] In the 1840s, the Bey of Tunis and the Sultan of Turkey took aggressive steps to end slavery. This was reported in American newspapers and lent credence to the abolitionists' arguments. It also challenged the trope of Islamic lands as static and unchanging and of slavery as being endemic to Islamic culture.[36] Thus, antebellum US attitudes toward the Turks and North African Muslims were not fixed but changed at different historical conjunctures and varied by multiple constituent groups within the nation. As Marr argues, American Orientalism in this period was elastic and "its protean meanings rel[ied] upon the historical circumstances, the performative situations, and the ideological intent of the different individuals who deploy[ed] its expressive grammar."[37]

The Postbellum Period

Travelers would continue to furnish information about the MENA region even in the postbellum era. Travelogues with descriptions of the Holy Land were immensely popular.[38] Mark Twain, who went on to become a staunch anti-imperialist, wrote in 1869 about his trip to the Holy Land in a book titled *The Innocents Abroad*, which sold nearly a hundred thousand copies.[39] While Twain witheringly (and hilariously) critiqued his fellow travelers for their hubris and lack of cultural sensitivity—a characteristic of American tourists that would continue into the next century and become grist for the Hollywood mill—he also had harsh words to say about Muslims. He called them "a people by nature and training filthy, brutish, ignorant, unprogressive [and] superstitious."[40] However, he seemed to have sympathy with suffering Syrians whom he called a people who "are naturally good hearted and intelligent" and who "with education and liberty, would be a happy and contented race."[41] Overall, however his assessment of Arabs was that they were "savages" and that Muslims were pagans. Thus, we see both a recourse to medieval tropes combined with a sense of racial superiority not unlike that witnessed in Europe.

Romantic notions of the Orient, however, featured the region as an exotic land to be admired and even emulated. Americans could brandish their cosmopolitan credentials through an interest in the Orient. Further, embracing Oriental styles became a means of resistance. Women suffragists, for example, advocated the wearing of Turkish trousers as more practical and masculine. Feminist leader Elizabeth Cady Stanton acknowledged that the "bloomer" (as it was called) was "an imitation in part of Turkish style."[42] Popular culture was dotted with such romantic notions. Illustrated versions of *The Arabian Nights* were widely sold, as were books about the Prophet.

Several best-selling novels like *Ben-Hur* (1880), *Quo Vadis* (1895), and *The Sign of the Cross* (1896) purported to give Americans a picture of the MENA region. In addition to novels and travelogues, a series of other popular media such as fairs and exhibitions, photographs, panoramas, and theme parks depicted the Holy Land in multiple forms that were readily available.[43] The disappointment that Americans felt at coming across local populations who failed to live up to the mediated images of the Holy Land, as American studies scholar Melani McAlister argues, lent "proof to the superiority of Christianity." The economic underdevelopment was viewed as both a failure of the Ottomans and a weakness in Muslim character.[44]

In nineteenth-century Europe, the Orientalist image of the backward and savage other coexisted with the romantic image of the exotic other, and US audiences readily adopted the latter. For instance, the American painter Frederick Bridgman produced dozens of sexually charged paintings of the East in line with those of his mentor, the French painter Jean-Léon Gérôme, famous for his paintings *The Snake Charmer* and *The Slave Market*.[45] Hollywood would further these exotic images in early silent films such as *The Arab* (1915), *Cleopatra* (1917), *Salomé* (1918), and *An Arabian Knight* (1920). Rudolph Valentino played the role of a sheik in two films, *The Sheik* (1921) and *Son of the Sheik* (1926), which among other things presented the East as sexually charged.

The Orient as sensual and sexual was channeled by advertisers in a form that McAlister refers to as "commodity orientalism." It was based on a logic that harnessed European Orientalist tropes of the East as excessive, luxurious, indulgent, and driven by sensuality, qualities that advertisers wanted to imbue in Americans. In these ways, the protestant ethic of frugality would be breached, marking the birth of an era of consumerism and self-indulgence. McAlister writes:

> Shopping in particular became linked to the exotic pleasure of the Orient, which allowed the new discourse of commodity culture to simultaneously praise the practice of indulgence and disavow it, by linking it to foreignness. In this moral geography, the East speaks of something missing in the world of the American work ethic; it is what one longs for; it is the iconography of sexual desire and the possibility of purchasing the feelings that go through with that desire—reverie, release, sensual pleasure—through the goods associated with it. And the department store, like the Orient itself, was grasped as an exhibition, a spectacle, even a dream.[46]

The dream of the Orient included South Asians as well. Edwin Weeks published his illustrated travelogue of his adventures in North Africa and India in *Harper's Monthly*. Media scholar Vivek Bald argues that his black and white sketches of India, which included mosques, palaces, exoticized images of Indian women, royalty, and markets, reproduced European Orientalist views of India.[47] Tobacco companies, Bald writes,

> made the fantasy of the palace and harem central to the branding and advertising of a wide range of their products. Smokers were offered a plethora of American manufactured tobacco products branded and marketed with "Near Eastern" names—Mecca, Red Kamel, Fatima, Bagdad—or explicitly East Indian ones. Americans could fill their pipes with Hindoo brand tobacco, smoke Royal Bengal cigars, or buy packs of Mogul cigarettes.[48]

In this context, Syrian immigrants to the United States were able to amass wealth by quickly making available "carpets, fine silks, and lace."[49] Historian Sarah Gualtieri has noted that Syrian immigrant merchants at the turn of the twentieth century became part of an "emerging transnational bourgeoisie who cleverly exploited America's desire to 'shop the Orient.'" Tens of thousands of Syrian immigrants, primarily Christian, settled in the United States during this period. They were part of the great wave of immigration that saw tens of millions come to the United States from eastern and southern Europe. Most Syrians were clustered in New York City or in the midwest, particularly Detroit.

Skin color and class position would influence how these new immigrants were regarded. A *New York Times* article describing the people in the Syrian enclave in New York City noted that "a good many of them are easily distinguishable by a rather dark complexion, and might by some be taken for Italians or Frenchmen from the South of France, but not a few are of quite light complexion, and with light-colored hair."[50] This latter group was more easily accepted. This parallels the experience of the tens of million southern and eastern European immigrants who also entered the United States in the same period who were known as "new immigrants." Race scholar David Roediger's analysis of these groups shows that they were at first racialized but, after World War II, accepted into whiteness.[51] He states that they occupied an "inbetween" space: "'Inbetween' hard racism and full inclusion neither securely white nor nonwhite—new immigrants were also chronologically inbetween sharply posed calls for their racially based exclusion . . . and far greater acceptance."[52]

Gualtieri similarly argues that the early Arab immigrants occupied a status between white and black. At first, and up until 1909, they were granted citizenship. However, in the context of racist arguments about citizenship and belonging, Syrians had to marshal all their resources to win legal battles around naturalization. They advanced arguments about their economic success and their Christian faith to prove that they were part of whiteness (the only means by which citizenship could be earned). Lawyers adduced civilizational arguments about the Holy Land to establish common ancestry. They also relied on social scientific explanations of human races to demonstrate the commonality between Syrian Christians and their white US counterparts. These efforts were more successful than those of their East and South Asian counterparts.[53] Within the racial hierarchy in the United States, East and South Asians were closer to blacks than they were to whites, as the Ozawa and Thind cases demonstrate.[54]

In the Immigration Act of 1917 (known as the Asiatic barred zone act), which prevented immigration from the Asian Pacific region, Syrians were exempted. This "exclusion of Syrians from the Asiatic barred zone helped consolidate [their whiteness]. Thus the legal construction of Syrian whiteness became part of a larger story of their disassociation from Asia and of the creation of a new category, the "Middle East" (which is, in fact, West Asia)."[55]

Arab Muslims had a more difficult time acquiring citizenship, Gualteiri argues. However, by the mid-1940s Arab Muslims were also incorporated into legal definitions of whiteness on the grounds that they were part of the Semitic race. The Immigration and Naturalization Services department argued that since the Semitic races had contributed to Western civilization, Arab Muslims could be granted citizenship. Thus, while Arab Americans were legally discriminated against in a process that we might understand as racism, it was a shifting and unstable form of racialization that did not target them specifically but was part of a system of oppression directed at all "new immigrants."

If Arab Americans were accepted into a proximity to whiteness, black Muslims faced a different situation. Starting in 1931, the FBI began a program of surveillance and intimidation of the members of the Moorish Science Temple of America (MSTA). For black Americans, Islam represented a mode of resistance in the postreconstruction era just as Protestantism was a means of challenging slavery in the antebellum period. At its height, the MSTA had tens of thousands of registered members.[56] Founded in 1926, it drew inspiration from a number of quarters, including the Ahmadiyya mission, which emerged in South Asia and sought to promote racial harmony. The MSTA not only advanced criticisms of white supremacy but also of Western imperialism in Muslim majority countries. African American studies scholar Sylvester Johnson writes that by

> conceptualizing the Moorish religion as encompassing a range of non-White races united by the experience of racism and colonialism, converts to Moorish Science developed a sense of national identity marked by political membership in a diasporic community—for them, Islam was not so much a confession of faith as a kind of citizenship in a racially defined civilization that spanned the globe.[57]

The group sought to restore its Moorish and transnational heritage.

When J. Edgar Hoover learned of the MSTA, he immediately "associated these African American Muslims with racial insurgence."[58] The FBI viewed the group's leaders as "fanatics" because of their advocacy of racial equality. To their mind, a group that challenged white supremacy and US imperialism was a danger to the status quo. This resulted in a widespread program of surveillance, the planting of infiltrators, and use of tactics of intimidation to disrupt the group's activities including through the use of the law. In the state of Mississippi, the MSTA was prosecuted for violating the state's antisedition laws. The group represented "racial enemies threatening the ability of the White race to control the government of Mississippi and that of the nation," Johnson writes.[59] This amounted to sedition. Once convicted, MSTA members were sentenced to jail as a warning to other black people of what would happen if they dared to challenge white supremacy. Similar efforts at intimidation and surveillance continued through to the 1960s against leaders of the Nation of Islam (NOI), including Malcolm X. Malcolm, like the MSTA, denounced white supremacy and US imperialism and used Islam as the glue to build a transnational identity for black people.

The national security state considered these black Muslims to be dangerous internal threats.[60] In 1955, the FBI had produced an intelligence report about the NOI titled "The Muslim Cult of Islam." Even though it changed the name of the report to the "Nation of Islam" in 1960, it continued, as communication scholar Sydney Pasquinelli argues, to call the group a "cult" or the "cult of Black Muslims." Such a designation was meant to discredit the NOI and its version of Islam, since the group was opposed to white supremacy. The 1955 report outlined the central tenets of what the FBI considered to be "orthodox" Islam (which it approved of), which were then contrasted with the NOI's practice, which was deemed "unorthodox." There was a "good" Islam and a "bad" or inauthentic Islam for the FBI. Further, the domestic good Muslims, as Pasquinelli writes, were "imams of Middle Eastern (rather than African) descent who were opposed to (Arab-, African-, and Black-) nationalism" who were then "treated as representatives of an authentic, peaceful Islam."[61]

If black Muslims were racialized as security threats by the FBI, Arab Americans were included into this framework starting in the late 1960s. Arab American studies scholars Elaine Hagopian, Nadine Naber, Louise Cainkar, and others have written about the ways in which anti-Arab racism operates through a transnational frame whereby empire targets Arabs living inside the United States when it goes to war in the MENA region.[62] Cainkar states that "once marginally white, and thus structurally privileged even if ideologically impugned, Arab Americans became racially excluded from whiteness in a later-emerging US American project: global US empire."[63] Naber traces the journey of Arab Americans from "model minority" to "problem minority."[64] Moreover, they have also argued that US support of Israel's settler colonial project plays an important role in how Arab Americans are treated inside the United States.

Building on this work, I have argued elsewhere that the project of terrorist racial formation occurred in the context of empire in crisis.[65] The national security state designated Arab Americans as "terrorists" or "potential terrorists" through the counterinsurgency logic of the Cold

War era that saw threats abroad and at home in similar ways. Operation Boulder, a modification of the infamous COINTELPRO project used to target the New Left and activists in the civil rights, black power, American Indian, Puerto Rican, anti-war, and other groups was deployed to target and racialize Arab Americans. As part of the effort to restore US hegemony, conservatives in the United States and Israel played a central role in advancing a counterterrorist program and imperialist agenda on a global scale. Two crucial conferences organized by the Israeli Jonathan Institute (discussed in Chapter 4) played a role in the development of the global "Arab terrorist" as a threat to democracy. More broadly, the attempt to resuscitate empire/colonialism, after successful national liberation movements had discredited colonialism not only in the minds of the colonized but also sympathetic sections in Western nations, provided the context for the evolution of terrorist racial formation. Moreover, the global economic crisis and the crisis of US imperialism in the late 1960s and 1970s created the conditions, I have argued, for two simultaneous racial projects: the criminalization of blacks and the terrorization of Arabs (and later Iranians, Muslims, and South Asians). The "black criminal" and the "brown terrorist" were birthed in the womb of a national security state seeking to quell threats to the restoration of US economic and political hegemony through the logic of counterinsurgency.

American Orientalism and Modernization Theory

After World War II, the United States emerged as one of two hegemonic nations on the global stage. It now became necessary to develop systematic knowledge about various parts of the world in order to facilitate imperial domination. As it set out to take the place of Britain and France in the MENA region and establish its dominance, it needed information to guide its policy. At first, it could only rely on young men who had grown up in the region, children of missionaries or university professors, known as the "Arabists." Additionally, US businesses in the Middle East, particularly oil companies, were a source of information. Finally, archeologists who had led expeditions in the area had created a body of knowledge.[66]

But in the context of the Cold War, and with the development of national liberation movements, the United States needed reliable information to further its interests in the region. The government as well as private foundations began to sponsor and fund "area studies" programs and departments that focused on the study of not only the Near East, but also Asia, Africa, and Latin America more broadly. Three foundations played a significant role in this process: the Carnegie Corporation, the Rockefeller Center, and the Ford Foundation. International relations scholar Inderjeet Parmar suggests that these "Big 3" foundations helped mobilize knowledge production within universities to "consolidate U.S. hegemony around the globe."[67] With large grants, US universities set out to create departments, centers, and programs instrumental to serving the needs of empire. Two approaches guided the study of the Middle East: Orientalism (which was still dominated by philologists) and social scientific research, from which a new model known as "modernization" would be developed. This latter model, while it claimed to be objective social science, was in fact imbued with notions of "exceptionalism and empire," as historian Osamah Khalil argues in his comprehensive book on knowledge production on the Middle East, *America's Dream Palace*.

One of the first universities to set up a Near East studies program was Princeton University. The Rockefeller and Carnegie foundations provided resources for this program, and the State Department expressed enthusiastic support. In 1947, Princeton organized a conference titled "The Arab and Moslem World: Studies and Problems." In attendance were prominent Orientalists like the Oxford scholar H. A. R. Gibb and the Austrian Gustave von Grunebaum. Attendees included members from the oil company ARAMCO, the State Department, and representatives from the Rockefeller Foundation, the Carnegie Corporation, and the American Council of Learned Societies.[68]

As it became clear that the imperial center was shifting across the Atlantic to the United States, prominent Orientalist scholars from Europe took up academic positions at US universities. For instance, Gibb left Oxford to take a position at Harvard University in 1955 and played a central role in the development of the Orientalist approach in the country. Grunebaum influenced a new generation of scholars at the University of Chicago and then UCLA.[69] Between them they brought Orientalist modes of analysis to the United States and continued the work of influential late-nineteenth-century Orientalists like Ernest Renan. Gibb, for instance, argued that the "Arab mind" and the "Muslim mind" had an essence that could be grasped by reading the classical texts of Islam. Grunebaum argued that a static Islamic culture could help explain all contemporary phenomena. Such sweeping generalizations, characteristic of Orientalist scholarship, were influential in the United States because they provided a quick and easy way to grasp a large and complex region.

In the ensuing decades, Orientalism was challenged by social scientific research to such a degree that Gibb acknowledged some of the shortcomings of the Orientalist method and urged social scientists and Orientalists to work together.[70] However, despite the publication of a number of works critical of its assumptions and methods in the period after the 1970s, Orientalism survived. Bernard Lewis, the British Orientalist, can be credited with continuing the legacy and influence of Orientalism. Lewis accepted a position at Princeton University in 1974 and has been a key figure in Orientalist thought in the United States ever since.

The United States, however, could not simply accept *in toto* the language of the old empires. Its own history of struggle against British imperialism meant that there were voices in the political sphere that resisted the mantle of imperialism. American exceptionalism is premised on differentiating the country from Europe and projecting it as a land of liberty and benevolence in international relations. This image erases not only its settler-colonial foundation, but also its territorial wars of expansion both with Canada and Mexico and its imperial interventions in Latin America during the nineteenth century, guided by the Monroe doctrine.[71]

The upheavals of World War II combined with decolonization struggles weakened the older empires and created a bipolar world oriented around two new powers, the United States and the Soviet Union. In this context, the United States hoped to loosen the aging imperial powers' grips on their colonial territories. The Truman and Eisenhower administrations therefore claimed to support anti-colonial national liberation movements; concretely, they announced their intention to aid developing nations by supporting projects that would build infrastructure and foster economic growth. But this economic aid came at a price—they demanded political allegiance. For instance, the United States first sought to bring Gamal Abdel Nasser's Egypt under its wing through promises of financial aid. Nasser sought relations with the Soviet Union, though, and the Eisenhower administration punished him by reneging on its promise to provide funding for the construction of a dam in Aswan. Nasser promptly nationalized the Suez Canal, which led Britain, France, and Israel to launch a war on Egypt. The United States leaned on them to end their aggression, allowing Egypt to finally get rid of its former colonial master—Britain. This example reveals the carrot-and-stick approach that the US elite employed again and again during the Cold War: using monetary incentives to win allies, punishing them when they strayed, but also acting to weaken the hold of former colonizer nations when possible.

Secretary of State John Foster Dulles said of the Suez crisis that what "the British and French have done is nothing but the straight, old-fashioned variety of colonialism of the most obvious sort."[72] In contrast, the United States crafted a new model of imperialism on the basis of what McAlister has called "benevolent supremacy." This model was premised on the notion that a US-dominated world would ensure liberty and democracy for all through the mechanism of free-market capitalism. Henry Luce, publisher of the magazines *Life* and *Time*, captured this new global role in an editorial titled "The New American Century." He argued that the United States was a "Good Samaritan" that would bring about "freedom and justice" around the world in the postwar period.[73]

McAlister states that, at the policy level, "benevolent supremacy" meant linking "US economic and military strength to a program that was anticommunist, anticolonial, and supportive of free markets."[74] The policy of anti-colonialism was about supplanting the old colonial powers and was therefore highly selective. While the United States rhetorically supported anti-colonial struggles in cases where its aims coincided with those of the anti-colonialists, it thwarted other struggles (for instance, it came in on the side of France in Algeria and Indochina), and it had a few of its own colonies in the Caribbean and the Pacific. Above all, newly decolonized nations were not to oppose economic imperialism and US access to markets and investment opportunities around the world. Schol-ar-activist Sidney Lens summarized US aims as follows: to establish an "open door" policy that allowed it to enter into otherwise blocked-off markets and establish multinational trade as the pillar of economic policy; to weaken and isolate forces that opposed the open door (which included both the former colonial powers as well as radical nationalists and communists); and to gain, as President Kennedy put it, "influence and control" over pliant governments, typically right-wing, through "grants and loans with conditions attached to them, military aid, equip-ment and training of puppet armies, military pacts, CIA-sponsored revolts, and on occasion, when these other methods were inade-quate . . . direct intervention by U.S. armed forces themselves."[75]

This new form of imperialism required a new language; that language was called "modernization theory." Area studies were dominated by this approach from the 1950s to the 1970s. Modernization theory drew on the work of Max Weber, distinguishing between "traditional" and "modern" societies. Traditional societies were agricultural and rural, slow to change, and politically authoritarian. Modern societies, on the other hand, were seen as industrial, quick to change, and politically democratic and egalitarian. The scholars who developed this approach offered various explanations for why traditional societies did not progress; some pointed to cultural factors, others to economic ones. At the end of the day, it was agreed that change would not come from within these societies but had to be brought from outside. Turner calls these theories "internalist" because they are based on the assumption

> that a society's capacity for change is retarded by certain archaic features of the beliefs or personalities of individuals, their traditionalist orientation to social problems, their magical beliefs or their inability to save for future growth. The absence of Weberian ingredients of growth—asceticism, rational law, bureaucracy, free labour—is an internal social virus which incapacitates the economic system... development is treated as a process through a series of necessary stages—primitive, pre-modern, modern, post-industrial—which lead to an end-state society. The actual process of development takes the form of a gradual evolutionary unfolding of some inner essence (ratio-nality) or the maturation of that essence (the modernisation process). The outcome of development is the achievement of a stationary end-state which is a faithful replica of the liberal democracies of Western capitalism.[76]

In short, these new theories simply articulated new ways to divide the world into "us" and "them." Modernization theorists postulated that "our" society was dynamic, scientifically oriented, rational, supportive of individual development, democratic, and egalitarian, whereas "their" societies were static, hidebound, despotic, and authoritarian. What was needed, then, was Western intervention to "help" traditional societies make the transition to modernity. This view was not so different from earlier Orientalist notions, but it was wrapped in the credibility of social science. Modernization theorists didn't speculate about contemporary societies based on classical texts: they conducted empirical research and gathered data, which was evaluated using quantitative data analysis tech-niques. These methods were not neutral and value-free but rather imbued with ethnocentric assumptions.

Daniel Lerner, author of the highly influential book *The Passing of Traditional Society: Modernizing the Middle East*, argued that people who live in modern societies are distinguished by their personalities, which he explained in psychological terms. Modern individuals have "empathy," which allows them to see themselves in the shoes of others and therefore to visualize and make possible social mobility. Traditional individuals do not have this capacity and are therefore in need of Western influence to help them shed their old, static ways.[77] Lerner's method of analysis was based on social scientific methods even while they reproduced Orientalist racist propositions. In the field of economics, Ragnar Nurkse's "vicious circle of poverty" theory and W. W. Rostow's "economic take-off" echoed similar assumptions.[78] In the field of mass communication, Everett Rogers's *Diffusion of Innovations* is about how new ideas could be spread in traditional societies. Rogers concluded that those who were not open to "innovation" introduced by the West were best understood as "laggards."[79] In short, those who resisted Western propaganda/"innovation" were seen not as individuals acting in their own interests or resisting imperial intervention but rather as hidebound traditionalists blocking progress. Through the logic of imperial ethnocentric racism, which sees the world from the vantage point of the United States and its geopolitical interests, people in the Global South were constructed as inferior races.

While Orientalism and modernization theory each had their own research traditions and methods, both shared a polarized view of the world that saw the East as inferior and the West as superior; both were based on deeply racist notions tied to biology and culture. Anti-Arab and anti-Muslim racism relies on biologizing culture to make culture appear natural and inherent.[80] Since neither theory could see change coming about internally in the Global South, both argued for imperial intervention, which they claimed would benefit native/traditional peoples. Overall, few if any questioned the premise that research on the Middle East (and in area studies in general) should be tailored to meet the needs of the US government. In 1958, the National Defense Education Act was passed with the aim of meeting the knowledge needs of the United States in the context of the Cold War, which spurred on area studies programs and these modes of thinking. This was the dominant trend until the 1970s. At that point, various factors, particularly the impact of successful national liberation struggles on the field of Middle East studies, led to a flurry of books and articles critical of both Orientalism and modernization theory. Policy makers found it more challenging to find scholars who fell in line with US imperial aims. This led to the rise of think tanks that established close ties to the US national security state, as Khalil demonstrates.[81] Unmoored from the standards of academic rigor, think tanks would play an instrumental role in furnishing empire with theory and policy.

Conclusion

This chapter explains how the United States, an inheritor of British imperialism, also produced racialized subjects in its own unique ways. However, from colonial America to the postbellum era, there was no singular conception of Muslims in the United States, be it of Turkish and North African rulers or enslaved Black Muslims. Rather, there were shifting and complex attitudes. While the newly formed American nation was purported to be founded on principles of democracy which it contrasted with the despotism of the Turks, how Muslims were viewed and treated varied by context. Orientalism as a contradictory ideology can be seen at work during much of this period. Significantly, there were no systems of racist oppression that corresponded to this ideology until the imperial domination of the MENA region after World War II. To be sure, in the early decades of the twentieth century, Arab American and South Asian immigrants experienced racism through discriminatory naturalization laws, and black Muslims were targeted by the FBI in addition to suffering other forms of racism that non-Muslim black people experienced. However, this was the legacy of previous white supremacist laws and practices. Arab Americans who had been accepted into a proximity to whiteness were targeted as "potential terrorists" after the Arab-Israeli war of 1967. This new project of terrorist racial formation evolved to incorporate Iranians after the Iranian revolution of 1979 and the hostage crisis. In the 1980s, the rise of various movements and parties of political Islam both in the MENA region and in Central/South Asia prompted an expansion of the category of "terrorist" to include Iranians, South Asians, and other Muslims. The "Arab terrorist," a creation of the late 1960s, evolved into the Arab, Iranian, and "Islamic terrorist" in the 1980s and then the Arab/Muslim/South Asian terrorist during the 1990s.[82] The events of 9/11 served to crystallize this association. I name this process *terror-craft* and refer the reader to my essay on this topic and my forthcoming book for a deeper analysis.[83]

This chapter, together with Chapters 4 and 5, demonstrates that empire is not a fixed structure cemented into place. This is why "race" is constantly shifting and evolving. While the ideology of anti-Muslim racism can be seen in earlier periods, it was the actual domination of the MENA region that created the conditions for the production of a racialized terrorist threat. As Ella Shohat and Robert Stam argue:

Racial categories are not natural but constructs, not absolutes but relative, situational, even narrative categories, engendered by historical
processes of differentiation. The categorization of the same person can
vary with time, location, and context.[84]

Significantly, they add, "Racism is above all a social relation . . . anchored
in material structures and embedded in historical configurations of
power."[85]

In line with these scholars I have argued that in the postwar era, Orientalism and modernization theory were the means through which the United
States realized its imperial ambitions during the Cold War. The racial
Muslim of the twenty-first century, discussed in Chapter 6, was born in
this Cold War context. Bernard Lewis played a key role in adapting Orientalism to the United States. In an essay titled "The Roots of Muslim Rage"
published in 1990, he explained anti-imperialist resistance by Muslims
through the framework of the "clash of civilizations" in which political
conflicts were displaced onto the realm of culture and religion.[86] Political
scientist Samuel Huntington, who has done much to popularize this
notion, published an essay with this title in the journal *Foreign Affairs* and
then the book *The Clash of Civilizations*. He argued that in the post–Cold
War world, conflict would be driven by culture rather than politics
between the seven or eight civilizations he named.[87] He wrote, "Western
ideas of individualism, liberalism, constitutionalism, human rights, equality, liberty, the rule of law, democracy, free markets, the separation of
church and state, often have little resonance in Islamic societies."[88] Culture
was both the basis of conflict and a mode of racializing Muslims. Thus,
Orientalist modes of thought were absorbed, repackaged, and represented
to serve US imperialism. In Chapter 3, I explore the continuity of the classical Orientalist corpus in the contemporary ideology of Islamophobia as
well as its rearticulations in new ways.

3

The Ideology of Islamophobia

A nine-minute interview with religion scholar Reza Aslan on CNN featured a news ticker at the bottom with the question: Does Islam promote violence? Anchor Alisyn Camerota began the program by stating that while defenders of Islam insist that it is a peaceful religion, "others disagree" and point to the "primitive treatment in Muslim countries of women and other minorities."[1] Co-anchor Don Lemon, who is African American, nodded as she spoke, signaling his overall agreement with her framework.[2] Aslan, visibly surprised by this question, responded that the conditions for women in Muslim-majority countries vary. While women could not drive in Saudi Arabia, in various other Muslim-majority countries women have been elected heads of state not once but several times. Before he could complete his sentence that the United States had yet to elect a woman as president, Lemon interrupted: "Be honest though, Reza, for the most part, it is not a free and open society for women in those states."

For Lemon, "Islam" and the "Muslim world" is a homogeneous space. In this imagined geography, as Edward Said has pointed out, "Islam" is the antithesis of the "West."[3] It is "primitive," as Camerota opined, and therefore anti-modern, misogynist, unfree, and violent. Lemon is so sure of this worldview that he feels vested with the authority to call out an established scholar of religion like Aslan for intellectual dishonesty. To add weight to this view, the program featured two clips, one from political commentator Bill Maher and the other from Israeli prime minister Benjamin Netanyahu. Aslan expertly countered their arguments. And while the anchors were unable to refute Aslan's points, they nevertheless felt confident to speak in generalities about what they think happens in "those states." Aslan repeatedly highlighted the diversity of Muslim-majority countries, even pointing out that to bring up two or three examples and then generalize to about 1.5 billion Muslims is the very "definition of bigotry." Yet despite all the evidence adduced by Aslan, for instance, how genital mutilation is more widespread in Christian-majority nations in Central Africa, the anchors remained undeterred in their opening thesis that Islam is violent because of "its" treatment of women. Thus, while the ticker posed a question about whether Islam promotes violence, the entire segment was about proving that it did.

This interview captures taken-for-granted ideological frameworks that have become common sense in the West. While these frames have a longer history, as seen in the previous chapter, Orientalism (or perhaps neo-Orientalism) was broadened and consolidated in the aftermath of 9/11.[4] The racialized Muslim was created as a composite group that could be understood through a handful of characteristics or beliefs. While race is dynamic, contingent, and contextual—with Muslims being variously cast as "bad" or "good" as the next chapter illustrates—the ideology of Islamophobia attempts to fix what it means to be Muslim and to create a reified Muslim whose behavior can be predicted, explained, and controlled.

All societies develop a set of assumptions or beliefs that are held in common and become "common sense," that is, taken for granted. These dominant beliefs then constitute an ideology that sets the limits of permissible thinking on a topic.[5] As Stuart Hall writes, ideologies

work most effectively when we are not aware that how we formulate and construct a statement about the world is underpinned by ideological premises; when our formations seem to be simply descriptive statements about how things are (i.e. must be), or of what we can "take-for-granted." "Little boys like playing rough games; little girls, however, are full of sugar and spice" is predicated on a whole set of ideological premises, though it seems to be an aphorism which is grounded, not in how masculinity and femininity have been historically and culturally constructed in society, but in Nature itself. *Ideologies tend to disappear from view into the taken-for-granted "naturalized" world of common sense.* Since (like gender) race appears to be "given" by Nature, racism is one of the most profoundly "naturalized" of existing ideologies [emphasis added].[6]

In other words, frameworks that help one to "understand" the world are in fact ideological and are based on a host of assumptions about the "natural" order of things. Anti-Muslim racism as an ideology operates in precisely this way. While blatant racism is obvious and recognizable as propaganda, assumptions about Muslim states as misogynist parade as truth statements, as simply how things are. The CNN interview is an excellent example of how this works. We also saw how any alternative framework is labeled as dishonest because it is "well known" that the "Muslim world" is undemocratic, sexist, violent, and anti-modern.

Hall also argues that the preferred cultural framing of an issue acquires dominance through a process of repetition within a context where competing frames are silenced. He notes that "in order for one meaning to be regularly produced, it ha[s] to win a kind of credibility, legitimacy or taken-for-grantedness for itself." Moreover, this takes place on a terrain where other constructions become "literally unthinkable or unsayable."⁷ While Aslan was given a space to voice his arguments, typically guests on these programs are those who reinforce the status quo. In this case, the interview ended with an acknowledgment of a plurality of "perspectives," a self-congratulatory stance on CNN's liberalism and multiculturalism. However, Camerota is quite clear that this is simply Aslan's point of view, presumably as a Muslim man, rather than a presentation of fact that countered the hegemonic narrative.

This chapter outlines the dominant assumptions that frame discussions of Islam and Muslims after 9/11. I focus primarily on political discourse, and I cite politicians, past and present military officials, religious leaders, influential ideologues, and other such "primary definers of news." As Hall and others explain, "the primary definition *sets the limit* for all subsequent discussion by *framing what the problem* is."⁸ They suggest that the relationship between "primary definers" and the media is such that

> it permits the institutional definers to establish the initial definition or *primary interpretation* of the topic in question. This interpretation then "commands the field" in all subsequent treatment and sets the terms of reference within which all further coverage or debate takes place [emphasis in original].⁹

The chapter draws from political discourse and outlines the frames used by dominant definers to discuss the "Islam" problem after 9/11. These frames are not new but often have a longer history rooted in Orientalist worldviews even if they are repackaged in new ways.

It must be acknowledged at the outset that there are exceptions to the dominant framing method outlined here. However, for the purposes of this chapter, I focus on the dominant narratives and offer six ideological frames that have been employed to represent Arabs, Iranians, South Asians, and the "Muslim world" after 9/11:

1. Islam is a monolithic religion.
2. Islam is uniquely sexist and Muslim women need to be liberated by the West.
3. Islam is anti-modern and does not separate religion and politics.
4. The "Muslim mind" is incapable of rationality and science.
5. Islam is inherently violent.
6. The West spreads democracy because Muslims are incapable of democratic self-rule.

I use the term "frame" to signify that these are particular constructions of the world rather than merely reflections. I subject each frame to critical examination to uncover how distorted or selective interpretations of history are mobilized to create the ideology of Islamophobia. By no means is this list exhaustive. Rather, it sets out to offer a framework from which other associated notions—such as Muslims as fifth columnists in western societies, as infiltrators, and as bent on replacing the secular West with an intolerant Islamic society—are built upon. These frames draw upon and build on earlier scholarship on Islamophobia and anti-Arab racism, such as that described by indigenous and Arab American studies scholar Steven Salaita and others.[10] Middle East studies specialist Stephen Shechi wrote one of the first books on the ideological campaign against Muslims in the United States.[11] I draw on his work and others to deconstruct the ideology of Islamophobia. I also show the continuity between contemporary Islamophobia and Orientalism. There are, however, differences as well. As Sheehi argued:

> The difference between previous strains of Orientalism and contemporary Islamophobia is that the sins of Arab Muslims are now visited on all Muslims. Now all Muslims are saddled with the failures, irrationalism, and backwardness that Orientalists previously defined as particular to the Semitic Arab culture and history.[12]

As discussed in previous chapters, the designation "Oriental" encompasses a broad group of people, including South Asians.

Frame 1: Islam Is a Monolithic Religion

It is often taken for granted that Islam is homogeneous. This is in large part because Orientalists propagated the myth that Islam is a monolith that can be fully understood through its classical texts. It is only when one works from such an assumption that one can make claims about a static entity, the "Muslim civilization," with a core set of unchanging values, or about the "Muslim mind" (viewed in the singular, as though all Muslims share a hive mind). By denying the diversity of Islamic history and practices, it becomes possible to state that "Islam" has certain inherent, unchanging characteristics that render it anti-democratic, violent, sexist, and so on.

Minoo Moallem argues that "the idea that a cultural or religious system can be intrinsic has its roots in European race relations and, in particular, in the discourse of anti-Semitism."[13] The religious othering of Jews and Muslims has often been intertwined (see Chapter 1). The process of creating a monolithic and unchanging religion or culture labeled "Islam" allows its proponents to "know" with certainty what happens in Muslim-majority countries, as seen in the CNN interview, or to predict how Muslims might behave as seen in various counterradicalization programs. A monolithic "Islam" serves as a default to stabilize the ideology of anti-Muslim racism even while it allows for "good" and "bad" Muslims.

Even a cursory look at the practice of Islam around the world shows this notion to be patently false. There are 1.8 billion Muslims in the world—85 percent are Sunni and 15 percent are Shi'a.[14] Within these two main denominations, there are many more branches. Muslim-majority countries and regions span the globe, from Indonesia (the most populous Muslim-majority country) to Pakistan and Bangladesh and to several central Asian countries. Countries with the largest populations of Muslims include Indonesia, Pakistan, Bangladesh, India, Turkey, and Iran. Moreover, Islam is the majority religion in several sub-Saharan African nations (Somalia, Sudan, and Senegal) and in nations considered European like Albania and Bosnia. These nations also contain other religious and nonreligious minorities (hence the term *Muslim-majority countries*). India, a predominantly Hindu country, is home to close to two hundred million Muslims. And about a third of Muslims live in countries that are not Muslim-majority nations.[15]

Islam looks different in each of these regions and countries, largely because as it spread, people imbued it with their own local customs and traditions. Sadiq al-Azm, professor of Middle East studies, notes:

> Islam as a living, dynamic, evolving faith responding to widely differing environments and rapidly shifting historical circumstances inconvertibly proved itself highly compatible with all the major types of polities and varied forms of social and economic organisation (sic) that human history produced and threw up in the lives of peoples and societies . . . In light of these palpable historical facts, adaptations and precedents it should be clear that Islam has had to be very plastic, adaptable, malleable and infinitely reinterpretable and revisable to survive and flourish under such contradictory conditions and widely varying circumstances.[16]

Thus, the Sufi Islam practiced in northern India is quite different from the Shi'a Islam practiced in Lebanon, which is in turn different from the Sunni Islam practiced in Pakistan. Even within a single branch of Islam, customs and practices vary by region and across time. The Islam of seventh-century Arabia is different from the Wahhabism that exists today in Saudi Arabia. Religious texts may be more or less fixed, but all of the world's religions, including Islam, have changed and adapted based on historical transformations.

Anthropologist Talal Asad has noted that "Islam is neither a distinctive social structure nor a heterogeneous collection of beliefs, artifacts, customs, and morals. It is a tradition."[17] By this he means that how Islam is practiced varies and is related to the past, present and future. "The variety of traditional Islamic practices in different times, places, and populations indicates the different Islamic reasonings that different social and historical conditions can or cannot sustain."[18] In short, Islam is not a fixed entity and must be understood within a context.

A significant dimension of the current Islamophobic rhetoric involves the demonization of Arabs. During his 2008 presidential campaign, Barack Obama was "accused" of being an Arab, which is shorthand for "Muslim" in some quarters. Let us note, therefore, a simple point: all Muslims are not Arabs, and all Arabs are not Muslims. Arab countries are home to Christians, Jews, Druze, and other religious minorities. Arabs are people who speak Arabic, share certain common cultural traditions, and claim a common Arab ethnic identity.[19] Nadine Naber suggests that while the term *Arab* is contested, it is used to signify cultural and linguistic similarity. She adds that, "Arab is also a national identity" and "Arabs share a language and a common cultural and imagined national community."[20] Since 1945, countries in which Arabic is the primary language combined to form the Arab League. This league consists of nations "considered Arab nations, including Algeria, Bahrain, Djibouti, Egypt, Iraq, Jordan, Kuwait, Lebanon, Libya, Morocco, Oman, Palestine, Qatar, Saudi Arabia, Somalia, Sudan, Syria, Tunisia, the United Arab Emirates, and Yemen."[21] Iran and Turkey are located in the Middle East and North Africa (MENA) but are not considered Arab because of linguistic and cultural differences.

Thus, even a cursory glance at the diversity of the people who follow Islam is enough to demonstrate that they are not a monolithic group. Yet this is precisely the logic we will find at work in the following frames, which assert that Islam is inherently sexist, irrational, violent, anti-modern, and undemocratic. The homogenization of "Islam" is assumed to be true, and it functions as the basis of all of the other frames. Said noted that the influential Orientalist Grunebaum "produced a solid *oeuvre* that concentrated on Islam as a holistic culture about which, from beginning to end of his career, he continued to make the same set of essentially reductive, negative generalizations."[22] This pattern can be found not only in scholarship but in popular culture as well.[23]

Frame 2: Islam Is Uniquely Sexist and Muslim Women Need to Be Liberated by the West

Fighting brutality against women and children is not the expression of a specific culture; it is the acceptance of our common humanity—a commitment shared by people of good will on every continent. The fight against terrorism is also a fight for the rights and dignity of women.

—First Lady Laura Bush

The rights of the women of Afghanistan will not be negotiable ... [w]hen the light is fully shed throughout all of Afghanistan, the United States is committed to working to ensure not only that the women of Afghanistan regain their place in the sun, but they have a place in their future government as well.

—Secretary of State Colin Powell

We have obviously serious problems with the Taliban government. They're an incredibly repressive government, a government that has a value system that's hard for many in America . . . to relate to. Incredibly repressive toward women.

—President George Bush

Nothing more symbolises the oppression of women than the burka, which is a very visible sign of the role of women in Afghanistan.

—Cherie Blair, wife of British prime minister Tony Blair[24]

During and after the invasion of Afghanistan, a series of political figures including Laura Bush, Cherie Blair, George Bush, Donald Rumsfeld, and Colin Powell argued that the United States had an obligation to uphold women's rights in Afghanistan and to root out the Taliban regime.[25] Subtle references to "our" culture and values, as can be seen in the quotes above, served to ground the rescue narrative within a "clash of civilizations" framework, which pits the "West" and "Islam" in a transhistoric battle. To be sure, conditions for women in Afghanistan were harsh. However, until they proved to be useful for empire, Afghan women warranted little coverage in the media. As Carol Stabile and I wrote, in broadcast media only thirty-seven programs focused on Afghan women in 1999. From January 2000 to September 11, 2001, there were thirty-three programs. From September 12, 2001 to January 1, 2002, the number of broadcast programs spiked to 628.[26] This sustained attention was due in no small part to the role that "primary definers" such as those quoted at the start of this section play in determining what is newsworthy and when. When the suffering of Afghan women proved useful to the war on terror and to US imperial aims in South and Central Asia, they became the subject of sustained media attention. In reality, Afghan women are no better off than they were before the war, particularly in the rural areas where things deteriorated after the US/NATO invasion. This point was made quite strongly by women's rights advocate Malalai Joya, the youngest woman ever elected to the Afghan parliament.[27] The United States responded by barring her entrance into the country for a speaking tour in 2011 until public protest erupted.

In *Do Muslim Women Need Saving?*, anthropologist Lila Abu-Lughod argues that the Afghan war gave rise to a new ubiquitous common sense that views militarism as the means to advance women's rights. She further analyzes the multiple venues, from scholarly work to memoirs and pulp nonfiction, through which the West portrays Muslim women as victims. We might argue that if Kipling coined the term "half devil, half child" to describe the colonized as a subject in need of discipline (as devil) and education/uplift (as child), then today we have the logic "half victim, half terrorist." While the terrorist, still largely gendered male, must be vanquished through wars and drone strikes, the (female) victim must be rescued and "liberated." In this process, a flattened monolithic female Muslim subject is created. Abu-Lughod highlights the diversity of Muslim women's experiences, pointing to class, region, nationality, the history and nature of political movements including national liberation struggles, and other factors that inform the status of women. Sociologist Valentine Moghadam has demonstrated with ample data that the conditions for women in the MENA region vary widely.[28] Outlining the role of women as agents of change working within constraining conditions, she shows how it is not "Islam" that impacts women's rights but socioeconomic and political conditions. Yet a particular image of the Muslim woman animates imperial feminism, which among other things erases MENA region and South Asian women's activism and advocacy.[29]

When France passed a ban on the hijab (couched as a ban on all religious symbols in schools), the argument was that this would "liberate" Muslim women. The reality, however, is that French Muslim women have not been liberated by these actions. The ban has only led to greater discrimination against, and ostracism of, Muslim women.[30] This is not new. The French have a long history of unveiling Muslim women as part of their projects of colonialism. In Algeria, sociologist Marnia Lazreg points out that poor and working class Algerian Muslim women were coerced to be part of a well-choreographed event in 1958 where their veils were publicly removed by French women in a purported demonstration of their liberation. In response, many women who did not previously veil adopted the veil as a symbol of protest. From that point on, the veil was no longer an article of religious clothing but became a "strategic devise, under which and out of which women and men alike carried out paramilitary action."[31] Sociologist Christine Delphy, following Lazreg, argues that the

> French did nothing to help North African women. But they carried out a few "un-veiling" campaigns during the Algerian War . . . under the pretext of "liberating women." In reality, the purpose of these campaigns—like the rapes committed by soldiers or the use of

"lascivious" native women in brothels—was to demoralize the Algerian men by "stealing" their last bit of property: women.[32]

Additionally, the attack on the veil and the attack on Islam were means by which to defang the national liberation movement that had used Islam as an ideological glue to bring people together to stand up to French imperialism.

Leila Ahmed traces the emergence of the "discourse of the veil" in the late nineteenth century and how it became the most visible marker of difference as well as the inferiority of Muslim societies.[33] In recent decades, the veil has been banned, scorned, or otherwise used to advance a taken-for-granted argument about the need for "enlightened" governments to rescue Muslim women.[34] Largely absent from this discourse are the voices of Muslim women who could speak to the complex reasons why they don the veil. Anthropologist Fadwa El Guindi outlines these reasons, stating that they range from an affirmation of cultural and religious identity, to taking a feminist stance against the male gaze, to being an expression of liberation from colonial legacies.[35]

The CNN interview with Aslan (described in the beginning of this chapter) captures well this ubiquitous ideological framework developed over two centuries in the West. Many scholars have written about what has variously been called "colonial feminism," "gendered Orientalism," and "imperial feminism." With its origins in European colonialism (see Chapter 1), this ideological framework rests on the construction of a barbaric misogynistic "Muslim world" that must be civilized by a liberal, enlightened West. As postcolonial studies scholar Gayatri Spivak famously put it, the narrative was of "White-men-saving-brown-women-from-brown-men." Commenting on Europe's nineteenth-century obsession with Muslim women, Lockman states that there "is no subject connected with Islam which Europeans have thought more important than the condition of Muslim women."[36] The dominant narrative presented Muslim women as either objects of desire in the harem or as severely subjugated, oppressed, and little more than slaves. Just as the Muslim despots tyrannized their subjects, it was argued, they also tyrannized their wives and daughters. Orientalist paintings visualized these arguments vividly. (To be sure, there were national differences in Orientalist paintings of Eastern women. For instance, while French painters depicted nudity, the British clothed the women of the harem.)[37]

Romantic Orientalist French painter Eugène Delacroix's *The Death of Sardanapalus* (1827) presents a monarch presiding over the death and torture of women and animals. The woman on the monarch's bed

Eugène Delacroix, *La Mort de Sardanapale* (*The Death of Sardanapalus*), 1827, Louvre, Paris.

appears to be dead while the rest are in stages of being killed by the monarch's slaves, who range from light-skinned to black. The bearded turbaned monarch and his turbaned light- and dark-skinned servants are predatory figures set against the helpless European-looking white women. The painting is based on Lord Byron's play of the same name in which Sardanapalus, defeated by his enemies, collects his prized possessions (including his concubines) and sets them and himself on fire. Delacroix embellishes that scene and presents the monarch as the epitome of brutality. While his servants are executing his order to possibly rape and torture the women and his horse, he watches on like a spectator, his arm propping up his head. Sardanapalus is the embodiment of the Oriental despot—cruel, powerful, and deviant in his sexuality. This painting is among the first in the harem genre of Oriental paintings and evokes disgust at Saradanapalus's treatment of women.[38] Amidst death, he appears calm in a room where red, evocative of blood, is the dominant color.

Cultural historian Rana Kabbani observes that in this painting the

> violence of the narrative is linked to its eroticism; indeed, the female bodies in the throes of death are made to take on positions of languor of sexual abandon. Their dying becomes exotic spectacle, voyeuristically observed by Sardanapalus and the spectator.[39]

The possible response by spectators, other than voyeuristic pleasure at the nudity and possible torture, is also disgust caused through an identification with the white-skinned French-looking women.

When he painted this, Delacroix had not yet visited the East; the characters he paints are of his imagination. In a previous painting, *The Massacre at Chios,* about the killing of Greeks at the hands of the Ottomans, he had used his mistress as a model.[40] In general, Kabbani notes that the

> desirable woman in Orientalist painting was hardly ever "foreign" looking. She conformed closely with conventional standards of European beauty. The more desirable prototypes were Circassian (the fair-skinned descendants of the Circassian subjects of the Ottoman Empire) since they were exotic without being unappetizingly dark.[41]

The same is true of the woman in Jean-Léon Gérôme's *The Slave Market* (1866).

Here a petite fair-skinned woman is being inspected by her prospective buyer who is examining her teeth. Her owner/seller has disrobed her and stands with her white veil in one hand and a cane in another. Her complete objectification and humiliation communicates to western audiences the inferiority of Muslim societies. While the painting is on the one hand titillating to a male heterosexual viewer, it also evokes disgust and a sense of western superiority. Not least, it validates the argument that the West needs to rescue Muslim women.

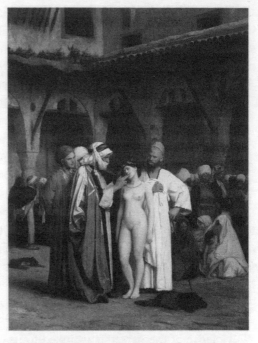

Jean-Léon Gérôme, *Le marché d'esclaves* (*The Slave Market*), c. 1866, Clark Art Institute, Massachusetts.

When Muslim men are present in Orientalist paintings, they are violent, predatory, and cruel. The owner/seller is darker skinned and has Moorish features in contrast to the buyer and his retinue. While the buyer wears a grand green robe, the seller wears more modest clothing. In several Orientalist paintings, class is signified by skin color. In Delacroix's *Women of Algiers in Their Apartment* (1834) and Gérôme's *Pool in a Harem* (1876), black women are presented as servants who attend to the needs of the fair-skinned wives and concubines of the male patriarch. Thus we see race, class, and gender portrayed in particular ways in the context of European debates over Atlantic slavery and various projects of racial formation. *The Slave Market* is part of a subgenre of Orientalist paintings that focus on slavery, which visualize for Western audiences sympathetic fair-skinned women as slaves.[42]

Another subgenre is paintings about the harem; since most European males did not have access to that space, these paintings were more a projection of their sexual fantasies than the reality of life in the gender segregated spaces in which women spent their time.[43] As various scholars have shown, European men who wrote about the plight of Muslim women had little access to these women to verify their assumptions.[44]

Coterminous accounts by western women of the Muslim women they encountered reveal a more complex reality.[45] Nevertheless, this narrative of the oppressed Muslim woman serviced the colonial enterprise. The Afghan war in 2001 elevated imperialist feminism. Furthermore, it has various other political and commercial uses.[46] For instance, in 2019 the far right-wing Alternative for Germany Party urged Europeans to vote for them using posters of the *The Slave Market* with the title "so that Europe doesn't become Eurabia."[47]

But what of Muslim women themselves? Are they oppressed? Some point to the fact that women's rights have been severely curtailed by right-wing Islamist regimes such as the Taliban in Afghanistan and the Conservative Alliance in Iran. We might respond to this point in two ways. First, the parties of political Islam adapt religion to serve their political goals in much the same way as American Christian fundamentalists have used Christianity to attack women's rights. However, these Islamist parties and organizations are not a monolith. Second, all of the world's major religions are to a greater or lesser extent sexist. Singling out Islam for its sexist practices in the mainstream media and public discourse is not a historical oversight but a systematic attempt to construct "our" values and religion as being enlightened in contrast with "theirs."

One could, for instance, point to sexism in the history of Christianity and in Christian-majority societies quite easily. The Christian creation myth tells us that Eve was created out of Adam's rib and that women's pain in childbirth is a punishment for Eve's disobedience to God. Women who were thought to be witches were burned at the stake not only in Europe but in colonial America, barely three centuries ago. Nicaragua, Chile, El Salvador, and Malta, all predominantly Catholic countries, ban abortion without exception, even if the woman's life is in danger.[48] The United States has yet to elect a female head of state, as Aslan pointed out, and it was only in 2020 that a woman of color was elected to the vice presidency.

Even if we examine Islam on its own terms, there is much debate about the role of women. The Quran, like any religious text, lends itself to multiple interpretations. Scholars like sociologist Fatima Mernissi and political scientist Asma Barlas have argued that Islam is not inherently misogynistic. Mernissi notes that while traditional interpretations of Islam seek to regulate women's sexuality and social space, she also argues that if "women's rights are a problem for some modern Muslim men, it is neither because of the Quran nor the Prophet, nor the Islamic tradition, but simply because those rights conflict with the interests of a male elite."[49] Barlas further points to the egalitarian passages in the Quran that suggest equality between men and women. She argues that sexist interpretations of the Quran are products of particular societies that need religious authority to justify sexual inequality.[50] Ahmed states that prior to the institutionalization of Islam, women in Arab society participated in warfare and religion and had sexual autonomy. Historian Montgomery Watt even goes so far as to argue that Arab society at the time was predominantly matrilineal.[51] However, Rodinson rejects this analysis, describing Arabia in this period instead as a patrilineal society where polyandrous practices, combined with substantial social roles for women, prevailed in certain regions.[52] Prophet Mohammad's first wife Khadija was a wealthy woman who was forty when she proposed to the twenty-five-year-old Mohammad. Khadija had been married twice before and was widowed; it was Mohammad's first marriage.

As Islam spread, it adopted the cultural practices of various empires, including those of the neighboring Persian and Byzantine empires. The Christians who populated the Middle East and the Mediterranean had more rigid customs associated with women. In the Christian Byzantine empire, the sexes were segregated. Women were not to be seen in public, they were veiled, and they were given only rudimentary education. As the expanding Islamic empire incorporated these regions, it also assimilated these cultural and social practices.[53] In other words, the particular misogynistic practices that Islam came to adopt were inherited from the Christian and Jewish religious customs of the neighboring societies that Muslims conquered. At the same time, however, as Samir Amin argues, the "model proposed by Islam" remained "entirely part of the tradition of patriarchal authority and the submission of women."[54] The significant point here is that sexist attitudes toward women, far from being unique to Islam, were prevalent among Christians and Jews as well.

Finally, a word on nongovernmental organizations (NGOs). In the neoliberal era, the withdrawal of state and public resources from the processes of social reproduction created a gap that NGOs have been able to fill. This has given birth to a privatized means by which to address and appropriate gender oppression. A network of well-funded NGOs, in collaboration with the UN and its various agencies, has produced what has been referred to as a *neoliberal aid regime*. Inderpal Grewal and Victoria Bernal noted that in 2000, NGOs disbursed between twelve and fifteen billion dollars and that by 2012, the NGO sector had become more powerful than the state in some parts of the world.[55] Sociologist Zakia Salime's analysis of the Moroccan context sheds light on the alliances between the state, feminist organizations, and the UN, highlighting how these alliances and NGO involvement are another means through which imperial feminism is reproduced.[56] NGOs, particularly those that receive large grants from corporate sources, have thus become the new missionaries of empire bolstering neoliberal capitalism. General Colin Powell observed that NGOs were a "force multiplier" and "an important part of our combat team" in the Afghan war.[57]

Frame 3: Islam Is Anti-modern and Does Not Separate Religion and Politics

The alleged "primitive" treatment of women in "Islam" that we saw in the CNN story builds on the notion that the West is advanced and civilized while the East is barbaric and anti-modern. In Europe, this discussion has played out under the rubric of the "crisis of multiculturalism." As media and cultural studies scholars Alana Lentin and Gavan Titley lay out, anti-Muslim racism has been revitalized through the rejection of multiculturalism, which is seen as enabling anti-modern practices. Multiculturalism, which promotes respect for cultural and religious practices, has created a situation, various conservatives and liberals have argued, where medieval norms are subverting European modernity. To counter this, the public has been won to banning veils and other symbols of Islam from public life. Muslims are accused of being anti-modern if they fail to take off their veils or if they take offense at hate speech (which is defended as free speech). The demands on Muslim immigrants to integrate bolsters a form of cultural racism that casts Europe as liberal and modern in opposition to Islam, which is seen as premodern.[58]

This argument that Islam is anti-modern flows from the belief that Muslim-majority societies have never seen a separation of religion and politics. Christian Europe critically examined and overcame its religious worldview through the Reformation and the Enlightenment, thus entering modernity; Islam and the "Muslim world" did not. The underlying assumption is that while Christianity was intellectually open to allowing views that challenged Christian dogma, Islam was not. The primary ideologues of the thesis that religion and politics have always been intertwined in the "Muslim world" are Bernard Lewis and Samuel Huntington.

Lewis sets out his argument as follows: he begins with the historic separation of religion and politics in Christianity and then states that such a separation has not occurred in Muslim societies, which, he argues, have not seen the equivalent of the Enlightenment. He asserts that whereas their own historical conflicts forced Christians and the West to learn to separate religion and politics, "Muslims experienced no such need and evolved no such doctrine."[59] As he put it, "the origins of secularism in the West may be found in two circumstances—in early Christian teachings, and, still more, experience, which created two institutions, church and state; and in later Christian conflicts which drove the two apart." In contrast, there was "no need for secularism in Islam."[60] Huntington, who popularized Lewis's "clash of civilizations" thesis, took this one step further and argued that the "underlying problem for the West is not Islamic fundamentalism. It is Islam, a different civilization whose people are convinced of the superiority of their culture, and are obsessed with the inferiority of their power."[61] What follows from this reasoning is that while certain "civilizations" understand the proper role of religion in society, others do not. Therefore, Islamist groups in contemporary society are a natural outgrowth of an anti-secular cultural tendency in "Islamic civilization."

It is true that Islam came into being as both a political and religious ideology. However, since at least the eighth century there has been a de facto separation of political and religious power.[62] Furthermore, there is nothing unique in Islam's political potential. When the papacy sought to unite Europe under the banner of Christianity, it unleashed the Crusades in the name of God. When George Bush launched the war on terror, he called it a "Crusade." More broadly, the United States remains a society where religious rituals are enacted within the state. Elected representatives swear allegiance to the nation on the Bible; a similar mandate to tell the truth in court proceedings has the ritual of placing one's hand on the Bible or other religious texts, and presidential speeches end with invoking God's blessings on the American people. However, the existence of religion in state spaces needs to be distinguished from its actual role in various societies at specific historical moments. Not unlike Christianity, Islam transformed itself to adapt to the needs of the societies in which it was practiced. A brief overview of Islam and its spread illustrates this trend.

The Prophet Mohammad, a merchant who traveled widely, understood that if the tribes who populated his city were to gain greater political and economic power in the region, they would need to unite under a common banner. Islam as envisioned by Mohammad combined spirituality with politics, economics, and social mores. He acted as both a political and a religious leader, and his authority in both realms was unquestioned.[63] This was not so with his successors, however. Shortly after his death there were conflicts over Mohammad's temporal successor (called the *caliph*). The fourth caliph, Ali, was opposed by several forces including one of the Prophet's wives. Followers of Mu'awiya (founder of the Umayyad dynasty) are known as Sunni Muslims, while followers of Ali are known as Shi'a Muslims. It was a struggle for political power rather than purely religious rivalry that led to the first division between Shi'a and Sunni, as political scientists Mohammed Ayoob and Danielle Lussier argue.[64]

Within a century of Mohammad's death, Muslim armies went on to conquer vast areas and to establish a powerful empire. It was in this context that a de facto separation of religious and political power began to take shape. While the heirs to the Prophet, or the caliphs, held religious authority, it was the monarchs, sultans, and emirs who wielded political power.[65] Ayoob and Lussier trace the continuity of this practice over many centuries and note that "the distinction between temporal and religious affairs and the temporal authority's de facto primacy over the religious establishment continued throughout the reign of the three great Sunni dynasties—the Umayyad, the Abbasid, and the Ottoman."[66]

The first Muslim empire, which brought together large numbers of people from various regions, sought to develop a set of laws that could be applied uniformly to all Muslim subjects. This need for a system of organization was the impetus behind the development of the Sharia—a set of rules codified into law. The ulama were entrusted with the task of formulating the Sharia. Various Sharia systems that emerged from this effort attempted to describe all human acts and activities and to classify them by permissibility: as forbidden, objectionable, recommended, and so on. These rules encompassed almost all spheres of life, from commerce and crime to marriage, divorce, property, hygiene, and various aspects of interpersonal relationships.[67] It was the responsibility of the religious establishment to promote adherence to the newly developed Sharia law.

This role of ensuring social discipline through religious law was pervasive, and in this realm the ulama did indeed hold power. However, in the realm of politics they had little sway.

[There] was a consensus that as long as a ruler could defend the territories of Islam (*dar al-Islam*) and did not prevent his Muslim subjects from practicing their religion, rebellion is forbidden, for *fitna* (anarchy) was worse than tyranny . . . Political quietism was the rule in most Muslim polities most of the time for a thousand years, from the eighth to the eighteenth century.[68]

A division of labor developed between the "men of the pen" and the "men of the sword." The former class, which included not only the ulama but also bureaucrats (who worked under the leadership of the political ruler), was charged with carrying out the administrative and judicial functions of government; the latter defended and expanded the empire and held political authority.[69] Whereas the Prophet Mohammad was both a political and religious leader, the needs of empire necessitated a de facto separation.

While this was the reality of the relationship between religion and politics, leading theologians went out of their way to demonstrate the opposite as a way to uphold their credibility. They have consistently done so through history, thereby creating the impression that religion and politics were more closely intertwined than they actually were. Not surprisingly, Orientalists—whose view of the world is driven by texts—fall easily into the trap of not separating religious claims from actual reality. That said, there are examples of more practically minded theologians, such as al-Ghazali (1058–1111), who openly advocated a division of labor between the caliph and the sultan.[70]

Thus, contrary to Lewis's claims about the indivisibility of religion and politics in Islam, Ayoob and Lussier argue that the

> historical trajectory of religion-state relations in Islam . . . has not been very different from that of Western Christianity. However, since Islam has never had a single locus of religious authority (like Christianity prior to the Reformation), the religious class did not pose the sort of challenge to temporal authority that the religious hierarchy the pope presided over did to emperors and kings in medieval and early modern Europe.[71]

As noted in Chapter 1, the English, in the context of the Protestant Reformation, curtailed the authority of the papacy and its representatives, thereby creating a situation where political power was concentrated within the monarchy. In contrast, the "dispersal of religious authority in Islam . . . normally prevented a direct clash between temporal and religious power such as happened in medieval Christendom."[72]

Significantly, while scientific thought existed within Muslim empires and thrived, the same was not true of Christian Europe. For instance, in the thirteenth century, the Syrian scholar and physician Ibn al-Nafis was the first to advance the notion of the pulmonary circulation of blood. Al-Nafis lived to the age of eighty and died in his bed. In contrast, the second scholar who put forward this argument was put to death by the Inquisition. The Spanish Michael Servetus was arrested in 1553 on charges of blasphemy and burned at the stake for refusing to recant.[73] This is not to say that Muslim scholars did not face punishment when they strayed too far from accepted truths. Rather, the kind of systemic and prolonged persecution that scientists faced under Christianity does not have an exact parallel in Islam, even if there were periods when scientists and dissidents were persecuted. In some Muslim empires such as the Mughals in India, the emperor Akbar (1556–1605) emphasized "the path of reason" rather than a "reliance on tradition."[74]

Frame 4: The "Muslim Mind" Is Incapable of Reason and Rationality

The reality is the use of military force against Iran would be very dangerous . . . [i]t would be very provocative. The only thing worse would be Iran being a nuclear power. It's the worst nightmare of the Cold War, isn't it? The nuclear weapons in the hands of an irrational person, an irrational force. Ahmadinijad is clearly irrational.
—Former New York City mayor Rudolph Giuliani

Quite obviously rational deduction does not have a place in the mentality of Hezbollah's leader, the Rev. Hassan Nasrallah, in the mentality of the Iranian leader Mahmoud Ahmadinejad, who raves on about how Israel must be destroyed and the misery he is going to cause America. Rational deduction does play a role in the mentality of the Israelis and the Americans.
—Editor and columnist Emmett Tyrrell[75]

In a 2006 speech titled "Faith, Reason, and the University," Pope Benedict XVI equated Catholicism with reason and Islam with violence and a lack of reason. Paraphrasing a fourteenth-century Byzantine emperor, he argued that when a religion (like Islam) is spread through violence, it goes against reason and also against nature, for "not to act in accordance with reason is contrary to God's nature."[76] In making this argument, the Pope joined a long line of Orientalists who have argued that reason, rationality, and science are alien to the world of Islam.

The French Orientalist Ernest Renan, who championed science and reason, stated in his 1883 essay "Islam and Science" that "early Islam and the Arabs who professed it were hostile to the scientific and philosophic spirit."[77] In a lecture at the Sorbonne, he said:

> Anyone with any knowledge of current affairs can see quite clearly the actual inferiority of the Muslim countries, the decadence of the states governed by Islam, the intellectual barrenness of the races that derive their culture and education from that religion alone. All those who have traveled to the East or to Africa have been struck by the totally narrow mind of the true believer, the kind of iron band around his head that closes him off completely from science and makes him quite incapable of learning anything or opening his mind to any new ideas.[78]

Renan made sweeping generalizations about the "narrow minds" of people who live in the East and in Africa, who because of their adherence to Islam are an intellectually barren race. Renan believed in a hierarchy of "peoples, languages, and cultures" and while the Semites (which he understood to include both Jews and Arabs)[79] were one of two "great and noble races," along with the Aryans, he argued that they had ceased to produce anything new because of "the terrible simplicity of the Semitic spirit, closing the human brain to every subtle idea, to every fine sentiment, to all rational research."[80] What we see here are not only racist assertions about Muslims but also the idea that Islam has stunted scientific growth. When challenged to explain the flourishing of science in Islamic empires in the Middle Ages, Renan replied that the Arabs, like other "Semites," were incapable of science; Arab science was a continuation of Greek science conducted not by Arabs but Persians and converted Greeks.[81] Thus, it was the "Aryans" who were responsible for this flowering of science, he argued.[82]

Cromer, whom we encountered in Chapter 1 in his pith helmet in Egypt, had this to say in his two-volume book *Modern Egypt*:

> The European is a close reasoner; his statements of fact are devoid of ambiguity; he is a natural logician, albeit he may not have studied logic; he is by nature skeptical and requires proof before he can accept the truth of any proposition; his trained intelligence works like a piece of mechanism. The mind of the Oriental, on the other hand, like his picturesque streets, is eminently wanting in symmetry. His reasoning is of the most slipshod description. Although the ancient Arabs acquired in a somewhat higher degree the science of dialectics, their descendants are singularly deficient in the logical faculty. They are

often incapable of drawing the most obvious conclusions from any
simple premises of which they may admit the truth.[83]

Unlike Renan, Cromer is kind enough to admit that Arabs and Muslims
once grasped the "science of dialectics"—but today, he claims, they are
completely deficient in logic and reasoning. This caricature persists even
in the early twenty-first century.

While today such blatantly racist arguments as Cromer's are advanced
only by those on the Far Right, it isn't hard to see how the overall logic of
irrationality pervades many discussions. For Europeans, Moallem
explains, "Islam represents a homogenous doctrine that is essentialized
as a force that limits the mental capacities of its adherents."[84] As communication scholar Karim H. Karim has argued, those who are seen as
"terrorists" are presented as crazed, irrational, and fanatical: as individuals who commit untold horrors with no clear reason or motivation.[85]
Palestinian suicide bombers, Talal Asad notes, are presented as rabid
lunatics rather than as people driven to extreme measures under conditions of occupation.[86] We are asked to believe that terrorists are driven by
irrational instincts rather than political motivations. The debate on
whether Iran should be allowed to have nuclear weapons also draws from
these arguments. As seen in the quote from Giuliani, nuclear weapons
"in the hands of an irrational person, an irrational force" would be a
disaster.[87] These lines of demarcation are familiar: "irrational" Iran and
the "rational" West. Little discussion is devoted to why Iran, as a rational
political actor, might want to acquire nuclear weapons; it is, after all,
surrounded by nuclear powers such as India, Pakistan, China, Russia,
and Israel, and by US bases in Qatar, Iraq, Turkey, and Afghanistan, any
of which might harbor nuclear weapons.

There are many ways to debunk this myth about Islam, science, and
rationality and many excellent books and articles that tear to shreds the
very concepts of biologically defined races and the spurious connection
between race and intellectual capacity.[88] Here, however, I will outline
briefly the vast contributions made by Muslim scholars to human knowledge. Islamic and Arabic science scholar George Saliba has demonstrated
that not only did science thrive in the Middle Ages in Muslim empires,
but the work of Muslim, Persian, and Arab scholars laid the basis for
Europe's Renaissance.[89] Saliba challenges the classical narrative about
Arabic and Islamic science, which suggests that Muslim scholars simply
translated the great works of antiquity and the contributions of the
Persians and Indians, while offering nothing new. He shows how, for

instance, Copernicus who advanced the heliocentric view of the solar system didn't posit his theory in isolation but built on previous work by Arab and Muslim scholars. Saliba argues against the classical narrative, which posits that when Europeans came out of their period of cultural stagnation in the eleventh century, they retranslated the work of classical antiquity back into Latin and went through a miniature renaissance in the twelfth century and that from then on Europe developed scientific knowledge sealed off from Arab and Muslim influences. In fact, according to this narrative Islamic science went into decline after the eleventh century with not simply the "death of science" but also the "total death of rationality in Islam."[90] Recent research, Saliba shows, demonstrates this to be a fabrication. He further asserts that it is only if one uses a Eurocentric model where science and religion must battle one another leading to the ultimate triumph of the former to measure other societies that one comes to the conclusion that Islam stifled science and remained intellectually stagnant. If "progress," Saliba argues, is narrowly defined as the "victory of science over the church" as "European progress was defined," only then can one say that there was a lack of progress in Muslim societies. This is also the basis from which to deny the many contributions that Muslims have made to Europe's progress. It is this kind of fallacious reasoning that allows one to argue that Islam is anti-modern and irrational.[91]

The Persian scholar Ibn Sina—known in Western histories as Avicenna—laid the basis for the study of logic, science, philosophy, politics, and medicine. Ibn Rushd systematized Aristotle's thought so as to introduce rationalism and anti-mysticism to a new audience; he also went beyond Aristotle to promote rational thought as a virtue in itself. Ibn Rawandi wrote several books questioning the basic principles not only of Christianity and Judaism but of Islam as well. Ibn Rawandi belonged to the Mu'tazilite sect, which went so far as to question whether the Quran was really a collection of the revelations that Mohammad received from God. As scholar-activist Tariq Ali notes, they used rationalist thinking, fragments of Greek philosophy, and their own observations to develop theories to explain the physical world.[92] In short, scientific thinking thrived in the world of the Islamic empires.

It is also significant that Pope Benedict, in denouncing Islam for lacking reason, failed to bring up the Catholic Church's hostile opposition to the scientific revolution and to the birth of nonreligious and rational ways of understanding the world. The scientific revolution, and more broadly, the Enlightenment, stood in opposition to Christian dogma and were viewed as a threat by the Church. Scientists who employed reason and rationality to explain the physical world were severely punished. Perhaps as significantly, Giordano Bruno, who extended the Copernican model, was imprisoned for eight years by the Roman and Venetian Inquisitions for refusing to recant his beliefs around the same time that Akbar published his treatises on reason and nondenominational rule in India. Bruno was later burned at the stake. Galileo was similarly brought before the Inquisition and placed under house arrest for the rest of his life after he recanted his scientific theories.

Benedict's speech is deeply rooted in Orientalist myths; it presents a particular vision of a rational and enlightened "West" while obscuring Christianity's own history of violence. He thus quoted the Byzantine emperor Manuel II Paleologus, who said, "Show me just what Mohammed brought that was new, and there you will find things only evil and inhuman, such as his command to spread by the sword the faith he preached."[93] It is ironic that Joseph Ratzinger—who was elected Pope Benedict XVI after serving as head of the Vatican office of the Congregation for the Doctrine of the Faith (formerly known as the Inquisition)—could denounce the spreading of religion through violence and face little or no criticism. This is how ideology operates. The repetition of taken-for-granted frames by "primary definers" prevents alternative explanations. Perhaps the most potent, and the longest surviving frame, is that Islam is at its core a violent religion.

Frame 5: Islam Is an Inherently Violent Religion

Barely moments after the Twin Towers came crashing down, US politicians and pundits began to associate that act of violence with Islam in ways not dissimilar to earlier constructions. From the public speeches of mainstream political figures to the rants of right-wingers such as Ann Coulter to the proclamations of the Pope and others, a slew of comments too numerous to list here connected the actions of a handful of people to the religion of Islam. This frame has a long history that goes back to the Crusades. However, its reproduction in later periods is the product of particular historical circumstances. Today, it serves to deflect attention from the violence of empire in the war on terror.

The Danish cartoon controversy illustrates how this frame of Islam and violence operates, and how it serves to desensitize western audiences to the mass killings of Muslims in Afghanistan, Iraq and elsewhere. In 2005, the Danish newspaper *Jyllands-Posten* (J-P) posted twelve depictions of the Prophet Mohammad, which were solicited by its cultural editor. One of these cartoons featured the Prophet with a bomb on his turban. This cartoon not only depicts Mohammad as a terrorist but Islam as being imbricated with violence from its origins. This argument was a staple of the Right, but made its way into a liberal newspaper in Denmark in 2005. The cultural editor claimed to be motivated by the desire to defend free speech even if that meant offending Muslims. Shortly before this, J-P had published a series of editorials and op-eds that were anti-immigrant and that portrayed Islam as a dangerous and belligerent religion.[94] The cartoons therefore didn't come out of nowhere. Anthropologist Peter Hervik has argued that the logic of J-P's cultural editor derives from what is called "entitlement racism," which involves "the right to offend and to humiliate" in the name of liberal principles.[95]

Muslims around the world protested these cartoons and some Islamists turned to violence. The response in Denmark and elsewhere was to point to Islam's illiberalism and anti-modern attitudes. In fact, Hervik argues that in the decade since the cartoons were published, the hegemonic position grew stronger so that "resistance to, or criticism of, the publication, even when set in a democratic dialogue" became a "sign of the opponent's lack of integration or of cowardice, and lack of character and courage to stand up for free speech."[96] At the time and since, liberal columnists endorsed J-P's position, defending the cartoonists on the grounds of free speech. Many US newspapers carried the cartoon of Mohammad with the bomb on the same grounds, without recognizing or acknowledging that the cartoon endorsed the frame of an inherently violent Islam. To be sure, the US has a long history of publishing anti-Arab and anti-Muslim cartoons and the republication of the J-P cartoon was not unique.[97]

This frame of Islam and violence is also peddled by "native informants," Muslims who aid empire, who play an authenticating role. Irshad Manji, the Bengali-Canadian author, in her book *The Trouble with Islam* compares the Prophet with terrorists and presents herself as the "good" Muslim speaking out against Islam's violence and backwardness. Anthropologist Zareena Grewal explains the problem with such accounts:

Native informer "tell-all" accounts do not explain how Islam figures in local contexts or in a broader history; they simply demonstrate that Islam explains every episode of Muslim violence in history, at every scale, from a dysfunctional nuclear family to war between medieval empires.[98]

Manji's arguments fit so well with the dominant ideology that various doors have been opened to her fallacious arguments. For instance, she was the first recipient of Oprah Winfrey's *O* magazine's Chutzpah award given to courageous women activists. Manji was honored for standing up to "Islamic bullies and terrorists."[99]

To be sure, Muslim rulers and their empires have deployed violence. In the two decades after the Prophet's death in 632 CE, Muslim armies defeated its two great neighbors, the Byzantine and Persian (Sassanian) empires, conquered large segments of their land, and set up an empire. One reason that they were able to defeat these two powerful empires was because constant warfare between the Byzantines and the Persians over the previous century had left the people war-weary. In other words, war was a constant fact of life at the time. Moreover, Christianity too rose to dominance through conquest and conversion, first in the Roman world and then in the neighboring areas of Europe, Armenia, Arabia, eastern Africa, and central Asia.[100] The Crusades, waged by European Christians from the eleventh century on, were another violent chapter in Christianity's history. During the First Crusade in 1099, Crusaders launched a killing spree after taking control of Jerusalem, murdering almost the entire population of Muslim men, women, and children. Jews, who fought side by side with the Muslims to defend the city, were not spared either. The Crusaders set fire to a synagogue in which Jews had taken refuge and made sure that every one of them burned to death.[101]

This was not an anomaly: Crusaders passing through Germany en route to Jerusalem murdered Jews in cold blood. Christians were not spared either. When the Crusaders attacked Constantinople in 1203, "for three days and nights, the Crusaders murdered, raped, looted or destroyed everyone and everything they could get their hands on. Untold thousands perished; many more were brutalized, maimed and left homeless."[102] King Richard of England (known as Richard the Lionheart) beheaded thousands of men in full view of their armies after a battle. In contrast, after Saladin, the sultan of Egypt, successfully retook Jerusalem from the Crusaders, he forbade acts of vengeance and violence against the Crusaders, gave Jews state money to rebuild synagogues, and left churches untouched.[103] This is why he was celebrated in Europe as a just and fair Muslim ruler.

Christian empires were no less brutal toward their own populations. This ranged from the persecution faced by non-Orthodox Christians in the Byzantine Empire to the Vatican's intolerance toward non-Catholic Christians and Jews. Still to come was the Inquisition, a series of movements orchestrated by the Catholic Church and Christian orthodoxy to reassert the Church's economic control over Europe. The Spanish Inquisition is remembered for its utter brutality, mass torture, and the burning of men and women at the stake. Many Jews either fled to other parts of Europe to escape the Inquisition or sought a new home under the Muslim Ottoman Empire (1299–1922). Although it was not devoid of persecution, Ottoman society was on the whole more tolerant; Jews and Christians lived peacefully there, and some attained high positions in the bureaucracy (sometimes even without converting to Islam).

Looking at Christianity's brutal history today, one might well advance an argument that all Catholics are bloodthirsty fanatics. Indeed, this logic would be analogous to the argument that Islam is inherently violent and that Muslims have a "predisposition" toward violence. Yet such a generalization is unthinkable. To my knowledge, no mainstream newspaper or magazine has drawn a straight line between the birth of Christ and various acts of terrorism committed by Christian fundamentalists. Furthermore, as Asad argues, the same people who call the actions of suicide bombers unjustified legitimize US wars in Iraq and Afghanistan, which have caused the deaths of hundreds of thousands. In short, within this ideology only the violence of certain groups, Muslims, is highlighted and coded as a product of those groups' religious affinity. The ideology of Islamophobia more broadly helps to reproduce and sustain empire. As Arun Kundnani put it:

> The racist and imperialist violence upon which US-led capitalism depends cannot be acknowledged in liberal society so it is transferred onto the personality of the Muslim and seen as emanating from "outside" the social order. Imperial violence is then only ever a proportionate response to the inherently aggressive and threatening nature of the fanatical Muslim enemy.[104]

Frame 6: The West Spreads Democracy Because Muslims Are Incapable of Democratic Self-rule

> I frankly believe that if Iraq was located anywhere else in the world, that a functioning democracy would likely emerge in the relatively short term. But it's not located anywhere in the world; it's in the Middle

East with the world's biggest sponsors of terror on its borders and nearby in the region.

—South Carolina senator Jim DeMint

Now as we work with the people of Iraq to develop a strong and vibrant and vital democracy here in the heart of the Middle East, we can do so assured that these values are universal . . . and America has always been at its best when it is securing, and providing for, and bringing those values to the rest of the world.

—US secretary of state Condoleezza Rice[105]

The classic version of this frame states that Islamic "civilization" is not capable of democracy and that it can only produce despotism. As we saw in Chapter 1, the notion of "Oriental despotism" was developed in the eighteenth century by writers like Montesquieu, who argued that the hot climate of the East made Orientals submissive and thus unable to resist tyranny. Orientalists put this theory on a seemingly sounder academic footing by stating that despotism was one of the core values of "Islamic civilization" and that political revolution and resistance to bad government was alien to Arab and Muslim cultures.[106] Modernization theory made this notion more scientific by suggesting that "traditional" societies were characterized by hierarchical systems of power. Thus, change would never come from within, and it was the burden of the West to civilize, modernize, and democratize the East.

Arthur James Balfour, who famously penned the Balfour Declaration recognizing Zionists' claim for a state in Palestine, put it this way in 1910:

First of all, look at the facts of the case. Western nations as soon as they emerge into history show the beginnings of those capacities for self-government . . . having merits of their own . . . You may look through the whole history of the Orientals in what is called, broadly speaking, the East, and you never find traces of self-government.[107]

In talking about the "Oriental" and the "East" in such broad terms, Balfour was homogenizing a vast swath of people in Asia. He went on to argue that Britain was in Egypt not only for the sake of the Egyptians but "for the sake of Europe at large." This was the burden of the great British Empire, he concluded, and it must bear it with grace and dignity.

What then if the ungrateful native should choose self-rule over the enlightened colonial overlord? What was Balfour's Britain to make of the movements for national liberation in Egypt, India, Palestine and other colonized nations? Such struggles for self-determination had to be explained away. One way this was done was to assert that the leaders of these movements were misguided agitators who could not understand what was in their own best interests. As Cromer argued, "the real future of Egypt . . . lies not in the direction of a narrow nationalism, which will only embrace native Egyptians . . . but rather in that of an enlarged cosmopolitanism."[108] In other words, the subject people should stop any effort toward self-government and realize that they are better off as members of the global British Empire.

Echoes of such attitudes were to be found in the United States as well. In 1907, President Theodore Roosevelt, who shared Balfour's and Cromer's views of Egyptians, stated that they were "a people of Moslem fellahin who have never in all time exercised any self-government whatever." A firm believer in race, he asserted that Muslims were an inferior people: "It is impossible to expect moral, intellectual and material well-being where Mohammedism is supreme."[109] Often these ideas were used to explain why it was that "democracy-loving" imperialists couldn't bring democracy to the countries they colonized—the people just weren't ready for it. At other times it has been suggested that colonialism paved the way for self-rule and that without such Western influence, democracy would not have taken root in the East.[110]

Almost a century later, the George W. Bush administration would use this framework to argue that the United States needed to stay in Iraq even though it had not found any weapons of mass destruction in the country, in order to bring democracy—a proposition that received widespread public support. The United States has similarly stated at various points that one of its goals in Afghanistan is "nation-building"—and liberals as well as anti-war feminists accepted this logic.[111] Additionally, as Jasbir Puar argues, large sections of the global gay left were also incorporated into this paradigm through a "wholesale acceptance of the Islamophobic rhetoric that fuels the war on terror," even going so far as to tacitly endorse the forces "pushing for an Iranian invasion" and occupation.[112] This embrace of imperial ethnocentric racism and the war on terror by gay subjects was met with an incorporation of certain homosexual constituencies within the United States's new national identity in a process that Puar calls "homonationalism."[113] US exceptionalism was embellished through its purported gay-friendly credentials. The imperial cooptation and incorporation of normative homosexuality also served to create Muslims as cultural and civilizational others.

In reality, the United States has never had an interest in bringing democracy, much less women's and gay rights, to the people of the MENA region. If anything, it has a long and sordid record of wrecking democratic movements and replacing them with dictatorships.[114] After World War II, national liberation struggles swept the globe. Between 1932 and 1962, Egypt, Iraq, Syria, Lebanon, Libya, Morocco, Tunisia, and Algeria all succeeded in shaking the hold of their colonial masters. In the wake of these struggles, there was a widespread desire for reform and change in the region, and new political and social forces emerged. Arab nationalism gained a stronghold, but socialist and communist parties also vied for political influence. The United States publicly supported national liberation struggles and rhetorically intervened when it saw an opportunity to weaken the hold of Britain and France; but its interests did not (and do not) lie in supporting democratic movements on their own terms. Thus, when Egypt nationalized the Suez Canal in 1956, which then prompted France, Britain, and Israel to declare war, the United States issued an injunction to these countries to cease their aggression.[115] This was the approach the United States used to establish its hegemony in the region and to displace the old colonial powers.

When nationalists failed to comply with US interests, they were reviled. John Foster Dulles, as Eisenhower's secretary of state, called Nasser and other Arab nationalists like him "pathological" for their suspicion of the West and referred to the nationalist Iranian leader Mohammad Mossadegh as "a wily Oriental."[116] Eisenhower believed that Arabs were incapable of democratic self-rule. He said: "If you go and live with these Arabs, you will find that they simply cannot understand our ideas of freedom and dignity . . . They have lived so long under dictatorships of one form or another, how can we expect them to run successfully a free government?"[117] In reality, the United States has consistently supported dictators and repressive regimes that can be relied upon to act in the interests of the West. It has further funded, trained, and armed the military and security forces of its dictatorial allies so as to prevent domestic challenges to their rule. This strategy has largely been successful until fairly recently; and should it fail, the United States continues to maintain powerful naval forces and military bases in the region.

Despite the hot weather, people in the MENA region and South Asia have fought for self-rule and progressive reforms. In 2011, a wave of mass struggle burst onto the historic stage. In a matter of weeks, grassroots movements in Tunisia and Egypt swept from power two pro-Western dictators who had ruled with an iron fist for decades. Democracy and political freedom were key demands in what was called the "Arab Spring" of 2011. International relations scholar Gilbert Achcar argues that Washington's response, when it became clear that its old (Egypt, Bahrain, Yemen) and new (Libya) allies could be swept aside, oscillated between co-opting sections of the opposition (as in Egypt, Yemen, Libya, Syria) as a way to limit the scope of change, and supporting the forces of counter-revolution (Bahrain, Egypt after 2013). The US agenda in the Arab region has never been to promote democracy, as heralded by President Obama in his 2009 Cairo speech. Instead, the security of Washington's rich clients and protégés, the Gulf's oil monarchies—and particularly the Saudi kingdom, arguably the most antidemocratic and anti-women state on earth—has animated US policy since World War II.[118]

Even after the Arab spring, Orientalist Bernard Lewis continued to maintain that democracy will not work for Arabs; a consultative system based on traditional Islamic culture would be better, he argued. As he put it:

> We, in the Western world particularly, tend to think of democracy in our own terms—that's natural and normal—to mean periodic elections in our style. But I think it's a great mistake to try and think of the Middle East in those terms and that can only lead to disastrous results, as you've already seen in various places.[119]

Echoing an older argument, he added that "they are simply not ready for free and fair elections . . . I think we should let them do it their way by consultative groups."[120] Lewis was speaking here to Western leaders; he seemed to be advising them that the "problem" of the various peoples' movements cannot be solved through Western-style elections because the "language of Western democracy is for the most part newly translated and not intelligible to the great masses."[121] Even in the twenty-first century, the natives, the unwashed masses, still don't know better. Their systematic organizing and Twitter-based publicity for free elections, more political parties, and greater political freedom are best ignored; instead the West, which still knows best, should guide them to accept Islamic forms of governance for which they are better suited. To be sure, there are alternative forms of governance that various people's movements have thrown up, including during the Iranian revolution of 1979, which are arguably more representative than the two-party system in the United States dominated by the slave era Electoral College system. However, such discussions are not possible in an ideological system where Western and US democratic systems are seen as the pinnacle of political development and freedom.

Conclusion

In this chapter, I examined six ideology frames that constitute the core of anti-Muslim racism. Both liberals and conservatives have entrenched and reproduced this ideology in the years since 2001. The focus in this chapter has been primarily on political and news media discourse. However, cultural products such as films and television shows are also important vehicles in the mobilization of the ideology of Islamophobia. The six frames can be seen in cultural products as well. For instance, media scholar Jack Shaheen shows how numerous films depict the Middle East and North Africa as anti-modern and medieval.[122] What he calls "Arabland" consists of deserts, harems, sheikhs on camels, dancing girls, tents, and oases.[123]

Evelyn Alsultany observes that since the 1990s the emphasis on multiculturalism has led to a shift where the "Other is portrayed sympathetically in order to project the United States as an enlightened country that has entered a postracial era."[124] Her analysis of television portrayals of Arabs and Muslims demonstrates that there are more complex representations in the post-9/11 era. Yet, even while these complex depictions appear to go beyond stereotypes, they in fact "promote logics that legitimate racist policies and practices."[125] In our analysis of the show *Homeland*, Arun Kundnani and I have argued that the series offers a liberal and more palatable alternative to the popular *24*, which was accused of being Islamophobic.[126] *Homeland* overcomes the detectable racism of *24*, through its liberal and multicultural approach. But in the end, it legitimates the national security state and its counterterrorism policies. In this sense, we argued that it "remains Islamophobic in its basic structure."[127]

4

"Good" and "Bad" Muslims: The Foreign Policy Establishment and the "Islamic Threat"

The relationship of the United States to "Islam"—that is, Islam as a social construct rather than a reflection of the religion and its adherents—is contradictory and flows from its foreign policy. Readers unfamiliar with this history might be surprised to learn that movements and organizations that interpret Islam in various ways to advance political goals were not always seen as enemies. There was no "Islamic threat" in the form of non-state or state actors in the early Cold War era. Until the 1970s, the US political elite allied with some of the forces seeking to project various interpretations of Islam on the political stage, such as the Saudi monarchy. In the 1970s, this approach changed in response to various factors, including the Iranian Revolution of 1979, which brought Ayatollah Khomeini and his Islamic Republican Party to power. After this, the US political class had it both ways: the parties and movements of political Islam were enemies in some cases, but not in others. Politics scholar Mahmood Mamdani coined the term "good Muslim, bad Muslim" to capture the duality of how those who support or oppose US imperial ambitions are understood.[1]

The good/bad Muslim typology can be understood as imperial ethnocentric racism in that it is productive of racialized constructions of "them" in contrast to "us" rooted in imperial ambitions. Those who agree with us are friends, even if that friendship is contingent, while those who disagree are enemies. Imperial ethnocentrism isn't simply about viewing the world from the vantage point of one's nation or ethnic group but also about the tendency to see those who are part of colonized or less power-ful nation states, or subordinated groups within imperial nations, as inferior. "They," whether as friend or enemy, are inferior or subordinate to "us." Even as allies they are at best adjuncts within a larger power dynamic. Such articulations are not readily legible as racist because they are so deeply ideological and naturalized. Moreover, these are unstable classifications, with "good" turning "bad" quite easily.

Furthermore, the movements that are inspired by Islam or that inter-pret the religion in a variety of ways to address social problems are not a monolith. To even use a singular term such as "Islamism" to categorize various Sunni and Shi'a groups that span the globe runs the risk of homogenization. Political scientist Khalil al-Anani refers to this homo-genizing tendency as the "ISISification" of Islamist politics, where the Islamic State of Iraq and Syria (ISIS, or we might say al-Qaeda before that) becomes the face of political Islam.[2] In reality, Islamist groups emerge from particular national and regional contexts and are influenced and shaped by these historical conditions; by no means can they be understood to be identical to one another. As Ayoob, Lussier and Dylan Welch argue, the "multidimensional nature of political Islam means that any attempt to categorize Islamist actors into neat, binary categories, such as violent and peaceful, radical and moderate, reformist and statist, etc." leads to inaccuracies and gross generalizations.[3] They show that strategy, politics, and goals differ greatly.

This chapter focuses on the foreign policy establishment, which includes politicians of both major parties as well as experts in various think tanks, and their debates about how to think of and frame policy around the "Islamic threat." I begin by outlining how various state and non-state actors that sought to mobilize Islam on the political stage were understood during the Cold War. This is the context in which Muslims were thought of as good or bad depending on their orientation toward US imperialism and through a process best understood as imperial ethnocentric racism. I then turn to the post–Cold War era to unpack how the two main wings of the foreign policy establishment, the neoconserva-tives and "realists" or liberal interventionists, view Islamist forces. I draw on international relations expert Fawaz Gerges's discussion of the "accommodationist" and "confrontationist" approach to the movements of political Islam to capture the debate within the foreign policy estab-lishment. I argue that differences both in rhetoric as well as policy, such as whether to accommodate or confront, have led to different forms of Islamophobia—liberal and conservative. Both are imperial forms of racism. This chapter and the next shed light on how empire is a process. To secure its interests, the United States constantly shifts strategy and tactics. Thus, while Iraq was obliterated in the name of 9/11, Saudi Arabia was not touched even though fifteen of the nineteen hijackers were of Saudi origin. Imperial racism is strategic and purposeful, hence "good" and "bad" Muslims.

"Good" and "Bad" Muslims during the Cold War

During the Cold War, the United States had a few key objectives in the Middle East and North Africa (MENA): to control the flow of oil, to create opportunities for US businesses, and to keep the Soviet Union out.[4] The question was how to realize these objectives. As one of two superpowers on the world stage, the United States had a steep learning curve. It did not have the same knowledge and experience as European colonial powers such as France and Britain. The Council on Foreign Relations (which publishes the influential journal *Foreign Affairs*) organized a series of conferences in the late 1940s and 1950s to work out a strategy for responding to the wave of decolonization struggles sweeping Africa, the Middle East, and Asia.[5] These study groups brought together members of the US government and the few experts who existed at the time. This period saw the growth and development of "area studies" programs at various universities to meet the knowledge needs of the US government. The end result was policy that was influenced by modernization theory that sought to foster capitalist development; another was Orientalism. As discussed in Chapter 2, these theories constructed people in the MENA region in racialized terms.

In 1949, President Harry Truman launched his Point Four Program, which promised financial and technical aid to developing nations. The administration had a particularly dismal view of the people in Muslim-majority countries, reflected in the following quote: "Seeing little but squalor and stagnation around him, [the Arab] will not admit to himself the obvious answer that he belongs to a peculiarly irresponsible and feckless race."[6] To prevent what was believed to be the natural racial tendency of Arabs toward political and religious extremism, it was argued, economic assistance was vital. Modernization theorists raised the alarm of revolution. Walt Rostow, author of *The Stages of Economic Growth: A Non-Communist Manifesto* and among the most influential modernization theorists, helped the Kennedy and Johnson administrations develop policy; he also influenced Henry Kissinger, who followed his precepts.[7]

The dominant thinking was that once freed from the colonial yoke, Muslim-majority countries, if left unchecked, would veer out of Western control and likely into the clutches of the Soviet Union. This was not an acceptable outcome for the US political class. At first, policymakers sought to bring nationalists like Egypt's Gamal Abdel Nasser and Iran's Mohammad Mossadegh onto their team. When this failed they had to devise new strategies. Eisenhower, who replaced Truman, developed a Middle East policy that took these circumstances into consideration. The Eisenhower doctrine, unveiled in 1957, promised financial and military assistance to countries in the MENA region that were under threat "from any nation controlled by international communism."[8] In short, in addition to financial incentives, Eisenhower also put the military option on the table.

One lesser-known aspect of the Eisenhower doctrine was the "Islam strategy." This strategy consisted of bolstering Islamist organizations against secular nationalists and of trying to create an Islamic pole of attraction in King Saud of Saudi Arabia.[9] In a letter to a confidante in the early fifties, Eisenhower wrote:

> We wanted to explore the possibilities of building up King Saud as a counterweight to Nasser. The king was a logical choice in this regard; he at least professed anti-Communism, and he enjoyed, on religious grounds, a high standing among all Arab nations.[10]

Some administrators even began to develop the notion of Saud as a kind of "Islamic Pope."[11] A year after Eisenhower wrote his letter about Saud, he received Said Ramadan, the son-in-law of the Muslim Brotherhood's founder Hassan al-Banna, at the White House. Even though the Brotherhood had resorted to violent actions, killing several Egyptian officials, Ramadan was to become a part of the United States's strategy in the Middle East.[12] Thus, we see that actions that would later be called "terrorism," such as political assassinations, were acceptable if carried out by allies.

The Orientalists who helped shape this strategy were convinced that the largely secular ideology of nationalism and atheist communism would hold little weight in the "Muslim world." At a conference organized and sponsored by the government at Princeton University in 1953, Orientalist scholars, policymakers, and various native informants (including Ramadan) concluded that the United States must use religion to win hearts and minds, ignoring the popularity of nationalist movements.[13] US propaganda efforts at the time thus emphasized the Christian and religious roots of American culture in contrast to the godlessness of the USSR.[14] The National Security Council reasoned in 1952 that the "three monotheistic religions in the area have in common a repugnance to the atheism of communist doctrine and this factor could become an important asset in promoting Western objectives in the area."[15]

Thus, in Egypt, the Muslim Brotherhood was cultivated to serve as a bulwark against Nasser, and in Iran, a group of clergy were encouraged as a challenge to Mossadegh.[16] When Mossadegh nationalized the oil industry in 1951, it showed the threat posed by nationalists to Western oil interests. If Mossadegh represented the potential for what radical nationalists in power might do, Nasser represented Washington's nightmare scenario in the region in his stated attempt to unite Arab nations. Nasser advocated a pan-Arabism that sought to bring together the separate Arab nation-states that had been created after World War I under the Sykes-Picot treaty. If this plan were to be realized, it would have strengthened their collective power and ability to resist US imperialism. Thus, in addition to other methods used to neutralize Nasser, the CIA began to cultivate the Muslim Brotherhood and to rely increasingly on Saudi Arabia as a counterbalance.[17] As one senior CIA official put it, the

> optic was the Cold War. The Cold War was the defining clarity of the time. We saw Nasser as socialist, anti-Western, anti-Baghdad Pact, and we were looking for some sort of counterfoil. Saudi efforts to Islamicize the region were seen as powerful and effective and likely to be successful. We loved that. We had an ally against communism.[18]

US officials attempted to promote Saudi Arabia as an Islamic alternative to radical nationalism. The strategy, however, was doomed to fail because it drew on homogenizing racist caricatures of people in the region. Historian Walter Laqueur, perhaps the only establishment political commentator who saw a problem with this approach, noted in 1956 that what "is decisive is that Islam has gradually ceased to be a serious competitor of Communism in the struggle for the souls of the present and potential *elites* in the countries of the Middle East" [emphasis in original].[19] Indeed, as political scientist Tareq Ismael shows, there were significant communist parties in several Arab countries.[20] Indonesia, the most populous Muslim-majority country, had the largest communist party in the world.

If communism was a pole of attraction, this was even more true of "third world nationalism," as it was known at the time. Not only elites but the general population as well gravitated toward Arab nationalism as seen, for instance, in the immense popularity of Nasser as well as Ba'athist parties in Syria and Iraq. Further, like many third world nationalist movements and parties from South Asia to sub-Saharan Africa, Arab nationalists also adopted various interpretations of socialism.[21] Nasserists and Ba'athists referred to themselves and their programs as "Arab social-ism." Though Nasser claimed that Islam's teachings were consistent with his view of "socialism," Nasserist ideology was largely secular.[22] In this context, nationalists and leftists who opposed US imperialism were cast not as bad "Muslims" but bad Arabs, Iranians, Afghans, or South Asians. Various leftists were not explicitly identified as bad Muslims. To the extent that "Islam" and "Muslims" were part of political discourse in the early Cold War era, the terms tended to be coded positively.[23] As I have argued elsewhere, Saudi Islam in service of empire was the "right" kind of Islam.[24] Moreover, the parties of political Islam such as the Egyptian Muslim Brotherhood (founded in 1928) or the Saudi monarchy and its state-sanctioned version of Islam known as Wahhabism were compar-atively less significant on the political stage.

The popularity of national liberation movements and left parties across the third world represented a desire to end colonialism. In this, people in the MENA region and South Asia were demonstrating in prac-tice that religion, while important in their private lives, was not a determining factor in the political sphere. This stood in contrast to the Orientalist perspective that mosque and state have never been separate in "Islam," as discussed in Chapter 3. An Orientalist racist perspective fails to recognize that Arabs, Iranians, and South Asians make political choices and decisions based on a number of factors and while religion plays a part (as it does in the United States), it is not the only or the primary decisive factor. Despite this reality, however, the Islam strategy continued without contradiction until the 1970s. It must be noted, however, that the strategy of cultivating Islamist groups was not uniformly accepted by the political class or even widely known to the public. What was clear was that nationalists who bucked US imperialism were enemies who had to be squashed by any means necessary.[25]

The new US security paradigm under the Nixon doctrine, announced in 1969, rested on building up three regional strongmen: Israel, the Shah's Iran, and Saudi Arabia. Officially, it was known as the "twin pillar" strat-egy, but in addition to Iran and Saudi Arabia, Israel, and later Egypt and

Turkey, helped secure US interests in the region. An alliance with Saudi Arabia meant US support for the kingdom's attempts to Islamize politics in the region. Meanwhile, it supported and encouraged the Shah in Iran, who waged a relentless campaign against Communists in the Tudeh Party and later dissolved all parties except for his own.[26] Because he led a program of modernization and rapid industrialization, and even though he had dealt a blow to political plurality and democracy, he was cast as a "good" secular Iranian since he fell in line with US capitalist imperial goals.

The Iranian Revolution of 1979 was the pivotal moment that shifted US attitudes against what the West soon labeled "Islamic fundamentalism." The popular revolt successfully toppled the US-backed Shah, who had ruled with an iron fist. The revolution was the product of deep discontent among workers, students, peasants, and traders (or *bazaaris*) against the Shah. Iran's workers, in particular its oil workers, were the key muscle that brought the Shah down, but were unable to play an independent role. This allowed Khomeini to maneuver between various factions over the course of two years and finally to take power for the Islamic Republican Party, as historian Nikki Keddie and others have argued.[27] When Khomeini took over the leadership of the revolution and established what he called an Islamic state, it provided inspiration to organizations of political Islam in the region, who saw their hopes and dreams realized. The United States ratcheted up the negative "Islam" frame. "Bad" Muslims had overthrown the "good" secular Shah. Nevertheless, the Reagan administration armed Iran during its war with Iraq, in what came to be known as the Iran-Contra scandal. Further, in the context of the Cold War, the US cultivated other Islamist formations in a proxy war against the Soviet Union. The Soviet Union invaded Afghanistan in 1979 and the United States armed and trained the Afghan mujahideen rebels, who policymakers viewed as advancing imperial interests. Al-Qaeda emerged out of the mujahideen. Thus began a period of contradiction when "Islam" was both a positive and negative construct depending on whether actors supported or militated against US imperial aims.

The Reagan administration used harsh language to denounce Iran, the "bad" Muslims; the administration referred to the "good" Muslims, the Afghan mujahideen, in positive ways. In a 1985 speech, Reagan described the mujahideen as "freedom fighters."[28] With the help of the Pakistani Inter-Services Intelligence, the Reagan administration armed and trained the mujahideen from Afghanistan and elsewhere.[29] He justified such support through the 1980s by stating that the mujahideen are "our brothers," and "we owe them our help."[30] One such brother was the Saudi billionaire Osama bin Laden, whose family had benefited from Saudi state contracts and US funding.[31] Bin Laden became interested in Afghanistan after the Soviet Union invaded the country in 1979. He had contacts with Afghan mujahideen leaders and moved to the country in 1982. Working with his former teacher Abdullah Azzam, he brought in and trained thousands of volunteers.[32] By the mid-1980s he had established several camps of his own and in 1988 he created a database of the volunteers who passed through his camp; the file was named al-Qaeda.[33]

The main foreign source of volunteers for the Afghan jihad was the Arab world. Thousands of people who came to be known as the "Afghan Arabs" poured in from Egypt, Saudi Arabia, Algeria, and several other countries. Until that point, those who believed that taking up arms might advance their political aims were in a minority and had no program outside of isolated acts of urban terror, Gerges argues. In fact, most were seen as outlaws in their countries of origin. The Afghan war served to unite them, train them, and give their movement life.[34] Gerges writes:

> In Afghanistan was assembled the first truly global army of Islamic warriors—the Afghan Arabs. Never before in modern times had so many Muslims from so many different lands speaking so many tongues journeyed to a Muslim country to fight against a common enemy— Egyptians, Saudis, Yemenis, Palestinians, Algerians, Sudanese, Iraqi Kurds, Kuwaitis, Turks, Jordanians, Syrians, Libyans, Tunisians, Moroccans, Lebanese, Pakistanis, Indians, Indonesians, Malaysians, and others.[35]

For the first time it seemed as if a global "community of believers" had come together to fight against infidel encroachment, thanks to the United States and its allies in the region.[36] The Soviet Union's retreat from Afghanistan in 1989 marked a high point for Islamists in the region, and it legitimized the extreme tactics of the militants in the eyes of others who now looked to them as a way forward. Their job complete in Afghanistan, the holy warriors now dispersed to other regions such as Bosnia, Kashmir, and elsewhere to carry on their struggles and to be dubbed "bad" from then on.[37] Similarly, Iraqi dictator Saddam Hussein was an ally of the United States during the 1980s, only to become a "new Hitler" in the context of the first US war on Iraq in 1990.[38] A secular-identified Arab leader, Hussein went from being a "good" Arab to a "bad" Arab.

The Clinton administration viewed Iran as a hub of international terrorism and Islamic "extremism" and instituted sanctions and banned trade with Iran. However, it consorted with the Taliban, whose ultra-conservative Deobandi philosophy had created horrific conditions for women in Afghanistan (as noted in Chapter 3), because of an interest in forging a pipeline deal that would, it was hoped, give US companies access to the oil and natural gas reserves in the Caspian Sea.[39] At the end of the day, Islamist forces that cooperated with a vision of the world adopted by the United States were allies, and those who did not were enemies and cast as "terrorists." This is how imperial ethnocentric racism works.

The word *terrorism* is put in quotation marks throughout this text not to deny the existence of groups like al-Qaeda or ISIS or to downplay the devastating attacks they have carried out, but rather to call attention to the kinds of acts of political violence that are seen as terrorism and those that are not. Although *terrorism* is often defined as violence targeted against civilians to inflict fear so as to advance political agendas, governments often label as *terrorist* those non-state actors that attempt to thwart their objectives while ignoring the political violence of allies.[40] Further, state violence and state-sponsored violence against civilians is rarely, if ever, categorized as terrorism irrespective of the number of lives lost. Perhaps most important to this discussion is the fact that the threat posed to Americans by the parties of political Islam is minuscule. Marc Sageman, former CIA operations officer and long-time government consultant on terrorism, provides the most comprehensive analysis of the actual threat, arguing that there is a "great inflation of the terrorist threat to the United States"[41] and "a dramatically inflated fear of the actual danger posed by neojihadists."[42]

The "Islamic Threat" in the Post–Cold War Era

The collapse of the Soviet Union and the emergence of a unipolar world, or what has been called a "unipolar moment," led to a reconfiguration of US imperialism. At the time, the discussion revolved around a "peace dividend" and a global order characterized by butter, not guns. The United States would create and police a "New World Order" in which it would show up anywhere it was needed, like a "globocop," to right wrongs, advance humanitarian goals, and save the day. The 1991 Gulf War demonstrated to the world that the end of "Communism" did not mean the end of the US military; instead of fighting the Russians, it would be used against other still-significant threats to international stability—rogue states, failed states, terrorists, and a host of others who refused to acquiesce to pax Americana. This was not going to be accomplished through the naked assertion of power, but through the logic of multiculturalism and benevolence.

Melani McAlister argues that the US military reconfigured itself in this period as a meritocratic institution in which women and people of color could thrive. General Colin Powell was a visible embodiment of this new branding effort. McAlister puts it this way:

> After the Gulf War, politicians and the press alike expected that the United States would now be able to intervene whenever and wherever its leaders felt necessary. The representations of the military provided the mandate for that power: the diversity of its armed forces made the United States a world citizen, with all the races and nations of the globe represented in its population. As the military would represent the diversity of the United States, the United States, as represented in its military, would contain the world.[43]

In the following decades, feminism, gay rights, and multiculturalism were absorbed into the US' representation of itself as a liberal empire.[44] As I have argued elsewhere, the brand shift from the Cold War to the war on terror involved a move away from the focus on white middle class masculinity as the face of imperial power to a multiracial, feminist neoliberal logic and form of representation.[45] Multicultural imperialism and a politics of inclusion effectively shields empire from charges of racism.

In the 1990s, the central goal shared by the (first) Bush and Clinton administrations was to expand US power and prevent the rise of any potential rival. Like their Cold War counterparts, these leaders sought to integrate the world into a capitalist order under their control. This time, instead of modernization, the model was neoliberalism with an emphasis on privatization, deregulation, a move away from public and social welfare policies, and the adoption of other free market principles. To realize what Bush described as the "New World Order," the United States militated against "rogue regimes" that refused to play by American rules and attempted to control regions whose instability could undo the smooth functioning of the capitalist system. Non-state actors outside US control had to be contained or removed.

In the 1990s, the MENA region was seen as perhaps the most strategically important region, chiefly because it houses the world's largest oil reserves—oil being the lifeblood of the world economy. The Center for Strategic and International Studies argued in 2000 that the

> Persian Gulf will remain the key marginal supplier of oil to the world market, with Saudi Arabia in the unchallenged lead. Indeed, if estimates of future demand are reasonably correct, the Persian Gulf must expand oil production by almost 80% during 2000–2020, achievable perhaps if foreign investment is allowed to participate and if Iran and Iraq are free of sanctions.[46]

US interventions in the region are related either directly or indirectly to the question of control over the flow of oil, the creation of opportunities for US businesses, and the advancement of US geopolitical interests. In this context, Islamist groups were cast as allies or enemies based on their degree of acquiescence to US aims. What shifted during this period was that non-state actors who resorted to terrorist tactics became a thorn in the side of the United States.

Beyond al-Qaeda, which had set the United States in its crosshairs, many of the militants who had fought in Afghanistan either returned home or traveled elsewhere.[47] Their training by the CIA and Pakistan's Inter-Services Intelligence and their war experience gave them the knowledge they needed to use violent tactics to advance their goals. This was a rather inconvenient outcome for empire. Inevitably, the United States would face the consequences of its support of militants in Afghanistan in the form of "blowback." Political scientist Chalmers Johnson, author of *Blowback: The Costs and Consequences of American Empire*, argued:

> The United States . . . is the world's most prominent target for blowback, being the world's lone imperial power, the primary source of the sort of secret and semisecret operations that shore up repressive regimes, and by far the largest seller of weapons generally.[48]

The 1993 bombing of the World Trade Center was the first example of a whole sequence of similar acts that would reach their apogee on 9/11.[49] The 1993 attack was followed by the Riyadh bombing in 1995, the Khobar bombing in 1996, the American embassy bombings in Kenya and Tanzania in 1998, and the bombing of the USS Cole in 2000. These attacks on

US diplomatic or military targets in the Middle East and Africa led the US military to a new concept it called "asymmetrical warfare," which viewed these new stateless and transnational groups as threats that needed to be monitored and tracked.[50] The Clinton administration designated several groups as "terrorist" and developed a defensive strategy to protect its military and diplomatic installations abroad. Clinton did not rule out the occasional cruise missile attack, however: he bombed "terrorist" targets in the Sudan and Afghanistan in 1998 in response to the Tanzanian and Kenyan embassy bombings. The supposed "terrorist" target in Sudan turned out to be a pharmaceutical company that provided much-needed drugs for people in the region.[51]

Even at this stage, though, "terrorists" did not replace the Soviet Union as the new global enemy of the United States; instead, the dominant thinking in policy circles was that Islamist organizations that used political violence were one force among many that could upset its post–Cold War vision. However, pockets of the ruling elite, particularly the neoconservatives, began to write about "Islamic fundamentalism" as a potential key threat to US interests. The Israeli political class similarly tried to win the United States and Europe to viewing Islamism as their new larger-than-life enemy.[52]

Gerges describes this as a debate between "confrontationists" and "accommodationists." The confrontationists argued that Islamism was the new post–Cold War "other" and that the United States must confront and challenge this adversary. The key ideologue leading this charge was Bernard Lewis, who as noted in previous chapters raised the alarm about an impending "clash of civilizations."[53] Samuel Huntington then popularized this concept in an essay titled "The Clash of Civilizations?" in *Foreign Affairs*, followed by a book with the same title (minus the question mark).[54] Huntington put forward the thesis that in the new post–Cold War era, conflict would be characterized by cultural differences between various civilizations. He named about seven or eight such civilizations, arguing that the Islamic civilization was among the more dangerous threats to the West.

This argument was reflected in a slew of other articles. For example, journalist Judith Miller, in a *Foreign Affairs* article in 1991, argued that US policymakers should not try to distinguish between "good" and "bad" Islamists because there was a consensus among all Islamists to defeat the West. As she put it: "In Islam's war against the West and the struggle to build Islamic states at home, the ends justified the means."[55] Confrontation, rather than co-optation or dialogue, was the only way to thwart this new enemy. Daniel Pipes (son of the neocon Cold Warrior Richard Pipes), Martin Indyk (who served on Bill Clinton's National Security Council), Jeane Kirkpatrick, and a variety of others added their voice to this chorus.[56] The "clash" thesis was not a partisan position; confront-ationists belonged to both political parties. The difference between the accommodationists and confrontationists was not over the goal of US hegemony, it was about strategy and rhetoric. For example, accommoda-tionists did not see the parties of political Islam as a new monolithic enemy; instead, they drew distinctions between "moderate" Islamists (the term *moderate* has historically been given to any force that is pro-US, including the ultra-orthodox Wahhabi Saudi monarchy), and the "extremist" minority (the use of this term *extremist* saw a shift from Arab nationalists to some of the parties of political Islam in this period). This kind of thinking, as noted above, is deeply problematic not least because such simplistic generalizations hide complex histories. Clinton took an accommodationist approach toward the Taliban because of oil and natural gas interests in the region.[57]

Significantly, both confrontationist and accommodationist positions are racist. Arun Kundnani argues that the conservative and liberal approaches to the problem of "Islamic extremism" are steeped in cultural racism. Conservatives believe that the problem arises from Islamic culture's failure to adapt to modernity (as discussed in Chapter 3), while liberals assert that it is not Islam but rather Islamism, seen as a totalitar-ian ideology like fascism or communism, that drives political violence. What is missing in both accounts are the historical conditions that drive Islamist parties and movements. Absent a historical analysis that sets out to explain human action within particular contexts, they posit that culture—whether Muslim culture (conservatives) or Islamism as totali-tarian culture (liberals)—drives the actions of extremists. Both, therefore, are forms of cultural racism that dehumanize people and turn them into empty vessels driven by demonic ideologies. As Kundnani puts it, in "the West, people make culture; in Islam, culture makes people."[58] Thus, the confrontationist and accommodationist approaches are both built on racism; one is of a conservative kind while the other is liberal, which reflect the limits of acceptable discourse in the political establishment.

During the 1990s, the accommodationist line dominated in Washing-ton. The Bush Sr. administration did not adopt the clash thesis. Instead, the position of the administration as articulated by an assistant secretary of state was that the

US government does not view Islam as the next "ism" confronting the West and threatening world peace. This is an overly simplistic response to a complex reality . . . The Cold War is not being replaced with a new competition between Islam and the West. The Crusades have been over for a long time. Americans recognize Islam as a historic civilizing force among the many that have influenced and enriched our culture.[59]

The Clinton administration continued to operate within this framework. As Anthony Lake, Clinton's National Security Advisor, put it:

In the Middle East and throughout the world, there is, indeed, a funda-mental divide. But the fault line runs not between civilizations or religions; no, it runs instead between oppression and responsive government, between isolation and openness, and between moder-ation and extremism.[60]

The Bush and Clinton administrations sought to win over Muslim-majority countries by appealing to universal values of freedom, tolerance, and responsive government. The term *liberal hegemony* has been used to capture this approach; it rests on the use of liberal tropes to present the racialized other as incapable of self-advancement (see Chapter 3). There was of course a difference between rhetoric and practice. The United States thus did little to pressure its authoritarian allies in the MENA region to open up their political systems or foster democratic processes. Instead, it maintained that openness and moderation would be achieved through neoliberal reforms. In the 1990s, liberal imperialism held the day.

The confrontationists, representatives of conservative Islamophobia, however, continued to fight for their position. While they would have little success in shaping foreign policy, they made headway in influencing media perceptions of the Islamic terrorist. Thus, after the World Trade Center bombing in 1993 they argued vociferously that an international network of Muslim terrorists was out to destroy the West. As I argue in Chapter 7, conservatives and the Right actively sought to cultivate the image of the existential "Islamic threat" against whom only a confront-ationist approach would work. They were successful to the extent that when the federal building in Oklahoma City was bombed in 1995 by Gulf War veteran Timothy McVeigh, the media were quick to jump to the conclusion that Muslims were to blame. The neocons were a central part of this strategy of confrontation.

The Neocons

The term *neoconservative* was coined in the early 1970s by Michael Harrington, a founding member of Democratic Socialists of America, as a way to distance former allies (some liberal, others socialist) who had started to gravitate to the right.[61] Harrington named figures such as Irving Kristol, Norman Podhoretz, Jeane Kirkpatrick, Michael Novak, Nathan Glazer, and Daniel Patrick Moynihan as turncoats who had moved away from democratic socialism. Most of the first generation of neocons supported the US war with Vietnam and resented the anti-war movement. They saw themselves as liberals who believed in the idea that America was a force for good in the world and that it should maintain global stability and intervene militarily when needed. They stood against the "bad liberals" who championed George McGovern's bid for the presidency in 1972, viewing them as operating with a politics of "appeasement" and liberal guilt.[62] Many opposed Lyndon Johnson's Great Society program of domestic reform as well.

The neocons' vision of imperialism is premised on the notion of American exceptionalism: "A pervasive faith in the uniqueness, immutability, and superiority of the country's founding liberal principles, accompanied by a conviction that the United States has a special destiny among nations."[63] This vision of the United States as a unique "beacon for other nations" because of its liberal values is taken for granted within the policy establishment as a whole.[64] However, what is different about the neocons is their singular commitment to unipolarism and militarism. As international relations scholar Danny Cooper writes, the neocons "have been nothing if not consistent in their belief that only overwhelming American military preponderance can prevent the outbreak of great power war . . . [and] that multipolar international orders lead to great power war." In short, what defines the neoconservatives is the notion of a unipolar world dominated by the United States, which they believe is in the interests of all: "American military preponderance is good for America, and good for the world."[65]

It follows, therefore, that they drew different conclusions than liberals about the role of the United States in the world after the defeat in Vietnam. As social ethicist Gary Dorrien notes, the liberal imperialism of the 1940s and 1950s "combined a liberal internationalist commitment to the United Nations and international law with a balance of power realism in diplomacy and an ideological abhorrence of Communism."[66] After

Vietnam, Cold War liberals backed away from open confrontation and intervention, a posture the neocons saw as weak. For them, any accommodation to the Soviet camp was surrendering to the enemy in the name of realism. Alternatively, they advocated an interventionist strategy with huge increases in military spending.

Several neocons, such as Bill Kristol (Irving Kristol's son), Richard Perle, Richard Pipes, and Paul Wolfowitz, held high positions during the Reagan era. They retained the *neo* prefix in order to differentiate themselves from the isolationist (noninterventionist) wing of conservatism. Some even stood to the right of Reagan—such as Norman Podhoretz, editor of the neocon magazine *Commentary*, who argued that liberals were fools and that gay people opposed war because of their lust for "helpless, good-looking boys."[67] Frank Gaffney, who founded the Center for Security Policy think tank, argued that the Soviet leader Mikhail Gorbachev had seduced Reagan with false promises.[68] (The central role of this think tank within the Far Right Islamophobic network is discussed in Chapter 7.)

The unipolar moment after the Cold War

When the Soviet Union collapsed, the next generation of neocons developed a vision for the post–Cold War world that was premised on the notion of US dominance in a unipolar world. Charles Krauthammer, a nationally syndicated journalist best known for his writing in the *Washington Post*, articulated this position in a 1990 piece titled "The Unipolar Moment," published in the preeminent foreign policy journal *Foreign Affairs*.[69] Krauthammer argued that the end of the Cold War had created a "single pole of world power." This single superpower, the United States, could therefore intervene anywhere it wanted around the world and set the terms of world politics. To realize this vision, Krauthammer continued, it was necessary to marginalize the arguments of the realists and the isolationists in the policy establishment, who did not realize how important it was for one hegemonic power to rule in order for there to be global stability.

This article was followed by a report prepared for the Pentagon by neocon Paul Wolfowitz (at the request of Dick Cheney) with the help of Scooter Libby, Richard Perle, Zalmay Khalilzad, and others. The *Defense Planning Guidance* report was not intended for public consumption but was leaked to the *New York Times* and the *Washington Post*. The document stated that the first objective of the United States should be to "prevent the re-emergence of a new rival."[70] It must "establish and protect a new order" so that potential competitors would realize that "they need not aspire to a greater role or pursue a more aggressive posture to protect their legitimate interests."[71] In short, a Pax Americana should be established on the military, political, and economic fronts. Even advanced industrialized nations would be discouraged from seeking to "overturn the [US] established political and economic order."[72] It followed from this that the United States would act alone if it needed to, in a unilateral manner, with no questions asked. This, the report stated, would guarantee world stability in a way that neither the UN nor any other multilateral coalitions could. In order to maintain world stability, the report continued, the United States had a right to wage preemptive war on any aggressor. It named a number of state actors as aggressors, from Iraq and North Korea to India and Japan. Post-Soviet Russia was also viewed as a potentially destabilizing force. Preemptive strikes were warranted against any threat to US interests.

At the time, the foreign policy establishment critiqued these ideas harshly; the report was a political embarrassment for the elder Bush. Joe Biden called it a prescription for "literally a Pax Americana," a US empire. Senator Alan Cranston (D-California) likewise ridiculed the document and its authors for wanting the United States to be "the one, the only main honcho on the world block, the global Big Enchilada."[73] The backlash was so strong that Wolfowitz believed his political career to be over. The document was revised, and a softer version replaced the original. It was not yet the neocons' time—the 1990s were to be the era of "humanitarian imperialism," led by Clinton and the liberal imperialists.

What is noteworthy about the document, though, is that the enemies it named were diverse, and the list of national interests was broad. These included "access to vital raw materials, primarily Persian Gulf oil; proliferation of weapons of mass destruction and ballistic missiles, threats to US citizens from terrorism or regional or local conflict, and threats to US society from narcotics trafficking."[74] Thus, "terrorism" was named as only one among several threats faced by the United States. In fact, Krauthammer's article didn't even mention terrorism, an omission for which he would later atone in an article where he stated that the "new threat [Islamism] is as evil as the old Evil Empire."[75] Several neocons and their sympathizers began to advance this notion that "Islamic terrorism" needed to be viewed as the new post–Cold War enemy. Daniel Pipes echoed this point, writing, "Like communism during the Cold War, Islam is a threat to the West."[76] In short, even before the events of 9/11, the neocons were attempting to replace the Soviet Union with a new archnemesis. However, only after 9/11 could this notion come to fruition. Podhoretz, in his 2007 book *World War IV: The Long Struggle against Islamofascism*, compared Islamism to fascism and argued that the struggle against "Islamofascism" was just as important as the previous world wars. In part, this line of argument, with its association between fascism and Islam, came from the neoconservatives' right wing, Likud-style Zionism.

The Israel connection

In a *Wall Street Journal* essay titled "What the Heck Is a 'Neocon'?," leading neocon Max Boot stated unequivocally that "support for Israel" has been and remains a "key tenet of neoconservatism."[77] For the neocons, Israel is instrumental in advancing US power.[78] If the United States was going to maintain its dominance in the Middle East, it followed that Israel, the most pro-American country in the region, had to be its key ally. This is not unique to the neocons but has been a bipartisan commitment. However, the neocons developed a relationship with their counterparts in Israel, the right-wing Likud Party, to develop the notion of the "terrorist" as a threat to democracy and civilization.

Three of the lobby groups/think tanks associated with neoconservatism focus solely on the Middle East—the Jewish Institute for National Security of America, the Washington Institute for Near East Policy (WINEP), and the Middle East Forum. All three are pro-Zionist institutions that spend time and resources analyzing US strategy in the Middle East and lobbying for Zionist positions. Additionally, neocons have held positions on the boards of other think tanks such as the conservative and pro-Zionist American Enterprise Institute, with which they are closely associated, as well as the right-wing Hudson Institute. A neocon and senior fellow of the Hudson Institute, the Israeli-born Meyrav Wurmser, established the Middle East Media Research Institute (MEMRI) in 1998. MEMRI mainly seeks out news media articles from Middle East sources that cast the region and its politics in a negative light and translates them for domestic media consumption. (The equivalent of this institute in the Middle East might be one that selectively translated Fox News broadcasts or the rants of televangelists on the Christian Broadcasting Network as the key lens through which to understand the United States.) Another co-founder was a former colonel in the Israeli military intelligence organization.[79] Before the establishment of Bill Kristol's *Weekly Standard* in 1997 (incidentally located in the same building as the American Enterprise Institute), the leading neocon publication was *Commentary*, which

Podhoretz edited for thirty-five years. The journal was published by the American Jewish Committee, whose stated mission is to "safeguard the welfare and security of Jews in the United States, in Israel and throughout the world."[80]

Concretely speaking, neocon positions on Israel are aligned with right-wing Zionist or Likud-style politics, combined with an abhorrence of any negotiations that show compromise and weakness. It follows, therefore, that the neocons were strongly opposed to the Oslo Accords, which at least in name was based on the principle of mutual recognition and an exchange of land for peace. When Yasser Arafat signed the agreement on the White House lawn in 1993, President Clinton told him that he could proclaim a "state" in the Occupied Territories and become its president. In exchange for US and Israeli recognition of this "state," Arafat was asked to sign away long-standing—and historically just— Palestinian claims on three major issues: the status of Jerusalem, Palestinian refugees and the right of return, and sovereignty over their land. These concessions led Edward Said to call the accords "an instrument of Palestinian surrender, a Palestinian Versailles."[81] Despite the deeply problematic nature of the Oslo Accords from a Palestinian perspective, the neocons considered it insufficiently favorable to Israel and opposed it. Even though Israel had no intention of upholding any of its pledges and the United States had no intention of forcing Israel to comply, the neocons vociferously opposed Oslo, seeing the deal as an Israeli, and by extension American, retreat. Consistent with their opposition to the deals Reagan struck with the Soviet Union, the neocons argued that Oslo would lead to the dissolution of Israeli power. Frank Gaffney and the Center for Security Policy stated that the "land for peace" formula was nothing more than a series of "*retreats* by Israel— unilateral, headlong surrenders of strategically vital real estate" to the Arabs who were "committed to its destruction."[82]

In 1996, the neocons advised Israeli prime minister Benjamin Netanyahu that Israel's security was based on destabilizing Arab governments. They published a document titled *A Clean Break: A New Strategy for Securing the Realm*, arguing that Israel should attack Syrian military targets in Lebanon and even Syria if necessary.[83] At the time, conventional wisdom saw Iraq as a major threat to Israel, and the neocons urged Netanyahu to support the Jordanian Hashemites' challenge to Iraq's borders. This argument was similar to a position developed in the 1980s by the right-wing Likud Party in Israel.[84] The argument went that Israel should fragment, dissolve, or otherwise weaken the neighboring Arab states as a way to shore up its own safety. The logic was that since most of the support for the Palestinian cause came from Arab nations, weakening the latter would help destroy the Palestinian movement. As Noam Chomsky put it:

> It is only natural to expect that Israel will seek to destabilize the surrounding states, for essentially the reasons that led South Africa on a similar course in the region. In fact, given continuing military tensions, that might be seen virtually as a security imperative.[85]

When Israel invaded Lebanon in 1982, it was pursuing this vision.

This thinking continued on both sides of the Atlantic. Political commentator Stephen Sniegoski argues that it was the basis for the invasion of Iraq in 2003 and the Bush plan to destabilize the Middle East in order to reconstruct it based on the neocons' vision:

> In contrast to the [United States'] traditional goal of stability [as a way to secure access to oil], the neocons called for destabilizing existing regimes. Of course, the neocons couched their policy in terms of the eventual *restabilization* of the region on a democratic basis . . . Likud-nik strategy saw the benefit of regional destabilization for its own sake—creating as it would an environment of weak, disunified states or statelets involved in internal and external conflicts that could be easily dominated by Israel . . . [and] without outside support, the Palestinians would be forced to accede to whatever type of peaceful solution Israel offered [emphasis in original].[86]

The logic of destabilization was articulated in the report published by the Project for the New American Century in 2000 (see Chapter 5).

Another avenue of cooperation between the neocons and Likud officials was the development of the notion of the "terrorist threat." Richard Pipes, Podhoretz, and even the neocon idol Senator Henry "Scoop" Jackson attended an important conference in Jerusalem on international terrorism in 1979. In addition to these figures, several Israeli politicians like Likud prime minister Menachem Begin, as well as the elder George Bush and high-level officials from European countries, were also in attendance.[87] The conference, held in Jerusalem, was organized by the Jonathan Institute, then headed by Benjamin Netanyahu. In his opening remarks at the conference, Netanyahu's father Benzion sought to project Israel's enemies—Palestinians who had taken up armed struggle for self-determination—as "terrorists" and to rally the rest of the world around the struggle against "terrorism."[88] The terrorist, Benzion continued, "speaks of 'humanitarian' and national causes, he pretends to fight for 'freedom' against oppression, he keeps speaking of 'legitimate rights.'" To counter this, he argued that this terrorist actually has "no moral restraints" and "respects no code of law." Instead, he belongs in the same camp as the Nazis: "In his genocidal attitude he takes toward the societies he assails, whether it is Ireland, Lebanon, or Israel, he is an offshoot of Nazi philosophy."[89] This equation of Arabs and later Muslims with the Nazis has a long history in Israel.[90] The conference was called therefore to "serve as the beginning of a new process—the process of rallying the democracies of the world to struggle against terrorism and the dangers it represents."[91]

This conference was a response to various resolutions that were passed by the UN General Assembly that legitimated the use of armed struggle in ending colonialism and that validated Palestinian self-determination.[92] Benjamin Netanyahu thus characterized the UN as being "incapable" of dealing with terrorism. For Netanyahu the UN's "legitimation of terror groups" was an "intolerable spectacle" that necessitated the 1979 conference.[93] One presenter at the conference argued that the PLO had served as an intermediary between Moscow and Iran's Ayatollah Khomeini in the plot to overthrow the US-backed Shah.[94] At this stage, the emphasis was on the PLO and the conflation of Arabs with terrorism. "Islamic terrorism" was barely referenced, and overall, Islam was marginal to this conference.[95]

This changed at the second International Conference on Terrorism, held in 1984 in Washington, DC. During his opening remarks, Benjamin Netanyahu stated that "modern terrorism has its roots in two movements that have assumed international prominence in the second half of the twentieth century, communist totalitarianism and Islamic (and Arab) radicalism."[96] By this stage, Iran had come to be a thorn in Israel's side with its support for Hezbollah in Lebanon, and Arab radicalism was bracketed while Islamism took center stage. In short, state actors—particularly the Soviet Union and Iran—were seen as giving life to international terrorism. The PLO was not omitted; its "terrorist mini-state in Lebanon" was presented as "a training center and launching group for what had become a kind of terrorist international."[97] Presenters at the conference included neocons such as Moynihan, Kirkpatrick, and Krauthammer, as well as Israeli leaders such as Yitzhak Rabin and US politicians such as former Secretary of State George Shultz. A new addition to this conference was a session on "Terrorism and the Islamic World," which included the Orientalists Bernard Lewis, Elie Kedourie, and Panyotidis Vatikiotis.

Lewis argued at the conference that the term "Islamic terrorism" was apt because "Islam is a political religion" and Mohammad, in contrast to other religious leaders, had "founded a state and governed it."[98] Lewis explained that it was "inevitable that when the Islamic world confronts the problem of terrorism, that problem, too, assumes a religious, indeed in a sense an Islamic, aspect."[99] Elie Kedourie began his speech by stating that there is "a prevalent—and justifiable—impression that an appreciable part of terrorist activities today originate, and frequently take place, in the world of Islam, and particularly in its Arab portion."[100] He then cherry-picked historical examples from various Muslim kingdoms, starting with the assassination of Ali, going on to the Assassins of the tenth century, and up to Khomeini's Iran, which "exemplifies the idea of a 'terrorist state,'" to knit together a narrative of transhistoric "Islamic terrorism."[101] He ended by raising the alarm that "terrorism in modern Islam is unlikely to prove a flash in the pan."[102] These two conferences were instrumental in the development of the ideology of a racialized terrorist threat.[103]

While the 1984 International Conference on Terrorism was held in Washington, DC, signaling that the United States would lead the world in the war on terrorists, its origins were in Israel. Israel was going through a series of changes in the 1980s. In the mid-1970s, the parties of the religious right (the *haredim*) started to play a greater role in domestic politics. These parties were also responsible for raising the level of hateful rhetoric against non-Jews. One rabbi stated:

> Arabs are a cancer, cancer, cancer in the midst of us . . . There is only one solution, no other, no partial solution: the Arabs out! Out! . . . Let me become defense minister for two months and you will not have a single cockroach around here.[104]

As international relations scholar Fred Halliday notes, it was in this context that anti-Arab and anti-Muslim racism came together to a much greater extent, especially among the settler community as well as the nationalist and religious parties.[105] However, this did not prevent the Likud Party from using the precursor organization to Hamas, the Mujamma' al-Islamiyya, for its own purposes. When the Israeli state recognized and formally licensed the Mujamma' in 1978, the logic was simple—the Islamists' hostility to the left made them useful entities.[106]

The most palpable impact of these conferences was on Reagan's foreign policy. The perceived failure of the Carter administration in dealing with the Iran hostage crisis created an opening for Ronald Reagan and the first war on terror in the 1980s. The day the hostages were released, Reagan used his inaugural speech to repudiate Carter's foreign policy and replace it with a militarist stance centered around terrorism. Top officials in the Reagan administration, such as George Shultz and Jeane Kirkpatrick, both attendees of the Jonathan Institute conferences, ensured that counterterrorism assumed a central focus. However, this militarized approach to terrorism did not persist in the same way under Bush and Clinton. After the Oslo agreement, Daniel Pipes, writing on behalf of the Middle East Forum in the 1990s, registered his opposition to this peace deal by casting suspicion on the intentions of the Arab leadership and warning of the "threat of militant Islam against America and the West."[107] But despite the efforts of the neocons and Israeli lobbyists, this attitude toward "Islamic terrorism" did not significantly impact the rhetoric or policy of the first Bush or Clinton administrations. The 1990s were the era of liberal imperialism, and the neocons would have to wait their turn.

Before turning to Clinton and humanitarian imperialism, however, it is worth noting that many of the think tanks and lobbying groups cited above are not exclusively neocon hubs. WINEP, for instance, has a "mix of neoconservative and Clintonite views," according to historian Maria Ryan.[108] WINEP was founded by Martin Indyk, who formerly served as the research director of the pro-Israel lobby group American Israeli Public Affairs Committee (AIPAC). James Woolsey, Perle, and Wolfowitz served on its board, and neocons Joshua Muravchik and Pipes were adjunct scholars. During the 1990s, though, WINEP was largely supportive of Clinton's policies and many of its leading lights, including Indyk, joined the Clinton administration. Unqualified support for Zionism is a bipartisan requirement in the US foreign policy establishment. As of 2007, the Jewish Institute for National Security of America think tank's board of fifty-five advisors included only four neocons. As we shall see in the next section, neocons are represented on the boards of various realist/ liberal imperialist think tanks as well. In short, the neocons are an integral part of a foreign policy establishment that is pro-Israel and pro-US imperialism. The differences, such as they are, are of tactics, strategy, and rhetoric.

Liberal Imperialism

Liberalism has long furnished justifications for empire and imperialism. Political scientist Uday Singh Mehta has argued that leading British liberal authors invoked "relevant categories such as history, ethnicity, civilizational hierarchies, and occasionally race and blood ties" to "fashion arguments" in service of empire.[109] Journalist Richard Seymour in his book *The Liberal Defence of Murder* argues that the

> tradition of imperial liberalism is almost as old and perplexing as liberalism itself. On the face of it, a doctrine that appears to stress human equality and universalism ought to have nothing to do with a violent system of domination and exploitation. Yet, for many liberals, the virtues of empire were then *very much as they are now* for "liberal interventionists": it promised pedagogy, cultural therapy, economic development, the rule of law, liberty, and even, sometimes, feminism [emphasis added].[110]

Feminism, gay liberation, and racial inclusion have all become hallmarks of liberal imperialism in the post–Cold War period.

In a similar vein, philosopher Jean Bricmont argues in his book *Humanitarian Imperialism: Using Human Rights to Sell War* that the

> ideology of our times, at least when it comes to legitimizing war, is no longer Christianity, nor Kipling's "white man's burden" or the "civilizing mission" of the French Republic, but is a certain discourse on human rights and democracy, mixed in with a particular representation of the Second World War. This discourse justifies Western interventions in the third world in the name of the defense of democracy and human rights or against the "new Hitlers."[111]

While Bricmont may be too hasty in dismissing the uses of the "white man's burden" logic (given the revitalization of Orientalism in the post-9/11 era as discussed in Chapter 3), he is correct to point to democracy and human rights as the key rationales for war. These liberal arguments, however, aren't only the tools of liberal imperialists—they are part of the neocons' arsenal as well. After all, the Bush administration used women's rights as justification for the 2001 war on Afghanistan and named "democracy-building" a goal in Iraq. The difference between the neoconservative and liberal imperialist wings of the policy establishment lies in the latter's recourse to multilateralism and coalition-building when possible (though not always), as well as a willingness to use diplomacy.

As international relations scholar Stephen Walt, who identifies with the realist tradition, states:

> The only important intellectual difference between neoconservatives and liberal interventionists is that the former have disdain for international institutions (which they see as constraints on U.S. power), and the latter see them as a useful way to legitimate American dominance. Both groups extol the virtues of democracy, both groups believe that U.S. power—and especially its military power—can be a highly effective tool of statecraft. Both groups are deeply alarmed at the prospect that WMD [weapons of mass destruction] might be in the hands of anybody but the United States and its closest allies, and both groups think it is America's right and responsibility to fix lots of problems all over the world. Both groups consistently over-estimate how easy it will be to do this, however, which is why each has a propensity to get us involved in conflicts where our vital interests are not engaged and that end up costing a lot more than they initially expect.[112]

He adds humorously that "liberal interventionists are just 'kinder, gentler' neocons, and neocons are just liberal interventionists on steroids."[113] Both strategies, however, have been employed by Republicans and Democrats. George H. W. Bush advocated US global dominance through the use of coalitions and bodies like the UN and eschewed advice from neocon circles. The Clinton administration, however, reworked the global image of the United States through the use of the language of "humanitarian intervention."

Anthony Lake, Clinton's national security advisor, argued that during "the Cold War we contained a global threat to market democracies." Now, after the collapse of the Soviet threat, it was possible to "consolidate the victory of democracy and open markets."[114] Consequently, the Clinton vision was about promoting democracy through neoliberal reforms. The world needed to be made safe for neoliberal capitalism—and Clinton took it upon himself to penetrate areas of the globe previously under Soviet control. As legal and global affairs scholar Jean-Marc Coicaud puts it, "Clinton made American economic success and free trade the defining aspect of his presidency."[115] Where military force was needed, Clinton resorted to multilateral institutions like the UN or NATO. The key voices in his foreign policy team were Lake, Madeleine Albright, Warren Christopher, and his close friend and advisor Strobe Talbott (of the centrist Brookings Institution). This team advocated the use of military power to pursue more humanitarian goals and underscored the priorities of democracy and human rights. They were also opposed to the "go it alone" style and advocated that, as much as possible, the United States should pursue a multilateral strategy.[116] Clinton's "new Wilsonian" view, which stood in contrast to the elder Bush's balance-of-power realism, was premised on the notion that US policy had entered, as Chomsky put it, a "noble phase" with a "saintly glow."[117]

The most important think tank associated with the multilateralist camp of the foreign policy establishment is the Council on Foreign Relations (CFR), which publishes the journal *Foreign Affairs*. The board of directors includes Richard Haass (CFR president since 2003), Zbigniew Brzezinski (former national security advisor to Jimmy Carter), Joseph Nye (theorist of "soft power"), Madeleine Albright, Colin Powell, Richard Holbrooke, Strobe Talbott, Fouad Ajami (who was part of the Bush inner circle that framed the response to 9/11), and neocon Elliott Abrams, who is a senior fellow.[118] While CFR veers toward the realist side, neocon views are represented within it. Similarly, the influential think tank Center for Strategic and International Studies includes realists like Sam Nunn, David Abshire, Richard Armitage, Henry Kissinger, Brent Scowcroft, and Joseph Nye as well as neocons like Zalmay Khalilzad.

It should therefore come as no surprise that these individuals talk to one another and vie for influence within the broader political arena. When they disagree it is typically around strategy or rhetoric; they all share the overall aim of maintaining US hegemony. For instance, back in the 1950s when the Orientalists were arguing that Islam and Communism were incompatible, the newly formed CFR (founded in 1954) took a position against this thesis. Its Middle East strategist at the time wrote:

> Islam cannot be counted on to serve as such a barrier [to the USSR]. The theory that communism and Soviet influence could never make inroads in the Moslem world because they are materialistic and atheistic has not been borne out. Religion does have a significant place in Middle Eastern society. It colors both popular and official attitudes. But it does not establish absolute immunity to a political virus such as fascism or communism.[119]

In short, CFR offered a realist view of how the United States might maintain its power in the Middle East. This is a difference of strategy, not of goals and outcomes.

The first "humanitarian" mission of the 1990s was Clinton's continuation of Bush's Operation Restore Hope in Somalia in 1993. UN troops,
under the leadership of the United States, were sent to address the food
crisis and feed the hungry—yet the troops arrived months after those
most threatened by hunger had already died of starvation. While the
United States and UN justified the invasion on humanitarian grounds,
US interests in Somalia's geostrategic location and oil resources played a
more significant role in the US decision to intervene. When eighteen US
soldiers were killed (in an incident that formed the basis for the film
Black Hawk Down), US troops departed and left the East African nation
worse off than when they arrived. The United States also killed hundreds
of Somali citizens.[120] This intervention prefigured what was to come.
Despite this, liberals provided cover for Clinton's "humanitarianism."
Former leftists like Paul Berman and Michael Ignatieff cheered on this
new imperialism, as did New Left icons like Daniel Cohn-Bendit.

Of course, the United States did not intervene in every humanitarian
crisis—the most famous case being the Rwandan genocide—nor would
the Clinton administration truly adopt multilateralism. For instance,
Washington refused to sign an agreement supported by a majority of the
world's countries to ban the use of antipersonnel landmines. The Clinton
administration did not always seek the consent of the UN Security
Council before waging war—the NATO-led war on Serbia in 1999 was
carried out without UN authorization, nor did it go through UN channels before bombing Iraq (with British help) in 1998. Political analyst
Phyllis Bennis, fellow at the progressive think tank Institute for Policy
Studies, shows convincingly that even while Clinton used the rhetoric of
"assertive multilateralism," he employed Bush Jr.-style unilateralism well
before 9/11. She adds that he cynically used the UN to provide "multilateral cover" for US goals and that Clinton's "humanitarian interventions"
were in reality a disguise for "unilateral militarism."[121] Moreover, the
genocidal sanctions regime in Iraq presided over by the Clinton administration was far from "humanitarian."

Despite this, the neocons continued to maintain their ideological
differences with Clinton, writing several critiques of his foreign policy. In
1996 Bill Kristol and Robert Kagan published an important essay in
Foreign Affairs titled "Toward a Neo-Reaganite Foreign Policy." Rejecting
balance-of-power realism, they argued that

in a world in which peace and American security depend on American
power and the will to use it, the main threat the United States faces now

and in the future is its own weakness. American hegemony is the only reliable defense against a breakdown of peace and international order. The appropriate goal of American foreign and defense policy, therefore, is to preserve that hegemony as far into the future as possible.[122]

This "neo-Reaganite" policy was called "benevolent global hegemony" because it asserted that what was good for the United States was generally good for the world as well. As an aside, we might note that this was not a radically new idea but rather a continuation of the "benevolent supremacy" that McAlister argues characterized US policy in the post–World War II era.[123] What was new in the late 1990s was the willingness among the adherents of this policy to use the word *empire* more openly. Whereas the United States shied away from this designation after World War II, not least to differentiate itself from colonial powers like Britain and France, the unipolar world created new conditions for the resurrection of imperial language.

One might argue that Clinton's vision was not so different from that of the neocons. It was, however, packaged in more sophisticated language. As Maria Ryan writes, there was

> significant convergence between the neoconservative objectives and those of the Clinton administration. To be sure, the language some of the neocons used was more explicit. They openly prioritized the credibility of NATO and were frank about why a US and NATO victory was important. Clinton presented a softer image, claiming he was also motivated by humanitarian considerations—and perhaps he was—but even for Clinton humanitarianism alone was not enough to compel intervention.[124]

Thus, liberalism and human rights discourse effectively masked imperial objectives and imperial violence. "Benevolent hegemony" is a reworking of the white man's burden and is based on the notion that the United States knows best what is in the interests of developing nations. While the rhetoric is no longer blatantly racist in neocon and realist/liberal circles, its assumptions that people in developing nations are incapable of self-rule or of change from within minus imperial intervention has been part of a bipartisan consensus for a while. Such an attitude still infantilizes and therefore racializes those who disagree with the imperial agenda. In the aftermath of World War II it was about the adoption of modernization programs; in the neoliberal era it is about structural adjustment programs and the neoliberalization of the economy.

Toward the end of the 1990s, the Clinton administration stated that the United States was an "indispensable nation" and that because of its unmatched power and its values it could "stand taller and see farther" than others. Therefore, its dominance of the world was necessarily benign: it was not based on coercion but rather on the attractiveness of American values, commodities, and popular culture.[125] This is what Joseph Nye refers to as "soft power." (Nye served in the Clinton administration and is on the board of the CFR.) While they might quibble over the details, this vision of US dominance was shared by all sections of the foreign policy establishment; that is, at least until Trump departed from this consensus, creating a new era of blatant racism and a rejection of the humanitarian mission of the post–Cold War era. While Trump's racism was obvious, imperial ethnocentric racism has informed US policy from the Cold War on.

Conclusion

This chapter outlined the evolving posture toward the movements of political Islam within the foreign policy establishment from the Cold War to the end of the 1990s. Until the 1970s, policy makers saw various state and non-state actors that mobilized Islam on the political stage as allies, but after the Iranian Revolution "bad" Islam and "bad" Muslims made an entrance. The development of the "Arab terrorist" and later the "Islamic terrorist" stock figure, a product largely of the neocon–Likud alliance, began in the late 1970s and continued through the 1980s. The confrontationist approach toward Islamists was not, however, adopted during the 1990s either by the Bush Sr. or Clinton administrations. During the 1990s, empire sought to craft itself through the lens of liberal hegemony. However, by the end of the 1990s, various US policies toward the Middle East were at a dead end. Significantly, with predictions that world energy demands would increase by 50 percent in the first two decades of the twenty-first century, it became necessary to find more effective ways to extract oil from the region. Gilbert Achcar writes that for "the Bush administration, as for U.S. capitalism as a whole, the need to put an end to the embargo imposed on Iraq was becoming urgent."[126] The attacks of 9/11 provided an opportunity to reshape the region; this moment and its aftermath are the focus of the next chapter.

5

Empire's Changing Clothes:
Bush, Obama, Trump

In September 2000, the neoconservative think tank Project for the New American Century released a document outlining its foreign policy vision. It called for the United States to use overwhelming military force to take control of the Persian Gulf region, for "maintaining global US preeminence . . . and [for] shaping the international security order in line with American principles and interests."[1] This goal, the report went on to add, was going to take some time to be realized "absent some catastrophic event—like a new Pearl Harbor."[2] On September 11, 2001, such an event did occur—at a time when the neoconservative wing of the foreign policy establishment held powerful positions in the administration of George W. Bush. The crisis of 9/11 positioned the neocons to realize their vision and to project US power on a global scale.

The attacks on that fateful day precipitated unanimous agreement in the foreign policy establishment that the war on terror would henceforth frame US foreign policy. Three days after the attacks, the Authorization for Use of Military Force Against Terrorists was passed, setting in motion an open-ended, perpetual, global war that has continued to this day.[3] Barely had the ashes settled from the Twin Towers when loud proclamations that "Islamic terrorists" represented existential threats to the United States began to echo in the public sphere. From then on, US foreign and domestic policy has been shaped by the rubric of "terrorism" and the corresponding security measures needed to allegedly keep Americans safe. As noted in previous chapters, the racialized terrorist as a national and global security threat has been part of imperial practice since the late 1960s; 9/11 brought it front and center and set the terms of what was to come in the decades after. It was the basis from which a new infrastructure of empire has been crafted.

Professor of politics and international affairs G. John Ikenberry captured the post-9/11 dynamic in the influential journal *Foreign Affairs*:

> For the first time since the dawn of the Cold War, a new grand strategy is taking shape in Washington. It is advanced most directly as a response to terrorism, but it also constitutes a broader view about how the United States should wield power and organize world order. According to this new paradigm, America is to be less bound to its partners and to global rules and institutions while it steps forward to play a more unilateral and anticipatory role in attacking terrorist threats and confronting rogue states seeking WMD (weapons of mass destruction). The United States will use its unrivaled military power to manage the global order.[4]

US imperialism was strengthened and bolstered after 9/11. The attacks provided policy makers with a larger than life enemy, "Islamic terrorism," against which a global war was necessary. Seizing the moral high ground of a nation under attack, the foreign policy establishment resurrected empire, as historian Rashid Khalidi argued in his book *Resurrecting Empire: Western Footprints and America's Perilous Path in the Middle East*.[5] The wars on Afghanistan and Iraq followed soon after. In fact, in the first two decades of the war on terror, as the Preface notes, hundreds of thousands have been killed while tens of millions have been displaced.

In this chapter, I outline the foreign policy of the Bush, Obama, and Trump administrations. I study various policy documents as well as influential articles and statements by policy makers to argue that while Trump represented a break with the bipartisan consensus around liberal hegemony with a turn toward nativism and the "America first" policy, there are also continuities among all three administrations. In place of the standard self-representation of the United States as a force of liberty and benevolence in international relations, the Trump administration marked a turn toward what has been called "illiberal hegemony."[6] Unlike his Republican predecessors, Trump did not operate through covert dog-whistle forms of racism; he threw away the whistle and adopted overt forms of racism consistent with that of the Far Right Islamophobic network discussed in Chapter 7. Moreover, if the neocons were liberal interventionists on steroids, as Stephen Walt claimed (see Chapter 4), Trump was a neocon on steroids minus a liberal human rights cover.

Liberal imperial racism was replaced by blatant racism for a period. With the election of Joe Biden and Kamala Harris in 2020, liberal multicultural imperialism was back on the agenda. The key argument in this chapter is that whether packaged in liberal or right-wing terms, racist policies have been central to all administrations since 9/11.

September 11 and the Bush Doctrine

Almost immediately after 9/11, the Bush administration started to look for ways to attack Iraq. As Richard Clarke, then "counterterrorism czar," reveals in his book *Against All Enemies*, President Bush took a few people aside and said to them:

> I know you have a lot to do and all . . . but I want you, as soon as you can, to go back over everything, everything. See if Saddam did this. See if he's linked in any way.[7]

This effort to target Iraq was part of the larger neocon strategy of destabilizing the Middle East (see Chapter 4). Destabilizing the region also meant transforming the cultural values of the Middle East and North Africa (MENA) to make them less hostile to Western powers, less supportive of the Palestinian cause, and more neoliberal. The Bush Doctrine, as it came to be known, laid out in the National Security Strategy (NSS) document released in 2002 enshrined neoconservative foreign policy.[8]

The key element of the Bush Doctrine was that it proclaimed the United States' unilateral right to wage preemptive war—to attack another sovereign nation not because it directly threatened the United States but because it could potentially pose a threat. It gave the president discretion to determine what constituted a threat. Thus, if a nation "harbored terrorists," developed weapons of mass destruction, or otherwise acted in ways that went against US interests, it would be subject to attack and invasion. Another key aspect of the Bush Doctrine was the imperative to put down the rise of any rival that might challenge US hegemony. The NSS document states: "Our forces will be strong enough to dissuade potential adversaries from pursuing a military buildup in hopes of surpassing, or equaling, the power of the United States."[9] This translated into US military presence in the Middle East and Central Asia, considered "hot spots" due to their oil and natural gas resources as well as their closeness to potential rivals like China, India, and Russia. The US wars in Afghanistan and Iraq were designed to accomplish both aims: to put down potential threats and dissuade potential adversaries. The Bush administration had intended to carry out regime change in Iran and Syria after it did so in Iraq. With the region under its control, Washington could then dictate terms to the other powers that rely on Middle East oil, particularly China.

The leaked Wolfowitz report *Defense Planning Guidance* from the early 1990s (see Chapter 4)—the report so roundly scorned by the policy establishment—was now being put into practice against the backdrop of the tragedy of 9/11. The neocons, as well as others sympathetic to their vision, understood the historic opportunity the 9/11 attacks presented. Condoleezza Rice, Bush's national security advisor and later secretary of state, put it succinctly when she told her senior national security staff shortly after 9/11 to think about how to "capitalize on these opportunities," which were "shifting the tectonic plates in international politics," to the advantage of the United States.[10]

Yet capitalizing on this opportunity to realize the neocon vision also meant orchestrating an elaborate public relations campaign designed to elicit public support and stifle criticism. Enter the war on terror. Stephen Sheehi points out that the rhetorical response to 9/11 was worked out by a group of academics, journalists, policy makers, and experts who were invited to strategy sessions at the White House. As Wolfowitz explained, "The US government, especially the Pentagon, is incapable of producing the kinds of ideas and strategy needed to deal with a crisis of the magnitude of 9/11."[11] Among those invited to help in generating the appropriate public response were Bernard Lewis, journalist and former *Newsweek* editor Fareed Zakaria, and Johns Hopkins professor Fouad Ajami, as well as several neocons.

Sheehi points to the different approaches Lewis and Zakaria took. He writes that if "Lewis locates the failures of Islam within the barbarism of the 'Arab mind,' then Zakaria locates the hate for the West in the failure of Arab political culture and economic organization."[12] Both are deeply racist positions. Zakaria, a student of Samuel Huntington, argued that the United States should promote free markets and democracy in the Middle East, channeling his mentor's modernization proclivities. For people like Zakaria, creating pliant, individualistic, consumerist neo-liberal citizens in the MENA region is possibly as important as US control over oil. However, not unlike the Orientalists of the preceding century, Zakaria declared that Arabs have seen the "reverse of the historical process in the Western world, where liberalism produced democracy and democracy fuels liberalism. The Arab path has produced dictatorship, which has bred terrorism."[13] This is a reworking of Oriental despotism built on the racist essentialization of the Arab other. This is Clinton-style liberal imperialism and liberal racism. It was made more palatable with women at the helm—Madeleine Albright as Clinton's secretary of state and Condoleezza Rice in the same role in Bush's second term. It was now the burden of white and black women to bring civilization to the benighted masses. The cultural shift that Zakaria and others were pushing was also designed to prevent insurgencies in the MENA region. Lewis took a position more closely aligned with the neocons. It is therefore not surprising that the neocons would turn to Lewis to provide the intellectual ballast needed to justify their foreign policy; as Danny Cooper puts it, the neocons "lionize Lewis."[14] According to journalist Bob Woodward, Lewis was "a Cheney favorite," and Cheney used Lewis's academic credentials and credibility repeatedly to justify his own policy positions.[15]

The "clash of civilizations" rhetoric therefore became dominant in the aftermath of 9/11 and was the ideological basis for the wars in Afghanistan and Iraq as well as the targeting of the racial Muslim domestically (see Chapter 6). For a time it appeared that the neocons were unstoppable—but they overplayed their hand. During its first term, the Bush administration built a "coalition of the willing" to invade Iraq, rejecting criticisms from allies it derogatorily labeled "old Europe." The Bush administration planned to carry out rolling regime changes throughout the region to install quisling governments obedient to Washington's dictates. One senior British official close to the administration captured this imperial plan in a characteristic masculinist pose[16] of the era: "Everyone wants to go to Baghdad. Real men want to go to Tehran."[17] The war on Iraq, however, did not go the way the neocons wanted it to. Instead of greeting US forces as liberators, the Iraqi people resisted and rejected US hegemony. The plan to carry out regime change in Iran and Syria was halted; if anything, Iran was strengthened by US actions. Not only was the neocon vision of a new Middle East in jeopardy, but the United States had alienated its former allies in Europe and strengthened China (as well as Russia and Venezuela). All of this led retired General William Odom to call the Iraq War "the greatest strategic disaster in US history."[18] This prompted an about-face in the Bush administration's policies, which moved toward the use of more multilateral tactics. Additionally, the administration moved away from "hard" power (such as the use of coercion and bribery) and toward winning "hearts and minds," as represented in the counterinsurgency strategy championed by its military commander in Afghanistan, General David Petraeus.

The military's 2006 counterinsurgency manual laid out how soft power would be used in the battlefield. In the Foreword, Petraeus noted that it had been twenty years since the US military had produced a field manual specifically on counterinsurgency and articulated this new doctrine as follows:

> A counterinsurgency campaign is, as described in this manual, a mix of offensive, defensive, and stability operations conducted along multiple lines of operations. It requires Soldiers and Marines to employ a mix of familiar combat tasks and skills more often associated with nonmilitary agencies. The balance between them depends on the local situation. Achieving this balance is not easy. It requires leaders at all levels to adjust their approach constantly. They must ensure that their Soldiers and Marines are ready to be greeted with either a handshake or a hand grenade . . . Soldiers and Marines are expected to be *nation builders as well as warriors*. They must be prepared to help reestablish institutions and local security forces and assist in rebuilding infrastructure and basic services. They must be able to facilitate establishing local governance and the rule of law. The list of such tasks is long; performing them involves extensive coordination and cooperation with many intergovernmental, host-nation, and international agencies [emphasis added].[19]

In short, it wasn't enough simply to kill and militarily defeat the enemy; soldiers needed to take part in building infrastructure, providing basic services, and being both "nation builders and warriors." A coauthor of this manual wrote that counterinsurgency involved "collecting information about the whole society, understanding local conditions, monitoring public opinion, and analyzing social and political relationships and networks."[20] To aid this effort, the following year the Pentagon recruited anthropologists through a $40 million program called the "Human Terrain System." It sent these anthropologists to Iraq and Afghanistan to gather cultural information in order to better prosecute the war on terror. It stated a clear goal: "Empathy will become a weapon."[21] Middle East studies scholar Laleh Khalili observes that the involvement of

> liberal human rights practitioners in the drafting of the *Counterinsurgency Field Manual* meant that population-centric counterinsurgency

[where the military would no longer be simply a tool of force but also one of modernization] is now considered a progressive form of warfare by many liberal interventionists in European and North American capitals.[22]

Thus, even under the neocon regime, liberal interventionist approaches became necessary.

By the end of Bush's second term, however, the failing occupations in Afghanistan and Iraq—as well as the economic crisis of 2007–2008, whose proportions were not seen since the Great Depression—meant that it was time for a change. The ruling elite also gave Obama their blessing, hoping to put a friendlier face on US imperialism. The other team of imperialists was ready with a plan to rehabilitate the global image of American empire and to secure its interests on the world stage.

Obama's Liberal Imperialism

In January 2007, a leadership group on US–Muslim relations headed by Madeleine Albright, Richard Armitage (former deputy secretary of state under George W. Bush), several academics like Vali Nasr and Jessica Stern, and Muslim Americans like Daisy Khan and Imam Feisal Abdul Rauf (who appear again in Chapter 7) produced a report titled *Changing Course: A New Direction for US Relations with the Muslim World*. The report was produced with the assistance of various "good Muslims," who had a seat at the table in the Obama administration. It received high praise from political figures like Republican Senator Dick Lugar and democrats like Congressman Howard Berman and Leon Panetta (soon to be CIA director and eventually secretary of defense), as well as former generals like Anthony Zinni.[23] In its opening pages, it states that distrust of the United States in Muslim-majority countries was the product of "policies and actions—not a clash of civilizations." It went on to argue that to defeat "violent extremists," military force was necessary but not sufficient and that the United States needed to forge "diplomatic, political, economic, and cultural initiatives." The report urged the US leadership to improve "mutual respect and understanding between Americans and Muslims," promote better "governance and improve civic participation," and help "catalyze job-creating growth" in Muslim-majority countries. This was a return to Clintonian liberal imperialism, with its emphasis on diplomacy and markets. The report's call to action stated that it would be vital for the next president to talk about improving relations with Muslim-majority countries in his or her inaugural speech and to reaffirm the US "commitment to prohibit all forms of torture."

Barack Obama was the ideal vehicle to model this new posture. Indeed, in his inaugural address, Obama did precisely as the policy group's document suggested. In one of his first speeches abroad, in Cairo, Obama rejected the "clash of civilizations" argument, emphasizing the shared common history and aspirations of the East and West. Whereas the "clash" discourse sees the West and the world of Islam as mutually exclusive and as polar opposites, Obama emphasized "common principles." He spoke of "civilization's debt to Islam," which "pav[ed] the way for Europe's Renaissance and Enlightenment," and he acknowledged Muslims' contributions to the development of science, medicine, navigation, architecture, calligraphy, and music. This was no doubt a remarkable admission for an American president, but one that Obama clearly saw as vital to bolstering the United States' badly damaged image in the "Muslim world."[24] Indeed, this speech marked a significant rhetorical shift from the Bush era.[25]

It was, however, consistent with the line argued by liberal imperialists. As Joseph Nye put it in *Foreign Affairs*:

> The current struggle against Islamist terrorism is much less a clash of civilizations than an ideological struggle within Islam. The United States cannot win unless the Muslim mainstream wins. There is very little likelihood that people like Osama bin Laden can ever be won over with soft power: hard power is needed to deal with such cases. But there is enormous diversity of opinion in the Muslim world. Many Muslims disagree with American values as well as American policies, but that does not mean that they agree with bin Laden. The United States and its allies cannot defeat Islamist terrorism if the number of people the extremists are recruiting is larger than the number of extremists killed or deterred. Soft power is needed to reduce the extremists' numbers and win the hearts and minds of the mainstream.[26]

The need for a cultural shift articulated earlier now became central under the Obama administration. Nye acknowledged the diversity of opinion in Muslim-majority countries from the MENA region to South Asia and advocated the use of soft power to win hearts and minds. The Obama era therefore came to be characterized by a shift to liberal imperialism and liberal Islamophobia. The key characteristics of liberal Islamophobia in the Obama era were the rejection of the "clash of civilizations" thesis, the elevation of "good Muslims" both domestically and internationally, and a concomitant willingness to work with "moderate" (or pro-American) Islamists. While Orientalists like Lewis and his neocon associates view the culture of Islam as backward and as instrumental in fomenting political violence, liberals differentiate between the mass of Muslims and "extremists." They view the latter as driven by a totalitarian ideology.[27] Liberal Islamophobia may be rhetorically gentler than conservative Islamophobia, but it is nonetheless imperial racism in that it takes for granted the "white man's burden." It doesn't occur to the likes of Nye, Albright, and Haass that it is for ordinary people in the Middle East and Central/South Asia to make decisions about their societies. As noted in Chapter 3, this belief that the United States can and should shape the destinies of other nations is a central frame in the ideology of anti-Muslim racism. Self-determination does not enter their framework—and "benevolent supremacy" remains unquestioned.

Obama claimed that his policy was a shift to the realist tradition of great power geopolitics. As he put it, "The truth is that my foreign policy is actually a return to the traditional bipartisan realistic policy of George Bush's father, of John F. Kennedy, and in some ways of Ronald Reagan."[28] Yet, as we saw above, during Bush's second term the neoconservatives were also gravitating toward this position because of the failure of their approach in Afghanistan and Iraq. Soon after taking office, Obama deployed 30,000 more troops to Afghanistan, expanded the war into Pakistan (through the "Af-Pak" strategy), tried to pressure Iraq into granting an extension of the US occupation (which failed), carried out drone attacks and "black ops" in Yemen and Somalia, and participated in the NATO war on a former ally in Libya, Muammar Gaddafi. This should not come as a surprise, since his inaugural staff included Bush personnel like defense secretary Bob Gates and General Petraeus, as well as Democratic Party hawks like Hillary Clinton and Joseph Biden. The Obama administration's strategy consisted of a return to multilateralism, using multilateral institutions to incorporate and subordinate international and regional rivals.

In his 2010 National Security Strategy document, Obama argued that the US should focus its

> engagement on strengthening international institutions and galvanizing the collective action that can serve common interests such as combating violent extremism; stopping the spread of nuclear weapons and securing nuclear materials; achieving balanced and sustainable

economic growth; and forging cooperative solutions to the threat of climate change, conflict, and pandemic disease.[29]

Yet, despite this multilateral strategy, the Obama administration still resorted to unilateral actions when needed— the assassination of Osama bin Laden, for example—as well as to bilateral agreements. Obama's vision was to secure, through this strategy of engagement, a world order under US management and in its interests.

In practice, this didn't go very smoothly. The NATO attempt to dominate Afghanistan began to lose its multilateral character, as various European nations started pulling out their forces in response to domestic opposition. By the end of the first decade of the new millennium, the "hearts and minds" approach and the counterinsurgency strategy had more or less failed. Obama therefore had to return to counterterrorism and say "good-bye to nation building and counter-insurgency operations."[30] The failure of the Bush policies he was pursuing ushered in a new phase in Obama's imperial strategy.

In the context of the Arab uprisings of 2011, known as the "Arab Spring," the Obama administration at first supported its dictatorial allies (such as Egypt's Hosni Mubarak, a personal friend of the Clinton family).[31] When it became clear that they were going to be swept from power, Obama embraced the Arab Spring, at least rhetorically, while at the same time supporting counterrevolutionary forces around the region. The United States continued to fund the Egyptian military, the key source of counter-revolution in that country. Elsewhere the Obama White House stayed silent—such as when Saudi Arabia not only repressed its Shi'a rebellion, but also sent troops to Bahrain to crush the uprising in that country. Had Obama wanted to intervene on the side of the pro-democracy demonstrators in Bahrain, he could have used the Fifth Fleet, which is stationed there. Instead, he opted to support pro-Western forces in Libya and Syria as a means of replacing inconsistent allies and deflating movements demanding meaningful social change.

In 2012, Obama's defense strategy approach, delineated in *Sustaining US Global Leadership: Priorities for 21st Century Defense*, refocused US foreign policy and its military structure.[32] It made clear that the United States would continue to fight against "violent extremists," even though the assassination of bin Laden had diminished al-Qaeda. As the report states, "its affiliates remain active in Pakistan, Afghanistan, Yemen, Somalia, and elsewhere"; the US military will "monitor" these groups and strike "the most dangerous groups and individuals when necessary."[33] In short, Obama intended to continue the war on terror on non-state actors through surveillance as well as drone attacks and the use of Special Operations Forces.

Drone strikes became the Obama administration's signature mode of warfare. In May 2012 the *New York Times* revealed that every Tuesday ("Terror Tuesdays"), Obama met with advisors to determine the list of people to be assassinated using drone strikes (the "kill list"). This list sometimes included US citizens like the Yemeni-born cleric Anwar al-Awlaki. In the same drone strike that killed al-Awlaki, his sixteen-year-old son Abdulrahman was also executed without as much as a trial or the presentation of evidence in a court of law.[34] Deep within the *Times* article, it was revealed that the Obama administration was able to make claims about low civilian casualty counts in drone strikes because it defined as a "combatant" (against whom drone warfare is sanctioned) any military age male who lived in an area being targeted by drone strikes "unless there is explicit intelligence posthumously proving them innocent."[35] Such a definition epitomizes racist dehumanization as it exposes tens of millions to vulnerability to premature death, an important dimension of racialization. Obama's sophisticated oratory and rebranding of the war on terror meant that the US public supported drone warfare. In June 2012, about 62 percent of the public approved of drone strikes. This stood in stark contrast to polls in Egypt, Jordan, and Turkey, where disapproval ranged from 81 to 89 percent.[36]

At any rate, the guidance document refocused attention on the Asia-Pacific area and named China and Iran as key state actors that needed to be contained. To deter and contain China, the United States would work with its "network of allies and partners."[37] Bypassing its long-term ally Pakistan, the document named India as furthering US aims in Asia. In a similar vein, the report also turned to allies in the Middle East, particularly the Gulf Cooperation Council nations, to "prevent Iran's development of a nuclear weapon capability and counter its destabilizing policies."[38] Needless to say, it affirmed the administration's commitment to "Israel's security and a comprehensive Middle East peace." Finally, it turned to its European allies and NATO to take on a greater share of the burden of maintaining global security, so that the United States may not only move some its forces from Europe but also downsize its military.

The Obama administration learned that interventions such as those in Iraq and Afghanistan were the wrong ways to project US power. As Obama noted in his preface to the guidance document, we will remember the lessons of history and avoid repeating the mistakes of the past when our military was left ill prepared for the future. As we end today's wars and reshape our Armed Forces, we will ensure that our military is agile, flexible, and ready for the full range of contingencies.[39]

The document continues, "US forces will no longer be sized to conduct large-scale, prolonged stability operations."[40] Instead, the political class drew the lesson that the way to achieve its objectives is through missions like the NATO military campaign in Libya, which involved air power and relied on local allies on the ground. In sum, Obama's imperial posture involved trying to establish US hegemony in Asia (preventing the rise of China) and in the Middle East (containing Iran) through multilateral alliances and the use of air strikes, drone attacks, counterterrorism, and special operations forces as well as cyber warfare. In short, despite the Right's charge that Obama was a "secret Muslim agent" working on behalf of foreign governments, he was in reality a liberal imperialist at the helm of a nation trying to reassert its domination in an increasingly multipolar world.

Trump's Illiberal Hegemony

Trump gained national prominence by amplifying right-wing attacks on Obama and the claim that he was Muslim and therefore more loyal to Muslim-majority countries than the United States. Along with Fox News, Trump popularized a conspiracy theory known as "birtherism" that claimed Obama was born in Kenya and therefore could not be president.[41] Despite the release of Obama's birth certificate, documenting his birth in Hawaii, Trump remained popular with the right-wing electoral base that brought him to power in 2016. Trump broke with the dog-whistle racism of the Republican Party, resorting instead to blatant right-wing racism and nativism. His domestic and foreign policy involved making "America Great" by putting "America First." This stance was interpreted in some quarters as a return to isolationism, a policy among some conservatives in an era before the rise of the neocons. In reality, as political scientist Barry Posen argued in *Foreign Affairs*, Trump adopted a different strategy for global dominance, one that might better be described as "illiberal hegemony."[42]

In a nutshell, illiberal hegemony translated into a policy of aggressive unilateralism and the abandonment of multilateral organizations,

treaties, and economic pacts through which the United States had dominated the world. It was neoconservatism on steroids combined with
Trump's transactional approach to deal making. This marked a break
with the bipartisan strategy of liberal or benevolent hegemony that the
political class had pursued since the Cold War. Moreover, the multicultural and feminist imperialism of the post–Cold War era was replaced by
white nationalism. Until the Trump administration, both parties were
committed to the US state superintending global capitalism behind the
veneer of benevolence. Their goal was to integrate the world's states into
a so-called rules-based neoliberal order of free trade globalization and to
prevent the rise of any peer competitor or rival alliance of states. In place
of this bipartisan consensus, Trump implemented a toxic combination of
economic nationalism, unilateral imperialism, and a transactional relationship with all states in the world system. While he promised an end to
"forever wars," he never intended to retreat from US dominion over the
MENA region and South and Central Asia. As he stated in his 2017
National Security Strategy statement in the early days of his administration, "Radical Islamist terror groups were flourishing. Terrorists had
taken control of vast swaths of the Middle East."[43] He therefore adopted
a policy, he states, to "crush" the Islamic State of Iraq and Syria (ISIS),
promising to continue to pursue "them until they are destroyed."[44]

However, Trump reoriented military strategy away from the war on
terror toward great power competition with China and Russia. In his second
term, Obama accomplished part of his "pivot to Asia" policy by bolstering
alliances with Asian states and redeploying the US Navy to the region. But
he failed to get the Trans-Pacific Partnership Agreement through Congress,
where it faced bipartisan opposition; Trump later abandoned it. Moreover,
after the rise of ISIS in Syria and Iraq as well as the Arab Spring, the Obama
administration was forced to remain focused on the MENA region and
could not fully pivot to Asia as planned. In order to contain Iran, the Obama
administration negotiated a nuclear accord—the Joint Comprehensive
Plan of Action—to protect the monopoly over nukes that the United States
and Israel have in the region. But Washington's allies, Israel and Saudi
Arabia, both opposed the deal and demanded a more hawkish approach of
greater sanctions as well as military action against Iran.

The Trump administration's approach dovetailed with that of Israel
and Saudi Arabia. Significantly, it tried to shift the United States away
from the MENA region and South and Central Asia, which had dominated US foreign policy since 9/11, to a greater focus on China and
Russia. As foreign affairs scholar Walter Russell Mead notes:

What gives Mr. Trump his opening is something many foreign-policy experts have yet to grasp: that America's post-Cold War national strategy has run out of gas. First, Mr. Trump knows that the post-Cold War policies can no longer be politically sustained. Second, he knows that China poses a new and dangerous challenge to American interests. Third, he sees that foreign policy must change in response. The old approach—on everything from trade and development, to military deployments and readiness, to religious freedom and women's issues— must be reassessed in the light of today's dangerous world.[45]

Trump abandoned the project of superintending global capitalism through multilateral institutions and alliances for a project of US nationalism. This meant abandoning some, but certainly not all, multilateral deals like the Trans-Pacific Partnership Agreement and the Joint Comprehensive Plan of Action. To maintain hegemony in the MENA region, Trump supported Israel and Saudi Arabia as counterweights to Iran and gave a green light to the use of military means to shore up their interests. He escalated Obama's drone war and Special Forces operations as the principal means for neutralizing non-state threats like al-Qaeda and ISIS. He took this several steps further by carrying out extrajudicial assassinations of state leaders such as Qasem Soleimani, commander of the Quds Force, a division of the Islamic Revolutionary Guards responsible for extraterritorial and clandestine operations.

To be sure, the US use of drones began first under the Clinton administration and steadily escalated; the highest number of attacks (under Obama) was later topped by Trump. Medea Benjamin demonstrates that in 2000 the Pentagon had fewer than fifty aerial drones, but by 2010 possessed nearly 7,500.[46] As a candidate, Trump famously promised to kill not only those accused of terrorism but their families as well.[47] The racist dehumanization was extended beyond "combatants" or military age men the Obama administration saw fit to kill to include their families as well. In power, Trump dramatically expanded the theater of operations from Afghanistan, Iraq, and Syria to Yemen, Pakistan, and Somalia. In just his first two years in office, he launched more strikes in each of these countries than Obama had. He staged 238 strikes in Yemen, Somalia, and Pakistan, more than Obama's 186 over a similar period. He carried out 176 attacks in Yemen in just two years, dwarfing Obama's total of 154 strikes in Yemen in eight years.[48] The total civilian casualty rate of these attacks is not known, because the Trump administration placed restrictions on the reporting of these figures. The corporate media have reported on some of the worst examples, like the bombing of a wedding party in Yemen that killed twenty people and wounded dozens of others, including the groom.[49] The Bureau of Investigative Journalism, which has tracked the drone wars in Pakistan, Afghanistan, Yemen, and Somalia from 2010 to 2020, reports that there were 14,000 strikes, killing between 8,000 and 9,000 people. Among those were as many as 2,000 civilians and close to 500 children.[50]

In Afghanistan, Trump initially continued Obama's policy. US troops trained and helped the Afghan government and the military in their war against the Taliban. However, he broke with previous counterinsurgency thinking about "hearts and minds" by adopting a more aggressive approach. As he put it, "We are not nation-building again. We are killing terrorists."[51] In 2017 the United States dropped the largest non-nuclear weapon in history—the so-called "Mother of All Bombs"— on an ISIS facility. The attack drew criticism from Afghanistan's former president Hamid Karzai, who declared: "This is not the war on terror but the inhuman and most brutal misuse of our country as testing ground for new and dangerous weapons. It is upon us, Afghans, to stop the USA."[52] This attack was the largest bombing campaign since the start of the war in 2001.[53] In 2019, the United States was responsible for larger numbers of civilian casualties than the Taliban.[54] Through the use of spectacular violence, Trump forced the Taliban to the bargaining table. In a break with previous administrations, Trump opened direct negotiations with the Taliban without including the Afghan government. The end result was a deal agreed to by both the Taliban and Afghan government. It reiterated US support for the Afghan government, encouraged negotiations between the government and the Taliban without preconditions, and promised the full withdrawal of US forces by 2021.[55]

In Iraq, Trump also continued Obama's policy, which was largely focused on defeating ISIS and trying to pressure the Iraqi government to break relations with Iran. As Trump prepared to enter the White House, the Obama administration led the largest bombing attack on Iraq since the 2003 "shock and awe" campaign targeting in particular ISIS forces in Mosul. Trump agreed with this campaign. He stated that once in office he would "bomb the shit"[56] out of ISIS and "take the oil" as part of the "spoils of war."[57] While Trump's national security team prevented him from appropriating the country's resources, he did succeed in extending Obama's bombing campaign against ISIS. The devastation was widespread and included the complete destruction of Mosul and the murder of more than 40,000 civilians.[58]

In Syria, the Trump administration continued Obama-era policies before extracting most US troops from the country. Obama criticized Bashar al-Assad's regime but refused to support the popular revolution in the country, preferring stability above all else, as Gilbert Achcar has argued in *Morbid Symptoms*.[59] The Obama administration intervened only after the rise of ISIS when an air war was launched on ISIS headquarters in Raqqa. The United States deployed military personnel to support various forces including the Kurdish Syrian Democratic Forces to help them seize territory from ISIS. Trump escalated Obama's air war against Raqqa, destroying 80 percent of the city's buildings.[60] However, the Trump administration also broke significantly with the Obama administration. While the latter chose not to attack the Assad regime after its use of chemical weapons in 2013, Trump carried out an airstrike on Syria's Shayrat Airbase in April 2017 to punish the regime for using them. However, this was more a warning than an actual attack in that it did little damage to the regime's ability to continue its war on the Syrian people. After the fall of Raqqa, in another break with Obama and most of the foreign policy establishment, the Trump administration drew down US troops in Syria, leaving only a small and largely symbolic force and abandoning the Kurds to a fight their enemy, Turkey, on their own. The key triumph of the Special Operations forces was the execution of the ISIS commander Abu Bakr al-Baghdadi in 2019. In sum, despite his campaign promises to end the "forever wars" in the MENA region and South and Central Asia, the Trump administration continued the war on terror in several countries, particularly Afghanistan, Iraq, and Syria.

The biggest break perhaps with Obama era policies lay with Iran. Not only did the Trump administration rip up the Joint Comprehensive Plan of Action, but the "maximum pressure" policy imposed a devastating new sanctions regime on Iran. These sanctions, which barred foreign investment and oil sales, have crippled the Iranian economy, contracting it by 4.8 percent in 2018 and 9.5 percent in 2019.[61] There was also an escalation of drone strikes and increased use of Special Forces operations against Iranian assets throughout the region, most famously the assassination of Soleimani in 2020. Iran responded with a largely symbolic counterattack on a US airbase in Erbil, Iraq. In the end, both sides drew back from the brink of war. However, the new sanctions regime has failed to have the intended impact. Despite Iran's economic crisis, it retained support from its regional allies as well as Russia and China. Moreover, it accelerated its nuclear program in defiance of the United States. As Middle East scholar Vali Nasr of the liberal interventionist camp wrote:

> The Trump administration has taught Iran—and all aspirants seeking to join the nuclear club—the wrong lessons: that they should have a bigger nuclear program before talking, negotiate incrementally, and give up nuclear assets slowly lest sanctions come back.[62]

Finally, Trump not only strengthened US ties to Israel and Saudi Arabia but green-lighted their most hawkish policies. He abandoned the long-held claim of the United States that it was an "honest broker" between Israel and the Palestinians, openly supporting Netanyahu's far right policies without criticism including Israel's continued colonization of Palestinian territory. He further recognized Jerusalem as Israel's capital and moved the US embassy there (the Biden administration retained this location). Trump unabashedly denounced Palestinians as terrorists, stating during his 2016 campaign that he would not be neutral toward Palestinians. As he put it, they have to "stop with the terror because what they're doing with the missiles and with the stabbings and with all of the other things that they do, it's horrible and it's gotta end."[63] In his first year in office, the administration dropped Washington's long-standing commitment to a two-state solution and a year later ended all funding to the United Nations Relief and Works Agency that provides services to five million Palestinian refugees. He cut another $200 million in funds to USAID programs that provided much-needed assistance, particularly in the Gaza Strip.[64] In the final days of the administration, Netanyahu and the Israeli political class's long-term efforts to equate criticism of Israeli policy with anti-Semitism was enshrined in a new classification of the Boycott, Divestment and Sanctions (BDS) movement as anti-Semitic. During a trip to Israel in 2020, former CIA director and secretary of state, Michael Pompeo, declared that the United States would henceforth categorize support for BDS as anti-Semitism, a stance warmly embraced by Netanyahu.[65]

Like his position on Israel, Trump adopted a policy of uncritical support for Saudi Arabia, turning a blind eye to the murder of former *Washington Post* journalist Jamal Khashoggi ordered by Saudi Crown Prince Mohammed bin Salman.[66] Thus, Trump continued the Obama administration's weapon sales to the regime and green-lighted its war in Yemen against Iran's Houthi allies. Saudi attacks have caused a massive humanitarian disaster. The destruction of whole swaths of the country as well as the impoverishment of the majority of the country's population has created a situation where millions are on the edge of starvation and only manage to survive by getting food from the UN.[67] In the six years since Obama entered the United States in the war in 2015, 100,000 Yemenis were killed and 250,000 people starved to death.[68] Empire has sanctioned such vulnerability to premature death both in its liberal and crude racist forms.

Conclusion

This chapter outlined US foreign policy since 9/11. The neocon wing of the policy establishment, out of power in the 1990s, was finally in a position of power to realize its vision. However, the confrontations in Afghanistan and Iraq did not go as planned. The implosion of the Bush agenda then saw the baton handed over to liberal imperialists, who instituted a rhetorical shift and continued the multilateral strategies adopted in Bush's second term to project and maintain US hegemony. This did not, however, change the realities of people's lives in the "Muslim world," which in some ways got worse under Obama. Even while we witnessed a rhetorical shift from the Bush to the Obama era, the fundamentals of how empire in the twenty-first century would function remained the same.

When Trump replaced Obama, it marked a shift from liberalism and liberal Islamophobia to a more blatant and overt form of racism not seen since the civil rights movement, which ushered in the so-called "postracial" era. One of Trump's first executive orders banned people from seven Muslim-majority countries—Iran, Iraq, Libya, Somalia, Syria, Sudan, and Yemen—from visiting the United States for ninety days and halted Syrian refugees from seeking asylum in the United States indefinitely. Liberals viewed this association of all people from certain countries with terrorism as an overt form of discrimination based on religious exclusion.[69] Trump's rhetoric and actions were not a return to the Bush era but were an amplification of far right, racial-nationalist forces and their ideologies. The neocons tend to eschew overt racism in favor of more covert and liberal rhetorical approaches. This is not true of all neocons, a section of whom are part of the Islamophobic right (see Chapter 7).

However, Trump's "illiberal hegemony" alienated much of the capitalist and imperialist establishment. Not only did members of the liberal foreign policy and security establishment support Biden, but leading figures from the Republican side did so as well. Seventy former national security officials launched a pro-Biden website called *Defending Democracy Together*, which stated:

> We are profoundly concerned about the course of our nation under the leadership of Donald Trump. Through his actions and rhetoric, Trump has demonstrated that he lacks the character and competence to lead this nation and has engaged in corrupt behavior that renders him unfit to serve as President.[70]

In the 2020 elections, Biden defeated Trump to assume the presidency.

Like Obama before him, Biden faces the task of rehabilitating empire and rebuilding multinational relationships. In his article in *Foreign Affairs* titled "Why America Must Lead Again," Biden has promised to do both and to restore Obama era policies.[71] As he states: "The triumph of democracy and liberalism over fascism and autocracy created the free world. But this contest does not just define our past. It will define our future, as well." This will translate into a return to soft power and a rejection of the blatant right-wing racism of the Trump era. Most significantly, Trump eschewed the "good Muslim, bad Muslim" approach (with the exception of Saudi Arabia) and opened the door to right-wing Islamophobia. Biden has rejected this approach. We might therefore expect a return to liberal Islamophobia and the accommodationist approach. However, Biden has stated his intention to continue Trump's policy to withdraw military forces from the "forever wars" and to use drone warfare instead. While he has promised to take a more critical stance toward Israel, this will likely involve a return to the Obama era during which Israel was supported with significant financial and military aid. Further, he has proposed to end the "maximum pressure" policy and reengage Tehran in negotiations. In short, as of this writing, it appears that the United States is headed into a third Obama term with a multiracial and female-heavy leadership team ensuring a process where neoliberal multiculturalism, as it has in the past, will paper over racist imperial policies.

6

Terrorizing Muslims: Domestic Security and the Racialized Threat

US wars abroad have dire consequences for those seen as domestic representatives of the foreign enemy. Race scholar Nikhil Pal Singh argues that "frontier wars, the wars of the early U.S. empire, and the twentieth century's world wars all illuminated affinities between war making and race making, activating or reaffirming distinctions between friend and enemy along an internal racial border."[1] Perhaps the most significant example of this process in the twentieth century involved the treatment of Japanese Americans after the attack on Pearl Harbor. More than 100,000 people of Japanese descent were rounded up and put into detention camps. Young and old were incarcerated simply for having a Japanese ancestor and forced into harsh conditions in makeshift camps, often without cooking or even plumbing facilities. Of those incarcerated, nearly three-quarters were US citizens.[2]

In his book *How Does it Feel to Be a Problem?*, Moustafa Bayoumi tells the stories of young Arab Americans caught in the dragnet of the national security state after 9/11.[3] In *Homeland Insecurity*, Louise Cainkar outlines the heightened sense of vulnerability experienced by Arab American and Muslim communities.[4] In *The Limits of Whiteness*, sociologist Neda Maghbouleh discusses the racialization of Iranian Americans from the turn of the twentieth century to the post–9/11 era and situates their contradictory race and class positions within American racial hierarchies.[5] In *Missing: Youth, Citizenship and Empire after 9/11*, Asian American studies scholar Sunaina Maira lays out the experience of South Asian Muslim youth from Pakistan, Bangladesh, and India after 9/11.[6] Other books and essays by scholars in various fields articulate the ways in which US wars in the Middle East, North Africa and South/Central Asia come back to impact Arab, Iranian, and South Asian Americans through various projects of domestic racialization.[7] Significantly, as Nadine Naber points out, "racial profiling 'here' is a key strategy of empire. It *is* empire [emphasis in original]".[8]

The result of such race making has been a nightmare for those targeted. In *The Feeling of Being Watched*, journalist Assia Boundaoui captures the fear, stress, and even paranoia that comes from being surveilled. The documentary is about the FBI surveillance program Vulgar Betrayal and the impact on Boundaoui's Arab American community in Bridgeview, Illinois. Vulgar Betrayal started in the 1990s and such programs have only amplified after 9/11. The result is that almost every Muslim family knows someone who has been caught up in the national security dragnet. Entire communities have been disrupted. For instance, at the beginning of the millennium, Brooklyn was home to about a quarter million people of Pakistani origin. By 2003, as many as 50,000–60,000 were reported to have left; they were either jailed, deported, or had fled the witch-hunt mentality pervading the city.[9] What was known as "little Pakistan," Junaid Rana argues, became a shell of its former self, with businesses shuttered and restaurants closed down.[10]

To be sure, the racial Muslim produced after 9/11 is not limited to people with ancestry in the countries and regions discussed above. The new racialized terrorist sutured all these aforementioned groups together with those who "look Muslim" such as Indian Sikhs and Hindus, Arab and Iranian Christians, and even brown skinned people from Latin American countries. However, those targeted by the security apparatus have been primarily Muslim. As Naber and Rana explain:

> Anti-Muslim racism operates in complicated and incongruous ways for a reason. Especially since 9/11, and under the name of the War on Terror, by constructing an enemy of the state as porous and boundless, as anywhere and everywhere, the U.S. justifies waging war against diverse people and regions all lumped together as "Muslims" whether or not they are Muslim or share a particular country of origin, political view, or appearance. Even as this rationale of racializing those who are deemed "Muslim-looking," it is Muslims across the United States who are the primary targets of policing under the War on Terror policies.[11]

In this chapter, I lay out how Muslims have been terrorized, that is, produced as terrorist threats or "potential terrorists" by the national security state and subject to terror through racist policies in the post-9/11 period. I focus on the racializing practices of the domestic security apparatus, which includes a number of institutions such as the Department of Homeland Security (DHS), FBI, the National Security Agency, the Department of Justice (DOJ), various city police departments, and the legal system. This separation of domestic security from international security apparatuses is of course artificial. Imperial forms of domination are used at home as well as abroad and vice versa. For instance, the CIA is supposed to operate on the global stage, yet it was intimately involved in the New York Police Department's (NYPD) surveillance program of Muslims in the tristate area. The same surveillance technology used in Iraq in the 2003 invasion, later used by the Obama administration in Yemen, Pakistan, and elsewhere, was deployed in New York, New Jersey, and Connecticut.[12] Empire and the national security state are at once both national and international.

The chapter outlines how the racial Muslim has been produced by the national security state through a series of coercive policies from surveillance to preemptive prosecution. It begins with Bush era policies but also traces continuities under Obama and Trump. Obama's "smarter" war on terror was replaced by Trump's dumber and more blatant racist policies. The key vehicle for this process of racialization is the belief that "Islam" as an ideology predisposes Muslims to violence. "Islam," particularly in theories of radicalization, as Arun Kundnani argues in his comprehensive book *The Muslims Are Coming!*, came to be understood as an ideology that places Muslims on a fast track to terrorism.[13] What is at work is the logic of cultural racism. Étienne Balibar notes that "culture can also function like a nature, and it can in particular function as a way of locking individuals and groups a priori into a genealogy, into a determination that is immutable and intangible in origin."[14] Thus, Islam as culture/ideology is understood to shape behavior in current forms of war on terror racism in ways not entirely dissimilar to earlier biological and civilizational notions of race (see Chapters 1 and 2).

Precursors to 9/11

Chapter 2 explained how the racialized terrorist threat emerged in the late 1960s and how various security policies such as Operation Boulder, an adaptation of COINTELPRO, were deployed against Arab Americans. The Iranian Revolution and the hostage crisis as well as various other developments then produced the "Islamic terrorist." The evolving project of terrorist racial formation has since incorporated various groups considered as threats. During the 1980s, Arabs, Iranians, and Muslims from other nations experienced an intensification of racism in their daily lives. Legal scholars Susan Akram and Kevin Johnson observe that after every crisis, hate crimes against those who "look Muslim" increased as perpetrators fail to "differentiate among persons based on religion or ethnic origin, from Pakistanis, Indians, Iranians, and Japanese to Muslims, Sikhs and Christian Arabs."[15] Thus, after the hijacking of TWA Flight 847 in June 1985, there were violent attacks on "Muslim looking" people, Arab American associations, and symbols of Islam such as Islamic centers and mosques.

In the context of Reagan's war on terror, a DOJ document titled *Alien Terrorists and Undesirables: A Contingency Plan* provided a blueprint for the FBI to round up and detain Arab Americans. The justification it provided was that terrorists originate from Arab countries and must therefore be detained in the name of national security.[16] The DOJ even identified an internment camp in rural Louisiana as the location where Arab Americans would be held.[17] While this plan was not put into practice, several legal cases, particularly the case against the LA 8, exemplified the state's program of racial targeting. In 1987, eight Palestinian activists and one Kenyan were arrested on charges that they had raised money for the Popular Front for the Liberation of Palestine (PFLP). They were then placed under FBI surveillance for three years, allegedly to prevent a terrorist attack.[18] The Zionist Anti-Defamation League (ADL) provided the names of these activists in 1985 to the FBI. Naber argues that the ADL followed the logic that "anyone speaking out in support of Palestinians is a terrorist and should be arrested by the FBI and deported by the INS."[19] This illustrates not only the influence of Israel in the functioning of the US national security state, but also the continuity with earlier anti-Communist measures which were revived to target Arab Americans.

The McCarran–Walter Act of 1952, used to arrest the LA 8, had its origins in the early Cold War period. As legal scholar Kathleen Moore explains, the act was "designed to restrict the entry of communists" into the United States, and if already inside, "allowed for the expulsion of an alien on the basis of confidential information without a hearing."[20] The PFLP, it was argued, was an organization that advocated "doctrines of world communism." Thus, support for such a group was punishable through the McCarran–Walter Act.[21] The threat of Communism and that of terrorism came together seamlessly. When the McCarran–Walter Act was repealed after the collapse of the Soviet Union in 1991, the government switched to the new "terrorist activities" provisions of the Immigration Act of 1990 to continue the case. It was finally thrown out in 2007. This case illustrates how the national security state adapts provisions originally designed to handle one threat to deal with new and evolving threats. The McCarran–Walter Act, COINTELPRO, and other such means of controlling Communists proved suitable for targeting racialized others as well. Moreover, mechanisms developed after 9/11 were then deployed against leaders of the Occupy Wall Street movement as well as environmental rights activists including Native Americans in Montana protesting the Keystone Pipeline.[22]

In 1991, Bush Sr. launched a surveillance program against Arab Americans during the first Gulf War, just as Carter had launched a similar program targeting Iranian students during the Iran hostage crisis.[23] The FBI interrogated Muslim leaders as well as activists, including anti-war demonstrators. The DOJ required Arab residents and immigrants to submit to fingerprinting, and the Federal Aviation Administration devised a system of racial profiling.[24]

During the Clinton administration, Congress enacted two laws that served as precursors to what was to come in the post-9/11 era. In 1996, in the wake of Timothy McVeigh's attack in Oklahoma, the Antiterrorism and Effective Death Penalty Act (AEDPA) and the Illegal Immigration Reform and Individual Responsibility Act were passed.[25] Even though McVeigh was not an immigrant, these laws made it legal to deport immigrants—or, as stated in the AEDPA, "alien terrorists"—based on secret evidence. In the LA 8 case, when the government presented secret evidence, the judge refused to accept it. The 1996 act sought to legalize such a process. The act also birthed the "material support statute," discussed below, which became the basis for prosecuting Muslim Americans for "expressing an 'ideology,'" Kundnani argues.[26] Islam as "ideology" became integral to domestic security policy in the post-9/11 era. In short, even before the events of 9/11, the groundwork had been laid for the legalized targeting of the racialized Muslim, a category with flexible boundaries that could incorporate new people and groups.[27]

9/11 and Its Aftermath

In the immediate aftermath of 9/11, Congress passed the USA PATRIOT Act, the Enhanced Border Security and Visa Entry Reform Act, and the Homeland Security Act.[28] These laws brought together terrorism and immigration and extended the policies of the Clinton administration. Specifically, they helped to enforce the Bush administration's directive to accomplish two goals: "deny entry into the United States of aliens associated with, suspected of being engaged in, or supporting terrorist activity" and "locate, detain, prosecute, or deport any such aliens already present in the United States."[29] The Homeland Security Act created the DHS, which brought together twenty-two different federal agencies and departments. The goal was to produce, as the DHS website states, "a strengthened homeland security enterprise and a more secure America that is better equipped to confront the range of threats we face."[30] The result of the aforementioned laws and the formation of the DHS was an expanded and fortified national security state.

Immediately after the attacks, about 1,200 Muslim citizens and non-citizens, most of them Arab and South Asian, were rounded up, summarily arrested, and questioned by the FBI, the Immigration and Naturalization Service, and various state and local law enforcement agencies. They were detained for varying periods of time, often in solitary confinement and with a shroud of secrecy surrounding the whole affair. In her important anthology *Civil Rights in Peril*, Elaine Hagopian points out that not one of these people was found to be a "terrorist" or to have any link whatsoever to 9/11.[31] A few months later, the DOJ announced that it had made a list of about eight thousand men between the ages of eighteen and thirty-three from specific (but unnamed) countries who had entered the United States after January 2000 who were to be "interviewed" by law enforcement personnel. Of this list, fewer than twenty were arrested on immigration charges and three on criminal charges, but *none* were shown to have any links to terrorism—similar to the results of Operation Boulder in the 1970s.[32] Even as Bush repeatedly assured the world that the United States was not at war with Islam or with Muslims, Muslims were being rounded up and terrorized (in both senses of the term), based on an understanding that "Islam" drives Muslims to violence.

Muslims and those who "look Muslim" were being produced as racialized threats even if explicitly racist language was not employed. Color blind security measures were at work to create the racialized Muslim as threat. To be sure, working class Arab Americans and South Asian Americans faced the brunt of such persecution.[33] As anthropologist Nazia Kazi explains, "Class and cultural capital play a key role in sheltering some Muslims from the full effect of Islamophobia and exposing others to the brunt of it."[34] Naber's ethnographic research shows that "middle–upper class individuals were more protected by legal aid and socialization within white middle class cultural norms (such as dress and speech) than their working class counterparts."[35]

Another program initiated in 2002, the National Security Entry-Exit Registration System (NSEERS), which had its origins in the 1996 AEDPA terrorism bill and was amended by the USA PATRIOT Act, required male immigrants sixteen and older from twenty-five countries to report to Immigration and Naturalization Service offices in order to be "fingerprinted, photographed, interviewed, and have their financial information copied, or to register when they enter the country, then re-register after thirty days," as legal scholar Nancy Murray writes.[36] The countries were named this time and included Muslim-majority and Middle Eastern countries as well as North Korea. "Terrorism" is a flexible and opportunistic category that is constantly shifting, in this case to include North Koreans. By fall 2003, more than 83,000 immigrant residents had registered under the program. As their reward for coming forward, 13,799 found themselves facing deportation proceedings. As for whether "terrorists" were apprehended by this program, eleven people were found to have "links" to terrorism. The program did not produce a single terrorism conviction.[37] It was eventually suspended in 2011, but its effects linger. Trump sought to revive this precedent in 2017 when he declared that it was necessary to create a Muslim registry to combat terrorism.

Cainkar argues that programs like NSEERs, which are based on "assumptions about the innate characteristics of persons who inhabit the grand categories of Arab and Muslim," lead to the "racialization of Arabs and Muslims because they give concrete meaning to essentialized, undifferentiated representations of Arabs and Muslims."[38] In 2003, another thousand people were arrested as part of a program to catch "absconders" from Middle Eastern nations who had overstayed their visas and who might have knowledge of "terrorist activity."[39] Many of these people were put "on planes to destinations where they knew no one. They left behind jobs, homes, and families, including American-born children."[40] American Civil Liberties Union (ACLU) National Legal Director David Cole has referred to these forms of persecution as the "new McCarthyism."[41] While the Cold War persecuted Communists in the United States, the war on terror targeted racialized subjects. Such a perception coded into law enabled the FBI to gather information about "concentrated ethnic communities," on the grounds that such information can aid in the analysis of "potential threats and vulnerabilities" and assist in "domain awareness," as legal expert Faiza Patel observes.[42] Put simply, the FBI is legally permitted to racially profile Muslims, though it does not use that term.[43] While federal law around anti-discrimination prevents profiling Muslims simply because they are Muslims, national security can be used to override these protections. Thus, it is legal to assume that a devout Muslim from a Middle Eastern country is linked to terrorism.[44] As legal scholar Leti Volpp has argued, after the events of 9/11 the "terrorist" was differentiated from the "citizen," so that civil liberties could be denied to the former.[45] Such a denial of rights is based on exclusionary racist logics.

In a nutshell, the FBI and other law enforcement agencies have operationalized one of the ideological frames discussed in Chapter 3: "Islam is inherently violent." As Kundnani argues, the

> war on terror paradigm . . . makes ideology the root cause of political violence [and] derives from the cold war theory of totalitarianism, which presumed a similar direct causal connection between ideology and the repressive practices of political control.[46]

Counterterrorism policy and practices of surveillance, indefinite detention, and arbitrary deportation flow from this logic.

Surveillance, Detention, and Deportation

In 2011, the Associated Press (AP) released a series of investigative reports on the NYPD's surveillance of Arab and Muslim communities. With training from the CIA, the NYPD spied on mosques (often using informers called "mosque crawlers"), community centers, Muslim-owned businesses, religious bookstores, universities, and a host of other locations deemed to be "hot spots."[47] The NYPD's "demographics unit" went undercover into minoritized neighborhoods in the tristate area to obtain information as part of what it called a "human mapping program." The AP reports received significant mainstream media attention and drew sharp criticisms of the program. The presidents of many of the targeted universities released statements condemning the NYPD's espionage.[48] The Newark mayor at the time, Cory Booker, stated that profiling based on religion was "a clear infringement on the core liberties of our citizenry."[49]

These revelations marked the first mainstream public discussion, a full decade after the events of 9/11, of the systematic violations of the civil liberties of Muslims and those who "look Muslim." The reports offered many Americans their first glimpse into the nightmare endured by the racialized Muslim. The NYPD surveillance program, however, was just the tip of the iceberg. Whistleblower Edward Snowden released his collection of documents from the National Security Agency in 2013, revealing the full extent of mass surveillance. In 2014, journalists Glenn Greenwald and Murtaza Hussain showed that the specific targets of National Security Agency surveillance were prominent Muslim Americans who had been put under surveillance despite there being no reasonable grounds for suspicion about criminal activity.[50] Investigative journalists Jeremy Scahill and Ryan Devereaux demonstrated that the number of people on the National Counterterrorism Center's no-fly list had increased tenfold to 47,000 in the Obama era. The leaked documents revealed that the center maintained a database of terrorism suspects worldwide, the "Terrorist Identities Datamart Environment." In 2013, it had a million names, twice the number from four years prior. The database included more than 20,000 people within the United States who were disproportionately concentrated in Dearborn, Michigan, with its significant Arab American population.[51] These stories about the targeting of Muslims and Arab Americans did not get the same attention as the initial Snowden revelations. This flows from a perception that while it is correct to object to the US government collecting private data on "ordinary" (read *white*) people, the racialized Muslim is a legitimate target of surveillance.

Perhaps for the same reasons, the media paid little attention to prisoners abused through indefinite detention, solitary confinement, and torture. While the torture of Muslim prisoners in places like Abu Ghraib or Guantánamo Bay did receive front-page attention after the release of scandalous photos, mainstream discussion continues to reflect a naive faith that justice prevails in the "land of the free." In an essay titled "Guantánamo at Home," political scientist Jeanne Theoharis wrote:

> The problem of torture and other human rights violations in America's "war on terror" has been framed as a problem that happens largely beyond our shores. The underlying assumption is that if

Guantánamo detainees were to be tried on United States soil and in federal courts (as many groups demand), such egregious abuses would not occur.[52]

In fact, as Theoharis argued, this assumption is false. The national security state uses similar methods both abroad and inside the United States.

A 2011 report appropriately titled *Under the Radar: Muslims Deported, Detained, and Denied on Unsubstantiated Terrorism Allegations*, released by the Center for Human Rights and Global Justice at New York University Law School, documented the ways in which the law has been used to "cast Muslims as dangerous threats to national security."[53] The report argued that "religious, cultural, and political affiliations and lawful activities of Muslims are being construed as dangerous terrorism-related factors to justify detention, deportation, and denial of immigration benefits."[54] Muslims have been presented as terrorists in cases that were actually about immigration violations. Charges brought against Muslim immigrants "are almost always ordinary immigration violations," the report states, yet the government has routinely insinuated connections to terrorism without providing any proof of these allegations.[55]

The story of Foad Farahi illustrates this practice. Farahi, an imam of Iranian descent, came to the United States in 1994 with a student visa and later applied for political asylum. After 9/11, the FBI approached him numerous times, asking him to become an informant and to spy on his community. He consistently refused, not wanting to be an agent of the state within his community. At his asylum hearing, law enforcement agents met him in court and told him that they had evidence demonstrating that he had supported a terrorist group. They gave him a choice: drop his case and leave the United States voluntarily or be charged as a terrorist. Farahi first opted for voluntary departure, no doubt frightened at the prospects of being "disappeared" like so many other Muslim men. Later, when he realized that the state had no case against him, he decided to fight. Despite repeated requests, the state refused to share information about the terrorism allegations with Farahi or his lawyer so that they might mount a defense. Eventually, Farahi's voluntary departure order was overturned and his asylum case was to be reopened.[56] Others who were not as brave as Farahi—or, perhaps, who had more to lose—succumbed to state pressure. As *Under the Radar* shows, the law enforcement community routinely uses threats based on little or no evidence to coerce people to cooperate in the war on terror and become snitches—or face the state's reprisal.

Another nightmare that Muslim citizens and immigrants have endured is arrest and detention for long periods of time. The law has been bent to allow such detentions in the name of national security. *Under the Radar* highlights a trend where Muslim immigrants are painted as threats and detained for minor immigration violations that do not normally warrant detention. Even those who have not broken the law sometimes find themselves in detention centers. In her book *Patriot Acts,* Alia Malek tells the story of a teenager who was detained on suspicion of being a terrorist:

On March 24, 2005, Adama Bah, a sixteen-year-old Muslim girl, awoke at dawn to discover nearly a dozen armed FBI agents inside her family's apartment in East Harlem. They arrested her and her father, Mamadou Bah, and transported them to separate detention facilities. A government document leaked to the press claimed that Adama was a potential suicide bomber but *failed to provide any evidence* to support this claim. Released after six weeks in detention, Adama was forced to live under partial house arrest with an ankle bracelet, a government-enforced curfew, and a court-issued gag order that prohibited her from speaking about her case. In August of 2006, Adama's father was deported back to Guinea, Africa. Adama, who had traveled to the United States with her parents from Guinea as a child, also found herself facing deportation. She would spend the next few years fighting for asylum and struggling to support her family in the United States and Guinea [emphasis added].[57]

West African Muslims like Bah were not the only teenagers to have experienced such trauma. Bayoumi tells the story of another Muslim teenager who was ripped from her life in Brooklyn and placed in detention. To protect her identity, Bayoumi refers to her as "Rasha." One night the FBI came to Rasha's home and placed her and her entire family in detention centers for months. Her family had an appeal pending about their immigration status, but they were locked up anyway. Bayoumi describes her experience in the detention facility:

For a while she stopped eating. She would lie on her bed sometimes for two or three days continuously, finally lugging herself out of bed one day when the cell door opened so she could join the others and eat. *Like lab rats*, she thought.

She slowly snapped out of her depression, but she couldn't stop feeling angry. She tried to transform her anger into a life lesson, to believe that God was trying to show her the nature of her humanity.

But she felt wronged. Never in her life had she thought that she would end up in jail unless she had committed a crime. So why was she here? For what? Because she had overstayed her visa and was now undocumented? She didn't commit a crime, and she was being punished for someone else's acts. For someone else's crime. She hadn't been convicted. She had been abducted.

This wasn't justice. It was revenge [emphasis added].[58]

Ultimately, Rasha's family was released. This has been the story of thousands of women and men—young and old, citizen and non-citizen—who have been arrested, detained, and deported in the name of the war on terror. This is how racism operates. When groups of people are dehumanized, violence against them is not only possible but considered reasonable by many. Moreover, those targeted include a wide range of people, from Arabs and South Asians to West Africans.

This process has also been called the "securitization of Islam," which involves treating entire communities as security threats because they are Muslim. The government has justified this treatment, even against those who have committed no crime, by stating that "preemptive prosecution" is essential to keep America safe. Preemptive prosecution is the domestic legal variant of the doctrine of "preemptive war," discussed in the previous chapter. If the rationale for "preemptive war" is to prevent the rise of a future rival to the United States on the global stage, "preemptive prosecution" is about apprehending "potential" terrorists.

Preemptive Prosecution

Preemptive prosecution involves targeting suspect communities through a range of tactics such as the use of agents provocateurs to incite people to do things they otherwise would not and the charge of "material support" for terrorists, which can be applied for something as innocuous as giving money to a charitable foundation. The logic underlying these cases is that Muslims are naturally "predisposed" to commit violent acts and should therefore be put away before they cause harm. This bizarre logic is reminiscent of Steven Spielberg's dystopian film *Minority Report*, based on Philip K. Dick's 1956 novella, about three "precogs" who can foresee crime before it occurs. Acting on this information, a police "precrime" unit then arrests people before they actually commit a crime and only because they might be "predisposed" to do so. In the movie, the unit is shut down. In real life, however, many are facing years in prison for crimes that they did not commit, in which no one had been killed and no property had been destroyed.

In a report titled *Inventing Terrorists: The Lawfare of Preemptive Prosecution*, lawyers Steve Downs and Kathy Manley analyzed the DOJ's list of terrorism and terrorism-related convictions from 2001 to 2010. They found that 72.4 percent of the convictions were cases of preemptive prosecution where the "defendant's perceived ideology and not . . . his/her criminal activity" was the basis of conviction. About 21.8 percent of the convictions involved people who engaged "in minor, non-terrorist criminal activity but whose cases were manipulated and inflated by the government to appear as though they were 'terrorists'".[59] In short, a majority of cases were based on a racialized and essentialized understanding of Muslims. Downs explains:

> To prove predisposition, the government claims that routine, normal behavior of the defendants—dress, religious observances, Islamic financial transactions, literature, etc.—indicate a "predisposition" to commit terrorism, based on the false stereotype that *all* Muslims are predisposed to commit terrorism. If they are sufficiently "Muslim," they are sufficiently "predisposed" [emphasis in original].[60]

Thus, simply being perceived as Muslim makes one suspicious. If the surveillance mechanisms designed in the late 1960s began a process of racializing Arabs, preemptive prosecution took it to a whole new level. The racialized Muslim so produced involved a wide swath of people subject to this form of persecution.

The racism at work here is not blatant or obvious. In fact, race does not enter the picture. Instead "security" practices are enacted which do the work of racializing suspect populations. These communities are then subject to a whole panoply of surveillance and criminalization, from arbitrary arrests, to indefinite detention, deportation, torture, solitary confinement, the use of secret evidence, and sentencing for crimes that white people would not be jailed for, such as speech, donations to charitable organizations, and other such acts considered "material support" for terrorism.[61] Kundnani's interviews with FBI and other security personnel shows that they do not believe they are racist; they think that they are doing their jobs to ensure safety and security.[62]

International relations scholar Clara Eroukhmanoff argues that "political actors can both securitise Islam and simultaneously declare that

'Islam is not a threat' or that 'Islamophobia is a shame.'" Statements like "Muslims are not the enemy" effectively construct Muslims as the enemy, even though the literal meaning of the phrase indicates the exact opposite because such speech activates, Eroukhmanoff argues, "an Orientalist set of assumptions about Islam" without the speaker having to resort to blatant and overt forms of racism.[63] It works in ways akin to dog whistle tactics where certain words stand in for fully developed racial meanings among racist constituencies. As she puts it, "pre-existing registers of meaning" are typically "activated when the codewords 'Islam' or 'Muslim' are interpellated in more covert forms of speech." She refers to this process as "indirect securitization."[64] Indirect securitizing speech inoculates the speaker and listeners from charges of racism. Thus, securitizing actors and audiences believe that they have not transgressed the bounds of a "post-racial," multicultural society. In this way, she argues, indirect securitization produces the conditions in which white people are constituted as victimized subjects, while Muslims are constructed as racially securitized terrorist threats.

"Material support" for terrorists

The charge of "material support" for terrorism has been used against people for a wide range of activities from donating to charitable organizations to participating in anti-war activities. Charity or zakat is one of the five pillars of Islam and is considered a religious obligation for all Muslims. After 9/11 the Bush administration shut down major Muslim charitable organizations operating in the United States and froze their assets, allegedly to prevent the flow of money to "terrorists." Muslims who made contributions to charitable organizations that then donated money to groups the US government designated "Foreign Terrorist Organizations" (FTOs) were tried in court for providing "material support" to terrorists. As lawyer Michael Ratner of the Center for Constitutional Rights explains, even limited contact, such as providing blankets to a hospital associated with an FTO or teaching nonviolent forms of conflict resolution to an FTO, is seen as material support.[65] Zakat has an element of political solidarity with struggles elsewhere, especially Palestine, which the security state has sought to control.

The largest Muslim charitable organization in the United States, the Holy Land Foundation, was alleged to be associated with Hamas and shut down by executive order shortly after 9/11. During the ensuing trial, it was well established that the Holy Land Foundation's leaders had not performed, supported, or encouraged any form of violence, and furthermore, that the money sent abroad was used to provide basic needs and services for the very poor, such as Palestinians in the Gaza Strip, whose living conditions constitute a humanitarian crisis. The government did not establish any direct funding ties for "terrorism." Instead, the case rested on the argument that the foundation had sent money to zakat committees controlled by Hamas. The defense argued that these charitable committees were the only means through which aid could get to the people who needed it—and that UN agencies and USAID had also used the same committees. Hamas controlled these committees, they explained, because Hamas is the elected government of Palestine.[66] Nevertheless, the prosecution managed to secure harsh convictions. Two of the defendants are serving sixty-five-year prison terms.[67]

"Material support" charges have been used to target a wide variety of people. While Muslims have been the key targets, non-Muslims have also been subject to similar treatment. In 2010, the FBI raided the homes and offices of anti-war activists (including Caucasian US citizens) in Illinois, Minnesota, and North Carolina. They were given grand jury subpoenas on the grounds that they provided material support for terrorism. The state not only equated their peace activism with providing material support to terrorists, but also infiltrated various leftist groups. FBI agents became active in the groups, formed friendships, and recorded private conversations.[68]

In yet another tragic case, Fahad Hashmi, a US citizen who grew up in Queens, New York, was arrested in 2006 and charged with providing material support to terrorists. Hashmi's crime was that he had allowed an acquaintance to stay in his London apartment, a man named Junaid Babar, who was carrying items that would later be delivered to al-Qaeda. These dangerous items included raincoats, ponchos, and waterproof socks. By the government's logic, Hashmi should have smelled a rat, knowing how deadly waterproof garments are and how decisively they would tip the balance of power in the direction of al-Qaeda. For this crime, he spent three years in pretrial solitary confinement.

The news media covered this story as though a "web of terror" had been discovered in New York City, hardly deviating from the official script. New York police chief Raymond Kelly claimed, "This arrest reinforces the fact that a terrorist may have roots in Queens and still betray us."[69] Hashmi, who was Jeanne Theoharis's student at Brooklyn College, was at the London School of Economics pursuing a master's degree when he was arrested. Theoharis describes Hashmi as a "devout Muslim and outspoken political activist" whose "spunk and stubborn willingness to question authority" she admired. A promising student and a young man of conviction, Hashmi should have had a bright future ahead of him. Instead, Theoharis describes his appalling treatment at the Metropolitan Correctional Center in lower Manhattan, where he was put under Special Administrative Measures forbidding contact with the external world:

> Fahad was allowed no contact with anyone outside his lawyer and, in very limited fashion, his parents—no calls, letters, or talking through the walls, because his cell was electronically monitored. He had to shower and relieve himself within view of the camera. He was allowed to write only one letter a week to a single member of his family, using no more than three pieces of paper. One parent was allowed to visit every two weeks, but often would be turned away at the door for bureaucratic reasons. Fahad was forbidden any contact—directly or through his lawyers—with the news media. He could read only portions of newspapers approved by his jailers—and not until 30 days after publication. Allowed only one hour out of his cell a day, he had no access to fresh air but was forced to exercise in a solitary cage.[70]

After four years of such treatment, the state managed to break Hashmi's spirit. Activists mobilized to support Hashmi, but the prosecution made sure that they would not be allowed into the courtroom and won a motion to have Fahad judged by an anonymous jury with extra security. Such measures ensured that the jury would likely be prejudiced before the trial even started. Weighing these factors, Hashmi accepted a plea bargain on one count of conspiracy to provide material support to terrorism. He was sentenced to fifteen years in jail.

The acquaintance who delivered the rain gear to al-Qaeda, Babar, was released on bail in 2008, and in 2010 his sentence was commuted to "time served." The judge noted that he "began cooperating even before his arrest."[71] This has led to speculation that Babar had become an agent provocateur for the government before he visited Hashmi's apartment and that he may even have been sent to "get" Hashmi because of his politics and criticism of US policy.

Agents provocateurs and entrapment

The US government's increased use of agents provocateurs has resulted in numerous cases of entrapment, where individuals have been enticed to participate in what they think are terror plots but are in fact plots the government has invented. Since 9/11, informants in mosques and in

Muslim communities have led to the prosecution of hundreds.[72] As of 2008, the FBI had a roster of 15,000 paid informants,[73] and it had 10,000 counterterrorism intelligence analysts as of 2013.[74] The Center for Human Rights and Global Justice report *Targeted and Entrapped* outlines various problems with the use of such informers, not the least of which is that they are recruited through threats, as mentioned above in the case of the Iranian imam, as well as bribes—such as reduced criminal charges or a change in immigration status, creating what the report calls "a dangerous incentive structure."[75] Its authors found that in the cases they studied, the "government's informants introduced and aggressively pushed ideas about violent jihad and moreover, actually *encouraged* the defendants to believe that it was their duty to take action against the United States" [emphasis in original].[76] The informants also goaded the defendants to acquire violent videos and weapons which were later used to convict them and even went so far as to pick the locations that were to be attacked. In short, without the active leadership of the agents provocateurs, the "foiled terror plots" would not have existed. Journalist Trevor Aaronson in his book *The Terror Factory: Inside the FBI's Manufactured War on Terrorism* has argued that the FBI does the work of creating terrorists as a way to justify the billions of dollars spent on counterterrorism activity.

The Newburgh Four case illustrates how entrapment works. This is the story of four African American men from poor families, two of whom had psychological issues, and all of whom had trouble with the law at various points. When David Williams was approached by an FBI informant, his younger brother had just been diagnosed with liver cancer. The family desperately needed money, and the FBI informant, Shahed Hussain, promised that and more. David's aunt Alicia McWilliams, who became an activist around his case, says that David "watched his brother almost die and be revived five times. He knew [his brother] Lord needed a liver. The whole experience took him for a loop." The informant capitalized on this vulnerability and incited David and three others to carry out a plan to bomb synagogues in the Bronx. Hussain not only picked the sites and drove the four men there, he provided them with what they were told were bombs—and even badgered one man who said he refused to kill women and children, eventually convincing him to go forward with the plan. Without Hussain, the "terror plot" would not have existed. As Ted Conover, a resident of the targeted Bronx community, asks:

> Why does the government's anti-terror net catch such unconvincing villains: black men near mosques who, in exchange for promises of

money, sign on to knuckleheaded schemes that would never exist if it weren't for the informants being handsomely paid to incite them?[77]

Conover, a distinguished writer at New York University's Arthur L. Carter Journalism Institute, observes that this was a perfect public relations moment for the law enforcement community. He states:

> The arrest of the Newburgh Four was choreographed to perfection. A police helicopter shot live video as Hussain drove them down the Saw Mill River Parkway. After he and the four others left fake bombs at the Riverdale Temple and Riverdale Jewish Center, located about a block from each other, a massive police presence revealed itself: a special semi-rig sealed off one end of the street and an armored truck the other; and a slew of plainclothes officers descended on the suspects, guns drawn, breaking their SUV's windows and pulling the men out. Within an hour, Mayor Michael Bloomberg, Police Chief Ray Kelly, and local elected and police officials were on the scene and in front of the television cameras, praising the capture of the dangerous criminals and the aversion of what, in the mayor's words, "could have been a terrible event in our city."[78]

Thus the specter of "Islamic terrorism" is kept alive even while the real threat is minimal. As of this writing (February 2021), the number of deaths in the United States from what is called "Jihadi terrorism" after 9/11 (2001) is 107.[79]

As noted earlier and bears repeating, former counterterrorism analyst Marc Sageman has shown in a comprehensive study that in the ten years after 9/11, western countries have experienced only a few dozen attacks or terror plots carried out by what he calls "neojihadists." He argues that the political violence of these forces has been "dramatically inflated" and has led to an "overreaction of the counterterrorist community" that threatens "fundamental civil liberties."[80] In his analysis of these plots and attacks, he shows that less than one in *one million* Muslims who live in the West (North America, Australia, New Zealand, and the European Union) turn to political violence each year. A similar argument has been made by a number of scholars.[81] Yet despite the minimal threat posed by those who turn to violence in the name of Islam, the national security apparatus has continued its racist targeting. One reason given for this is the "potential" threat posed by those seen as Muslim who should be monitored at all times, it is argued, to prevent another

9/11-scale attack. The racialized Muslim, which includes a wide group of people, are the scapegoats of an imperial project that operates on a national and international scale. Various theories of radicalization have bolstered this logic.

Theories of Radicalization

In 2007, the NYPD produced a document titled *Radicalization in the West: The Homegrown Threat*, in which it posited four stages of radicalization: pre-radicalization, self-identification, indoctrination, and jihadization.[82] According to this model, all young Muslim males fall into the preradicalization stage. In short, simply being a member of a religious faith, whether citizen or resident, placed one on a conveyor belt toward "radicalization." Now if, by some chance, a member of this group should give up smoking, drinking, and gambling and start to grow a beard (the focus is on males) and wear traditional Islamic clothing, he is on the fast track toward acquiring "Jihadi-Salafist ideology," which puts him squarely in the next stage: "self-identification." Another characteristic of "self-identification" is political awareness and community activism. By the third stage, "indoctrination," the NYPD tells us, the person has withdrawn from the mosque and has become politicized around a set of new beliefs leading to the fourth stage, "jihadization," which is when he becomes ready to plan a terrorist attack. Signs of reaching this fourth stage include conducting research on the internet, performing reconnaissance activity, and acquiring materials. While the report states that there is no profile for a potential terrorist, the thrust of its analysis is precisely about creating such a profile and predicting the activity of potential terrorists. Based on data from a grand total of ten cases, the report states that there is "remarkable consistency in the behaviors and trajectory of each of the plots across the stages" and that "this consistency provides a tool for predictability."[83] Theories like this are used to justify the kind of human mapping program discussed earlier, where infiltrators were sent to bookstores, community centers, mosques, and other "hot spots" where Muslim citizens and immigrants spend their time.

One does not need a doctorate in sociology or psychology to see that this is an inherently racist behavioral model fraught with double standards. For instance, the same kind of surveillance does not take place in white communities, even though white supremacist organizations have been responsible for the murder of more people in the United States than those supposedly driven by Islam since 9/11.[84] A DHS report released in 2009 cautioned against violence by white supremacist groups:

> The threat posed by lone wolves and small terrorist cells is more pronounced than in past years. In addition, the historical election of an African American president and the prospect of policy changes are proving to be a driving force for rightwing extremist recruitment and radicalization.[85]

The report also named the recession following the 2007–2008 financial crisis and economic insecurity as factors that spur the growth of domestic terrorism. One of the key differences between the DHS report and the aforementioned NYPD report is that race, gender, and religion are incidental to the DHS's analysis. While it speaks about the anti-black, anti-immigrant, xenophobic, and pro-gun politics of white supremacist groups, it fails to make the leap to the conclusion that there is a four-step process of radicalization that begins with a person simply being a white Christian male. Naturally, there is no systematic program to infiltrate white communities to see how these dangerous men eat, worship, play, or shop. More mainstream attention has been paid to these forces after the armed attack on the Capitol in Washington, DC on January 6, 2021. Some media outlets even noted the role of police and ex-military personnel in the attack.[86]

It should come as no surprise that even beyond declining to profile all white men, the civil liberties of far right groups are respected by the law enforcement community. There is no preemptive prosecution of these groups, which span a wide ideological range that includes white supremacists, neo-Nazis, and various Christian fundamentalist tendencies, even though many such groups form militias and hold regular paramilitary training camps. As Downs notes:

> Nobody bothers them because indoctrination and weapons training is constitutionally protected free speech and exercise of the Second Amendment right to bear arms. The criminal line is crossed only when such groups conspire to commit a specific crime. However, preemptive prosecution makes an exception for Muslims.[87]

In short, while white supremacists are allowed to train with guns at sites all over the United States, a Muslim American who acquires a weapon is deemed suspicious. As *Targeted and Entrapped* notes, the "evidence" that is routinely used in court cases to prove radicalization and a predisposition to commit violence by Muslims includes items such as violent videos, radical religious speeches, or weapons.[88] Kundnani's analysis of various radicalization theories leads him to the conclusion that "radicalization discourse was, from the beginning, circumscribed to the demands of counterterrorism policy makers rather than an attempt to objectively study how terrorism comes into being."[89]

The Brennan report notes that there are differences within the security and law enforcement community on the question of radicalization. The NYPD (as well other local law enforcement agencies) and the FBI advocate stage-based models for radicalization, which put Islam at the "front and center of their analysis."[90] The FBI believes that surveilling Muslims is not sufficient since risks can develop quite quickly, in a matter of months. This is why they use agents provocatuers.[91] On the other hand, the DHS and the National Counterterrorism Center have shied away from this stage approach, emphasizing the complexity of the process. They have also suggested that while Islam can be used to justify acts of terrorism, radicalization is not caused by Islam. While all sides within the national security establishment agree with the theory of radicalization and the need to apprehend "Muslim terrorists," they disagree on practical implementation.

The dichotomy between the conservative wing of the security apparatus and what might be called a "realist" wing is similar to that which exists in the foreign policy establishment. That such parallel views should exist within the security community is hardly surprising, given the interconnections between the political establishment, the military, and the legal system. Personnel often move from one realm to the other, carrying with them their backgrounds and points of view. For instance, about a third of the FBI's counterterrorism staff has past military service in the Middle East.[92] The "Muslim enemy" abroad and the one at home is fought using similar methods. The domestic war on terror, however, was largely kept under the radar. In 2009 this started to shift with the "homegrown terrorist" receiving more attention.

Manufacturing the Green Scare

In the early years of the war on terror, the public emphasis was on the wars in Afghanistan and Iraq. As Bush put it: "We're fighting them there so we don't have to fight them here."[93] In a West Point speech in 2002, he stated: "We must take the battle to the enemy, disrupt his plans and confront the worst threats."[94] The "terrorists" in our midst were those sent from the outside who "hate our freedoms." Thus, even though in the aftermath of 9/11, thousands of people perceived as Muslims were racially profiled and targeted, as noted above, the emphasis wasn't on "home-grown terrorism." This changed during the Obama era when a "green scare" analogous to the "red scare" of the Cold War era was fomented. (Green is the color of Islam.)

In 2009, several US citizens or legal residents were arrested for alleged connections to terrorist activity. In the latter part of the year these became high-profile cases that drew sustained media attention.[95] The first prominent case was that of Najibullah Zazi, an Afghan citizen and legal US resident who was arrested in September 2009 on charges of conspiracy to use weapons of mass destruction. This was followed by David Coleman Headley, a US citizen arrested in October for planning to attack a Danish newspaper. In December, revelations surfaced that Headley may have conspired with operatives of Lashkar-e-Taiba, a Pakistani group, in the 2008 Mumbai attacks. In March 2010 he pled guilty to all charges in an Indian court. On November 5, Major Nidal Malik Hasan killed thirteen people and wounded thirty at Fort Hood outside Killeen, Texas. The ensuing media circus focused on Hasan's religion and continued the trend of conflating Islam and violence.[96] Later that month, the federal government indicted eight people in Minnesota for allegedly recruiting approximately two dozen Somali Americans (citizens and legal residents) to fight with an insurgent group in Somalia. That December, five young men from northern Virginia were arrested in Sargodha, Pakistan, accused of traveling there to fight alongside Taliban militants in Afghanistan.

Coming as they did in quick succession, these cases spurred the rapid development of a new media lexicon around "homegrown terrorism." The *Washington Post* was typical:

> The arrests came at a time of growing concern about homegrown terrorism after the recent shootings at the Fort Hood, Tex., military base [by Hasan] and charges filed this week against a Chicago man [Headley] accused of playing a role in last year's terrorist attacks in Mumbai.[97]

Even though scores of Muslim Americans from West Africa to South Asia had been arrested in the preceding years, often with little or no basis, as noted above, this consistent attention cast Muslim citizens and legal residents as enemies of the state, marking a new turn in the rhetoric of the war on terror.

The most virulent expression of this new green scare was articulated by New York University professor Tunku Varadarajan. In a November 2009 *Forbes* article titled "Going Muslim," Varadarajan argued that what precipitated the tragedy at Fort Hood was a condition that he suggested was inherent to all Muslims: the tendency toward violence.[98] He argued that Hasan didn't "go postal"— that is, break down and become violent. (The term became popular after a 1986 shooting by a postal worker.) Hasan was simply enacting, in a cold and calculated manner, the teachings of Islam. He was "going Muslim." As Varadarajan put it:

> This phrase ["going Muslim"] would describe the turn of events where a seemingly integrated Muslim-American—a friendly donut vendor [Zazi] in New York, say, or an officer in the U.S. Army at Fort Hood— discards his apparent integration into American society and elects to vindicate his religion in an act of messianic violence against his fellow Americans.

In short, for Varadarajan, all Muslim Americans are "imminently violent," and while they appear to be integrated into American society, they are in fact ticking time bombs who could explode into violent, murderous rage. Kundnani argues that Hasan carried out the attack in large part due to the fear that he would be deployed to a Muslim-majority country and become complicit in war crimes against Muslims. He adds that Hasan also may have acted because the authorities had refused to investigate allegations of war crimes that had emerged in his counseling sessions with army patients.[99] Discounting these real lived circumstances that might have explained his actions, cultural racism was deployed to make the argument that Muslims are driven by "Islam" to be violent. The homegrown terrorist, predominantly identified as brown, male, and Muslim, is inherently violent despite all semblances to the contrary. What made the racialized Muslim a threat (and this category occasionally includes white Muslims like Colleen LaRose who was arrested on terrorism related charges in 2010) is their religion; they are culturally programmed by Islam to carry out murder and mayhem. In making this argument, Varadarajan was simply echoing the logic of "preemptive prosecution" and theories of radicalization employed by the law enforcement apparatus.

Following hard upon this controversy, in 2011 the HBO series *Homeland* featured a white Muslim terrorist sympathizer, Nick Brody. Brody, an all-American white male, is shown to have been corrupted by "Islam" into turning against his nation. "Islam" as ideology became a security threat. *Homeland* treats Islam as the insidious driving force behind all of the terror plots in the show, whether planned and perpetrated by foreign Muslims or by white American Muslim converts.[100] This racist logic has informed counterterrorism programs both within the United States and in several European nations. For instance, the notion of terrorists in our midst who must be apprehended before they can act prompted counterterrorism practices such as the United Kingdom's Preventing Violent Extremism program. These would be adopted in the United States during the Obama presidency through the Countering Violent Extremism program.

From Obama's "Smarter" War on Terror to Trump's Blatant Racism

The securitization of Islam and the racialization of Muslims initiated by the Bush administration were strengthened during the Obama era. The failed wars in Afghanistan and Iraq, not to mention the absence of weapons of mass destruction in Iraq, had called the credibility of the Bush administration into question. Both on the international and domestic front, Obama launched a "smarter" war on terror. Here I lay out a few ways in which the Obama administration built on and deepened the policies developed by Bush, but also how it replaced programs that had come under fire. Just as with the global war on terror where Obama initiated a new rhetorical posture, the domestic war on terror also acquired a more liberal veneer. As journalist Jeremy Scahill notes in his book *Dirty Wars: The World is a Battlefield,* one of the most comprehensive journalistic accounts of the expansion of empire after 9/11, "the war on terror, launched under a Republican administration, was ultimately legitimized and expanded by a popular Democratic president."[101]

Domestically, Obama furthered Bush's policies and the racialized Muslim continued to be targeted by the state. Obama went further than Bush in several ways. He secured for the president the power to execute US citizens suspected of ties to terrorism without so much as a trial or the apparently unnecessary burden of proof; the cleric and US citizen Anwar al-Awlaki was summarily executed in 2011. The Bush administration's practice of indefinite detention had stripped non-citizens of their habeas corpus rights. Obama, the lawyer, did not repudiate this practice. In fact, he signed into law the National Defense Authorization Act (NDAA) that not only institutionalized this process but also expanded its use to include US citizens. Although this is both unconstitutional and illegal, according to the ACLU,[102] and even though this process has torn Muslim families apart, Obama adopted Bush's policies and codified them into law. The NDAA also legitimated the dissemination of propaganda to US citizens. As journalist Naomi Wolf wrote, the NDAA "legalizes something that has been illegal for decades: the direct funding of pro-government or pro-military messaging in media, without disclosure, aimed at American citizens."[103]

The use of "soft" power was a hallmark of the Obama presidency. This meant that Bush era programs that were blatant propaganda had to be discontinued. One such program was the color-coded terror alert system. Tom Ridge, secretary of DHS, had praised the program when it was launched but then grew skeptical, stating that he was urged to raise the terror alert level as a way to bolster George W. Bush's presidential campaign in 2004.[104] The Obama administration replaced this program with the National Terrorism Advisory System, which is more subtle. In 2010 DHS launched the nationwide "See Something, Say Something" campaign, which took a multicultural approach to fighting terrorism. As I have argued elsewhere, counterterrorism propaganda took a decidedly anti-racist hue, with white terrorists as the bad guys in DHS YouTube videos and brown and black people as the good informants.[105] Obama's national security leadership team consisted of significantly more women and people of color. The process begun in the early post–Cold War era was taken to new levels in the Obama administration as multicultural imperial feminism became more prominent.[106]

Moreover, the role of citizens in watching for signs of radicalization among their neighbors, friends, and community members was now deemed important. (This was the case in the United Kingdom, from which the United States borrowed its own domestic counter-radicalization program.) Giving credence to radicalization programs in the law enforcement community, Obama unveiled his "counter-radicalization" strategy in 2011. In the opening statement of his strategy document, Obama stated:

> [M]ost recently, al-Qa'ida and its affiliates have attempted to recruit and radicalize people here in the United States, as we have seen in several plots and attacks, including the deadly attack two years ago on our service members at Fort Hood.

The Obama administration sought to actively recruit "good Muslims" to the war on terror by enlisting the help of patriotic citizens. He stated that

Muslims are "best positioned to take the lead because they know their communities best." Heaping praise on Muslim Americans who have worked with the law enforcement community, he called for more such work. The document in turn solicited the support of teachers, coaches, and community members, who were to be turned into a McCarthy-type informant system.[107] Liberal Islamophobia sets out to include Muslims to the extent that they give their consent to the war on terror abroad and at home.

However, being a "good" Muslim doesn't guarantee acceptance, as Reda Shata learned. He worked with the FBI and the police, inviting officers to his mosque for breakfast and even dining with Mayor Bloomberg. He personified everything that US imperialism has defined as a "good Muslim." Yet an undercover police officer and an informant were assigned to spy on him and to keep tabs on his mosque. When he learned that he was viewed as a suspect by the very people he had invited into his mosque, Shata said: "This is very sad . . . What is your feeling if you see this about people you trusted?" Indeed. As CBS news noted:

> The dichotomy between simultaneously being partner and suspect is common among some of New York's Muslims. Some of the same mosques that city leaders visited to hail their strong alliances with the Muslim community have also been placed under NYPD surveillance—in some cases infiltrated by undercover police officers and informants.[108]

The Obama administration contributed federal funds for the NYPD spying program.[109]

Adhering to the precepts of liberal Islamophobia, the aforementioned Obama report went on to state that "we must counter al-Qa'ida's propaganda that the United States is somehow at war with Islam" and instead affirm that "Islam is part of America, a country that cherishes the active participation of all its citizens, regardless of background and belief. We live what al-Qa'ida violently rejects—religious freedom and pluralism." Obama added that "our rich diversity of backgrounds and faiths makes us stronger."

This is the modus operandi of liberal Islamophobia: to roundly reject Islam-bashing—and then proceed to institute proposals that target and racialize Muslims. When representative Peter King held his McCarthy-style hearings in March 2011 to determine the extent of Muslim radicalization in the United States, he was rightly criticized by liberals.

However, that August, when Obama institutionalized this process through his "counter-radicalization" strategy, there was silence.

The Countering Violent Extremism program is deeply invasive and sinks its tentacles deep into Muslim communities. In fact, it serves to deputize members of the Muslim community as arms of the security apparatus.[110] As legal scholar Sahar Aziz writes:

> Community policing co-opts Muslim community leaders into gathering and sharing intelligence on Muslims' political beliefs, religious practices, and other information otherwise unavailable to law enforcement due to constitutional constraints. Believing they are serving the best interests of Muslim communities, many unwitting participants disclose the goings-on of the community and provide information about the politics of community leaders and mosques. This enables law enforcement's investigative arm to reach deeper into Muslim communities' affairs than they could otherwise, resulting in a de facto deputizing effect. All the while, aggressive counterterrorism enforcement practices and policies focused exclusively on Muslims remain unchanged.[111]

While all Americans are urged to pass on tips of suspicious activities, which are turned into Suspicious Activity Reports, the Countering Violent Extremism program sets out to recruit Muslims as active agents of the security state.

Donald Trump as candidate and then president shattered the liberal consensus cultivated by the Obama administration. Trump's overt forms of racism were of the kind seen in far right-wing quarters. Dispensing with "political correctness," Trump proposed the idea of a Muslim registry, where all Muslims would be forced to register with the US government. At one point the Kansas Secretary of State, Kris Kobach, was photographed carrying documents requiring "special registration" of immigrants and refugees from certain "high risk" countries, a code word for Muslim-majority countries. Trump and his advisors pointed to the Bush era NSEERS program discussed above as a precedent. In the end, Trump retreated from implementing such a registry.

He did, however, impose a Muslim ban. From the day he entered office, he issued a series of executive orders barring the entry of migrants from Muslim-majority countries. His first order suspended admission of all refugees for 120 days; stopped the admission of all Syrian refugees; and banned residents of Iraq, Syria, Iran, Sudan, Libya, Somalia, and

Yemen from traveling to the United States. The order triggered a wave of protests at airports by activists across the country. In New York City, taxi drivers (many of whom are Muslim) staged a political strike, effectively shutting down its airports.[112] They joined activists at a mass rally at JFK airport to protest the ban.[113] The next week Yemeni American business owners instituted a one day strike, shutting down over 1,000 bodegas in New York City.[114] The ACLU waged an unrelenting challenge to Trump's repeated attempts to implement the ban, blocking several in the courts. Significantly, the libertarian Cato Institute published a report stating that immigrants from these countries had not committed a single terrorist act between 1975 and 2015.[115] Trump's rhetoric was crass and threatened to undo the subtle and covert forms of racism that sustain the war on terror.

Trump legal advisor (and former New York City mayor) Rudy Giuliani attempted to provide a legal cover for the ban; he argued that it was not a ban at all and that Muslims were not being targeted specifically because they were Muslim. According to Giuliani, "we focused on, instead of religion, danger—the areas of the world that create danger for us, which is a factual basis, not a religious basis. Perfectly legal, perfectly sensible."[116] Indeed, such logic has been deployed for decades. Thus, the Supreme Court upheld the final iteration in 2018 on these grounds, arguing that the president of the United States could limit entry to those seen as security threats. The Court also struck down the 1944 *Korematsu* case that upheld Japanese internment which was based on the notion that people of Japanese descent constituted a race that represented a threat to the United States. Yet they refused to apply the same logic to the Muslim ban. In the minority opinion, Judge Sotomayor argued that the two were the same and that discrimination was a work based on "a superficial claim of national security." While she did not use the term *race*, Naber and Rana appropriately noted that "the racism of Japanese internment is the racism of the Muslim travel ban. Racism based on nationality is the racism based on religious group."[117]

Trump secured this victory in the Supreme Court by stipulating conditions used by Clinton, Bush, and Obama to enact similar albeit more moderate restrictions on admission of refugees, migrants, and visitors. Trump's statements and policies were thus extreme expressions of political elites' long history of using national security to deploy racist policies. The impact has been devastating particularly in the context of a massive refugee crisis taking place around the world, in particular from Muslim-majority countries devastated by US wars, counterrevolution, civil wars, economic crisis, and climate change. Trump banned these migrants from coming to the United States and capped overall refugee numbers at a historic low of 15,000 a year.[118]

Conclusion

This chapter outlined how the racialized Muslim was constructed as a security threat in the post-9/11 era. While there are precursors going back to the 1960s, the post-9/11 "racial Muslim" is a fluid category that includes a wide variety of people from West Africa to Bangladesh. Additionally, others get included in this category such as the half-white/half-Jamaican "shoe bomber" Richard Reid and the Puerto Rican José Padilla. Muslims and those perceived as Muslims were targeted in a variety of ways from airport screenings, registries, detention, deportation, entrapment, preemptive prosecution, and intrusive surveillance. Additionally, the security state sought to recruit informants using both incentives and coercion. During the Obama administration, the Countering Violent Extremism program used a "friendlier" and kinder form of community-based surveillance. Theories of radicalization that justified various practices of preemptive prosecution were modes of racializing the "Muslim" and turning a diverse group of people into a "race" of people who had to be monitored and disciplined lest they carry out violence. These theories are based on the supposition that "Islam" is a dangerous ideology that drives Muslims to violence. The "Arab terrorist" of the 1960s has evolved into a composite and flexible terrorist figure.

Thus, the NYPD surveillance program included not just Muslim Americans but liberal political groups as well.[119] Similarly, the FBI used agents provocateurs to entrap activists in the Occupy Wall Street movement.[120] The Black Lives Matter (BLM) hashtag and movement, begun in 2013 after the murder of Trayvon Martin, has been called "terrorist." In her book *When They Call You a Terrorist: A Black Lives Matter Memoir,* BLM co-founder Patrisse Khan-Cullors outlines not only how the rhetoric of terrorism is used to discredit the Movement for Black Lives but also how it normalizes violence against black and brown people. Terrorism as a category is fluid and opportunistic and can be expanded to include new and emerging threats. In the context of the mass multiracial BLM uprisings against police violence in the summer of 2020, Trump declared his intention to designate the anti-fascist political movement Antifa as a terrorist organization. This should not surprise anyone since measures used to control Communists and later the New Left, anti-war, and civil rights activists like COINTELPRO were applied to Arab Americans and later Iranian Americans. The McCarran–Walter Act originally designed to target leftists was expanded to include supporters of Palestinian rights. Whether during the Cold War and the "red scare" or the war on terror and the "green scare," the imperial state is ever vigilant, seeking to quell insurgency before it can threaten the system. Those seeking justice and equity have nothing to gain from supporting the war on terror.

7

The New McCarthyites:
The Right-wing Islamophobia
Network and Their Liberal Enablers

The Trump presidency was the most Islamophobic in US history. During Trump's time in office, anti-Muslim racism in its blatant and far right-wing form was legitimated, particularly among the tens of millions of his most ardent supporters. After the civil rights movement, Republicans had to resort to dog whistle tactics to appeal to racist voters, but Trump was able to overcome "political correctness" and to bring overt racism into the mainstream. His bigoted rhetoric and policies created a spike in hate crimes and bias incidents carried out by both state agencies and right-wing vigilantes. The Council on American-Islamic Relations (CAIR) reported 10,015 anti-Muslim acts between 2014 and 2019, with a 94 percent jump in 2017 in the wake of the first iteration of the Muslim ban. Over that five-year period, CAIR documented 1,164 hate crimes, 506 attacks on mosques, and 2,783 acts of discrimination by state agencies including the FBI, the Transportation Security Administration, and the US Customs and Border Protection.[1]

Trump was assisted by a number of Islamophobes who were appointed to positions of power such as Michael Pompeo, John Bolton, and Stephen Miller. I will return to these figures later, but a quote from Monica Crowley who was made assistant secretary for public affairs in 2019 provides a flavor of the kinds of beliefs held by right-wing Trump appointees. Crowley is a contributor to Fox News, a columnist, and a syndicated radio host most known for spreading conspiracy theories that Obama was a secret Muslim who took orders from terrorist organizations. As she put it:

Obama was born to a Muslim father, which under Islam automatically made him a Muslim. He says he converted to Christianity as an adult, which under Islam makes him an apostate . . . He grew up in Indonesia, which is the most populous Muslim nation on Earth. His stepfather was also a Muslim. He was steeped in Islam throughout his formative years, so it should come as no surprise that he has loyalties to Islam . . . The question is: can he be both loyal to Islam and loyal to the United States?[2]

Such individuals were elevated under the Trump administration since he himself had advocated similar positions, from questioning Obama's place of birth to his suggestion that Obama had a secret terrorist agenda.[3]

Trump and his ilk belong to what religion specialist Nathan Lean has called the "Islamophobia industry."[4] The Center for American Progress (CAP) published a comprehensive report on this network of individuals and groups titled *Fear, Inc.: The Roots of the Islamophobia Network in America* in 2011.[5] This well-researched report documents the connections between various right-wing groups, political figures, think tanks, conservative foundations, and the mainstream and right-wing media. However, the thrust of the argument is that Islamophobia, which they understand as religious intolerance rather than as anti-Muslim racism, is propagated by a "small, tightly networked group" that exists outside the mainstream.[6] In a follow-up publication in 2015, titled *Fear, Inc. 2.0*, the authors doubled down on their argument that Islamophobia is "not indicative of mainstream American views" and that only a small "fringe" that seeks to influence the mainstream is responsible for this ideology.[7] This chapter sets out to disprove this claim. As the entire book has argued, Islamophobia, better understood as anti-Muslim racism, emerges from the bowels of empire and goes far beyond fringe right-wing elements.

In his book *The Great Fear*, historian David Caute showed that McCarthyism wasn't simply about one out-of-control senator, but a political system (including both Democrats and Republicans) that allowed a figure like Joseph McCarthy to set the political agenda.[8] McCarthy was a useful tool in prosecuting the Cold War—particularly in creating a climate of fear where dissent could be punished and neutralized. The right-wing Islamophobic warriors play a similar role during the era of the war on terror. They are not "alien outsiders" but emerge from within the political establishment, the security apparatus, the academy, think tanks, and the mainstream media. Thus, far from "infiltrating" an otherwise sound democratic system, the "new McCarthyites," as I call them, are a product of, and sit comfortably within, the structures of US empire; their role is to elevate and legitimize overt racism.

The new McCarthyites do not operate in isolation from other political and social actors. Rather, there is a dialectical relationship between far-right racism and liberal racism. All these racisms sit on a spectrum with each influencing the other. While the Far Right and sections of the neoconservative camp have forwarded conspiracy theories about Muslims that are obviously and blatantly racist (such as the claim that 80 percent of mosques in the United States promote or support violence, discussed below), establishment liberals put forward arguments that are more subtle but nevertheless racist. The so-called "Ground Zero Mosque" controversy in 2010 is a good case study of the way in which overt right-wing Islamophobia interacts with liberal Islamophobia to produce the "Muslim" as a racialized other.

This chapter begins with an analysis of the Ground Zero Mosque controversy to demonstrate how even while the new McCarthyites were responsible for the hysteria generated, their arguments were enabled by the liberal establishment. The year 2010 was an important turning point for these forces, and the mosque controversy positioned the Islamo-phobic network to grow its influence. But this was not the first project of Muslim-bashing that the new McCarthyites had initiated. In the post–Cold War era, the Islamophobia network has been involved in silencing dissent by targeting scholars in the field of Middle Eastern studies, attack-ing Palestinian rights supporters, and attempting to shut down and delegitimize symbols of the Muslim community such as Islamic schools, mosques, and community centers. Various groups have come together to form this coalition of the new McCarthyites. These include sections of the neocon elite, the Christian Right, Zionist groups, and various "ex-Muslims." Finally, I discuss how establishment liberals enable and help to amplify Far Right anti-Muslim racism. Drawing on various schol-ars, I also outline how mainstream Muslim organizations inadvertently play a role in legitimizing the war on terror and therefore fueling the very racism they seek to oppose.

The Ground Zero Mosque Controversy

In 2009, Imam Feisal Abdul Rauf, who had served as a cleric in down-town Manhattan for more than a quarter century, proposed the construction of a center modeled on the 92nd Street Y and the Jewish

Community Center in Manhattan. The goal of the proposed center was to promote greater understanding of the Muslim community, he argued. Its name, Cordoba House, refers to the city of Córdoba, Spain, a leading cultural center during the high point of Muslim rule in the Iberian Peninsula. Córdoba represented not only a pinnacle of intellectual development, but also a period of relatively peaceful coexistence among Muslims, Christians, and Jews.

Rauf, who positions himself as a "moderate Muslim," envisioned a community center with recreation facilities like a swimming pool, basketball court, gym, culinary school, art studios, a childcare center, and badly needed prayer space for the neighborhood Muslim community. His plan was to enable people of all faiths to interact. Rauf is an establishment figure who has conducted training speeches for the FBI and the State Department after 9/11; he was also associated with the 2007 policy group's advice on improving US relations with the "Muslim world" (discussed in Chapter 5). The Obama era, it was believed, would be a time when "good Muslims" could reshape the political agenda. Rauf's book *What's Right with Islam* (2005) tries to explain Islam to the West and offers a "new vision" for western Muslims.[9] In so doing, it presents Islamophobia as a misunderstanding rather than a systematic form of racism tied to empire.

When the *New York Times* ran a front-page story on Cordoba House in December 2009, the overall tone was positive, even though it noted with some alarm what it might mean for a Muslim community center to be built so close to Ground Zero. Feisal was quoted saying that "we want to push back against the extremists."[10] A mother of a 9/11 victim publicly backed the Islamic center.[11] New York Mayor Michael Bloomberg supported the project, as did city officials. Even right-wing Fox News anchor Laura Ingraham seemed unperturbed: in an interview with Cordoba House co-founder Daisy Khan in December 2009, Ingraham supported the project. Even while arguing that Muslim-majority countries from Saudi Arabia to Lebanon are intolerant toward Christians, she told Khan, "I can't find many people who really have a problem with it . . . I like what you're trying to do."[12] When members of the political class agree on an issue, the media rarely challenge their assumptions.[13]

This story might have been lost in the media landscape had it not been for the mobilization of the new McCarthyites. On May 6, 2010, the New York City Community Board voted unanimously to approve the project. In response to the board's decision, Pamela Geller, a right-wing blogger, posted an entry titled "Monster Mosque Pushes Ahead in Shadow of

World Trade Center Islamic Death and Destruction." In it, she wrote, "This is Islamic domination and expansionism. The location is no accident. Just as Al-Aqsa was built on top of the Temple in Jerusalem." Casting it as a religious conflict and a provocation, Geller sought to inflame her base. The next day, her group Stop Islamization of America, which she co-founded with Robert Spencer, launched "Campaign Offensive: Stop the 911 Mosque!"[14] While this was not the first time the network had blogged about the community center, its moment had finally arrived. The immediate backdrop was the "homegrown terrorism" hysteria and the green scare (see Chapter 6), which created space for the Far Right to push the rhetoric further to the right.

For Geller, this was an example of Muslims trying to take over the United States. Stop Islamization of America called a protest for May 29 against what Geller called the "911 Monster Mosque." In this, Geller was contributing the US version of a conspiracy theory developed in Europe that Muslims and Arabs were out to destroy western civilization and create "Eurabia."[15] Geller is connected to the Far Right Dutch politician Geert Wilders, who gave a glowing blurb for the book she co-authored on the Obama presidency. She is also an admirer of open fascists and street gangs such as the English Defence League that routinely attack Muslims and immigrants. She once claimed that black South Africans are launching a "genocide" against whites.[16] A staunch Zionist, she wrote a column in an Israeli newspaper in which she referred to the term *Palestinian* as "fallacious" and exhorted Israelis to "stand loud and proud. Give up nothing. Turn over not a pebble. For every rocket fired, drop a MOAB. Take back Gaza. Secure Judea and Samaria."[17]

In protesting the proposed Islamic center, Geller and her ilk were likely trying to reproduce the success of the Swiss referendum the previous year to ban the construction of minarets. At the time of the vote, there were only four minarets in all of Switzerland, and yet the majority of Swiss voters supported the ban. There is a global Islamophobia network that works cooperatively together. Known as the "counter-jihad" movement, it works across borders sharing strategies, theories, and rhetoric.[18] Sociologist David Miller's non-profit organization, Public Interest Investigations, posted a report on its Spinwatch website in 2019 on the global counterjihad movement and its sources of funding. The Spinwatch report states that "the US counterjihad movement has been critical to facilitating the flows of ideas, people and money into Europe via its transatlantic network."[19] The Norwegian Anders Behring Breivik, who killed seventy-seven people in a bombing and mass shooting in 2011, cited several prominent US Islamophobes in his manifesto. Co-founder of Stop Islam-ization of America with Geller, Robert Spencer, led the pack, receiving 162 mentions in the racist diatribe.[20] Buoyed by the victory in Switzer-land in 2009, Geller and Spencer set out to reproduce the phenomenon of generating hatred for the symbols of Islam in New York City.

Geller's blog drew the attention of the right-wing *New York Post*, which began running articles that extensively quoted Geller. One article falsely claimed that Cordoba House's opening date was set for September 11, 2011.[21] This was the moment when this story spread like wildfire, gaining media attention not only on Fox News and other conservative outlets but also in the mainstream media.[22] However, even at this stage, the community center was still far from becoming a symbol of Muslim "insensitivity." When Mark Williams, a Tea Party leader, attacked Imam Rauf, New York City politicians came out against Williams and asserted their support for the center.[23] Williams's blog posts were quite extreme in their rhetoric. He wrote:

> The animals of allah for whom any day is a great day for a massacre are drooling over the positive response that they are getting from New York City officials over a proposal to build a thirteen-story monument to the 9/11 Muslims who hijacked those four airliners. The monument would consist of a Mosque for the worship of the terrorists' monkey-god and a "cultural center" to propagandize for the extermination of all things not approved by their cult.[24]

The curious addition of a Hindu deity (the monkey god Hanuman) into the mix demonstrates how racisms don't keep to prefixed borders and often combine various racialized groups.

The conservative blog Pajamas Media (now PJ Media), which received $3.5 million from the right-wing figure Aubrey Chernick (discussed below), used its platform to bring together voices of opposition to the community center.[25] Neocon Frank Gaffney wrote in June that the "Ground Zero mosque is designed to be a permanent, in-our-face beach-head for Shariah, a platform for inspiring the triumphalist ambitions of the faithful."[26] Republican politician Newt Gingrich echoed this point on Fox News, stating that the center represented Muslim "triumphalism."[27] The talking points were well orchestrated; neocon Daniel Pipes used the same wording, stating that the building "reeks of Islamic triumphalism."[28] Cordoba House was turned into a symbol of the Muslim invasion of the United States and a step toward the American equivalent of "Eurabia."

This kind of rhetoric is easy to identify as overt and blatant racism. Barbara and Karen Fields have called this form of racism "troglodyte racism" in that it is obviously reactionary. Such overt racism sits comfortably in the right-wing public sphere within its various online, print, and television outlets. And more generally, as noted in the introduction, Americans are taught that only this kind of hate speech is what counts as racism. However, in this instance, it spilled over from the right-wing media world of Fox News, the *Washington Times*, and the *New York Post* into the mainstream when figures such as former speaker of the House Newt Gingrich and former vice-presidential candidate Sarah Palin added their voices to the issue. Gingrich's comment was replayed in other parts of the mainstream media:

> Nazis don't have the right to put up a sign next to the Holocaust Museum in Washington. We would never accept the Japanese putting up a site next to Pearl Harbor. There is no reason to accept a mosque next to the World Trade Center.[29]

Because Muslims were so vilified after 9/11 and were turned into a "race" that bears collective responsibility for the attacks, such an argument by Gingrich which compared Muslims to Nazis (or a nation-state at war with the United States) seemed acceptable. Muslims as a whole were to blame for 9/11, and therefore any symbol of Islam close to what is considered "hallowed ground" was an affront. Soon, more and more voices critical of the project and particularly of its location started to find a home in the mainstream media.

The Anti-Defamation League (ADL), which has a long history of using anti-Muslim racism to bolster support for Israeli colonization,[30] weighed in, saying that it was insensitive to build the center "in the shadow" of the World Trade Center because it would cause pain to the victims of 9/11.[31] Former New York City mayor Rudy Giuliani called the mosque a "desecration."[32] To be sure, some of the mainstream media defended Muslims, the Islamic center, and by extension, the image of the United States as a tolerant multiracial society. Mayor Bloomberg defended it in a speech delivered with the Statue of Liberty in the background.[33] The *New York Times* featured a front-page story titled "When an Arab Enclave Thrived Downtown," advancing the proposition that Arabs (and Muslims) are an integral part of American society.[34] *Time* did a cover story that asked, "Is America Islamophobic?"[35] Under this question on the cover is the symbol of Islam, the crescent and star, filled in with the US flag. While *Time* defended Muslims against racist attacks, its article stopped short of showing the connections between Islamophobia and the war on terror.[36] Instead, it drew on the patriotic theme of the United States as a melting pot that welcomes immigrants.

Mainstream liberal media personalities such as Keith Olbermann, Jon Stewart, and Stephen Colbert also took a tough line against the Right, arguing for religious freedom and opposing the overt racism of the Far Right. However, the main line of defense was one of religious freedom and tolerance. What was at stake for these actors was a defense of multiculturalism and the image of the United States as a tolerant, immigrant-friendly nation. However, there is a long history of racist and exclusionary citizenship laws preventing non-white immigrants from acceptance into the body politic (see Chapter 2). Even those considered white today such as the Irish, Italians, and Eastern Europeans were not incorporated into whiteness until after World War II when the defeat of the Nazis discredited blatant racism. Moreover, Islamophobia in these venues was understood as a cultural misunderstanding or as the unwillingness of some, particularly the Far Right, to include and tolerate religious difference. Few, if any, called it anti-Muslim racism or connected it to empire. This is precisely the logic found in the CAP report as well.

The Islamophobia network's effort to brand the center as the "Ground Zero Mosque," even though it was several blocks from the site of the former World Trade Center, succeeded. Their construction of the victims of 9/11 erased the multiracial and multinational character of the dead. The narrative was one of white victimhood at the hands of the racialized Muslim, which has a longer history in the United States. As shown in Chapter 2, there was a groundswell of demand at the turn of the nineteenth century not only for Native American captivity stories but also the white US captive stories related to the Barbary Coast. Implicit and explicit white supremacy centered on white victimhood served not only to erase the Muslims who died on that day but to homogenize all Muslims. The Right was so successful in setting the terms of discussion that polls taken at the time showed that anywhere between 54 and 68 percent of Americans expressed opposition to the project at its proposed location.[37]

This success, however, was in no small part due to the role played by the liberal establishment. In the months prior, the media had whipped up hysteria around the threat of "homegrown terrorism." This green scare was integral to Obama's announcement to deploy 33,000 more troops to Afghanistan. In short, even though the right-wing Islamophobia network had been active for a few decades, the climate created by official liberalism in the form of support for more security measures to ferret out the "terrorists" in our midst bolstered their ability to take the argument further. Liberal Islamophobia interacts dialectically with conservative and Far Right Islamophobia to produce the "Muslim" as a threatening race.

Democratic Party politicians took positions that ranged from neutral to blatantly hostile. House Speaker Nancy Pelosi asked about the opposition funders, a tepid response. The following day she added that the location of the project was a "local decision" and that freedom of religion was a constitutional right.[38] Within the context of this national controversy, this would turn out to be the most positive response from a Democratic Party official: a rather lukewarm defense of the constitution rather than a denunciation of the new McCarthyites and their overt racism. Pelosi's counterpart in the Senate, Majority Leader Harry Reid, didn't offer even a tepid defense but spoke out against the project. He argued that while the First Amendment protects freedom of religion, he believed that the "mosque should be built someplace else."[39] Democrat Jeff Greene of Florida, running in the Senate primary, said that "common sense and respect for those who lost their lives and loved ones gives sensible reason to build the mosque someplace else."[40] Then came liberal Democrat Howard Dean, who argued that this was "a real affront to people who lost their lives" in the 9/11 attacks. In an interview with a New York radio station, he said he would like to see the center built in another, less controversial location.[41]

Thus, the terms of debate ranged between "Islamic triumphalism" on the one hand and an argument about the "proper" location of the proposed center on the other. One is overtly racist while the other appears more reasonable, upholding the Constitution and the right to religion while questioning this particular decision to build a community center in the proposed location. Tacitly or blatantly, both sides were in agreement that Muslims as a whole were connected to and shared blame for the destruction of the World Trade Center. This is how the homogenizing logic of racism works, where the actions of a few individuals are generalized to an entire group. For the Islamophobia network, the community center marked Muslim "triumph," or the ability to destroy the World Trade Center and raise a building with a mosque "on top of it." For liberals, "sensitivity" for the victims meant that any symbol of Islam close to the World Trade Center was an affront. For both, "Islam" was tied directly to the events of 9/11. Some like the public intellectual and scholar Tariq Ramadan took a position in the middle, arguing that while Muslims were not to blame for 9/11, it would not be a "wise decision" to build the center at the proposed location "considering the collective sensitivities in American society."[42]

As this "debate" unfolded, Obama qualified his earlier statements in support of the project by stating that while he affirms the religious rights of all people, he was not commenting "on the wisdom of making a decision to put a mosque there."[43] Obama was quickly adapting to right-wing pressure; when Gainesville, Florida, minister Terry Jones announced his plan to burn the Quran on September 11, Obama did not argue that such an act was offensive, that it constituted an attack on religious freedom, or that it was reminiscent of Ku Klux Klan cross burnings in the South, but that it threatened "national security" and that it would put US soldiers in Iraq and Afghanistan "in harm's way": "This could increase the recruitment of individuals who'd be willing to blow themselves up in American cities or European cities."[44] Obama's summoning of the specter of suicide bombers in US cities only gave further ground to the new McCarthyites.

What this controversy demonstrates is a dynamic in which Far Right-wing and liberal Islamophobia act as mutually reinforcing ideologies that serve to bolster empire. "Good" Muslims like Rauf and Khan, who had proposed the Islamic center and who believed that support for the war on terror would give them a seat at the table and therefore the ability to push back against Islamophobia, were sidelined. Moreover, the Obama era saw the rise of anti-Muslim racist groups driven not only by contempt for the first black president (and according to segments of the Far Right, first Muslim president), but also as a backlash against the shift to liberalism and multiculturalism within establishment politics. The Southern Poverty Law Center, which tracks hate groups, reported that the number of anti-Muslim groups tripled in 2011.[45] The report attributed this growth to a few key events, including what it called the "fever pitch" of Islamophobia during the Ground Zero Mosque controversy the previous year. Thus, the Far Right was able to consolidate its rhetorical victory in the form of a proliferation of organized racist groups.

Yet, it was not an outright victory since a mosque was opened in an existing building at the planned location.[46] This is in no small part due to the role played by grassroots interfaith, liberal, and left-wing groups in mobilizing a large and successful counter-demonstration against the Right (discussed in the conclusion). However, it is also true to say that the Islamophobia network received a boost from this controversy. Their success generated mainstream media attention. A series of articles and reports appeared in 2011 that sought to shed light on the organized nature of the Islamophobia network, its sources of funding, and its international scope. For instance, the lawyer David Yerushalmi, who masterminded the ban on the use of Sharia or Islamic law in US courts, was featured in a lengthy *New York Times* report.[47] Steven Emerson, Frank Gaffney, and other new McCarthyites were named in an investigative report on the Islamophobes' sources of funds.[48] This attention was not necessarily positive, but it demonstrated that the new McCarthyites were now a national force to be reckoned with.

The Rise of the Islamophobia Network

The Cordoba House controversy was not the Islamophobia network's first attempt to put troglodyte racism on the public stage. As journalist Max Blumenthal argued, the Ground Zero Mosque controversy was "the fruit of an organized, long-term campaign by a tight confederation of right-wing activists and operatives who first focused on Islamophobia soon after the September 11th attacks, but only attained critical mass during the Obama era."[49] He explains that their efforts began in the early 2000s when a coalition of pro-Israeli groups ranging from the ADL and the American Jewish Committee (AJC) to American Israel Public Affairs Committee (AIPAC) came together to address what they saw as a sudden increase in pro-Palestinian activism on college campuses. The key targets on campuses were scholars who studied the Middle East, whose work challenged the right-wing narrative generally and that of Israel in particular.

Martin Kramer's *Ivory Towers on Sand: The Failures of Middle Eastern Studies in America* provided the intellectual ballast necessary to make the argument that Middle East scholars were un-American because of their criticisms of Israeli and US foreign policy.[50] Kramer, who studied under Bernard Lewis, produced a book that fueled an effort to target and stifle critical thought. As historian Joel Beinin notes, "Kramer and his ilk were emboldened by their links to officials in the upper-mid levels of the Bush administration," and particularly to the neocons who shared their worldview.[51] He adds that the "neo-cons have much more powerful political connections than those that the AJC, the ADL and AIPAC were able to mobilize." But this unity was not coincidental. Rather, if Lewis, Zakaria, and others were the intellectual core that were brought together to formulate the propaganda war after 9/11 (see Chapter 5), Kramer, Daniel Pipes,

David Horowitz, and others served as the activists out in the world policing critical thought. Their job was to ensure that the war on terror brand
remained uncontested and that their propaganda was not punctured by
scholars with the knowledge and ability to expose it. Bush even nomi-
nated Pipes to a seat on the board of directors of the federally funded
United States Institute of Peace, which was assigned to produce knowledge to aid in conflict resolution. While Pipes's nomination was scuttled,
this event sheds light on the neocons' penchant for intellectual
domination.

Pipes went on to found the website Campus Watch, which asserts that
Middle East scholars are un-American. In terms that barely disguise its
contempt for the targeted scholars, the website explains why this might
be so; one page, since removed, stated that "Middle East studies in the
United States has become the preserve of Middle East Arabs" who "have
brought their views with them."[52] One such pernicious view is support for
the Palestinian cause and criticism of Israeli settler colonialism. The next
logical step was to target Arabs and Arab Americans. Indeed, Campus
Watch's first prominent attack occurred against Professor Joseph Massad
of Columbia University. The David Project, a Hillel-funded group
founded explicitly to influence campus debates on Israel, produced a
documentary film titled *Columbia Unbecoming*, which claimed that
Jewish students were being intimidated by Arab American professors
and that Columbia's campus climate was rife with anti-Semitism. David
Horowitz contributed to this attack by calling Massad "dangerous" in his
book *The Professors: The 101 Most Dangerous Academics in America*.[53]
Funds poured in from a network of sources and pressure on the Columbia administration intensified. Democratic congressman Anthony
Weiner added fuel to the fire by calling for Massad to be dismissed. In the
end, however, Columbia students and faculty launched a campaign in
defense of Massad that defeated the new McCarthyites. Massad not only
earned tenure but won the prestigious Lionel Trilling Award for excellence in scholarship.

Undaunted by this defeat, the David Project turned its attention to the
Islamic Society of Boston, which had been trying to build a center to
serve the Muslim population in Roxbury. The David Project unleashed a
campaign of lawsuits and propaganda, claiming that the center was
receiving money from sources such as the Muslim Brotherhood and the
Wahhabis in Saudi Arabia. The right-wing media amplified this argument from Murdoch's *Boston Herald* to the local Fox affiliates. The *Boston
Globe* also echoed this argument in a series of reports that advanced the

notion that the center could become a place to train underground terror cells.[54] Yet again, however, the Islamophobia network failed. This time it was defeated by an interfaith effort launched by liberal Jews, who success-fully resisted the Right. In 2008, the community center was built and the David Project's dire predictions were not realized. However, Blumenthal notes that the

> local crusade established an effective blueprint for generating hysteria against the establishment of Islamic centers and mosques across the country, while galvanizing a cast of characters who would form an anti-Muslim network which would gain attention and success in the years to come.[55]

Indeed, their first success was a campaign against the Arab American schoolteacher Debbie Almontaser, who was to serve as the principal of Khalil Gibran International Academy. The academy, a secular public elementary school with an English-Arabic curriculum, was proposed for construction in Brooklyn as one of sixty-seven bilingual schools in the New York City system. Almontaser, a longtime educator of Yemeni descent, was accused of being a jihadist and a 9/11 denier by Stop the Madrassa, a coalition launched by the Islamophobia network. Geller, who was just cutting her teeth as an Islamophobic warrior, blogged that Almontaser "opposed the war on terror," was associated with CAIR, and had even had the audacity to accept an award from this "radical" group. She went on to accuse Almontaser of "whitewash[ing] the genocide against the Jews."[56] Daniel Pipes, who was involved in the campaign against Massad and the Boston Islamic center, claimed that the school should be stopped because "Arabic-language instruction is inevitably laden with Pan-Arabist and Islamist baggage."[57] The campaign reached fever pitch when the new McCarthyites found a picture of a T-shirt with the slogan "Intifada NYC" produced by the group Arab Women Active in the Arts and Media (AWAAM), a local Arab feminist organization. The connection between AWAAM and Almontaser was that they shared an office with the Yemeni-American association on whose board Almon-taser sits. This was all the "evidence" that the Islamophobic warriors needed to brand Almontaser as a "jihadist" since she supported Palestin-ian rights.

The *New York Post* carried a story that stated that the T-shirt was "apparently a call for a Gaza-style uprising in the Big Apple."[58] Almontas-er's efforts to explain the meaning and significance of the term *intifada* were countered by an ADL spokesperson who called AWAAM "an active supporter of the terrorist groups Hezbollah and Hamas."[59] The usual anti-Palestinian crowd all chimed in and the pressure mounted. After enduring an intense campaign of personal harassment and intimidation, Almontaser was forced to resign when her former supporter, Mayor Bloomberg, caved. However, the Khalil Gibran International Academy was eventually established, and Almontaser sued the city. But the Islamophobia network learned valuable lessons on how to wage a successful campaign and apply pressure on elected officials. It wasn't long before they found another opportunity, the Cordoba House project, to carry out a similar campaign. Since then, attacks on mosques and community centers across the country have increased. And new McCarthyist-type "lists" have appeared on the internet such as the "Professors Watchlist" that draw from and build on Horowitz's *101 Most Dangerous* professors list mentioned above.

The New McCarthyites

Four interconnected groups of people have come together to project the image of a vicious and menacing "Muslim enemy" and to generate fear and hatred. They include sections of the neocon camp who have devoted themselves to ferreting out the "Islamic terrorist"; closely connected to them are Zionists whose goal of policing criticism of Israel dovetails with anti-Muslim racism. The Christian Right has joined the ranks of the Islamophobic warriors, as have a group of former Muslims (and Christians) from the Middle East and South Asia who have profited from Islam bashing.

The neocons and Zionists

Frank Gaffney and Daniel Pipes are two leading neocons who have focused on the politics of Islamophobia. Gaffney was a Reagan-era deputy assistant defense secretary who served under Richard Perle (1983–87). For Gaffney, it was an easy shift from Cold Warrior to Islamophobic warrior. He was a senior adviser to the group Americans for Victory Over Terrorism (AVOT), which was a subsidiary of the Project for the New American Century (PNAC).[60] AVOT was founded shortly after 9/11 by Republican Party stalwart William Bennett, also a founding member of PNAC. AVOT merged with the right-wing Claremont institute and appears to have ceased operations in 2017. However, the individuals involved in its creation remain active in various spaces. It is therefore worth examining the goals and objectives of this signature institution.

The group hosted a website that stated that it was "dedicated to victory in the War on Terrorism" through "the shaping of public opinion, the encouragement of a foreign policy based on the founding principles of America, increased research about Islam and Islamism and a steadfast commitment to attacking those who would blame America first."[61] This statement captures the strategy adopted by the neocons to "win" the war on terror. A crucial part of this strategy is the battle for public opinion. Within the journals of the foreign policy establishment, the neocons had strongly put forward their vision and polemicized against other foreign policy paradigms such as those of the realists (see Chapter 4). The pivotal 1996 essay by Kristol and Kagan that appeared in *Foreign Affairs* about "benevolent global hegemony"[62] not only argued against realism and stressed that US domination of the world would be benevolent and act in the interests of all nations; it also maintained that the US public would have to be "educated" and "inspired" to accept their special responsibilities as citizens of empire.[63] This meant not only serving in the military but also developing an ideological "sense of mission" in imperialist interventions, based on a faith in "American greatness."[64]

September 11 provided the neocons with the enemy they needed to promote their vision. As Danny Cooper notes, the neoconservatives are "most comfortable when they have . . . an ideological competitor against which they can define themselves."[65] While neocons like Norman Podhoretz celebrated the collapse of the Soviet Union, Cooper notes that, lacking a new rival, he was "clearly lost."[66] This sentiment applies across the board. Gary Dorrien's interviews with prominent neocons for his book *Imperial Designs* leads him to observe that "most were anxious to find a substitute for the energizing and unifying role that the cold war played for them."[67] This new enemy took the form of "Islam," a "totalitarian ideology" the neocons believe is akin to Communism. As the AVOT statement makes clear, it is not simply Islamists who use violent tactics that they wish to "research," but "Islam and Islamism" as a whole. By this logic, simply being Muslim made one suspicious; this is a form of cultural racism that relies on the homogenization and essentialization of the world's 1.8 billion Muslims. Drawing a page from the McCarthyist playbook, Gaffney was one of many who claimed that Obama was a "secret Muslim."[68] To be a Muslim was to be automatically suspicious, just as being a Communist meant that one was unfit to be a government representative. To be sure, establishment liberals too were party to this line of attack.[69]

Not only did AVOT set out to influence public opinion, it also sought to silence dissenting views. As its website declared, AVOT has a "steadfast commitment to attacking those who would blame America first." This was part of a larger strategy that targeted all dissenters but particularly, as noted above, the Arab American Left. The neocons have vigorously argued that the United States has been a force for good in the Middle East and that people in that region therefore had only themselves to blame for the state of their countries. This argument has been articulated not just by the likes of Pipes and Lewis, but also by mainstream figures like Fareed Zakaria and Thomas Friedman.[70] Neocon Ayaan Hirsi Ali has given legitimacy to this argument through her status as a "native informer." Ali, who blames Islam for her difficult childhood in Somalia (and pretty much everything else), asks: "Why are Muslims so hypersensitive to criticism and why don't they do anything with it except to respond by denying it or playing the victim?"[71] In short, Muslims who attempt to articulate criticisms of US policy do not have any legitimate grounds. Irshad Manji, another ideological collaborator with empire, puts it more condescendingly when she tells her "fellow Muslims" to "grow up," lecturing forcefully that the United States has been a champion of human rights and that "neither Israel or America lies at the root of Muslim misery."[72] As demonstrated in Chapter 3, these claims are far from true.

The attack on the Left, particularly the academic Left, was led by Project David and Campus Watch. Kramer's book *Ivory Towers on Sand* was followed by *Unholy Alliance: Radical Islam and the American Left* by the ex-leftist David Horowitz and by Andrew McCarthy's *The Grand Jihad: How Islam and the Left Sabotage America*.[73] Building on Kramer's early polemic that Middle East studies departments are wrong about US policy, these books attempted to spread the net more widely, condemning the Left as a whole, including the white Left, and constructing a conspiratorial alliance between Islamists and the Left.[74] The Norwegian Breivik adopted this argument and turned it into the basis for the murder of teenagers at a camp run by the social-democratic Norwegian Labor Party. The neocons disavowed Breivik's actions, yet their goal of silencing dissenting views and intimidating activists can be interpreted by those prone to violence like Breivik in these ways. The modus operandi of the neocons and the Islamophobia network is intimidation carried out through smear campaigns and harassment.

In addition to AVOT, Gaffney's Center for Security Policy (CSP) has been instrumental in promoting anti-Muslim propaganda. As the authors of *Fear Inc.* write, CSP is "a key source for right-wing politicians, pundits, and grassroots organizations, providing them with a steady stream of reports mischaracterizing Islam and warning of the dangers of Islam and American Muslims."[75] In addition to CSP, the other leading sources of anti-Muslim racism are Pipes's Middle East Forum, Robert Spencer's Jihad Watch, Pamela Geller and Robert Spencer's Stop Islamization of America, Steven Emerson's Investigative Project on Terrorism, and David Yerushalmi's Society of Americans for National Existence. Together, these groups have developed the notion that there is a conspiracy by Muslims to take over the United States and that Islamists have "infiltrated" all levels of society. They make no distinction between Islam and the parties and organizations of political Islam. Further, they contend that Muslim Americans have ties to terrorist organizations and want to replace the US Constitution with Islamic law. This form of troglodyte racism is overt and easy to identify. It has therefore been more challenging for its proponents to win legitimacy in the public sphere—until the Trump presidency.

This is not to say that they have been shut out of the mainstream. Far from it. For instance, in 1994, PBS aired Steven Emerson's film *Jihad in America*, which argued that secret terrorist groups operating in the United States posed a grave threat to national security. Emerson made his name as a journalist working for *US News and World Report*, where he rose to become a senior editor in the area of national security issues and went on to write about terrorism for CNN. Not only did *Jihad in America* run on PBS, but it also won the prestigious George Polk Award for best television documentary. Emerson formed the Investigative Project on Terrorism in 1995 in order to more consistently propagate conspiracy theories about the "Islamic threat." His books include *American Jihad: The Terrorists Living Among Us* and *Jihad Incorporated: A Guide to Militant Islam in the US*.[76] For Emerson and his ilk, there are no "good Muslims." When Republican governor Chris Christie appointed a Muslim lawyer for a New Jersey state judgeship, Emerson accused Christie of "having a strange relationship with radical Islam."[77] Not to be outdone, blogger Debbie Schlussel called Christie a "halal pig" stating that Judge Sohail Mohammed was a Hamas supporter.[78]

The legal apparatus has been an important arena for the new McCarthyites. David Yerushalmi works as the legal counsel for CSP. He was also actively involved in the Cordoba House controversy as legal counsel for

Stop Islamization of America. In June 2011, Yerushalmi wrote a widely cited report in Daniel Pipes's Middle East Forum journal *Middle East Quarterly* that claimed that 80 percent of US mosques promote or support violence.[79] Perhaps his most important contribution to the Islamophobia network is that he laid the legal basis for the anti-Sharia campaign. Yerushalmi co-authored with Frank Gaffney a CSP report titled *Shariah: The Threat to America* that became a central vehicle to consider banning Sharia's use.[80] Between 2010 and 2017, as many as 201 bills were introduced in forty-three states to ban the use of Sharia.[81] Yerushalmi is not so much an outsider trying to corrupt an otherwise just system as he is an insider and a new McCarthyite pushing the system further to the right.

David Gaubatz helped Yerushalmi gather early information by taking charge of his *Mapping Shari'a in America: Knowing the Enemy campaign*.[82] Prior to his life as an Islamophobic warrior, Gaubatz worked in the Middle East for the Air Force's Office of Special Investigations. He built his career after 9/11 by arguing that Muslim civil rights groups such as CAIR are actually front groups for terrorist organizations. He is co-author of *Muslim Mafia: Inside the Secret Underworld That's Conspiring to Islamize America*, which has been used by right-wing politicians to target CAIR and other groups.[83] David Horowitz has added his voice to this campaign by attacking the Muslim Student Association (MSA), a campus group with dozens of chapters in universities across the country. Horowitz claimed that the MSA is

> lying about its core mission—which is to advance the Islamic jihad against the Jews and Christians of the Middle East, and ultimately against the United States . . . Unfortunately the lies of the MSA (like its sister organizations CAIR and the Muslim American Society) are successful in snookering the willing accomplices of the political left and the unwitting accomplices of the inattentive middle to support and protect them.[84]

The logic of these new McCarthyites is that there are no "good Muslims" and that Muslim organizations, despite their stated intentions, are really front groups for the Muslim Brotherhood or the Wahhabis, who intend to attack Jews and Christians. While this rhetoric is extreme and represents the conspiracy theories of right-wing racists, they are just one step removed from the FBI and New York Police Department "radicalization" theories discussed in Chapter 6. The propaganda video *The Third Jihad*, which was shown to New York City police officers as part of their training, demonstrates this overlap between the new McCarthyites and the security establishment. The list of interviewees for this pseudodocumentary included not just right-wing Islamophobes but also figures such as New York City police commissioner Ray Kelly, former New York City mayor Rudolph Giuliani, former CIA director James Woolsey, former head of Homeland Security Tom Ridge, and Connecticut senator Joe Lieberman.[85] In their division of labor, the role for people like Horowitz is to win over public opinion through propaganda. Horowitz organized Islamofascism Awareness Week, which brought prominent anti-Muslim zealots to college campuses in 2007. His Freedom Center is affiliated with Robert Spencer's Jihad Watch, and Spencer's articles on jihad appear regularly in Horowitz's *Front Page* magazine.

Fear Inc. shows the interconnections between various Islamophobic warriors and the extent to which they coordinate their activities. The Islamophobia campaign has brought neocons together with other kindred spirits. In short, right-wingers of all stripes have united to foster anti-Muslim racism. However, as the Cordoba House controversy showed, the liberal establishment, which had initially supported the project, caved under pressure. This became the moment when the new McCarthyites could expand their base and, as stated above, triple the number of anti-Muslim hate groups within a year.

A note on the sources of funding for these groups is in order. Seven foundations contributed close to $43 million to these new McCarthyites between 2001 and 2009. The main funders were the Donors Capital Fund (DCP), the Richard Mellon Scaife Foundations, the Lynde and Harry Bradley Foundation, the Newton D. and Rochelle F. Becker Foundation and charitable trust, the Russell Berrie Foundation, Anchorage Charitable Fund and William Rosenwald Family Fund, and the Fairbrook Foundation.[86] Of these, the DCP, an offshoot of Donors Capital (DC), is associated with the Koch brothers. In 2008 alone, they poured $17 million into the distribution of the film *Obsession: Radical Islam's War with the West*, which postulates that the threat of "Islam" is comparable to Nazism.[87] Between the years 2009 and 2015, the biggest recipient of DCP/DC funds was Pipes's Middle East Forum, but Gaffney's CSP and Horowitz's Freedom Center also benefited from their money.[88] These Islamophobic groups continue to thrive and to channel ideas and funds to their European counterparts. The Spinwatch report shows that three giant corporate donor-advised funds (Fidelity, Vanguard, and Schwab Charitable Fund) have contributed millions to the Islamophobia network.[89]

The Becker and Berrie foundations are explicitly committed to promoting what they see as the interests of the Jewish community (specifically Zionism), and a third, the Fairbrook Foundation, is even more extreme in its Zionist orientation. Since the publication of *Fear Inc.* in 2011, these three foundations have stopped direct donations to Islamophobic groups. However, the 2019 Spinwatch report shows that they use donor-advised funds such as those mentioned above and others to achieve these aims.[90] Fairbrook is run by Aubrey and Joyce Chernick and "has provided funding to groups ranging from the Anti-Defamation League (ADL) and CAMERA, a right-wing, pro-Israel, media-watchdog outfit, to violent Israeli settlers living on Palestinian lands and figures like the pseudo-academic author Robert Spencer," according to Blumenthal.[91] Chernick also contributes to Washington Institute for Near East Policy and the Hudson Institute. These right-wing foundations and groups do not represent the views of the majority of Jewish Americans, even though they may claim to. An August 2011 Gallup poll asked respondents in various religious groups if they thought that American Muslims are sympathetic to al-Qaeda. Seventy percent of Jewish Americans said no; the only groups with higher "no" percentages were Muslims and atheists.[92] Further, Jewish Voice for Peace, a national organization with a powerful social media platform, has not only fought for Palestinian rights but also against Islamophobia. In short, what on the surface appears to be an issue of religious intolerance is, at its core, a political and racialized issue. Conservatives of all stripes see Islamophobia as instrumental to advancing their agendas.

The Christian Far Right
The Christian Right is an integral part of the Islamophobia network; it too ardently supports Israeli occupation and settlement of Palestinian lands. For the Christian evangelical movement, Israel is of crucial importance; they believe that Jews will go back to Israel before the return of Christ. And while they also believe that Jews would be converted to Christianity, they firmly support a Jewish state in Palestine.[93] Thus, the Christian Right has lined up with other Zionists in demonizing Palestinians. At least since the 1980s, the Christian Right has been an important base for the Republican Party. In fact, the Christian Right and the GOP have become some of the most extreme Zionists (even if they believe that Jews can't get into heaven). This marks a shift from the 1970s and earlier, when Israel had a "social democratic" world image and liberal Democrats were the most ardent supporters of Zionism. The events of 9/11 further

solidified the Christian Right–neocon–Zionist alliance. The alignment of US and Israeli policy has meant, as Elaine Hagopian writes, "defining Arab/Muslim states and/or movements within them as terrorist or supporters of terrorism."[94] For the evangelicals, "the attacks on Israel by Palestinian suicide bombers are an important test in the global fight against Islamic terrorism."[95]

Thus, established, well-known evangelicals like John Hagee, Pat Robertson, Jerry Falwell, Franklin Graham, and Ralph Reed have added to Islam-bashing and extreme anti-Muslim racism. Graham has called Islam "a very evil and wicked religion." For Graham, "true Islam" advocates the beating of wives and the murder of adulterous children and therefore "cannot be practiced" in the United States.[96] Other imitators, such as the Florida pastor Terry Jones have capitalized on this hatemongering.[97] There are numerous connections between the religious Right and the rest of the Islamophobia network, including groups such as Christians United for Israel and the Tea Party movement. State and local groups, particularly in Tennessee, North Orange (California), and Florida enthusiastically climbed onto the Islamophobia gravy train.[98]

In Murfreesboro, Tennessee, the Tea Party and the religious Right ganged up to stop the construction of an Islamic center. They were assisted by groups like ACT! for America, founded by Lebanese-American Brigitte Gabriel (who is Christian), whose members were involved in rallies not only in Tennessee but also in Florida and other states. People like Gabriel play an important role in the Islamophobia network—they legitimize the racist attacks on Muslims through their personal testimony. Gabriel travels the country to promote the idea that Muslims are horrible people, based on her experience growing up in Lebanon. At a counterterrorism event at Duke University in 2004, she explained the differences between Muslims and Israeli Jews as follows: "It's barbarism versus civilization. It's democracy versus dictatorship. It's goodness versus evil."[99] Tellingly, her first book was titled *Because They Hate: A Survivor of Islamic Terror Warns America.*[100]

Ex-Muslims

A whole slew of people, mostly "ex-Muslims," have played a role in the legitimation of anti-Muslim racism. It is profitable to be an ex-Muslim because of the lucrative book deals, honoraria to speak at private and state-funded conferences, access to a wide network of media for self-publicity, and the ability to make connections to people in positions of power who can help advance careers. One such ideologue, Nonie

Darwish, is the director of Former Muslims United, co-founded by Wafa Sultan, Walid Shoebat, and Ibn Warraq. Darwish is of Egyptian origin and was raised in Gaza. She believes that Islam "will destroy itself because it's not a true religion."[101] Her books (*Now They Call Me Infidel: Why I Renounced Jihad for America, Israel and the War on Terror*, and *Cruel and Unusual Punishment: The Terrifying Global Implications of Islamic Law*) have been endorsed and supported by Pipes, Spencer, and Horowitz.[102]

Darwish and Shoebat, along with Walid Phares, a professor at the National Defense University and a Fox News contributor, regularly give lectures to the law enforcement community on "terrorism."[103] Phares leads seminars for government employees and addresses law enforcement and homeland security conferences. He offers courses on terrorism for the Centre for Counterintelligence and Security Studies (CI CENTRE), one of several Far Right operations that populate the antiterrorism training industry. As lawyer Thomas Cincotta writes, this antiterrorism training industry consists of "a panoply of companies that offer instruction in surveillance tactics, cyber-security, bomb detection, school safety, and critical infrastructure."[104] A subset of this industry consists of groups that offer courses to law enforcement agencies on "jihad" and the threat it poses to national security. Phares fills the minds of his audience with his conspiracy theories about a jihadist strategy to infiltrate key institutions in the United States such as the defense sector, the academy, and community organizations. His books include *Future Jihad: Terrorist Strategies Against America*, *The War of Ideas: Jihadism Against Democracy*, and *The Confrontation: Winning the War Against Future Jihad*.[105]

Shoebat similarly tells his audiences that CAIR and the Islamic Society of North America are "the terrorist arms of the lawmaker: Sharia, Koran and Hadith."[106] Shoebat is even more extreme than his fellow ex-Muslims. His newfound Christian beliefs hold that during the "end times" of biblical prophecy, Muslims will fight alongside Satan on Earth.[107] Despite these outlandish claims (or perhaps because of them), he is enthusiastically promoted by his colleagues in the Islamophobia network. Gaffney gushed, "In the twenty-five years I have been in Washington I have never heard anything so extraordinary and *the truth* told so eloquently by someone like this," [emphasis added].[108] In 2011, he was paid $5,000 by the Department of Homeland Security to speak at a South Dakota law enforcement conference.[109]

The New McCarthyites, the Media, and the Security Establishment

The promotion of people with such extreme views as "educators" to the law enforcement community prompted Cincotta and Political Research Associates to issue a report on three counterterrorism training organizations: the International Counter-Terrorism Officers Association, Security Solutions International, and the CI CENTRE. These groups employ right-wing Islamophobes and regularly organize conferences for law enforcement personnel. In this environment, the new McCarthyites don't stick out for their outlandish views; in fact, they fit quite comfortably within the established legal and political structures and often share a stage with mainstream figures from the security establishment.

For instance, CI CENTRE's 2010 "Spy Cruise," an intelligence-themed conference held on a cruise ship, listed former CIA directors Porter Goss and Michael Hayden as speakers. (Goss's speech had the telling title "Radical Fundamentalism and [Judeo-Christian] Western Civilization are Irreconcilable.")[110] When the FBI uses the work of Robert Spencer and the Orientalist Raphael Patai in its trainings, it does so because that work fits with their existing ideological framework, or to be precise with the views of the conservative section of the FBI and the security apparatus. *Wired* magazine found and exposed a PowerPoint presentation by the FBI's Law Enforcement Communications Unit that drew from the Islamophobic warriors' highly distorted view of Islam.[111] In response to this and perhaps other revelations, the Obama administration called for a reexamination of the counterterrorism material used by government agencies.[112] Indeed, there are differences within various branches of government about how to view "Islamic terrorism," as previous chapters have illustrated.

In addition to this "educational" role within the security apparatus, the Islamophobia network also broadcasts its views to the public. It does so not only through the right-wing media, such as the Christian Broadcasting Network, Fox News, and the rest of the Murdoch empire, but also through the mainstream media, where their troglodyte racism goes mostly unchallenged. Apart from a few reports such as those by Anderson Cooper of CNN, who did an exposé on Walid Shoebat,[113] and a few stories on NPR, this disturbing trend has been largely ignored. In fact, people like Steven Emerson have easy and ready access to the mainstream media. Leading newspapers have quoted him as a "terrorism expert," his columns have appeared in the *Wall Street Journal,* and NBC employed him as a terrorism analyst—featuring him fifty times in just the first two months after 9/11.[114] Similarly, between September 2001 and September 2002, Daniel Pipes appeared 110 times on television and did 450 radio interviews.[115]

One example illustrates how Islamophobic propaganda is amplified in the mainstream media. The new McCarthyites have long claimed that 80 percent of mosques are controlled by jihadists. In 2004, Republican congressman Peter King stated on the Fox News network's *Sean Hannity Show* that "eighty to eighty-five percent of mosques in this country are controlled by Islamic fundamentalists." He backed up his claim by citing the research of Emerson and Pipes.[116] This story was repeated again and again by the Islamophobes, even in the mainstream media. In 2010, Pamela Geller stated that "four out of five mosques preach hate" on CNN.[117] In March 2011, Republican representative Peter King held hearings on the supposed radicalization in American Muslim communities. A few months later, in June 2011, Yerushalmi made the same claim in the spurious report mentioned above. Gaffney immediately endorsed the findings in his column in the *Washington Times*.[118] The upshot of this propaganda is that few in the media challenged the King hearings, giving credence to the notion that Muslims are in fact being "radicalized" and need to be questioned and monitored in ways similar to the "reds" in the Cold War era. This was also the year when Obama unveiled his Countering Violent Extremism program, which set out to uncover radicalization by deputizing members of the Muslim community to act as surveillance agents.

The overall dynamic is one in which the right-wing media are the hubs of Islamophobic propaganda, which then spills over into the mainstream media through the Islamophobic warriors or through sympathetic politicians. The political center then adapts and moves further to the right. In the case of the Cordoba House controversy, the Democrats added fuel to the fire and helped to bring Islamophobic rhetoric into the mainstream albeit in less crass ways and through the language of liberal Islamophobia. Several mainstream figures have also played this role, and it is to them that we turn next.

Mainstream and Liberal Enablers

The more sophisticated counterparts to Gabriel, Shoebat, and Phares are people like Ayaan Hirsi Ali, Fouad Ajami, Azar Nafisi, Irshad Manji, Kanan Makiya, and Ibn Warraq. These individuals have much more access to the mainstream media because their language is more "reasonable," and they are promoted by powerful political figures. Hamid Dabashi, in his book *Brown Skin, White Masks*, argues that these people, to whom he refers as "native informers," reinforce anti-Muslim racism through their dismal accounts of their countries of origin. Immediately after 9/11,

> comprador intellectuals [particularly of Iranian, Arab, and Pakistani origin] were actively sought out by the militant ideologues of the US empire. Their task was to feign authority, authenticity, and native knowledge by informing the American public of the atrocities taking place in the region of their birth, thereby justifying the imperial designs of the United States as a liberation.[119]

He adds that this logic "has been at times explicit, as in the writings of Fouad Ajami and Kanan Makiya during the build up to the invasion of Iraq; at times implicit, as in the cases of Nafisi and Hirsi Ali."[120]

Ayaan Hirsi Ali had a short career in Dutch politics before accepting a position at the neocon-dominated American Enterprise Institute think tank. Ali, who is originally from Somalia, was forced to resign her seat in Parliament after it was revealed that she lied in her application for political asylum in the Netherlands.[121] The neocons welcomed her with open arms, and her book *Infidel* became a *New York Times* bestseller for a few weeks. After her journey across the Atlantic, she penned *Nomad: From Islam to America: A Personal Journey through the Clash of Civilizations*, recycling the tired myths of the supposed clash in values between Islam and the West. In 2015 she published *Heretic: Why Islam Needs a Reformation Now*.[122]

Azar Nafisi similarly journeyed from Iran to the United States, where she became a protégé of Bernard Lewis, a colleague of Fouad Ajami at Johns Hopkins, and an employee of Paul Wolfowitz.[123] Her memoir *Reading Lolita in Tehran* is the story of how she saved seven students in Tehran by inviting them to her house to teach them about Nabokov's *Lolita* and other literary classics in the Western canon.[124] In so doing, Nafisi succeeds in rewriting Iran's history and turning its people into caricatures. As Dabashi writes, the "entirety of Iran as a nation, a culture, a society, a reality fades out behind the tale of a self-indulgent diva very pleased with her heroic deeds and quixotic victories."[125] Yet *Reading Lolita in Tehran* is much more subtle than the blatant propaganda of the far right. As Persian literature scholar Fatemeh Keshavarz writes, new

Orientalist narratives do "not necessarily support overt colonial ambitions" but they do have a "preference for a western political and cultural takeover" even while they erase "the complexity and richness of the local culture."[126] As a result, *Reading Lolita in Tehran* "prepare[s] the American public for a tough line on Iran. The seldom smiling monsters that emerge from the memoir do not seem to be doing anything other than hating, fighting, suppressing women, and trampling the American flag."[127] The book was on the *New York Times* bestseller list for more than a hundred weeks. It was translated into dozens of languages and has been widely adopted into course syllabi in campuses across the United States. Meanwhile, Moustafa Bayoumi came under attack for the use of *How Does it Feel to Be a Problem?* in classes for "force feeding" students with only "one point of view."[128] Racism thrives and is promoted, anti-racism is attacked.

Ali, Nafisi, and Manji (a Canadian of Egyptian and South Asian descent) have contributed most to the argument that the United States should defend human rights and women's rights in the "Muslim world." To quote Dabashi again:

> Next to national-security interests, human rights and women's rights in particular are now routinely cited as principal objectives of American imperial interventions. The role of Hirsi Ali, Nafisi, Irshad Manji, and their ilk is to speak on behalf of such insights as integral to the humanitarian mission at the heart of American imperialism. Offering, in English for the American and European market, a fierce critique of women's rights in Iran (Nafisi) or genital mutilation in Africa (Hirsi Ali) or gay and lesbian rights in Islam across the board (Irshad Manji) places the authority to right those wrongs in the hands of foreign readers and their elected officials, rather than the societies affected.[129]

Thus, rather than stand in solidarity with men and women in Muslim-majority countries who are fighting for rights of various kinds and against US-backed dictators, Ali and company invoke the rhetoric of the white man's burden.

The discourse of human rights has been central to the neocon propaganda war, even if sections have taken a more blatantly racist position. It is therefore important to recognize that recourse to such liberal rhetoric isn't simply the bastion of the liberal imperialists; it is at the heart of neoconservatism as well. What is different in the rhetoric of the liberal imperialists is that it attempts to separate Islam from Islamism as seen in the work of the late Christopher Hitchens, Paul Berman, Martin Amis,

Nick Cohen, Bernard-Henri Lévy, and Andrew Anthony.[130] Kundnani writes that these

> new liberals (correctly) put aside these arguments about the nature of Islam and the patterns of Islamic history [as articulated by Lewis and the Orientalists] and, instead, focus their attention on Islamism, a modern political movement, which they (incorrectly) take to be analogous to Stalinism or fascism. Islamism is regarded as an appropriation of modern European totalitarianism that is basically alien to "traditional Islam."[131]

The distinction between Islam and Islamism is important, not least because it insulates the liberals from straightforward charges of racism. If the focus is on a twentieth-century political ideology with European roots rather than a religion, then it is seen as legitimate.

Christopher Hitchens, once a regular columnist for the *Nation* magazine, became in his later years an outspoken liberal Islamophobe. In his book *God Is Not Great*, he took aim at all religions, arguing that religion "poisons everything" and was responsible for creating tyrannical regimes both in ancient and modern times.[132] His criticisms, however, were selective: he indicted Saddam Hussein for using Islam for political gain but had nothing to say about the born-again George W. Bush and his recourse to religion to justify his policy objectives. Hitchens went on to blame Islam for the horrible state of Iraq after the US-led invasion and occupation. In the final analysis, despite his equal-opportunity critique of the world's major religions, his book serves to prop up US foreign policy and erase the millions killed by US wars and sanctions. This is hardly surprising given that he "gravitated towards the neoconservatives, [was] feature[d] frequently on right-wing talk-shows, and [was] regularly seen with David Horowitz."[133] Hitchens, along with evolutionary biologist Richard Dawkins and author Sam Harris, are a trio called the "new atheists." Unlike the religious section of the right-wing Islamophobes, these authors have used atheism to target Islam, although the rhetoric often resembles the hysterical denunciations from the Right. As Lean writes, the "new Atheists became the new Islamophobes, their invectives against Muslims resembling the rowdy, uneducated ramblings of backwoods racists rather than appraisals based on intellect, rationality and reason."[134] Dawkins has praised Geert Wilders, whose blatantly racist comments about Muslims are quite shocking. Wilders referred to Moroccan immigrants as "scum" who make Dutch streets "unsafe."[135]

In contrast, other liberal imperialists like Michael Ignatieff and Paul Berman are more hesitant to be openly associated with the Right and with neoconservatives.[136] Berman, who is part of what he calls the "anti-totalitarian" left, supported the 2003 war on Iraq because "al-Qaeda . . . and Saddam's Baath Party are two of the tendencies within a much larger phenomenon, which is a Muslim totalitarianism."[137] As Kundnani notes, Hitchens shared with Berman the view that

> as soon as the West had won its historic battle against communism, a new totalitarianism—Islamism—emerged as a political force. The West, it is argued, is morally obliged to expunge this totalitarian threat both in the Islamic world and among its own Muslim communities.[138]

Thus, although liberal racists tend to use more subtle language, they ultimately end up making a similar argument to the neocons and the Islamophobic warriors.[139] All are united in their support for imperialism, and racism furnishes them with tools to justify empire. Like his liberal counterparts, Daniel Pipes has argued that "what Nazism or fascism was to World War II and Marxist/Leninism was to the Cold War, militant Islam is to this war [the war on terror]."[140]

Last but not least are groups like the ADL who enjoy a reputation as being civil rights organizations, but who have participated in the normalization of anti-Muslim racism. The ADL, as noted above, is funded by right-wing organizations and has been part of a systematic effort to target Muslims and pro-Palestinian activists. It hired George Selim who played a key role in the Department of Homeland Security Countering Violent Extremism program as the director of its anti-bias education program.[141] A 2020 primer on the ADL titled *The ADL Is Not an Ally* stated that while the ADL claims to oppose Islamophobia, "even offering anti-Islamophobia training as part of its anti-bias package," it does so on its own terms. The report notes that

> when the targets of US and Israeli Islamophobia and state violence speak for themselves, the ADL attacks them. (The same is true of anti-Black racism: the ADL says it opposes it, but polices Black organizers, attacking when it decides that they "misunderstand" racism or have been "distracted" by intersectional organizing with Arabs, Muslims, or Palestinians.)

The ADL belongs in the liberal camp since it does not use the crass language of the Far Right. It has also promoted the notion of a "good

Muslim," thereby "reinforcing both the idea of an existential conflict between Muslims and the West, and its own credentials as a promoter of 'tolerance.'"[142] For the ADL, Islamophobia is about religious intolerance, which it opposes, and not anti-Muslim racism rooted in empire, which it eschews, not unlike the authors of the *Fear Inc.* report.

Sadly, various Muslim groups have accepted this moniker of "good Muslim." In a deeply racist society, oppressed groups, through a process that W. E. B. Du Bois calls "double consciousness," come to see themselves through dominant categories.[143] Thus, as Zareena Grewal writes, "Muslim Americans leaders-turned spokespeople affirm their positive identification with the US as good, flag-waving citizens, identifying Islam in terms of normative definitions of a good religion and claiming a space in the cultural mainstream through the disavowal and identification of bad Muslims and bad Islam."[144] The rabid racism of the Far Right fuels a defensive response, which comes from an understandable desire to demonstrate that American Muslim organizations are not terrorist fronts and that the overwhelming majority of Muslims do not turn to terrorist tactics. Thus, CAIR has stated on its website that it believes that "it is both our civic and religious duty to work with law enforcement to protect our nation."[145] However, as Stephen Sheehi argues, this posture is also part of a "long tradition of Muslim American and Arab American communities' collective, communal collaboration with white America and the U.S. government" which results in these "communities' complicity with race and class privilege in the United States."[146] When groups like Islamic Society of North America and CAIR set out to demonstrate that Muslim Americans "are patriotic, civilly engaged, philanthropic, and politically active (especially as voters)," they play a role in legitimizing "the American government's geopolitical interests."[147] In assuming responsibility for national security and routinely denouncing "bad Muslims," these groups validate the war on terror and liberal Islamophobia.

Sheehi argues that Middle Eastern (both Arab and Iranian) and South Asian Muslims, who make up 45 percent of American Muslims, are overwhelmingly upper-middle class. This class position explains their assimilationist approach, which allows them to "maintain a sense of ethnic belonging while also benefiting from the class privileges that are firmly rooted in middle-class white America."[148] Not surprisingly, he adds that even while some CAIR chapters and other groups have endorsed Black Lives Matter and taken anti-racist positions, they prefer to eschew talking about race and racism altogether. Thus, they engage Islamophobia in terms of religious tolerance rather than as the racism that enables empire. Nazia Kazi similarly highlights the class background of mainstream Muslim organizations. Her important ethnographic research shows that "without fail, Muslim sermons, panel discussions, and community events" include "a condemnation of ISIS, terrorism, or violence against civilians." While it is not wrong to denounce such violence, to do so without a similar denunciation of the far greater violence of the United States lends itself to an acceptance of the war on terror as the appropriate way to deal with groups like ISIS. In trying to gain legitimacy in the mainstream, Kazi argues that these "good Muslims" fall into a "slippery slope" between condemning violence and "being an implicit advocate for the US 'war on terror.'"[149] This process validates imperial ethnocentric racism, which categorizes people as either "good" or "bad" Muslims based on their support for empire and gives credence to the war on terror.

Liberal Islamophobia enthusiastically incorporates "good Muslims" as a way to counter and diffuse charges of racism. In the lead up to the 2016 elections, Trump's blatant anti-Muslim racism was countered by Hillary Clinton's campaign through the use of "good" Muslims. Khizr Khan, the father of a fallen soldier and an avowed patriot, offered his copy of the constitution to Trump.[150] The terms of inclusion involved an acceptance of empire: his son had to give his life in service to US militarism and Khizr Khan had to overlook the Democrats' bending of the constitution and violations of international law.

Conclusion

This chapter demonstrates that a wide range of people and groups have participated in constructing a diabolical "Islamic threat." Together they are responsible for the most blatant and right-wing forms of anti-Muslim racism. The Islamophobia network includes a section of the neocons, Zionist organizations, Christian fundamentalists, and right-wing ex-Muslims from the Middle East and South Asia. A significant number of these new McCarthyites have connections with establishment figures or are themselves from the foreign policy establishment, the military, the CIA, the Department of Defense, or other branches of the security apparatus. They sit comfortably with one another at conferences and counterterrorism training sessions. Their arguments are made more palatable by the liberal Islamophobes who populate the academy, the mainstream media, and various think tanks. In short, the new

McCarthyites aren't aberrations in an otherwise fair and neutral system, despite their rabidly racist views, but an integral part of it.

The dynamic is one where liberal and conservative Islamophobia create fertile ground for right-wing Islamophobia to flower. If the range of acceptable political discussion goes from a differentiation between "good" and "bad" Muslims (imperial ethnocentric racism) to a denunciation of Islam as the driving force of violence (neoconservative anti-Muslim racism), then conspiracy theories that Muslims are a fifth column trying to take over the United States and create an Islamic state find greater resonance. The Ground Zero Mosque controversy demonstrated this dynamic at work. In the context of a Far Right attack using language that harks back to the Crusades, the best arguments from the political class were weak defenses of religious freedom. Instead of taking a principled anti-racist position that states that Muslims are no more to blame for the events of 9/11 than Christians are for the violence of Christian fundamentalists, the liberal establishment chose to question the location of the proposed Islamic center. While less blatant than the rabid Islamophobes who were accusing Muslims of "triumphalism," such an argument tacitly endorsed collective blame on all Muslims for the attacks on the Twin Towers. Obama further chose to counter the Far Right, raising the specter of suicide bombing, thereby justifying his own security measures. Such "indirect securitization," however, also essentializes and homogenizes Muslims. Liberal racism of this sort then feeds right-wing conspiracy theories.

This is also the context in which to make sense of Trump's election victory in 2016. Trump's victory was possible in part because he was able to tap into a base of supporters inclined to believe his conspiracy theories. The "silent majority" swept him to victory. His appointment of rabid right-wing Islamophobes strengthened troglodyte racism. Michael Pompeo, secretary of state in the Trump administration, was such a racist. After the Boston Marathon bombing, he claimed that the supposed silence of Muslim leaders made them "potentially complicit in these acts and, more importantly still, those that may well follow."[151] Brigitte Gabriel of ACT for America stated that Pompeo has been "a steadfast ally of ours since the day he was elected to Congress." Pompeo was given the "highest honor" bestowed by ACT in 2016, the National Security Eagle Award. Gaffney describes Pompeo as "one of the most intelligent men I know in public life." Along with Yerushalmi, Pompeo believes that mainstream Muslim American organizations are fronts for the Muslim Brotherhood.[152]

John Bolton was another Trump appointee closely associated with the Islamophobia network. He has served as chairman of the notorious anti-Muslim think tank, the Gatestone Institute. While he oversaw the group, it published articles like "Islam's 'Quiet Conquest' of Europe" and "Refugees of an Occupation Army?" He also was the keynote speaker at a conference entitled "Islam and Western Civilization: Can They Coexist?" organized by the Far Right American Freedom Alliance. He has a long history of collaboration with Pamela Geller and Robert Spencer and wrote the Foreword for their 2010 book, *The Post-American Presidency: The Obama Administration's War on America.*[153] But it is perhaps Stephen Miller who was the most notorious of Trump's various appointees. As a member of the Conservative Union at Duke University, Miller consorted with Richard Spencer and would go on to invent the term "alt-right" and become one of the leading white nationalists in the country. Miller has long been an advocate of framing the fight against terrorism in religious terms. While at Duke, he launched the Terrorism Awareness Project that organized "Islamo-Fascism Awareness Week" to raise awareness about "the Islamic jihad and the terrorist threat, and to mobilize support for the defense of America and the civilization of the West."[154] He was the main architect of Trump's domestic attacks on Muslims and immigrants.

When the authors of *Fear Inc.* insist that the Islamophobic Right are a "fringe" and that anti-Muslim racism is not a significant problem in the United States, they not only fail to acknowledge how the individuals they name sit comfortably within the imperial infrastructure but also discount the dialectical relationship between liberal, conservative, and Far Right racism. After all, more than 70 million people voted for Trump in 2020.[155] It is no wonder then that by 2020, QAnon, the internet-based social movement with religious underpinnings that peddles a range of conspiracy theories, gained ascendance.[156] The core claim of this movement is that an elite Satan-worshiping cabal has corrupted the United States and runs a global child-sex trafficking ring. QAnon followers believe that top military generals recruited Trump to run for the presidency in 2016 in order to break up this cabal. Largely a fringe movement, it went mainstream in the summer of 2020, spreading conspiracies about Covid-19, the Black Lives Matter protests, and the presidential election. QAnon also claimed that wearing masks during the pandemic will lead to the full burqa in a few years and the institution of Sharia in the United States.[157]

With the election of Joe Biden in 2020, troglodyte racism is not going to have the same platform as it did under Trump. However, these forces are not marginal but very much a central part of US imperialism. In this sense, their overt racism exists on a continuum with covert racism. As Hilary Aked, Melissa Jones, and David Miller, authors of the important Spinwatch report, argue, official counterterrorism and counterextremism policy sets the terrain on which the counterjihad movement and the Far Right can operate. Indeed, various models of radicalization combined with the Obama administration's Countering Violent Extremism initiative put a spotlight on "homegrown terrorism." This "green scare" then created fertile grounds for the growth and expanded reach of the conspiracy theories of the Right. Thus, to see the counterjihad movement, or the new McCarthyites, in isolation is to miss the broader dynamic at work. At the end of the day, the Islamophobia network is one part of an overall system that serves to reproduce empire. It is to this system, the "matrix of anti-Muslim racism," that we turn to next in the Conclusion.

Conclusion: Empire and the Matrix of Anti-Muslim Racism

This book has argued that empire, in various forms, has served as the crucible of anti-Muslim racism. In Chapter 1 we saw how Spain, the leading empire in the period of mercantile imperialism, developed possibly the first biological notion of race through its blood purity laws. The full force of these laws was applied first to Sephardic Jews and then to Spanish Muslims. Both groups faced systematic discrimination over a long period of time and were expelled in a process that we would today call ethnic cleansing. However, this was still a nascent form of racism, or protoracism, since it combined religious persecution with modern bodily or somatic notions of race. Muslim converts or *moriscos* occupied a liminal space between inferiority and superiority, the latter due in no small part to their association with the powerful Ottoman Empire and various kingdoms of North Africa. As such, the early modern era, the period of transition from the Middle Ages to the modern era, retained certain social relations from the previous period while also prefiguring what was to come next.

The rise of Britain and its hegemony in the period of capitalist imperialism gave rise to modern post-Enlightenment forms of anti-Muslim racism. Britain in the early modern era was in no position to dominate the formidable Ottomans, and the Turks were seen as equals if not superior to other European empires. While there were contradictory representations in various spheres, in the political and economic spheres the Turks were respected. A combination of factors changed this attitude, not least among them various revolutions including the Industrial Revolution and the American, French, and Haitian Revolutions, which brought about tumultuous changes ushering in the modern era based ostensibly on equal rights. I argued that two ingredients were necessary for full-blown anti-Muslim racism: the notion of "free" societies and the ability of European nations, like Britain and France, to finally challenge and dominate once powerful Muslim empires. Institutional Orientalism as a mode of colonial rule gave rise to *Homo islamicus,* which created Muslims in the Middle East and North Africa (MENA) as a homogeneous race. South Asian Muslims and Hindus were also part of a complex process of creating essentialized colonial subjects collectively understood as "Orientals." Religious forms of othering that were central in earlier periods of colonialism gave way to scientific racism.

Spanish, British, French, and US imperialisms have all been important vessels for the development of anti-Muslim racism, each with its own specific national characteristics and variations. Chapter 2 laid out how colonial America and the United States inherited British modes of racializing Muslims. Anglo settlers and colonial administrators deployed similar derogatory tropes against Native Americans and Turks. While Orientalism has a complex history in the United States, I argued that it is US imperial domination of the MENA region and South and Central Asia after World War II that led to the creation of anti-Muslim racism as an ideology and systematic practice of oppression. Postwar US imperialism set the stage for vulnerability to premature death for people in the MENA region and South and Central Asia and racist targeting inside the United States. Chapter 3 presented six ideological frames that constitute the core of Islamophobia. Chapter 4 focused on imperial ethnocentric racism and the construction of "good" and "bad" Muslims as well as on liberal and neoconservative Islamophobia. In Chapter 5, I traced the continuities and discontinuities between the Bush, Obama and Trump administrations in terms of foreign policy and the racialized Muslim abroad. Chapter 6 discussed domestic policy and the terrorization of the racial Muslim. In Chapter 7, I demonstrated the dialectical relationship between liberal, conservative, and right-wing Islamophobia.

Here I outline the infrastructure of empire created in the post–World War II era to shed light on the multiple spheres that are productive of anti-Muslim racism. I bring together the various arguments advanced in this book to offer a map that I call the "matrix of anti-Muslim racism."

The Infrastructure of Empire

The 1947 National Security Act made security a key element of the postwar order, creating the Office of the Secretary of Defense, the Joint Chiefs of Staff, the National Security Council, and the Central Intelligence Agency. This new and growing infrastructure of the postwar imperial state was presented not as an expansion of US power and hegemony on the global stage, but rather as a form of defensive security, most evident in the renaming of the Department of War as the Department of Defense. Cold War liberals insisted that the United States was not an empire like other European colonial powers. Instead, drawing on a dominant myth in US politics regarding its place in the world, they argued that it was an exceptional state, a beacon for other nations because of its unique history and foundation. During the Cold War, the United States projected the image of itself as a stronghold of democracy and free markets, which was pitted against Soviet totalitarianism.

According to historian Thomas McCormick, the United States fought World War II "not simply to vanquish their enemies, but to create the geopolitical basis for a postwar world order that they would both build and lead." Viewing the United States as the worthy successor to Britain, diplomat Norman Davis asserted that "we shall in effect be the heirs of empire."[1] The most famous example of this strategic approach to the war was the 1944 Bretton Woods conference, where Washington succeeded in establishing the institutional architecture that would govern the postwar global economy and reinforce US dominance in international commerce and finance. US objectives, moreover, could only be met by abandoning any effort to distinguish between national and global security.

The building of a postwar global economy under US hegemony was no easy task, however, if only because of the devastation of European economies, decolonization movements that threatened access to raw materials, the spread of capitalism in the third world, and a domestic US public that was very reluctant to support the level of spending necessary to meet US imperial ambitions. To move ahead with postwar plans, it would become necessary to pursue a Cold War posture that was both much more militaristic and more third world oriented and that ultimately depended on "scar[ing] the hell out of the American public."[2] Fear mongering has been central to the Cold War and the war on terror; it is an important mechanism through which a vast imperial infrastructure is maintained.

The postwar grand strategy came to be embodied in the secret 1950 document "United States Objectives and Programs for National Security" (NSC 68), described by McCormick as one "of the most pivotal policy documents in American history." "In its final form," McCormick writes, "NSC 68 called not only for massive military spending but for significant tax increases to fund it, a reduction of social welfare programs and all services not related to military needs."[3] It also called for a civil defense program to ensure loyalty among the citizenry, a media propaganda campaign to build and sustain public support, and psychological warfare and propaganda programs abroad. Every aspect of life—social, political, intellectual, and economic—was conceived as playing a role in national defense, and a massive security establishment was constructed. A military-industrial complex was put in place.

Colin Powell has referred to this complex as the "terror industrial complex" in the twenty-first century, suggesting a continuity with the Cold War.[4] This terror industrial complex provides the infrastructure of what I call the "matrix of anti-Muslim racism." In what follows, I outline the spheres discussed throughout this book and place them together to illustrate the joint and interactive processes involved in the production of Islamophobia. The matrix, however, isn't the last word on this question. One could fruitfully expand a structural analysis of this sort with an examination of social media, privatized military and policing agencies, NGOs, charitable foundations, defense contractors, and various public and private entities, all of which are part of the terror industrial complex in the neoliberal era.

The Matrix of Anti-Muslim Racism

The graphic titled "Matrix of Anti-Muslim Racism," below on page 215, is a visual depiction of the key sources of Islamophobia and their impact on public discourse and policy. At the top are some of the leading institutions that set the terms of discussion and modes of organization. While the political and security apparatuses are central to the configuration of empire, the production of knowledge in the academy and in think tanks is also relevant. To be sure, these spheres are not equal in size and impact, with the political and security apparatuses (and the larger terror industrial complex) having an outsized role in shaping imperial politics both domestically and internationally. However, for the sake of symmetry the boxes are all the same size in the chart.

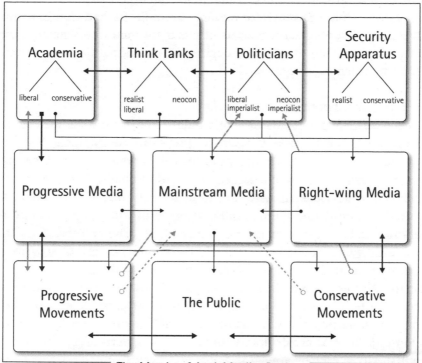

The Matrix of Anti-Muslim Racism

Moreover, these spheres are not monolithic, but consist of a plurality of visions broadly organized around liberal and conservative wings. Further, each of the domains is connected to one another as ideas and practices, and personnel from each move across these spaces. This is indicated by the arrows that connect the boxes. In terms of personnel, military generals become politicians, politicians take up positions within the academy, academics are recruited to be part of government task forces, and people in all of these spheres are part of the same think tanks. Significant numbers who inhabit these spaces also have ties to private industry, from military contractors to video game producers. In what follows, I clarify the role of each of these spheres as articulated in previous chapters and reiterate how the media, the public, and social movements play a role in the struggle for hegemony.

Significantly, the matrix is a way to visualize anti-Muslim racism as a process rather than as a fixed, close-ended project. As I have argued throughout, "race" once produced does not endure in the same form across time. While projects of racialization draw from past legacies, as well as coterminous racial regimes, context is central to how racism but also anti-racism operate. I have therefore employed a dialectical materialist mode of analysis that can capture contradiction and change within the totality of empire. The matrix with its many boxes, and the lines and arrows connecting these boxes, depicts the processual nature of racism and the struggle for hegemony.

The security apparatus

The security apparatus consists of a number of institutions such as the Department of Homeland Security, the FBI, the National Security Agency, the CIA, the Department of Justice, various city police departments, the military, and the legal system. Additionally, there are "fusion centers," where federal, state, and local security institutions cooperate and share knowledge. Fusion centers are government-run public–private entities and are part of a larger "homeland security enterprise," as the Department of Homeland Security puts it.[5] Yet, "homeland" security is intimately tied to overseas interests.

In Chapter 6, I outlined how these institutions together police and control the "suspect population" of Muslims. While the chapter focused on the domestic context, it also noted that practices developed in the domestic context are deployed abroad and vice versa. As political scientist Alfred McCoy argued in *Policing America's Empire*, practices of warfare, surveillance, and information gathering deployed to crush the resistance to US imperialism in the Philippines in the early twentieth century were brought back to the United States and informed the development of surveillance regimes domestically.[6] In subjugating the Filipinos, American soldiers often used anti-black racial epithets that they brought with them from home. In its decade-long pacification campaign, the US colonial regime created highly modern police and intelligence units, which developed innovative security techniques that helped to shape a new national security apparatus during World War I. These would be deployed successfully against dissident populations including black and brown activists. McCoy further suggests that the mass incarceration of Japanese Americans during World War II as well as the targeting of activists in the movements of the 1960s is the result of tactics developed in the Philippines. As we saw in Chapter 2, black Muslims in the Moorish Science Temple of America were surveilled and intimidated by the FBI in the 1930s; the Nation of Islam and its leaders were similarly targeted from the 1940s on. Arab Americans, Christian and Muslim, became part of this process in the late 1960s.

The period after 9/11 intensified the securitization of Islam. It generated a homogeneous "Muslim threat" that included not only Arab Americans but also South Asian Americans and black Muslims, among others. The racial Muslim was created as a security threat to be quelled domestically and internationally. On the global front, the wars on Afghanistan and Iraq were expanded to several other countries through drone warfare and other measures. The various branches of the military assisted by the CIA and other public and private security institutions have pursued US geopolitical interests under the guise of fighting terrorism. While some Islamists do turn to violence, the threat is exaggerated. Sociologist Charles Kurzman argues in *The Missing Martyrs: Why There Are so Few Muslim Terrorists* that while there is legitimate anger at imperialism in Muslim-majority nations, only a small number of people turn to terrorist tactics.[7] Yet, the actions of this minority have been deployed to generate a moral panic that sustains a massive national security state capable of advancing US imperial interests. In the process, tens of millions have been displaced and millions killed. The racialization at work involves a dehumanization of people targeted by the United States in various countries around the world who are subject not only to surveillance and torture but also drone warfare and airstrikes—in short, to a vulnerability to premature death.

The political class

Elected representatives in government at all levels have played an instrumental role in mobilizing Islamophobia. Posturing as "tough on terror" is a useful tactic during election season and plays a similar role to the "tough on crime" stance. Numerous politicians in both the Republican and Democratic Parties have resorted to anti-Muslim racism to advance their political careers. While Republican candidates are more blatant in their racist arguments, Democrats too deploy liberal Islamophobia as we saw in the analysis of the "Ground Zero Mosque" controversy. Liberal Islamophobes employ a politics of inclusion with the price tag involving an acceptance of empire and a willingness to aid the war on terror. Conservative and right-wing Islamophobes operate on the logic of exclusion such as bans and/or the removal of Muslim symbols from public spaces. Moreover, liberal, conservative, and right-wing anti-Muslim racism do not line up neatly along party lines. In 2015, in the lead-up to the presidential elections, the Institute for Public Accuracy compiled a list of statements by dozens of political figures to show that Trump's blatant anti-Muslim racism was simply part of a spectrum.[8]

Chapter 4 on the foreign policy establishment demonstrated that the "Islamic threat" has been mobilized by both the neocon and realist camps. Muslims, Arabs, Iranians, and South/Central Asians are deemed "good" or "bad" depending on whether they are for or against US aims—in other words, through the logic of imperial ethnocentric racism. While the neocons and liberal interventionists disagree on tactics and strategy, they are united in a shared vision of US global dominance. Chapter 5 explained the continuities and discontinuities between the Bush, Obama, and Trump administrations. When the strategy employed by the neocons in the Bush administration failed to accomplish their goals, the liberal interventionists resorted to new approaches in the Obama administration. Trump continued policies of previous administrations and introduced new ones. His illiberal hegemony, however, earned him the disapproval of the security establishment. He was replaced by Biden and the liberal interventionist camp. Through this period liberal and conservative anti-Muslim racisms have mutually reinforced one another, with one form or the other predominant at any moment. The price paid by the global victims of empire has been devastating. Moreover, while the two imperial camps disagree with one another, they also come together within bipartisan think tanks such as the Council on Foreign Relations and its influential journal *Foreign Affairs*.

Think tanks and academia

Knowledge production in think tanks and academic institutions has been critical for US imperial domination after World War II. The 1958 National Defense Education Act was passed with the aim of turning universities into centers for the generation of knowledge that would aid the Cold War aims of the United States. As described in Chapter 2, Orientalist modes of thinking made their way across the Atlantic both as bodies of work and through the movement of the actual bodies of scholars like Gibb and Lewis who trained generations of thinkers. Additionally, the particular mode of US economic imperialism laid the basis for modernization theory that was then applied to developing nations around the world. Both Orientalism and modernization theory were based on fundamentally racist notions about Muslim-majority countries and their people. Area studies programs, including Middle East studies, were dominated by these frameworks. Various academic institutions, with ample funding from the "Big 3" foundations (Ford, Rockefeller, and Carnegie), set up centers and programs to aid US imperial ambitions in the MENA region.

The rise of national liberation movements from India to Algeria in the postwar period brought new scholarship that challenged Orientalism and the modernization paradigm. Academics became less reliable as sources of instrumental knowledge. After the 1970s, the state developed a greater reliance on think tanks. In his book *Foreign Policy, Inc.: Privatizing America's National Interest*, historian Lawrence Davidson argues that the best-funded think tanks play a decisive role in shaping foreign policy and setting the terms of public discussion through their members' frequent appearances as "experts" in the mainstream media.[9] In Chapter 4, I outlined the various think tanks that have been central in shaping US attitudes toward the parties and movements of political Islam. Zionist think tanks and groups have played no small role in this process. Further, the collaboration between political elites in the United States and Israel created the conditions for the development of the Arab and later the Islamic terrorist threat. Two pivotal conferences organized by the Israeli Jonathan Institute brought together academics with political figures to create the groundwork for the production of the racialized terrorist threat.

Zionist think tanks and foundations are also part of the Islamophobia network, as Chapter 7 lays out. Various groups constitute the new McCarthyite configuration responsible for producing the most blatant and overt forms of anti-Muslim racism. The intellectual leadership is held by neoconservatives and the think tank Center for Security Policy (CSP). CSP played an important role in the anti-Sharia campaign, but it didn't act alone. Members who fit in the various boxes at the top of the figure on page 215 constantly interact and share ideas with one another. This can be seen, for instance, in the CSP report *Shariah: The Threat to America*.[10] This report featured articles by leading figures in the Islamophobia network but also by military generals (William Boykin, Edward Soyster), FBI and CIA officials (John Guandolo, James Woolsey), and others from the security establishment.[11] The range of interacting individuals and institutions is conveyed in the matrix by the connections between the boxes.

I am not aware of progressive think tanks that focus specifically on Islamophobia and take critical positions on the war on terror to the same extent as the think tanks that shore up centrist to right-wing positions. Thus, there is no line and arrow from think tanks to progressive media since it is not, as of this writing, a significant trend. However, various centers do contribute such perspectives as noted in several chapters, such as the Brennan Center for Justice, the Center for Constitutional

Rights, and the Institute for Policy Studies. George Soros's Open Society Foundations has spent millions of dollars in the United States supporting work that focuses on challenging Islamophobia, at least in overt forms, as part of its National Security and Human Rights program. Amnesty International and Human Rights Watch have also occasionally published reports and raised concerns about the treatment of Muslims in the United States.

Chapter 7 also described how notorious Islamophobes who peddle conspiracy theories have given lectures at security conferences and have held training workshops. *Wired* magazine's investigative reporting found that the "U.S. military taught its future leaders that a 'total war' against the world's 1.4 billion Muslims would be necessary to protect America from Islamic terrorists."[12] Among the various options that were put forward was to wipe out whole cities as was done with Hiroshima and to target the "civilian population wherever necessary." The Pentagon has since suspended such training, yet the officer responsible for giving these lectures, Army Lt. Col. Matthew A. Dooley, maintains his position within the military and the "commanders, lieutenant colonels, captains and colonels" who took his course and listened to his theories have since been placed in higher-level assignments in the military.[13] Under the Trump administration the far right was elevated to various positions of authority. Their think tanks and "experts" were able to push their agenda more successfully. Yet, in the struggle for ideological dominance there are very real debates between members of the political class, the security establishment, think tanks, and the academy. These debates play out in the establishment media, but social media also play a significant role.

The media
In *Policing the Crisis*, Hall et. al. argued that "folk devils" are produced by state actors whose repeated homogeneous statements typically present the menace as "out of all proportion to the actual threat offered."[14] Police officials, juridical actors, and politicians who are the "primary definers" formulate the rhetoric. The media, who are dependent on these official sources, then amplify the moral panic as secondary definers. As I have argued elsewhere and outlined in Chapter 2, the economic, social, and political crisis in the United States created the conditions for the genesis of the racialized Arab terrorist. However, there was no moral panic around the "Islamic terrorist" until after the events of 9/11. Since then a similar dynamic can be observed in the construction of the racialized terrorist threat by the primary definers in the top four boxes of the chart,

although academics critical of racism and empire have far less access to the corporate media.

During the Trump administration, fake news assumed a significant role in public life, and new dynamics came into play so that the boundary between primary and secondary definers was blurred.[15] Illegitimate news sites proliferated. In 2020, QAnon became a primary definer and source of news and information among certain segments of the population. Moreover, the primary definers do not all speak with a single voice even if they agree on the general premise that a war on terror, out of proportion to the actual threat presented by Islamists who turn to political violence, is necessary. Anti-Muslim racism manifests in reactionary, conservative, and liberal forms; all are articulated in the corporate media. During moments of crisis, such as a terrorist attack or a spectacle like the manufactured "Ground Zero Mosque" controversy, more extreme right-wing views enter the mainstream media through establishment political figures as well as right-wing pundits. But even during normal times, "journalists" like Steven Emerson have found outlets, such as on PBS, for their conspiracy theories. This is because the ideology of Islamophobia is ubiquitous, as demonstrated in Chapter 3. The six implicit ideological frames structure how journalists and news media producers view Muslims and Muslim-majority countries and as such they have become both primary and secondary definers policing the boundaries of what is considered to be the acceptable range of discussion. However, the media are contradictory institutions and can be pressured by both conservative and progressive movements.[16] In the figure, this is indicated by the dotted lines from the movements to the media. I have used dotted lines because movements are not a constant feature but rise up and become visible at certain moments, when they are covered by the corporate media, before retreating back into obscurity.

Further, the media are not a monolith and media and cultural products do not simply reflect dominant positions but play a constitutive role. As Kundnani and I have argued:

> The 9/11 Commission report, released in 2004, famously identified a "failure of imagination" as the basic problem with US national security policy. "Imagination is not a gift usually associated with bureaucracies," noted the report's authors. Preventing terrorist attacks in the future would require finding "a way of routinizing, even bureaucratizing, the exercise of imagination."[17] It was noted at the time that Tom Clancy's 1994 novel *Debt of Honor* had already imagined an airline

pilot flying a Boeing 747 into the US Capitol during a joint session of Congress, yet intelligence agencies themselves had not anticipated this possibility. In the War on Terror, it seemed, the erstwhile inability of security bureaucracies to imagine potential threat scenarios might be remedied by drawing on the creativity of Hollywood scriptwriters and right-wing pulp novelists. What was needed, it was thought, was to get inventive in conjuring up potential threats, as well as breaking down pre-existing assumptions of how best to prevent them. Hollywood was elevated in its role and became as significant as Arlington, Fort Meade, and Langley in the landscape of the US national-security state.[18]

There is a vast and well-funded right-wing media complex that spans legacy media such as Fox News, the Christian Broadcasting Network, the *New York Post,* and online platforms. In the digital age, bloggers such as Pamela Geller have risen to prominence, as noted in Chapter 7. Further, the Right has been involved in the production of documentaries that are widely distributed. For instance, the Clarion Project has financed and distributed a number of documentary films. In 2008, in the lead-up to the elections, a DVD copy of *Obsession: Radical Islam's War against the West* was inserted into seventy different newspapers and mailed to 28 million voters in swing states. *The Third Jihad* was shown to New York Police Department (NYPD) officers as part of their training.[19] The Clarion project was also responsible for a slick documentary called *Honor Diaries* that features a long list of native informants including Ayaan Hirsi Ali, who was also the film's executive producer.[20] Hirsi Ali also produced the Dutch film *Submission,* which similarly peddles imperial feminist tropes. Because so many foundations fund the activities of the Islamophobia network on a global scale, their media are significantly larger and more powerful than those of progressives. In the figure, the boxes representing progressive and right-wing media are the same size, but they are by no means equal in terms of resources or public impact as of this writing.

Progressive media do give voice to anti-racist arguments. Progressive media exist in a variety of forms from print media publications such as the *Nation* and *Teen Vogue*; radio and online news outlets like *Democracy Now!,* magazines like *Jacobin* as well as a slew of other alternative news websites such as the *Intercept*, Truthout and Commondreams; television shows on premium and network channels like *Last Week Tonight* with John Oliver or *Patriot Act* with Hasan Minhaj; and documentaries and short films. Further, civil rights and advocacy groups take out billboard campaigns and produce videos to fight Islamophobia. To be sure, as noted in the introduction, progressive media are also home to liberal Islamophobia. This too is contested space. Nevertheless, these sources more consistently give space to alternative and dissenting voices around empire, the war on terror, and anti-Muslim racism. Liberal and left-wing academics routinely contribute to progressive media as noted by the line connecting academia to progressive media. Academics, as well as some members in all the top boxes, also contribute to right-wing media; in the figure, the lines connecting the institutions at the top flow into the right-wing media as well.

Some members of the political class do contribute to pushing back against Islamophobia and the logic of the war on terror. This has been a perceptible trend after the election of four women of color in 2018 who together have been called "the Squad." Consisting of Alexandria Ocasio-Cortez of New York, Ilhan Omar of Minnesota, Ayanna Pressley of Massachusetts, and Rashida Tlaib of Michigan, the Squad have used their platforms as primary definers to bring anti-racist politics into the mainstream. Ilhan Omar and Rashida Tlaib have articulated positions against anti-Muslim racism and in support of Palestinian rights within the corporate media. However, an analysis of their appearances is likely to show that they face an uphill battle in trying to puncture the dominant Islamophobic ideology, not unlike what scholar Reza Aslan encounters (see Chapter 3). Progressive news shows like Stephen Colbert's *The Late Show* and others have amplified the voices of the members of the Squad as these shows reach a younger demographic more open to such critical positions. Additionally, the Squad have utilized social media to great effect. Indeed, the role of social media needs to be examined in greater depth to understand how resistance to anti-Muslim racism is both artic-ulated and mobilized for social justice.[21] One pivotal space in which resistance has been articulated is music. In his book *Rebel Music,* scholar Hisham Aidi explores the musical subcultures created by young Muslims around the world in the war on terror era.[22] He shows how hip hop and other musical genres including rock and reggae have articulated resis-tance to war on terror policies.

Social movements and the public

Three boxes appear at the bottom of the graph on page 215. The public is placed between conservative and progressive movements because both movements recruit from the public and attempt to influence public opinion.

Each of these movements shapes and is shaped by the mainstream media even while each is associated with mediated outlets that showcase its positions. Right-wing media and movements have far more resources that their progressive counterparts. This is likely to be the case for the foreseeable future until progressive movements are able to build stable grassroots institutions that attempt, among other things, to democratize the media and the political system.

Yet progressive movements even in the here and now have the ability to reshape the discussion and push back against racism, thereby impacting what political figures say and even pushing them a little further left, as indicated by the line from progressive movements to the politicians box. For instance, when Florida pastor Terry Jones threatened to burn Qurans, progressive protest movements erupted that pressured political figures to speak out against Jones. No Qurans were burned.

Resistance has been organized in various ways. Grassroots groups have mobilized against anti-Muslim bigotry, and communities of progressive lawyers have provided much-needed legal defense for besieged community members. The families of those targeted have been a continuous and constant source of resistance against anti-Muslim racism. Along with progressive lawyers, they have fought to win justice for their family members and to raise public consciousness and awareness. After the NYPD's "human mapping program" became public, DRUM (Desis Rising Up and Moving), a South Asian community organization that has been active around anti-Muslim racism, called demonstrations and press conferences. Activists in the Occupy Wall Street movement then took up this issue, helping to build rallies to call for the resignation of NYPD commissioner Ray Kelly. At these rallies, activists explicitly connected the NYPD's targeting of the black and Latino communities and the savage repression of Occupy Wall Street protestors with its racial profiling of Arabs and Muslims.

West coast social movement organizing in the Bay Area has brought together various anti-racist and immigrant rights groups. As Naber argues, 9/11 "expanded the possibilities for coalition building among activists engaged in homeland struggles in the diaspora (such as Palestinian or Filipino liberation)."[23] She shines a spotlight on how people with origins in the Philippines have been targeted inside the United States as a result of an imperial conception that the Philippines is al-Qaeda territory. These shared experiences of state persecution were productive of multiracial organizing in the aftermath of 9/11. However, one of the challenges that anti-racist movements have encountered, as Naber and Rana argue, is a failure to perceive anti-Muslim racism as racism rather than as religious discrimination.[24]

Liberal and radical students and faculty have long been a part of anti-racist and anti-imperial movements, and their participation often spills over into their research and teaching. The line from progressive movements to progressive media and the academy indicates this relationship between these three boxes. At times, the forces in these boxes do impact the mainstream media as well. For instance, in the context of the Ground Zero Mosque controversy, several scholars and activists were given platforms within the mainstream media. On September 11, 2010, progressives far outnumbered the Islamophobia network in two parallel demonstrations in downtown Manhattan. Thousands of New Yorkers of all shades and sizes marched to oppose the Far Right, chanting, "*Asalamu alaikum*, Muslims are welcome here." Because our movement grew so big and was so vocal, in the lead-up to and on the day of the protest, many dissenting voices were given time in the mainstream media. For instance, I was invited to speak on BBC's *Newshour* program, broadcast around the world, as one of the media spokespersons of our coalition. The protest poster, which several of us designed, is now displayed in the Museum of the City of New York as part of its installation marking significant protest movements in the city over the twentieth and twenty-first centuries. I say this not to toot my own horn but to make the point, from my own first-hand experiences, that struggle and resistance matter. Importantly, the forces of the Right who were largely bussed in from outside the city retreated in the face of a wide swath of forces coming together and standing up in opposition to their agenda. A mosque was created in downtown Manhattan in the proposed space. Through struggle, progressive actors were able to defeat the Right and, for a brief period, articulate anti-racist positions in the mainstream.

Thus, the imperial matrix contains its own contradictions. If anti-Muslim racism is produced and sustained within the infrastructure of empire, it can also be resisted. The matrix is a heuristic device that can help us understand how the balance of forces at any moment shapes anti-Muslim racism. It is open ended and context dependent so that an input at one end from one of the boxes at the top of the matrix does not guarantee a predetermined outcome in the media and in public opinion. While power is held by elites, this power is not absolute. The box I call the "Public" consists of people who are pulled both by progressive and conservative politics. A majority in this box are members of the working class, who have been ravaged in the neoliberal era and have sought explanations both on the Left and Right. In the context of mass struggles against neoliberal priorities, from the anti-globalization/global justice movements of the 2000s to Occupy Wall Street, the public can be won to a platform of progressive and even structural change. Indeed, at the height of the Black Lives Matter protests in June 2020, as much as 67 percent of the US public articulated support.[25] Race scholar Robin D. G. Kelley noted the multiracial character of these protests in contrast to earlier periods, which had fewer whites.[26] We might say that such protest movements, with deep organized roots in the community and in workplaces, have the capacity to move majorities in the direction of an anti-racist, anti-imperial, and anti-capitalist politics. The strikes of essential workers lacking supplies and support needed to deal adequately with the Covid pandemic were also an important part of the rebellion of the summer of 2020. Thus, in the heart of the imperial matrix are contradictions in the form of social forces that can not only challenge but also potentially tear the system down.

Yet, there is a lot of educational work to be done. Naber and Rana observe that for

> US social movements committed to dismantling US empire and racism there is a lot to gain from developing a clearer analysis of anti-Muslim racism and the ways it operates with ongoing US settler colonialism, the racist criminalization of Brown and Black immigrants, police violence, and the prison industrial complex.[27]

This book is a contribution to the existing work on these interconnections. I have argued that it is crucial to center anti-Muslim racism within empire, which is a global political and economic formation and which impacts a multitude of people. Understood this way, Islamophobia is not simply a form of religious misunderstanding or intolerance. Thus, while interfaith dialogue and education about Islam is useful, it is not enough. We also have to organize demonstrations, rallies, and other actions to make our collective voices heard when threats arise. But we need a strategy that not only deals with the immediate threats posed by the Far Right emboldened by the Trumps of the world, but also addresses the root causes that make these (and other) threats possible. In other words, we need to devise short-term tactics that put out fires in the present but without undermining the prospects for long-term change and thereby forcing us to confront even larger and more frequent fires in the medium to long term.

Combating anti-Muslim racism and various interconnected racisms more generally will require a great deal more than uniting in opposition to its most egregious manifestations. Moreover, it is necessary to recognize that anti-Muslim racism is systemic and not the product of a few "fringe" elements. From this flows the task of dismantling the institutional and structural foundations upon which anti-Muslim racism is built and which provide sustenance to its liberal, conservative, and reactionary variants. In other words, it is going to require a radical approach, one that gets at the very root of the problem, and that means, at a minimum, putting an end to the war on terror, dismantling the national security state, and undoing the class power that underpins that apparatus. That in turn is going to require the adoption of a politics that brings together various forms of oppression, racism alongside sexism, homophobia, transphobia, and ableism, both within workplace struggles and mass social movements on a global scale. This may seem like a tall order, but if we set our sights on anything short of that, we would be underestimating both the real threat that the world faces at this moment and how best to fight it.

Throughout this book I have adopted the Italian Marxist Antonio Gramsci's precept: pessimism of the intellect, optimism of the will. I ended the first edition of *Islamophobia* with the hope and optimism offered by the political revolutions known as the Arab Spring that began in the MENA region and spread around the world. In the years since I completed the first edition, there have been periods of rising struggle and defeat. However, the conditions that led to massive rebellions against the ravages of empire and the failures of the neoliberal system remain. Thus, in 2019 a new wave of struggle emerged that is being called the "second Arab spring."[28]

Conclusion

At the end of the day, the vast majority of people around the world are forced to live under a profoundly unjust and unequal system. The mass revolts in 2011 showed that this system and its warped priorities will not go unchallenged. The uprisings in Tunisia and Egypt spread not only to other countries in the region but also to Europe and the United States. Protestors learned strategy and tactics from one another as public spaces became key focal points for the movements. From Tahrir Square in Egypt to Pearl Square in Bahrain, the Puerta del Sol in Madrid, Syntagma Square in Athens, and Zuccotti Park in New York City, protest moments

self-consciously honored one another through solidarity greetings and
the imitation of tactics. In Madison, Wisconsin the fight against Republican Governor Scott Walker was seen as similar to that of the Egyptians
against Hosni Mubarak. Protestors carried signs that said, "Fight like an
Egyptian." Despite local differences, all of the movements were directed
against the neoliberal regime of the 1 percent and were both political and
economic struggles. Instead of feeling pity for their Arab and Muslim
brothers and sisters, activists in the West took inspiration from the
successes of their counterparts in Tunisia, Egypt, and Iran. In place of
the "white man's burden," a politics of international solidarity became
more visible.

To be sure, such international solidarity had existed in decades prior
to the 2010s. The national liberation struggles that swept the world from
India to Algeria in the postwar period rattled the centers of imperialism,
even as struggles were beginning to emerge inside Europe and the United
States. By the 1960s, radical social movements in countries around the
world rose up against capitalism, racism, and imperialism. Today, we are
in a similar but also different and new era. This is an era of victories but
also defeats, of highs and lows, of revolutions and counterrevolutions.
What is undeniable is the desire for change. What this brings is the
potential to create a brand new world free of racism and imperialism: a
new world where every individual will be treated with respect; a world
that will destroy empire and dump anti-Muslim racism into the dustbin
of history, and that will be the end of that.

Acknowledgments

I have acknowledged the various communities of scholars, students, and activists that I have had the privilege of being a part of in the introduction so here I will focus on the time, resources, and support that allowed me to finish my extensive revisions to this book. Rutgers University's Research Council Grant enabled to me obtain research help. In terms of time, I thank my union, the Rutgers AAUP-AFT, for the inaugural Paul Robeson fellowship that came with a course release. I thank Todd Wolfson for taking over the almost full-time job of the presidency of the union from me. Susan Keith helped free me from teaching duties in Fall 2020. All the revisions to the book were done in the late summer and fall, thanks to the time these wonderful colleagues created. I thank these brilliant people for reading small or large parts of this second edition and offering helpful feedback (in alphabetical order by first name): Ashley Smith, Bob Vitalis, Danielle Lussier, David Camfield, Gilbert Achcar, Helen Scott, Nazia Kazi, Patrick Barrett, and Peter Hervick. Arun Kundnani and Nadine Naber read the original draft of this manuscript, which was much longer. I deeply appreciate their brilliance, generosity, and extremely valuable feedback. I thank dear ones for intellectual as well as emotional support through various bouts of illness over the years (in alphabetical order by last name): Patrick Barrett, Anjali Ganapathy, Arun Kundnani, Scott LaMorte, Regina Marchi and Helen Scott. Finally, no work critical of empire is possible without political and personal support. I thank my union for its solidarity when Fox News attacked me in 2015. I was deluged by hate mail, death threats, and threats of sexual assault. My colleagues, comrades, and my union had my back. Sherry Wolf in particular was a rock. Without networks of solidarity this book would not exist. I thank Verso, and particularly Tariq Ali, for publishing this second edition.

Notes

Foreword

1. Ted Chaiban, "Palestinian Child Killed and Four Severely Injured in the West Bank in Past Two Weeks," UNICEF, December 4, 2020, unicef.org.
2. "Records on Countering Violent Extremism Program Reveal Previously Unknown Law Enforcement Ties," Henry Luce Foundation, September 10, 2020, hluce.org. Nicole Nguyen, *Suspect Communities: Anti-Muslim Racism and the Domestic War on Terror*, Minneapolis: University of Minnesota Press, 2019.
3. Laila Ujayli, "Biden and Global Islamophobia," *Reponsible Statecraft*, August 26, 2020, responsiblestatecraft.org.

Preface

1. David Vine, Cala Coffman, Katalina Khoury, Madison Lovasz, Helen Bush, Rachael Leduc, and Jennifer Walkup, *Creating Refugees: Displacement Caused by the United States' Post–9/11 Wars*, Brown University Costs of War Project, watson.brown.edu. Neta C. Crawford and Catherine Lutz, *Human Cost of Post–9/11 Wars: Direct War Deaths in Major War Zones, Afghanistan and Pakistan (October 2001–October 2019) Iraq (March 2003–October 2019); Syria (September 2014–October 2019); Yemen (October 2002–October 2019); and Other*, Brown University Costs of War Research Series, November 13, 2019, watson.brown.edu.
2. Jo Becker and Shane Scott, "Secret 'Kill List' Proves a Test of Obama's Principles and Will: Taking Personal Role in War on Al Qaeda," *New York Times*, May 29, 2012, A1.
3. Ruth Wilson Gilmore, *Golden Gulag: Prisons, Surplus, Crisis and Opposition in Globalizing California*, Berkeley: University of California Press, 2007, 28.

4. George Petras, Karina Zaiets, and Veronica Bravo, "Exclusive: US Counterterrorism Operations Touched 85 Countries in the Last 3 Years Alone," *USA Today*, February 25, 2021.

5. "Summary of Findings," Brown University Costs of War Research Series, n.d., watson.brown.edu.

6. Steve Garner and Saher Selod, "The Racialization of Muslims: Empirical Studies of Islamophobia," *Critical Sociology* 41: 1, 2015, 9–19.

Introduction: Islamophobia Is Anti-Muslim Racism

1. Albert Memmi, *The Colonizer and the Colonized*, Boston: Beacon Press, 1991, 85.

2. Andrew Shyrock argues that Islamophilia is the mirror opposite of Islamophobia. The latter is characterized by enmity and hatred, the former by friendship and affection. Both, he argues, essentialize and homogenize Muslims. Andrew Shyrock, ed., *Islamophobia/Islamophilia: Beyond the Politics of Enemy and Friend*, Bloomington: Indiana University Press, 2010.

3. Osamah Khalil, *America's Dream Palace: Middle East Expertise and the Rise of the National Security State*, Cambridge, MA: Harvard University Press, 2016, 4.

4. Khalil, *America's Dream Palace*.

5. Junaid Rana, *Terrifying Muslims: Race and Labor in the South Asian Diaspora*, Durham, NC: Duke University Press, 2011, 75.

6. For an overview of this scholarship, see Nadine Naber's introduction in Amaney Jamal and Nadine Naber, eds., *Race and Arab Americans Before and After 9/11: From Invisible Citizens to Visible Subjects*, Syracuse: Syracuse University Press, 2008.

7. Leila Ahmed, *Women and Gender in Islam*, New Haven: Yale University Press, 1992. Fatima Mernissi, *Beyond the Veil: Male–Female Dynamics in a Muslim Society*, London: Saqi Books, 1985.

8. Paul Blumenthal, "The Largest Protest Ever Was 15 Years Ago. The Iraq War Isn't Over. What Happened?" *Huffington Post*, February 15, 2018.

9. Edward W. Said, *Orientalism*, New York: Vintage, 1978.

10. Gilbert Achcar, *Eastern Cauldron: Islam, Afghanistan, Palestine, and Iraq in a Marxist Mirror*, Monthly Review Press, 2003; Rashid Khalidi, *Resurrecting Empire: Western Footprints and America's Perilous Path in the Middle East*, Beacon Press, 2005.

11. Ella Shohat and Robert Stam, *Unthinking Eurocentrism: Multiculturalism and the Media*, New York: Routledge, 1994, 19.

12. Deepa Kumar, "Danish Cartoons: Racism Has no Place on the Left," *MROnline.org*, February 21, 2006.

13. Norimitsu Onishi and Constant Méheut, "France's Hardening Defense of Cartoons of Muhammad Could Lead to 'a Trap,'" *New York Times*, October 30, 2020.

14. Kumar, "Danish Cartoons."

15. Uday Singh Mehta, *Liberalism and Empire: A Study in Nineteenth-Century British Liberal Thought*, Chicago: University of Chicago Press, 1999.

16. Jasbir Puar, *Terrorist Assemblages: Homonationalism in Queer Times*, Tenth Anniversary Expanded Edition, Durham, NC: Duke University Press, 2017.

17. Nadine Naber, "Look, Muhammed the Terrorist Is Coming!" in Jamal and Naber, eds., *Race and Arab Americans Before and After 9/11*, 276–303, 278.

18. Naber, "Look, Muhammed the Terrorist Is Coming!" 279.

19. Moustafa Bayoumi, "Racing Religion," *The New Centennial Review* 6: 2, Fall 2006, 267–93, 287.

20. Arun Kundnani and Deepa Kumar, "Race, Surveillance and Empire," *International Socialist Review*, no. 96, Spring 2015.

21. Barbara J. Fields and Karen E. Fields, *Racecraft: The Soul of Inequality in American Life*, London: Verso, 2012; Michael Omi and Howard Winant, *Racial Formation in the United States*, New York: Routledge, 1986.

22. Fields and Fields, *Racecraft*.

23. See the debate between Nancy Fraser and Michael Dawson on racial capitalism. In addition to the processes of exploitation and expropriation, I would add exclusion to account for legal processes of racialization from the Page Act and Chinese Exclusion Laws to the Muslim Ban. See Nancy Fraser, "Expropriation and Exploitation in Racialized Capitalism: A Reply to Michael Dawson," *Critical Historical Studies* 3: 1, 2016, 163–78; Michael C. Dawson, "Hidden in Plain Sight: A Note on Legitimation Crises and the Racial Order," *Critical Historical Studies* 3: 1, 2016, 143–61.

24. Nadine Naber and Junaid Rana, "The 21st Century Problem of Anti-Muslim Racism"; Steve Garner and Saher Selod, "The Racialization of Muslims: Empirical Studies of Islamophobia," *Critical Sociology* 41: 1, 2015, 9–19.

25. Quoted in Shyrock, ed., *Islamophobia/Islamophilia*, 4.

26. Chamlers Johnson, "Blowback: US Actions Abroad Have Repeatedly Lead to Unintended, Indefensible Consequences," *Nation*, September 27, 2001.

27. Marc Sageman, *Misunderstanding Terrorism*, Philadelphia: University of Pennsylvania Press, 2016; John Mueller, *Overblown: How Politicians and the Terrorism Industry Inflate National Security Threats, and Why We Believe Them*, New York: Free Press, 2006; Charles Kurzman, *The Missing Martyrs: Why There Are So Few Muslim Terrorists*, Oxford: Oxford University Press, 2011.

28. Sageman, *Misunderstanding Terrorism*.

29. A study by the Watson Institute at Brown University estimates that close to 400,000 are direct war deaths from the wars on Afghanistan, Iraq and Pakistan, and 800,000 civilians have been killed as an indirect consequence of war. Neta C. Crawford, "The Costs of War," online at watson.brown.edu.

30. See, for instance, Rana, *Terrifying Muslims* and the introduction to Gershon Shafir, Everard Meade, William Aceves (eds.), *Lessons and Legacies of the War on Terror: From Moral Panic to Permanent War,* Routledge Critical Terrorism Studies, London: Routledge, 2013.

31. Stuart Hall, Chas Critcher, Tony Jefferson, John Clarke, and Brian Roberts, *Policing the Crisis: Mugging, the State, and Law and Order*, 2d ed., London: Red Globe Press, 2013.

32. I develop this argument in more detail in my article "Terrorcraft: Empire and the Making of the Racialized Terrorist Threat," *Race and Class*, 62: 2, 2020, 34–60.

33. Saree Makdisi, *Making England Western: Orientalism, Race and Imperial Culture*, Chicago: University of Chicago Press, 2014.

34. See Fields and Fields, *Racecraft*; Shohat and Stam; Patrick Wolfe, *Traces of History: Elementary Structures of Race*, London: Verso, 2016.

35. Kumar, "Terrorcraft."

36. Chris Moody and Kristen Holmes, "Donald Trump's History of Suggesting Obama Is a Muslim," cnn.com, September 18, 2015.

37. As Neil Lazarus has argued, scholars in various fields including postcolonial studies fall into the trap of seeing the West as a homogeneous entity. Neal Lazarus, "The Fetish of the 'West' in Postcolonial Studies," in Crystal Bartolovich and Neal Lazarus, eds., *Marxism, Modernity and Postcolonial Studies*, Cambridge: Cambridge University Press, 2004, 43–64.

38. A. Sivanandan, "Challenging Racism: Strategies for the 1980s," *Race and Class* 25: 2, 1983.

39. Stuart Hall made a similar argument in his essay "Encoding, Decoding," in S. During, ed., *The Cultural Studies Reader*, London: Routledge, 1991, 90–103.

40. Bertolt Brecht, *Measures Taken and Other Lehrstucke*, London: Bloomsbury Methuen Drama, 1977, 34.

1. Empire, Race, Orientalism: The Case of Spain, Britain, and France

1. Albert Hourani, *Islam in European Thought*, Cambridge: Cambridge University Press, 1991, 282.

2. Hourani, *Islam in European Thought*, 230.

3. Janet L. Abu-Lughod, *Before European Hegemony: The World System A.D. 1250–135*, Oxford: Oxford University Press, 1991, 33.

4. Abu-Lughod, *Before European Hegemony*, 354, emphasis in original. See also Alex Anievas and Kerem Nisancioglu, *How the West Came to Rule: The Geopolitical Origins of Capitalism*, London: Pluto Press, 2015, for a global account of the rise of capitalism and Western hegemony.

5. On the years that mark this period, I am drawing from Étienne Balibar who suggests that 1500 is the starting point of modernity characterized by overseas expansion and mercantilism. I see the end of the modern era as one marked by the rise of industrial capitalism as well as the French, American, and Haitian revolutions that usher in a new era marked, at least in theory, by equality and equal rights.

6. Benno Teschke, *The Myth of 1648: Class, Geopolitics, and the Making of Modern International Relations*, London: Verso, 2003, 199.

7. Frederick Weaver, *Latin America in the World Economy: Mercantile Colonialism to Global Capitalism*, Boulder, CO: Westview Press, 2000.

8. Weaver, *Latin America in the World Economy*, 7.

9. Wood argues that this mode of imperial expansion relied on dispersing economic and political power locally while an imperial state governed from a distance. Ellen M. Wood, *Empire of Capital*, London: Verso, 2005.

10. Teschke, *The Myth of 1648*, 202.

11. Hourani, *Islam in European Thought*, 231–33.

12. Hourani, 234

13. Both quotes are in Hourani, *Islam in European Thought*, 230.

14. Zachary Lockman, *Contending Visions of the Middle East: The History and Politics of Orientalism*, 2d ed., Cambridge: Cambridge University Press, 2010, 42.

15. Nabil Matar, *Islam in Britain, 1558–1685*, Cambridge: Cambridge University Press, 1998.

16. On medieval Arab views of Europe and Europeans, see Nizar F. Hermes, *The [European] Other in Medieval Arabic Literature and Culture, Ninth-Twelfth Century AD*, New York: Palgrave Macmillan, 2012, and Daniel G. König, *Arabic-Islamic Views of the Latin West: Tracing the Emergence of Medieval Europe*, Oxford: Oxford University Press, 2015.

17. Nabil Matar, *Turks, Moors, and Englishmen in the Age of Discovery*, New York: Columbia University Press, 1999, 15.

18. Matar, *Islam in Britain*, 13.

19. Matar, *Turks, Moors, and Englishmen in the Age of Discovery*, 8.

20. Matar, *Turks, Moors, and Englishmen in the Age of Discovery*, 9.

21. Matar, *Islam in Britain*, 189.

22. David Brion Davis, *Inhuman Bondage: The Rise and Fall of Slavery in the New World*, Oxford: Oxford University Press, 2006, 58.

23. Jonathan Ray, *The Jew in Medieval Iberia, 1100–1500*, Brighton, MA: Academic Studies Press, 2011.

24. George M. Frederickson, *Racism: A Short History*, Princeton, NJ: Princeton University Press, 2002, 31.

25. J. H. Elliot, *Imperial Spain: 1469–1716*, London: Penguin Books, 1963, 108.

26. Elliot, *Imperial Spain*, 108.

27. Francisco Bethencourt, *Racisms: From the Crusades to the Twentieth Century*, Princeton, NJ: Princeton University Press, 2013, 151.

28. Bethencourt, *Racisms*, 150–51.

29. Bethencourt, *Racisms*, 141.

30. Bethencourt, *Racisms*, 138.

31. The expulsion of Jews and Muslims in Portugal, for instance, was handled differently. While Jewish children were not permitted to leave with their parents, Muslim children were. Fear of retribution against Christians in Muslim empires' lands translated into less harsh treatment of Muslims in comparison to Jews. See L. P. Harvey, *Muslims in Spain, 1500 to 1614*, Chicago: University of Chicago Press, 2005, 19–20.

32. Frederickson, *Racism*, 40.

33. Olivia Remie Constable, *To Live Like a Moor: Christian Perceptions of Muslim Identity in Medieval and Early Modern Spain*, Philadelphia: University of Pennsylvania Press, 2018.

34. Miguel de Cervantes, *Don Quixote*, translated by Edith Bloom, New York: HarperCollins, 2005, 879.

35. Cervantes, *Don Quixote*, 880-881.

36. Emmanuel Chukwudi Eze, *Race and the Enlightenment: A Reader*, Oxford: Blackwell, 1997, 5.

37. Frederickson, *Racism*.

38. Nell Irvin Painter, *The History of White People*, New York: Norton, 2010. See her chapter on Blumenbach.

39. Painter, *The History of White People*, 77.

40. Frederickson, *Racism*, 60.

41. Frederickson, *Racism*, 57.

42. For an overview of the relationship between capitalism and racism, see Helen Scott, "Was There a Time before Race? Capitalist Modernity and the Origins of Racism," in Crystal Bartolovich and Neal Lazarus, eds., *Marxism, Modernity and Postcolonial Studies*, Cambridge: Cambridge University Press, 2004, 167–84.

43. Maxime Rodinson, *Europe and the Mystique of Islam*, Roger Veinus, trans., London: I.B. Tauris, 1988, 46–47.

44. Norman Daniel, *Islam and the West: The Making of an Image*, 3d ed., rev., London: Oneworld, 2009, 312.

45. Hourani, *Islam in European Thought*, 236–37.

46. Rodinson, *Europe and the Mystique of Islam*, 65.

47. Quote in Melani McAlister, *Epic Encounters: Culture, Media and US Interests in the Middle East since 1945,* Berkeley: University of California Press, 2005, 9.

48. Wood, *Empire of Capital*.

49. David McNally, *Blood and Money: War, Slavery, Finance, and Empire*, Chicago: Haymarket Books, 2020, 96–97.

50. McNally, *Blood and Money*, 104–5.

51. Wood, *Empire of Capital*.

52. Weaver, *Latin America in the World Economy,* 33. Both Weaver and Wood note that aspects of mercantile imperialism persisted within British imperialism, as seen for instance in Britain's relationship with India.

53. Weaver, *Latin America in the World Economy,* 29.

54. Saree Makdisi, *Making England Western: Orientalism, Race and Imperial Culture*, Chicago: University of Chicago Press, 2014.

55. Makdisi, *Making England Western*, xiii.

56. Makdisi, *Making England Western*, xv.

57. Makdisi, *Making England Western*, xv.

58. Makdisi, *Making England Western*, xvi.

59. Matar, *Turks, Moors and Englishmen in the Age of Discovery*, 13.

60. Matar, *Turks, Moors and Englishmen in the Age of Discovery*, 170–72.

61. Leila Ahmed, *Women and Gender in Islam,* New Haven, CT: Yale University Press, 1992, 150.

62. Ahmed, *Women and Gender in Islam,* 152.

63. Ahmed, *Women and Gender in Islam,* 153.

64. Ahmed, *Women and Gender in Islam,* 151.

65. Ahmed, *Women and Gender in Islam,* 155–65.

66. Antoinette Burton, *Burdens of History: British Women, Indian Women, and Imperial Culture, 1865–1915,* Chapel Hill: University of North Carolina Press, 1994.

67. Inderpal Grewal, *Home and Harem: Nation, Gender, Empire and the Cultures of Travel,* Durham, NC: Duke University Press, 1996, 65.

68. Edward Said, *Orientalism,* New York: Random House, 1978.

69. Arthur Goldschmidt Jr. and Lawrence Davidson, *A Concise History of the Middle East*, 9th ed., Boulder, CO: Westview Press, 2010, 162.

70. Hourani, *Islam in European Thought*, 235.

71. Said, *Orientalism*, 82.

72. Said, *Orientalism*, 83–84.

73. Said, *Orientalism*, 87.

74. Anouar Abdel-Malek, "Orientalism in Crisis," in Alexander Lyon Macfie, ed.,

Orientalism: A Reader, New York: New York University Press, 2000, 47–56, 48, and Hourani, *Islam in European Thought*, 255–6.

75. Hourani, *Islam in European Thought*, 48.

76. Hourani, *Islam in European Thought*, 281.

77. Aijaz Ahmad, and before him Sadiq Jalal al-Azm, have critiqued Said for homogenizing the West, and for presenting all work about the East done in the West as being necessarily influenced by Orientalism. Al-Azm, one of the first to advance this argument, contended that while Said sought to challenge the ways in which Orientalists ascribe an essential nature to the East and West, which makes them not only ontologically different but that renders one superior to another, Said was himself guilty of essentializing the West. By tracing Orientalist attitudes all the way back to Homer, Said seems to suggest that there is something inherent in knowledge production in the West that renders it Orientalist. Additionally, even though one of Said's definitions of Orientalism is as a thoroughly modern phenomenon, his other definitions and his grand sweep of references muddy the historical context and the specificity of Orientalist modes of thought. Such a sweep that compares discourses produced in the capitalist and pre-capitalist eras, Ahmed argued, is one that even Foucault would have objected to. It leads Said to a place where the explanation for anti-Muslim/Arab caricatures comes out of the "European mind," which is for Said, as al-Azm puts it, "inherently bent on distorting all human realities other than its own for the sake of its own aggrandisement." Such a unilinear, essentialist and idealist understanding of Orientalism does not, al-Azm argues, serve Said well in his attempt to find an approach to how one might study other cultures and peoples in a non-repressive manner. See A. Abdel-Malek, "Orientalism in Crisis"; H. Dabashi, *Post-Orientalism: Knowledge and Power in Time of Terror*, New Brunswick: Transaction Publishers, 2009; A. Ahmed, *In Theory: Classes, Nations, Literatures*, Delhi: Oxford University Press, 1994; Gilbert Achar, *Marxism, Orientalism, Cosmopolitanism*, Chicago: Haymarket Books, 2013.

78. Abdel-Malek, "Orientalism in Crisis."

79. Hourani, *Islam in European Thought*, 285.

80. Hamid Dabashi, *Post-Orientalism: Knowledge and Power in Time of Terror*, New Brunswick: Transaction publishers, 2009, 30.

81. Abdel-Malek, "Orientalism in Crisis," 49.

82. Alexander Lyon Macfie, "Introduction," in Macfie, ed., *Orientalism*, 1–10, 1.

83. Extracts of the work of these scholars and full citations for their essays and books can be found in Alexander Lyon Macfie (ed.), *Orientalism*.

84. Macfie, "Introduction," 2.

85. Lisa Lowe, *Critical Terrains: French and British Orientalisms*, Ithaca, NY: Cornell University Press, 1991.

86. Lockman, *Contending Visions of the Middle East*, 69.

87. John McKinzie, *Orientalism: History, Theory and the Arts*, Manchester: Manchester University Press, 1995, 215.

88. Lockman, *Contending Visions of the Middle East*, 69.

89. Lockman, *Contending Visions of the Middle East*, 58.

90. Quoted in Hourani, *Islam in European Thought*, 247.

91. Hourani, *Islam in European Thought*, 247.

92. Hourani, *Islam in European Thought*, 248–49.

93. Hourani, *Islam in European Thought*, 249.

94. Abdel-Malek, "Orientalism in Crisis," 50.

95. Lockman, *Contending Visions of the Middle East*, 47.

96. Aslı Çırakman, *From the "Terror of the Word" to the "Sick Man of Europe": European Images of the Ottoman Empire from the Seventeenth Century to the Nineteenth*, New York: Peter Land, 2002, 125.

97. Bryan Turner, *Marx and the End of Orientalism*, Boston: Allen and Unwin, 1978, 7.

98. Rodinson, *Europe and the Mystique of Islam*, 60.

99. Abdel-Malek, "Orientalism in Crisis."

100. Lockman, *Contending Visions of the Middle East*, 78.

101. Quoted in Lockman, *Contending Visions of the Middle East*, 94.

102. David Spurr, *The Rhetoric of Empire*, Durham, NC: Duke University Press, 1993, 113.

103. Quoted in Richard Seymour, *The Liberal Defence of Murder*, London: Verso, 2008, 99.

104. Samir Amin, *Eurocentrism*, 2d ed., New York: Monthly Review Press, 2010, 14.

105. Edward Said, *Edward Said on Orientalism* (documentary), Amherst: Media Education Foundation.

106. Uday Singh Mehta, *Liberalism and Empire: A Study of Nineteenth-Century British Liberal Thought*, Chicago: University of Chicago Press, 1999, 32–33.

107. Karen E. Fields and Barbara J. Fields, *Racecraft: The Soul of Inequality in American Life*, London: Verso Books, 2014, 128.

108. Patrick Wolfe, *Traces of History: Elementary Structures of Race*, London: Verso, 2016, 7.

109. Raphael Patai, *The Arab Mind*, rev. ed., New York: Hatherleigh Press, 2002.

110. Jeremy Scahill, *Dirty Wars: The World Is a Battlefield*, New York: Nation Books, 2013.

2. The United States, Orientalism, and Modernization

1. Anthony Arnove, ed., *Iraq Under Siege: The Deadly Impact of Sanctions and War*, rev., Boston: South End Press, 2003.

2. John Pilger, "John Pilger on Why We Ignored Iraq in the 1990s—and Why the Media Is Doing So Again," *New Statesman*, October 4, 2004.

3. H. C. von Sponeck, *A Different Kind of War: The UN Sanctions Regime in Iraq*, Oxford, NY: Bergham Books, 2006.

4. Madeleine Albright, interview by Leslie Stahl, *60 Minutes*, CBS, May 12, 1996, http://www.youtube.com/watch?v=FbIX1CP9qr4.

5. This paragraph draws on Robert Kagan, *Dangerous Nation: America's Foreign Policy from Its Earliest Days to the Dawn of the Twentieth Century,* New York: Vintage, 2007, Chapter 1.

6. Sven Beckert, *Empire of Cotton: A Global History,* New York: Vintage, 2015, 117, 119.

7. Quoted in Zachary Lockman, *Contending Visions of the Middle East: The History and Politics of Orientalism*, 2d ed., Cambridge: Cambridge University Press, 2010, 78.

8. Kambiz GhaneaBassiri, *A History of Islam in America,* Cambridge: Cambridge University Press, 2010.

9. Allan D. Austin, *African Muslims in Antebellum America: Transatlantic Stories and Spiritual Struggles*, New York: Routledge, 1997.

10. Sylviane A. Diouf, *Servants of Allah: African Muslims Enslaved in the Americas,* 2d ed., New York: New York University Press, 70.

11. Michael Gomez, *Black Crescent: The Experience and Legacy of African Muslims in the Americas*, Cambridge: Cambridge University Press, 2005, x.

12. Sherman Jackson, *Islam and Black America: Looking Toward the Third Resurrection*, Oxford: Oxford University Press, 2014, 35.

13. Jackson, *Islam and Black America,* 38–40.

14. Sylvia Chan-Malik, "'Common Cause': On the Black-Immigrant Debate and Constructing the Muslim-American," *Journal of Race, Ethnicity and Religion* 2: 8, 2011, 1–39.

15. Timothy Marr, *The Cultural Roots of American Islamicism*, New York: Cambridge University Press, 2006, 28.

16. Marr, *The Cultural Roots of American Islamicism*, 2–3.

17. Khaled Beydoun argues that "criminalizing religion was vital to the project of stripping the humanity of Africans and reducing them to 'beasts of burden.'" Khaled Beydoun, *American Islamophobia: Understanding the Roots and Rise of Fear*, Oakland: University of California Press, 2018, 57. However, he provides no evidence that Islam was criminalized in colonial America. While his overall point that black Muslim slaves were reduced to property and therefore denied the right to practice their religion and even made to convert to Christianity is indeed accurate, it is not clear that religion was criminalized through any specific laws or acts. At least, I have not found legal scholarship to suggest that

there were processes at work that we today understand as the "securitization of Islam" or the criminalization of Islam back in the colonial and antebellum era.

18. GhaneaBassiri, *A History of Islam in America*, 29.

19. The first such instance of such a process can be seen in the twentieth century with those associated with the Moorish Science temple; see Sylvester Johnson and Steven Weitzman, eds., *The FBI and Religion*, Oakland: University of California Press, 2017.

20. Laws in late seventeenth century Virginia stipulated that conversion to Christianity did not entail freedom; George M. Frederickson, *Racism: A Short History*, Princeton, NJ: Princeton University Press, 2002, 45. A 1667 decree denied freedom based on conversion with the rationale that "baptisme doth not alter the condition of the person as to his bondage or freedom." Quoted in Lerone Bennett Jr., *The Shaping of Black America*, Chicago: Johnson, 1975, 67.

21. Bennett, *The Shaping of Black America*, 67.

22. Fuad Shaban, *Islam and Arabs in Early American Thought: Roots of Orientalism in America*, Durham, NC: Acorn Press, 1991.

23. Shaban, *Islam and Arabs in Early American Thought*, 62.

24. See Marr, *The Cultural Roots of American Islamicism*, Chapter 1.

25. Douglas Little, *American Orientalism: The United States and the Middle East since 1945*, Chapel Hill: University of North Carolina Press, 2002, 12.

26. Marr, *The Cultural Roots of American Islamicism*, Chapter 1.

27. Marr, *The Cultural Roots of American Islamicism*, 37.

28. Quoted in Shaban, *Islam and Arabs in Early American Thought*, 84.

29. Shaban, *Islam and Arabs in Early American Thought*, 85.

30. Paul M. Baepler, *White Slaves, African Masters: An Anthology of American Barbary Captivity Narratives*, Chicago: University of Chicago Press, 1999.

31. Baepler, *White Slaves, African Masters*.

32. Quoted in Marr, *The Cultural Roots of American Islamicism*, 54.

33. Baepler, *White Slaves, African Masters*.

34. See Marr, *The Cultural Roots of American Islamicism*, 142.

35. Marr, *The Cultural Roots of American Islamicism*, 156.

36. Marr, *The Cultural Roots of American Islamicism*, 150–51.

37. Marr, *The Cultural Roots of American Islamicism*, 297.

38. Melani McAlister, *Epic Encounters: Culture, Media and US Interests in the Middle East since 1945*, Berkeley: University of California Press, 2005.

39. Little, *American Orientalism*, 13.

40. Little, *American Orientalism*, 13.

41. Shaban, *Islam and Arabs in Early American Thought*, xviii.

42. Cited in Marr, *The Cultural Roots of American Islamicism*, 283.

43. McAlister, *Epic Encounters*, 14–20.

44. McAlister, *Epic Encounters*, 18.

45. Little, *American Orientalism*, 13.

46. McAlister, *Epic Encounters*, 22.

47. Vivek Bald, "The Only Good Muslim: Immigration Law, Popular Culture, and the Structures of Acceptability" in Sohail Daulatzai and Junaid Rana, eds., *With Stones in Our Hands: Writings on Muslims, Racism, and Empire*, Minneapolis: University of Minnesota Press, 2018.

48. Bald, "The Only Good Muslim," 143.

49. Sarah Gualtieri, *Between Arab and White: Race and Ethnicity in the Early Syrian American Diaspora*, Berkeley: University of California Press, 2006, 48.

50. Quoted in Gualtieri, *Between Arab and White*, 47.

51. David R. Roediger, *Working Towards Whiteness: How America's Immigrants Became White*, New York: Basic Books, 2005.

52. Roediger, *Working Towards Whiteness*, 12.

53. Roediger, *Working Towards Whiteness*, 76.

54. In 1922, Takao Ozawa, a Japanese immigrant who had lived in the US for many years, went to the US Supreme Court to challenge the law that prevented Asians from becoming naturalized citizens. In *Ozawa v. the United States*, he argued that his skin was actually lighter than many white people's, so if Italians and other Europeans could become US citizens, why not Asians? The Supreme Court ruled that race was an issue of blood, not skin color, and that no matter how light an Asian person's skin, they could never be considered "white," but would always be "foreign." One year later in 1923, an Asian-Indian immigrant, Bhagat Singh Thind, argued that he had the right to be a US citizen because he was an upper-caste Hindu, descended from white Aryans who had settled in India. Thus, his blood was white. The Supreme Court responded in *United States v. Thind* that race was not a scientific category but a social one and that no matter how much white blood an Asian might have, he was still "foreign" and could never be an American. The court gave up on using expert testimony and stated that the "common" American simply knew Thind was not white. "Common speech" and "popular understanding" were to be the new tests of whiteness.

55. Gualtieri, *Between Arab and White*, 77.

56. Sylvester Johnson, "The FBI and the Moorish Science Temple of America, 1926–1960," in Sylvester A. Johnson and Steven Weitzman, eds., *The FBI and Religion: Faith and National Security before and after 9/11*, Oakland: University of California Press, 2017, 55–66.

57. Johnson, "The FBI and the Moorish Science Temple of America, 1926–1960," 57–58.

58. Johnson, "The FBI and the Moorish Science Temple of America, 1926–1960," 58.

59. Johnson, "The FBI and the Moorish Science Temple of America, 1926–1960," 63.

60. Karl Evanzz, "The FBI and the Nation of Islam" in Johnson and Weitzman, eds., *The FBI and Religion*, 148–67; Arun Kundnani, *The Muslims Are Coming: Islamophobia, Extremism, and the Domestic War on Terror*, London: Verso, 2015.

61. This entire paragraph draws on the research of Sydney Pasquinelli and her analysis of FBI documents. See Sydney Pasquinelli, "The Lesser-Evils Paradigm for Imagining Islam: U.S. Executive Branch (Re)Framing of Islam in the Early Cold War Era of Racialized Empire Building," diss., University of Pittsburgh, 2018, 59.

62. Elaine C. Hagopian, ed., *Civil Rights in Peril: The Targeting of Arabs and Muslims*, London: Pluto Press, 2004; Nadine Naber, *Arab America: Gender, Cultural Politics, and Activism*, New York: New York University Press, 2012. See also Amanay Jamal and Nadine Naber, eds., *Race and Arab Americans before and after 9/11: From Invisible Citizens to Visible Subjects*, Syracuse, NY: Syracuse University Press, 2008.

63. Louise Cainkar, "Fluid Terror Threat: A Genealogy of the Racialization of Arab, Muslim, and South Asian Americans," *Amerasia Journal* 44: 1, 2018, 27–59, 29.

64. See Naber, *Arab America*, Chapter 1.

65. Deepa Kumar, "Terrorcraft: Empire and the Making of the Racialized Terrorist Threat," *Race and Class* 62: 2, 2020, 34–60.

66. Osamah Khalil, *America's Dream Palace: Middle East Expertise and the Rise of the National Security State*, Cambridge, MA: Harvard University Press, 2016, 11.

67. Inderjeet Parmar, *Foundations of the American Century*, New York: Columbia University Press, 2012, 2.

68. Khalil, *America's Dream Palace*, 80–81.

69. Edward Said, *Orientalism*, New York: Random House, 1978, 296.

70. Lockman, *Contending Visions of the Middle East*, 129–30.

71. Brian Loveman, *No Higher Law: American Foreign Policy and the Western Hemisphere since 1776*, Chapel Hill: University of North Carolina Press, 2010.

72. McAlister, *Epic Encounters*, 45.

73. McAlister, *Epic Encounters*, 47.

74. McAlister, *Epic Encounters*, 55.

75. Sidney Lens, *The Forging of the American Empire: From the Revolution to Vietnam: A History of U.S. Imperialism*, London: Pluto Press, 2003, 367–68.

76. Bryan Turner, *Marx and the End of Orientalism*, Boston: Allen and Unwin, 1978, 11.

77. Daniel Lerner, *The Passing of Traditional Society: Modernizing the Middle East*, New York: Free Press, 1965.

78. See Turner, *Marx and the End of Orientalism*, 11.

79. Everett Rogers, *Diffusion of Innovations*, 5th ed., New York: Free Press, 2003.
80. Nadine Naber, "Look, Mohammed the Terrorist Is Coming!" in Jamal and Naber, eds., *Race and Arab Americans Before and After 9/11*.
81. Khalil, *America's Dream Palace*.
82. Naber, "Look, Mohammed the Terrorist Is Coming!"
83. Kumar, "Terrorcraft." The book is tentatively titled *Terrorcraft: Empire, Race and Security.*
84. Ella Shohat and Robert Stam, *Unthinking Eurocentrism: Multiculturalism and the Media*, New York: Routledge, 1994, 19.
85. Shohat and Stam, *Unthinking Eurocentrism*, 19.
86. Bernard Lewis, "The Roots of Muslim Rage," *The Atlantic*, September 1990.
87. Samuel P. Huntington, "The Clash of Civilizations?" *Foreign Affairs* 72: 3, 1993, 22–49; Samuel P. Huntington, *The Clash of Civiliations and the Remaking of World Order*, New York: Touchstone, 1996. See Mahmood Mamdani, "Culture Talk; or How not to Talk about Islam and Politics," in *Good Muslim, Bad Muslim: America, The Cold War, and the Roots of Terror*, New York: Doubleday, 2004, for a critique of this approach. See also Edward Said, "The Clash of Definitions," in Emran Qureshi and Michael E. Sells, eds., *The New Crusades: Constructing the Muslim Enemy*, New York: Columbia University Press, 2003.
88. Quoted in John L. Esposito, *The Islamic Threat: Myth or Reality?* New York: Oxford University Press, 1999, 230.

3. The Ideology of Islamophobia

1. Media Matters Staff, "On CNN, Reza Aslan Explains How the Media Is Failing in Its Reporting on Islam," Media Matters, September 29, 2014, mediamatters.org.
2. For the role of African Americans in popular culture as a means to represent the benevolence of US imperialism and its "post-racial" character, see Moustafa Bayoumi, "The Race Is On: Muslims and Arabs in the American Imagination," *MERIP*, March 10, 2020; Kevin Alexander Gray, Jeffrey St. Clair, and JoAnn Wypijewski, eds., *Killing Trayvons: An Anthology of American Violence*, Petrolia, CA: CounterPunch Books, 2014.
3. Edward W. Said, *Covering Islam: How the Media and the Experts Determine How We See the Rest of the World*, New York: Vintage Books, 1981.
4. As noted in the introduction, the field of Arab American studies had examined this phenomenon in relation to Arab Americans and Muslim Americans since the late 1960s.
5. Stuart Hall, Chas Critcher, Tony Jefferson, John Clarke, and Brian Roberts, *Policing the Crisis: Mugging, the State, and Law and Order*, 2d ed., London: Red Globe Press, 2013.

6. Stuart Hall, "The Whites of their Eyes: Racist Ideologies in the Media," in Gail Dines and Jean M. Humez, eds., *Gender, Race, and Class in the Media*, 2d ed., Thousand Oaks, CA: Sage, 1995, 90, emphasis added.

7. Stuart Hall, "The Rediscovery of 'Ideology,'" in Julie Rivkin and Michael Ryan, eds., *Literary Theory: An Anthology*, Oxford: Blackwell, 1998, 1050–64, 1050.

8. Hall et al., *Policing the Crisis*, 59.

9. Hall et al., *Policing the Crisis*, 58, emphasis in original.

10. Steven Salaita, *Anti-Arab Racism in the USA: Where It Comes from and What It Means for Politics Today*, London: Pluto Press, 2006; Andrew Shryock, ed., *Islamophobia, Islamophilia: Beyond the Politics of Enemy and Friend*, Bloomington: Indiana University Press, 2010. The Runnymede Trust report mentioned in the introduction also identified several of the frames discussed in this chapter. For a quick summary of the Runnymede frames, see Todd Green, *The Fear of Islam: An Introduction to Islamophobia in the West*, Minneapolis, MN: Fortress Press, 2015, Chapter 1.

11. Stephen Sheehi, *Islamophobia: The Ideological Campaign against Muslims*, Atlanta: Clarity Press, 2011.

12. Sheehi, *Islamophobia*, 39.

13. Minoo Moallem, *Between Warrior Brother and Veiled Sister: Islamic Fundamentalism and the Politics of Patriarchy in Iran*, Berkeley: University of California Press, 2005, 41.

14. Jeff Diamant, "The Countries with the 10 Largest Christian Populations and the 10 Largest Muslim Populations," Pew Research Center, April 1, 2019, pewresearch.org.

15. Diamant, "The Countries with the 10 Largest Christian Populations."

16. Sadiq al-Azm, *Is Islam Secularizable? Challenging Political and Religious Taboos*, Berlin: Gerlach Press, 2014, 13.

17. Talal Asad, *The Idea of an Anthropology of Islam*, Washington, DC: Georgetown University, Center for Contemporary Arab Studies, 1986, 14.

18. Asad, *The Idea of an Anthropology of Islam*, 16.

19. Maxime Rodinson, *The Arabs*, Chicago: University of Chicago Press, 1979.

20. Nadine Naber, "Introduction," in Amaney Jamal and Nadine Naber, eds., *Race and Arab Americans Before and After 9/11: From Invisible Citizens to Visible Subjects*, Syracuse: Syracuse University Press, 2008, 5.

21. Naber, "Introduction," 5.

22. Edward Said, *Orientalism*, New York: Random House, 1978, 296.

23. Peter Morey and Amina Yaqin, *Framing Muslims*, Cambridge, MA: Harvard University Press, 2011; Jack Shaheen, *Reel Bad Arabs: How Hollywood Vilifies a People*, 2d ed., New York: Olive Branch Press, 2009.

24. The four epigraphs are taken from the following: Laura Bush, "Radio Address by Laura Bush to the Nation," The Avalon Project, November 17, 2001, avalon.law. yale.edu; G. Alcorn, "US Politicians Rush to Embrace Women's Rights in Afghanistan," *The Age* (Melbourne, Australia), November 22, 2001; B. Sammon, "Bush Urges Afghans to Help Oust Taliban," *Washington Times*, September 26, 2001. H. Rumbelow, "Cherie's Veiled Criticism," *The Times* (London), November 20, 2001.

25. Carol Stabile and Deepa Kumar, "Unveiling Imperialism: Media, Gender, and the War on Afghanistan," Media, Culture and Society 27: 5, 2005, 765–82.

26. Stabile and Kumar, "Unveiling Imperialism," 771–72.

27. Malalai Joya, *A Woman Among Warlords*, New York: Scribner, 2009.

28. Valentine M. Moghadam, *Modernizing Women: Gender and Social Change in the Middle East*, 3d. ed., Boulder, CO: Lynne Rienner, 2013.

29. Valentine Moghadam, ed., *From Patriarchy to Empowerment: Women's Participation, Movements, and Rights in the Middle East, North Africa, and South Asia*, Syracuse, NY: Syracuse University Press, 2007; Rabab Abdulhadi, Evelyn Alsultany, and Nadine Naber, eds., *Arab and Arab American Feminisms: Gender, Violence, and Belonging*, Syracuse, NY: Syracuse University Press, 2011.

30. Naima Bouteldja, "French Hijab Ban: One Year On," *Red Pepper Europe*, May 1, 2005, redpepper.org.uk. See also Christine Delphy, *Separate and Dominate: Feminism and Racism after the War on Terror*, London: Verso: 2015.

31. Marnia Lazreg, *The Eloquence of Silence: Algerian Women in Question*, Oxon, UK: Routledge, 1994, 135.

32. Delphy, *Separate and Dominate*, 111.

33. Leila Ahmed, *Women and Gender in Islam*, New Haven, CT: Yale University Press, 1992.

34. For an analysis of the veil debates in the French context, see Joan Walsh Scott, *The Politics of the Veil*, Princeton, NJ: Princeton University Press, 2010. For France and several other countries, see Hilal Elver, *The Headscarf Controversy: Secularism and Freedom of Religion*, Oxford: Oxford University Press, 2012. For a discussion in the United States, see Sylvia Chan-Malik, *Being Muslim: A Cultural History of Women of Color in American Islam*, New York: New York University Press, 2018, Chapter 4. For Canada, see Jasmin Zine, "Unveiled Sentiments: Gendered Islamophobia and Experiences of Veiling among Muslim Girls in a Canadian Islamic School," *Equity and Excellence in Education* 38: 3, 2006, 239–52.

35. Fadwa El Guindi, *Veil: Modesty, Privacy and Resistance (Dress, Body, Culture)*, Oxford, UK: Berg, 1999.

36. Zachary Lockman, *Contending Visions of the Middle East: The History and*

Politics of Orientalism, 2d ed., Cambridge: Cambridge University Press, 2010, 69.

37. See Isra Ali, "The Harem Fantasy in Nineteenth-century Orientalist Paintings," *Dialectical Anthropology* 39, 2015, 33–46, 39.

38. Petre Zoltán, "The Romantic Eugène Delacroix and Orientalism," *Astra Salvensis* 1: 2, 2019, 27–42, 35.

39. Rana Kabbani, *Imperial Fictions: Europe's Myths of Orient*, London: Saqi Books, 2008, 124–25.

40. Zoltán, "The Romantic Eugène Delacroix and Orientalism," 34.

41. Kabbani, *Imperial Fictions*, 133.

42. Kabbani, *Imperial Fictions*, 129.

43. This tradition of presenting Arab women as objects of desire continued in other media as well, such as picture postcards sent by the French from Algeria in the first three decades of the twentieth century. See Malek Alloula, *The Colonial Harem*, trans. Myrna Godzich and Wlad Godzich, Minneapolis: University of Minnesota Press, 1986.

44. For a general accounting of this narrative, see Lila Abu-Lughod, *Do Muslim Women Need Saving?* Cambridge: Harvard University Press, 2013. See also Lazreg, *The Eloquence of Silence*.

45. See for instance Reina Lewis, *Rethinking Orientalism: Women, Travel, and the Ottoman Harem*, New Brunswick, NJ: Rutgers University Press, 2004; Reina Lewis and Nancy Micklewright, eds., *Gender, Modernity and Liberty: Middle Eastern and Western Women's Writings: A Critical Sourcebook*, London: I.B. Tauris, 2006; Sara Mills, *Discourses of Difference: An Analysis of Women's Travel Writing and Colonialism*, New York: Routledge, 1991, all of which have analyzed European women's contributions to discourse on the "East" in the eighteenth and nineteenth centuries. What these authors show is that while some of the dominant myths about Muslim women are echoed here, there are also other accounts that contest the notion of Muslim women as horribly oppressed.

46. For an analysis of various popular and profitable novels with these themes (and also for how NGOs mobilize these tropes for fundraising purposes), see Abu-Lughod, *Do Muslim Women Need Saving?*

47. "US Museum Demands German Anti-Islam Party Stop Using 19th-Century 'Slave Market' Painting," cbsnews.com, April 30, 2019.

48. N. C. Aizenman, "Nicaragua's Total Ban on Abortion Spurs Critics," *Washington Post*, November 28, 2006.

49. Fatima Mernissi, *The Veil and the Male Elite: A Feminist Interpretation of Women's Rights in Islam*, Reading, MA: Addison Wesley, 1991, ix.

50. Asma Barlas, *"Believing Women" in Islam: Unreading Patriarchal Interpretations of the Qur'an*, Austin: University of Texas Press, 2002.

51. See Montgomery Watt, *Muhammad at Medina,* Oxford: Clarendon Press, 1956, cited in Leila Ahmed, *Women and Gender in Islam,* New Haven, CT: Yale University Press, 1992, 43.

52. Maxime Rodinson, *Muhammad,* trans. Anne Carter, New York: NYRB Classics, 2021, 230.

53. Ahmed, *Women and Gender in Islam,* 62.

54. Samir Amin, *Eurocentrism,* trans. Russell Moore and James Membrez, New York: Monthly Review Press, 2009, 59.

55. Inderpal Grewal and Victoria Bernal, *Theorizing NGOs: States, Feminism, and Neoliberalism,* Durham, NC: Duke University Press, 2014.

56. Zakia Salime, *Between Feminism and Islam: Human Rights and Sharia Law in Morocco,* Minneapolis: University of Minnesota Press, 2011.

57. Cited in Deepa Kumar, "Imperialist Feminism," *International Socialist Review,* no. 102, 2016, https://isreview.org/issue/102/imperialist-feminism

58. Alana Lentin and Gavan Titley, *The Crisis of Multiculturalism: Racism in a Neoliberal Age,* London: Zed Books, 2011.

59. Bernard Lewis, "The Roots of Muslim Rage," *Atlantic,* September 1990.

60. Lewis, "The Roots of Muslim Rage."

61. Samuel Huntington, *The Clash of Civilizations and the Remaking of World Order,* New York: Simon and Schuster, 1997, 217.

62. Olivier Roy, *The Failure of Political Islam,* Cambridge, MA: Harvard University Press, 1996, 13–14.

63. Arthur Goldschmidt Jr. and Lawrence Davidson, *A Concise History of the Middle East,* 9th ed., Boulder, CO: Westview, 2010, Chapter 3.

64. Mohammed Ayoob and Danielle N. Lussier, *The Many Faces of Political Islam: Religion and Politics in Muslim Societies,* Ann Arbor: University of Michigan Press, 2020.

65. Roy, *The Failure of Political Islam,* 14.

66. Roy, *The Failure of Political Islam,* 28.

67. Goldschmidt and Davidson, *A Concise History of the Middle East,* 108–109.

68. Ayoob and Lussier, *The Many Faces of Political Islam,* 28.

69. Goldschmidt and Davidson, *A Concise History of the Middle East,* 114.

70. Ayoob and Lussier, *The Many Faces of Political Islam,* 22.

71. Ayoob and Lussier, *The Many Faces of Political Islam,* 12.

72. Ayoob and Lussier, *The Many Faces of Political Islam,* 12.

73. Neil Davidson, "Islam and the Enlightenment," *Socialist Review,* no. 304, 2006.

74. Davidson, "Islam and the Enlightenment."

75. Epigraphs are from the Associated Press, Republican Debate, May 4, 2007; Emmet Tyrrell, "Defanging the Nihilists," *New York Sun,* August 10, 2006, 9.

76. Pope Benedict XVI, "Lecture of the Holy Father," September 12, 2006, in Regensburg, Germany, news.bbc.co.uk.

77. Quoted in Mahmood Mamdani, *Good Muslim, Bad Muslim*, New York: Doubleday, 2005, 45.

78. Quoted in Maxime Rodinson, *Marxism and the Muslim World*, New York: Monthly Review Press, 1981, 50.

79. Paul L. Rose, "Renan versus Gobineau: Semitism and Antisemitism, Ancient Races and Modern Liberal Nations," *History of European Ideas* 39: 4, 2013, 528–40.

80. Quoted in Albert Hourani, *Islam in European Thought*, Cambridge: Cambridge University Press, 1991, 251–52.

81. Hourani, *Islam in European Thought*, 252.

82. Lockman, *Contending Visions of the Middle East*, 79–80.

83. Quoted in Said, *Orientalism*, 38.

84. Moallem, *Between Warrior Brother and Veiled Sister*.

85. Karim H. Karim, *Islamic Peril: Media and Global Violence*, 2d ed., New York: Black Rose Books, 2003.

86. Talal Asad, *On Suicide Bombing*, New York: Columbia University Press, 2007.

87. Rudolph Guiliani, remarks delivered at Republican presidential debate, May 3, 2007, in Simi Valley, CA, 2008election.procon.org.

88. See, for instance, the various excellent critiques of the book *The Bell Curve*. See also Stephen Jay Gould's excellent *The Mismeasure of Man*, rev. and expanded ed., New York: W.W. Norton, 1996.

89. George Saliba, *Islamic Science and the Making of the European Renaissance*, Cambridge, MA: MIT Press, 2007.

90. Saliba, *Islamic Science and the Making of the European Renaissance*, 233.

91. Saliba, *Islamic Science and the Making of the European Renaissance*, 234.

92. Tariq Ali, *The Clash of Fundamentalisms: Crusades, Jihad, and Modernity*, London: Verso, 2002, 54.

93. Pope Benedict XVI, "Lecture of the Holy Father."

94. Peter Hervik, *The Annoying Difference: The Emergence of Danish Nationalism, Neo-racism, and Populism in the post–1989 World*, New York: Berghahn Books, 2011.

95. Peter Hervik, "Ten Years after the Danish Muhammad Cartoon News Stories: Terror and Radicalization as Predictable Media Events," *Television and New Media* 19: 2, 2018.

96. Hervik, "Ten Years after the Danish Muhammad Cartoon News Stories."

97. Peter Gottschalk and Gabriel Greenberg, *Islamophobia: Making Muslims the Enemy*, Lanham, MD: Rowman and Littlefield, 2008.

98. Zareena Grewal, *Islam Is a Foreign Country: American Muslims and the Global Crisis of Authority*, New York: New York University Press, 2013, 20.

99. "She's Got Chutzpah," *O* magazine, May 2004, 234, 240.

100. Lockman, *Contending Visions of the Middle East*, 19.

101. Ali, *Clash of Fundamentalisms*, 40.

102. Colin Wells cited in John Feffer, *Crusade 2.0: The West's Resurgent War on Islam*, San Francisco: City Lights Books, 2012, 36.

103. Andrew Curry, "The First Holy War," *U.S. News and World Report*, August 23, 2005.

104. Arun Kundnani, "Islamophobia as Lay Ideology of US-led Empire," kundnani.org.

105. Epigraphs from the Federal News Service, Hearing of the Senate Foreign Relations Committee, Subject: Iraq: The Crocker-Petraeus Report, September 11, 2007; Condoleezza Rice, "Rice Urges Iraqis to Pursue Inclusive Political Process," January 18, 2010, america.gov (accessed July 2011).

106. Orientalists like Lewis and Vatikiotis have argued that there is no concept of revolution among Arabs and Muslims. See Turner, *Marx and the End of Orientalism*, 68–69.

107. Quoted in Said, *Orientalism*, 32–33.

108. Quoted in Said, *Orientalism*, 37.

109. Quoted in Douglas Little, *American Orientalism: The United States and the Middle East since 1945*, Chapel Hill: University of North Carolina Press, 2002, 15.

110. See the critique of Nial Fergusson's book *Empire* for this. Paul D'Amato, "When Britannia Waived the Rules," *International Socialist Review*, no. 32, November–December 2003, isreview.org.

111. After a week in Afghanistan, Medea Benjamin of Code Pink took an about-turn in her anti-war position. See Aunohita Mojumdar, "Code Pink Rethinks Its Call for Afghanistan Pull Out," *Christian Science Monitor*, October 6, 2009. The Feminist Majority supported the US/NATO war; see Stabile and Kumar, "Unveiling Imperialism"; see also Jasbir Puar, *Terrorist Assemblages: Homonationalism in Queer Times*, Durham, NC: Duke University Press, 2017. Puar discusses how various feminists including the Feminist Majority signed on to the US war and even erased the work of Afghan feminist organizations such as the Revolutionary Association of the Women of Afghanistan, 5–7.

112. Puar, *Terrorist Assemblages*, xix.

113. Puar, *Terrorist Assemblages*, xxxii.

114. Sidney Lens, *The Forging of the American Empire: From the Revolution to Vietnam: A History of U.S. Imperialism*, London: Pluto Press, 2003; William Blum, *Rogue State*, Monroe, ME: Common Courage Press, 2000; Stephen Kinzer, *Overthrow: America's Century of Regime Change from Hawaii to Iraq*, New York: Times Books, 2006.

115. Gilbert Achcar, *Eastern Cauldron: Islam, Afghanistan, Palestine and Iraq in a Marxist Mirror*, New York: Monthly Review Press, 2004.

116. Quoted in Little, *American Orientalism*, 28.

117. Little, *American Orientalism*, 27–28.

118. Gilbert Achcar, *The People Want: A Radical Exploration of the Arab Uprising*, Berkeley: University of California Press, 2013.

119. David Horowitz, "A Mass Expression of Outrage against Injustice" (interview), *Jerusalem Post*, February 25, 2011, jpost.com.

120. Horowitz, "A Mass Expression of Outrage against Injustice."

121. Horowitz, "A Mass Expression of Outrage against Injustice."

122. Shaheen, *Reel Bad Arabs*.

123. Jack Shaheen, *Reel Bad Arabs*, Media Education Foundation documentary, 2006, shop.mediaed.org.

124. Evelyn Alsultany, *Arabs and Muslims in the Media: Race and Representation after 9/11*, New York: New York University Press, 2012, 16.

125. Alsultany, *Arabs and Muslims in the Media*, 21.

126. Deepa Kumar and A. Kundnani, "Imagining National Security: The CIA, Hollywood, and the War on Terror," *Democratic Communiqué* 26: 2, 2014, 72–83.

127. Kumar and Kundnani, "Imagining National Security," 80.

4. "Good" and "Bad" Muslims: The Foreign Policy Establishment and the "Islamic Threat"

1. Mahmood Mamdani, *Good Muslim, Bad Muslim*, New York: Doubleday, 2005.

2. Khalil al-Anani, *Inside the Muslim Brotherhood*, New York: Oxford University Press, 2016.

3. Mohammed Ayoob and Danielle N. Lussier, *The Many Faces of Political Islam: Religion and Politics in Muslim Societies*, Ann Arbor: University of Michigan Press, 2020, 17.

4. In his book *Oilcraft*, political scientist Robert Vitalis offers a new perspective on the US' relationship to oil in the region. He argues that between the 1940s and 1973, the belief was that US firms operating Middle East concessions would translate into a strategic good for the US state. After 1973, US policy makers talked about guaranteeing access, not control (because the private firms had lost their concessions) over oil. Thus, he argues that it was never about control over oil. Robert Vitalis, *Oilcraft: The Myths of Scarcity and Security That Haunt U.S. Energy Policy*, Stanford, CA: Stanford University Press, 2020.

5. Douglas Little, *American Orientalism: The United States and the Middle East since 1945*, Chapel Hill: University of North Carolina Press, 2002, 194–95.

6. Little, *American Orientalism*, 27.

7. Little, *American Orientalism*, 195–96.

8. Dwight D. Eisenhower, "The Eisenhower Doctrine on the Middle East, A Message to Congress," *The Department of State Bulletin* 36: 917, January 21, 1957, 83–87, fordham.edu.

9. Richard Dreyfus, *Devil's Game: How the United States Helped Unleash Fundamentalist Islam*, New York: Henry Holt, 2005.

10. Quoted in Dreyfus, *Devil's Game*, 121.

11. Rachel Bronson, *Thicker than Oil: America's Uneasy Partnership with Saudi Arabia*, Oxford: Oxford University Press, 2006, 74.

12. Dreyfus, *Devil's Game*, 72–73.

13. Dreyfus, *Devil's Game*, 76–85.

14. Joyce Battle, ed., *US Propaganda in the Middle East: The Early Cold War Version*, National Security Archive Briefing Book 78, Washington, DC: National Security Archive, 2002, gwu.edu.

15. Battle, ed., *US Propaganda in the Middle East*, 20.

16. Dreyfus, *Devil's Game*.

17. Dreyfus, *Devil's Game*, 97–104.

18. Dreyfus, *Devil's Game*, 125.

19. Walter Laqueur, *Communism and Nationalism in the Middle East*, New York: Praeger, 1956, 6, emphasis in original.

20. Tareq Ismael, *The Communist Movement in the Arab World*, New York: Routledge, 2005.

21. Other examples of such nationalism in North Africa and South Asia include the National Liberation Front (FLN by its French initials) in Algeria, Sukarno in Indonesia, and Zulfikar Ali Bhutto in Pakistan.

22. Maxime Rodinson, *The Arabs*, Chicago: University of Chicago Press, 1979, 111.

23. Deepa Kumar, "The Right Kind of 'Islam': News Media Representations of US–Saudi Relations during the Cold War," *Journalism Studies* 19: 8, 2018, 1079–97.

24. Kumar, "The Right Kind of 'Islam.'"

25. Fawaz Gerges, *America and Political Islam: Clash of Cultures or Clash of Interests?* Cambridge: Cambridge University Press, 1999, 40.

26. Ervand Abrahamian, *Iran Between Two Revolutions*, Princeton, NJ: Princeton University Press, 1982.

27. For more about the dynamics of the Iranian Revolution, see Nikki Keddie, *Modern Iran: Roots and Results of Revolution*, New Haven, CT: Yale University Press, 2003; Maryam Poya, "Iran 1979: Long Live Revolution . . . Long Live Islam?" in Colin Barker, ed., *Revolutionary Rehearsals*, London: Bookmarks, 1987; and Saman Sepehri, "The Iranian Revolution," *International Socialist Review* 9, August–September 2000.

28. Ronald Reagan, "Remarks at the Annual Dinner of the Conservative Political Action Conference," speech delivered March 1, 1985, *Public Papers of the Presidents of the United States: Ronald Reagan, 1985, Book 1*, Washington, DC: United States Government Printing Office, 1988, 228.

29. S. Coll, "Anatomy of a Victory: CIA's Covert Afghan War," *Washington Post*, July 19, 1992, A1.

30. Reagan, "Remarks," 228.

31. Eisenhower approved $500,000 in aid for the reconstruction of a railroad to the holy sites of Islam. When King Saud visited the United States in 1957, he was promised $180 million in military and financial aid. Upon returning home, he commissioned the Bin Laden family to undertake reconstruction of the Grand Mosque in Mecca, and it was through this contract that the latter would amass great wealth. Madawi al-Rasheed, *A History of Saudi Arabia*, New York: Cambridge University Press, 2002, 118.

32. Gilles Kepel, *Jihad: The Trail of Political Islam*, Cambridge, MA: Belknap Press, 2003, 315.

33. Kepel, *Jihad*, 315.

34. Mamdani, *Good Muslim, Bad Muslim*, 130.

35. Gerges, *Journey of a Jihadist: Inside Islamic Militancy*, Boston: Mariner Press, 2007, 111.

36. Gerges, *Journey of a Jihadist*.

37. Kepel, *Jihad*, 10.

38. Tom Raum, "Bush Says Saddam Even Worse Than Hitler," AP News, November 1, 1990, apnews.com.

39. A. Rashid, *Taliban: Militant Islam, Oil and Fundamentalism in Central Asia*, New Haven, CT: Yale University Press, 2000.

40. R. Jackson, M. B. Smyth, and J. Gunning, eds., *Critical Terrorism Studies: A New Research Agenda*, New York: Routledge, 2009; E. Herman, *The Real Terror Network: Terrorism in Fact and Propaganda*, Boston, MA: South End Press, 1982.

41. Marc Sageman, *Misunderstanding Terrorism*, Philadelphia: University of Pennsylvania Press, 2017, 21.

42. Sageman, *Misunderstanding Terrorism*, 22.

43. M. McAlister, *Epic Encounters: Culture, Media, and US Interests in the Middle East since 1945*, Berkeley: University of California Press, 2005, 250.

44. Jasbir Puar, *Terrorist Assemblages: Homonationalism in Queer Times*, Durham, NC: Duke University Press, 2017; N. Fraser, *Fortunes of Feminism*, London: Verso, 2013.

45. Deepa Kumar, "National Security Culture: Gender, Race, and Class in the Production of Imperial Citizenship," *International Journal of Communication* 11, May 2017, 2154–77.

46. Quoted in Gilbert Achcar, *Eastern Cauldron: Islam, Afghanistan, Palestine and Iraq in a Marxist Mirror*, New York: Monthly Review Press, 2004, 37.

47. Kepel, *Jihad*, 10.

48. Chalmers Johnson, *Blowback: The Costs and Consequences of American Empire*, New York: Henry Holt, 2000, 11.

49. Lawrence Wright has suggested that Ramzi Yousef, the perpetrator of the attack, had spent time in an al-Qaeda camp in Afghanistan. Lawrence Wright, *The Looming Tower: Al-Qaeda and the Road to 9/11*, New York: Vintage, 2007.

50. Samih Farsoun, "Roots of the American Antiterrorism Crusade," in Elaine C. Hagopian, ed., *Civil Rights in Peril: The Targeting of Arabs and Muslims*, London: Pluto Press, 2004, 137.

51. James Astill, "Strike One," *Guardian*, October 2, 2001.

52. Gerges, *America and Political Islam*, 52.

53. Bernard Lewis, "The Roots of Muslim Rage," *Atlantic*, September 1990.

54. Samuel Huntington, *The Clash of Civilizations and the Remaking of World Order*, New York: Simon and Schuster, 1997.

55. Judith Miller, "The Challenge of Radical Islam," *Foreign Affairs*, Spring 1993.

56. See Gerges, *America and Political Islam*, 20–28.

57. One US diplomat expressed the logic and the underlying lack of regard for women's rights: "Taliban will develop like the Saudis did. There will be Aramco, pipelines, an emir, no parliament and lots of Sharia law. We can live with that." Quoted in Rashid, *Taliban*, 179.

58. Arun Kundnani, *The Muslims Are Coming: Islamophobia, Extremism, and the Domestic War on Terror*, London: Verso, 2015, 58.

59. This was a speech delivered by Edward Djerejian in 1992 and is quoted in Gerges, *America and Political Islam*, 80.

60. Gerges, *America and Political Islam*, 91.

61. Gary Dorien, *Imperial Designs: Neoconservatives and the New Pax Americana*, New York: Routledge, 2004.

62. Dorien, *Imperial Designs*, 7.

63. Stewart Patrick and Shepard Forman, *Multilateralism and US Foreign Policy: Ambivalent Engagement*, Boulder, CO: Lynne Rienner, 2002, 7.

64. Patrick and Forman, *Multilateralism and US Foreign Policy*, 7.

65. Danny Cooper, *Neoconservatism and American Foreign Policy: A Critical Analysis*, New York: Routledge, 2011, 14.

66. Dorien, *Imperial Designs*, 21.

67. Quoted in Dorien, *Imperial Designs*, 11.

68. Dorien, *Imperial Designs*, 13.

69. Charles Krauthammer, "The Unipolar Moment," *Foreign Affairs*, 1990.

70. Dorien, *Imperial Designs*, 39.

71. Dorien, *Imperial Designs*, 40.

72. Dorien, *Imperial Designs*, 40.

73. Andrew Bacevich, *American Empire: The Results and Consequences of US Diplomacy*, Cambridge: Harvard University Press, 2002, 45.

74. Maria Ryan, *Neoconservatism and the New American Century*, New York: Palgrave McMillan, 2010, 22.

75. Ryan, *Neoconservatism and the New American Century*, 14.

76. Quoted in Gerges, *America and Political Islam*, 24.

77. Max Boot, "What the Heck Is a 'Neocon'?," *Wall Street Journal*, December 30, 2002.

78. Richard Seymour, *The Liberal Defence of Murder*, London: Verso, 2008, 159–60.

79. Stephen Sniegoski, *The Transparent Cabal: The Neoconservative Agenda, War in the Middle East, and the National Interest of Israel*, Norfolk, VA: Enigma Editions, 2008, 84.

80. Sniegoski, *The Transparent Cabal*, 26.

81. Edward Said, "The Morning After," *London Review of Books*, October 21, 1993.

82. Quoted in Ryan, *Neoconservatism and the New American Century*, 34.

83. Dorien, *Imperial Designs*, 197.

84. Sniegoski, *Transparent Cabal*, 52.

85. Noam Chomsky, *The Fateful Triangle: The United States, Israel and the Palestinians*, Cambridge, MA: South End Press, 1999, 455.

86. Sniegoski, *The Transparent Cabal*, 5, emphasis in original.

87. Benjamin Netanyahu, ed., *International Terrorism: Challenge and Response*, New Brunswick, NJ: Transaction Books, 1981.

88. Netanyahu, ed., *International Terrorism*, 6.

89. All quotes taken from Netanyahu, ed., *International Terrorism*, 5.

90. Gilbert Achcar, *Arabs and the Holocaust: The Arab-Israeli War of Narratives*, New York: Metropolitan Books, 2009.

91. Achcar, *Arabs and the Holocaust*, 6.

92. Deepa Kumar, "Terrorcraft: Empire and the Making of the Racialized Terrorist Threat," *Race and Class* 62: 2, 2020, 34–60.

93. Netanyahu, foreword to *International Terrorism*.

94. Robert Moss, "The Terrorist State," in Netanyahu, ed., *International Terrorism*, 128.

95. Mordecai Abir, "The Arab World, Oil and Terrorism," in Netanyahu, ed., *International Terrorism*, 135–41.

96. Benjamin Netanyahu, ed., *Terrorism: How the West Can Win*, New York: Farrar, Strauss & Giroux, 1986, 12.

97. Netanyahu, ed., *Terrorism*, 11.

98. Bernard Lewis, "Islamic Terrorism?" in Netanyahu, ed., *International Terrorism*, 66.

99. Lewis, "Islamic Terrorism?" in Netanyahu, ed., *International Terrorism*, 67.

100. Elie Kedourie, "Political Terrorism in the Muslim World," in Netanyahu, ed., *International Terrorism*, 70.

101. Kedourie, "Political Terrorism in the Muslim World," 72.

102. Kedourie, "Political Terrorism in the Muslim World," 76.

103. Kumar, "Terrorcraft."

104. Quoted in Fred Halliday, *Islam and the Myth of Confrontation*, New York: I. B. Tauris, 2003, 190–91.

105. Halliday, *Islam and the Myth of Confrontation*.

106. Kumar, "Terrorcraft."

107. Ryan, *Neoconservatism and the New American Century*, 57.

108. Ryan, *Neoconservatism and the New American Century*, 57.

109. Uday Singh Mehta, *Liberalism and Empire: A Study in Nineteenth-Century British Liberal Thought*, Chicago: University of Chicago Press, 1999, 2.

110. Seymour, *Liberal Defence*, 23, emphasis added.

111. Jean Bricmont, *Humanitarian Imperialism: Using Human Rights to Sell War*, New York: Monthly Review Press, 2006, 20.

112. Stephen M. Walt, "What Intervention in Libya Tells Us about the Neocon-Liberal Alliance," *Foreign Policy*, March 21, 2011; on Walt's identification as a realist, see Stephen Walt, "Is Barack Obama More of a Realist Than I Am?," *Foreign Policy*, August 19, 2014.

113. Walt, "What Intervention in Libya Tells Us."

114. Quoted in Noam Chomsky, *The New Military Humanism*, Monroe, ME: Common Courage Press, 1999, 14.

115. Jean-Marc Coicaud, *Beyond the National Interest: The Failure of UN Peacekeeping and Multilateralism in an Era of U.S. Primacy*, Washington, DC: United States Institute of Peace Press, 2007, 119.

116. Coicaud, *Beyond the National Interest*, 117.

117. Chomsky, *The New Military Humanism*, 14.

118. See Stephen Sheehi, *Islamophobia: The Ideological Campaign against Muslims*, Atlanta, GA: Clarity Press, 2011.

119. Dreyfus, *Devil's Game*, 85.

120. Lee Wengraf, "Operation Restore Hope, 1992–1994," *International Socialist Review* 77, May–June 2011.

121. Phyllis Bennis, *Challenging Empire: How People, Governments, and the UN Defy US Power*, Northampton, MA: Olive Branch Press, 2006.

122. Quoted in Ryan, *Neoconservatism*, 78.

123. McAlister, *Epic Encounters*.

124. McAlister, *Epic Encounters*, 142.

125. Patrick and Fornan, *Multilateralism and US Foreign Policy*, 23.

126. Achcar, *Eastern Cauldron*, 38.

5. Empire's Changing Clothes: Bush, Obama, Trump

1. Project for the New American Century, *Rebuilding America's Defenses: Strategy, Forces and Resources for a New Century*, Washington, DC: Project for the New American Century, 2000, 9, newamericancentury.org.

2. Project for the New American Century, *Rebuilding America's Defenses*, 83.

3. Alex Lubin, *Never-Ending War on Terror*, Oakland: University of California Press, 2001.

4. G. John Ikenberry, "America's Imperial Ambition," *Foreign Affairs*, September/October 2002, 49.

5. Rashid Khalidi, *Resurrecting Empire: Western Footprints and America's Perilous Path in the Middle East*, Boston: Beacon Press, 2004.

6. Barry Posen, "The Rise of Illiberal Hegemony," *Foreign Affairs*, March/April 2018.

7. Richard A. Clarke, *Against All Enemies: Inside America's War on Terror*, New York: Free Press, 2004, 32.

8. United States Department of Defense, *National Security Strategy* (2010 USNSS 2), Washington, DC: Author, 2010.

9. United States Department of Defense, *National Security Strategy*.

10. Quoted in Anthony Arnove, "The Decade of the 'War on Terror,'" *Socialist Worker*, September 11, 2011.

11. Stephen Sheehi, *Islamophobia: The Ideological Campaign against Muslims*, Atlanta, GA: Clarity Press, 2011, 44.

12. Sheehi, *Islamophobia*, 78.

13. Quoted in Sheehi, *Islamophobia*, 78.

14. Danny Cooper, *Neoconservatism and American Foreign Policy: A Critical Analysis*, New York: Routledge, 2011, 92.

15. Sheehi, *Islamophobia*, 56.

16. Susan Faludi, *The Terror Dream: Fear and Fantasy in Post–9/11 America*, New York: Metropolitan Books, 2007.

17. Newsweek Staff, "Periscope," *Newsweek*, August 18, 2002.

18. Democracy Now, "Ret. Army General William Odom: The U.S. Should 'Cut and Run' from Iraq," *Democracy Now!*, October 5, 2005.

19. United States Army, *Insurgencies and Counterinsurgency*, Washington, DC: United States Department of Defense, 2006, fas.org, emphasis added.

20. Quoted in Laleh Khalili, *Time in the Shadow: Confinement in Counterinsurgencies*, Stanford, CA: Stanford University Press, 2013, 47.

21. James Udris, Michael Udris, and James Der Derian, *Human Terrain*, DVD, UDRIS Film and OXYOPIA Productions, Oley, PA: Bullfrog Films, 2010.

22. Khalili, *Time in the Shadow*, 47.

23. Leadership Group on U.S.–Muslim Engagement, "Changing Course: A New Direction for U.S. Relations with the Muslim World," Washington, DC: U.S.–Muslim Engagement Project, 2009, sfcg.org.

24. Barack Obama, "A New Beginning," YouTube, speech delivered in Cairo, Egypt, June 4, 2009.

25. Deepa Kumar, "Obama's Cairo Speech: A Rhetorical Shift in US Imperialism," MROnline, June 12, 2009, mronline.org.

26. Joseph S. Nye Sr., "Get Smart: Combining Hard and Soft Power," *Foreign Affairs*, July 2009.

27. Kundnani has argued that both liberals and conservatives view Islamism through the lens of totalitarianism as if it were akin to communism and fascism.

28. Ryan Lizza, "The Consequentialist," *New Yorker*, May 2, 2011.

29. United States Department of Defense, *National Security Strategy*, 3.

30. Ty Cobb, "The Defense Strategic Guidance: What's New, What Is the Focus, Is It Realistic?" *Harvard Law School National Security Journal*, January 8, 2012.

31. Kirit Radia, "Struggling to Control the Message, Hillary Clinton Completes Tough Trip Abroad," ABC News, November 4, 2009, abcnews.go.com.

32. United States Department of Defense, *Sustaining US Global Leadership: Priorities for 21st Century Defense*, Washington, DC: Author, 2012, permanent.fdlp.gov.

33. United States Department of Defense, *Sustaining U.S. Global Leadership*, 1.

34. Deepa Kumar, "Judicial Ruling Disastrous for Americans," limaohio.com, April 19, 2014.

35. Jo Becker and Shane Scott, "Secret 'Kill List' Proves a Test of Obama's Principles and Will: Taking Personal Role in War on Al Qaeda," *New York Times*, May 29, 2012.

36. Medea Benjamin, *Drone Warfare: Killing by Remote Control*, New York: OR Books, 2012, 9.

37. Benjamin, *Drone Warfare*, 2.

38. Benjamin, *Drone Warfare*, 2.

39. Benjamin, *Drone Warfare*, preface.

40. Benjamin, *Drone Warfare*, 6.

41. Adam Serwer, "Birtherism of a Nation," *Atlantic*, May 13, 2020.

42. Barry Posen, "The Rise of Illiberal Hegemony," *Foreign Affairs*, March/April 2018.

43. United States, *National Security Strategy*, December 2017, whitehouse.gov.

44. United States, *National Security Strategy*.

45. Walter Russell Mead, "Trump Brings Foreign Policy Back to Earth," *Wall Street Journal*, November 29, 2017.

46. Benjamin, *Drone Warfare.*

47. "Part Four: You Think Our Country's So Innocent?," *Intercepted*, October 19, 2020, theintercept.com.

48. S.E. Cupp, "Under Donald Trump, Drone Strikes Far Exceed Obama's Numbers," *Chicago Sun Times*, May 8, 2019.

49. Shuaib Almosawa, "Wedding Is Hit by Airstrike in Yemen, Killing More Than 20," *New York Times*, April 23, 2018.

50. The Bureau of Investigative Journalism, "Drone Warfare," thebureauinvestigates.com.

51. "Part Four: You Think Our Country's So Innocent?," *Intercepted.*

52. Helene Cooper and Mujib Mashal, "US Drops Mother of All Bombs on ISIS Caves in Afghanistan," *New York Times*, April 13, 2017.

53. US Air Forces Central, "Airpower Effects," September 20, 2020, afcent.af.mil.

54. Mujib Mashal, "Afghan and U.S. Forces Blamed for Killing More Civilians This Year Than Taliban Have," *New York Times*, July 30, 2019.

55. Congressional Research Service, "Afghanistan: Background and US Policy: In Brief," November 10, 2020, fas.org.

56. Donald Trump, "I Would Bomb the Shit out of 'em," YouTube, November 12, 2015.

57. Steve Mufson, "Trump's Illegal, Impossible, and 'Beyond Goofy' Idea of Seizing Iraq's Oil," *Washington Post*, September 9, 2016.

58. Igor Kosov, "Mosul Is Completely Destroyed," *Atlantic*, July 10, 2017.

59. Gilbert Achcar, *Morbid Symptoms*, Stanford, CA: Stanford University Press, 2016, 15–65.

60. Ruth Sherlock, "'This Is Not Liberation': Life in the Rubble of Raqqa, Syria," NPR, October 26, 2018, npr.org.

61. BBC News, "Six Charts That Show How Hard US Sanctions Have Hit Iran," BBC News, December 9, 2019.

62. Vali Nasr, "Trump's Policies Have Convinced Iran to Build a More Advanced Nuclear Program Before Negotiating," *Foreign Policy*, September 21, 2020.

63. Nolan McCaskell, "Trump Backs Away from 'Neutral Stance' on Israel," *Politico*, March 21, 2016.

64. Peter Beaumont and Oliver Holmes, "US Confirms Ending UN Funding for Palestinian Refugees," *Guardian*, August 31, 2018.

65. David Halbfinger and Isabel Kershner, "Pompeo Visits West Bank Settlement and Offers Parting Gifts to Israeli Right," *New York Times*, November 19, 2020.

66. David Herszenhorn, "Trump Praises Saudi Crown Prince, Ignores Questions on Khashoggi Killing," Politico, June 29, 2019.

67. Murtaza Hussain, "Trump, the War President, Leaves a Trail of Civilians Dead in Yemen," *Intercept*, October 29, 2020.

68. "Yemen: Biden to End US Offensive Support for Saudi-Led Assault, But Will the War Actually End?," *Democracy Now!*, February 5, 2021.

69. For a timeline, see ACLU, "Timeline of the Muslim Ban," aclu-wa.org.

70. Defending Democracy Together, "A Statement by Former Republican National Security Officials," defendingdemocracytogether.org.

71. Joseph Biden, Jr., "Why America Must Lead Again," *Foreign Affairs*, March/April 2020.

6. Terrorizing Muslims: Domestic Security and the Racialized Threat

1. Nikhil Pal Singh, *Race and America's Long War*, Oakland: University of California Press, 2017, xii.

2. Stephen Downs, *Victims of America's Dirty Wars: Tactics and Reasons from COINTELPRO to the War on Terror*, Albany, NY: Project Salam, 2012, 71, projectsalam.org.

3. Moustafa Bayoumi, *How Does it Feel to Be a Problem? Being Young and Arab in America*, New York: Penguin Books, 2008.

4. Louise Cainkar, *Homeland Insecurity: The Arab American and Muslim American Experience after 9/11*, New York: Russell Sage Foundation, 2011.

5. Neda Maghbouleh takes a long view of the Iranian American experience; she notes that the "specter of Iran was a racial hinge between white Europe and non-white Asia: a face, a body, a culture, and a concept that could open or close the door to whiteness as needed. Excavating Iranians out of the margins of these cases reveals how they have been rhetorically positioned both inside and outside white citizenship in the United States for over a century." Neda Maghbouleh, *The Limits of Whiteness: Iranian Americans and the Everyday Politics of Race*, Palo Alto, CA: Stanford University Press, 2017, 10.

6. Sunaina Maira, *Missing: Youth, Citizenship and Empire after 9/11*, Durham, NC: Duke University Press, 2009.

7. For an overview of various projects of race making, see Louise Cainkar, "Fluid Terror Threat: A Genealogy of the Racialization of Arab, Muslim, and South Asian Americans," *Amerasia Journal* 44: 1, 2018, 27–59. On South Asians, race, and ethnicity, see Junaid Rana, *Terrifying Muslims: Race and Labor in the South Asian Diaspora*, Durham, NC: Duke University Press, 2011; Sridevi Menon, "Where Is West Asia in Asian America? 'Asia' and the Politics of Space in Asian America," *Social Text* 24: 1, 2006, 55–79; Susan Koshy, "Category Crisis: South Asian Americans and the Question of Race and Ethnicity," *Diaspora* 7: 3, 1998, 285–320, 302; Vijay Prashad, *The Karma of Brown Folks*, Minneapolis:

University of Minnesota Press, 2001; Karen Leonard, *Making Ethnic Choices: California's Punjabi Mexican Americans*, Philadelphia, PA: Temple University Press, 1992.

8. Nadine Naber, "Imperial Whiteness and the Diasporas of Empire," *American Quarterly* 66: 4, 2014, 1107–15, 1112, emphasis in original.

9. Stephen Salisbury, *Mohamed's Ghosts: An American Story of Love and Fear in the Homeland*, New York: Nation Books, 2019, 128.

10. Junaid Rana, "The Racial Infrastructure of the Terror-Industrial Complex," *Social Text* 34: 4, 2016, 111–38.

11. Nadine Naber and Junaid Rana, "The 21st Century Problem of Anti-Muslim Racism," nadinenaber.com, n.d.

12. Naber, "Imperial Whiteness," 1112–13.

13. Arun Kundnani, *The Muslims Are Coming! Islamophobia, Extremism, and the Domestic War on Terror*, London: Verso, 2015.

14. Étienne Balibar, "Is There a 'Neo-Racism'?" in Étienne Balibar and Immanuel Wallerstein, *Race, Nation, Class: Ambiguous Identities*, London: Verso, 1991, 21.

15. Susan M. Akram and Kevin R. Johnson, "Race and Civil Rights Pre-September 11, 2001: The Targeting of Arabs and Muslims," in Elaine C. Hagopian, ed., *Civil Rights in Peril: The Targeting of Arabs and Muslims*, Chicago, Il: Haymarket Books, 2004, 9–26, 16.

16. Cited in Eric Love, *Islamophobia and Racism in America,* New York: New York University Press, 2017, 99.

17. Love, *Islamophobia and Racism.*

18. Love, *Islamophobia and Racism*, 99.

19. Nadine Naber, "Introduction" in Amaney Jamal and Nadine Naber, eds., *Race and Arab Americans Before and After 9/11: From Invisible Citizens to Visible Subjects*, Syracuse, NY: Syracuse University Press, 2008, 36.

20. Kathleen Moore, "A Closer Look at Anti-Terrorism Law: Arab-American Anti-Discrimination Committee v. Reno and the Construction of Aliens' Rights," in Michael Suleiman, ed., *Arabs in America: Building a New Future*, Philadelphia, PA: Temple University Press, 1999, 84–99, 89.

21. Moore, "A Closer Look at Anti-Terrorism Law," 90.

22. Will Parrish and Sam Levin, "'Treating Protest as Terrorism': US Plans Crackdown on Keystone XL Activists," *Guardian*, September 20, 2018.

23. Sahar Aziz, "A Muslim Registry: The Precursor to Internment?," *Brigham Young University Law Review* 101, 2018, 120.

24. Elaine C. Hagopian, ed., *Civil Rights in Peril: The Targeting of Arabs and Muslims*, London: Pluto Press, 2004, 18–19.

25. Akram and Johnson, "Race and Civil Rights."

26. Arun Kundnani, *The Muslims Are Coming*, 47.

27. Assia Boundaoui filed Freedom of Information Act (FOIA) requests and won a court case compelling the FBI to release information on Operation Vulgar Betrayal. In her documentary, some South Asians in the midst of a largely Arab American community were the targets of the operation. Various Pakistani Islamist groups were added to the Foreign Terrorist Organization list in the 1990s. It is likely that South Asians were also being surveilled through programs like Operation Vulgar Betrayal. We will not know the full extent of state surveillance of Arabs, Muslims, and South Asians until more FOIA requests are filed. See A. Boundaoui, *The Feeling of Being Watched*, documentary film, feelingofbeing-watched.com.

28. Uniting and Strengthening America by Providing Appropriate Tools Required to Intercept and Obstruct Terrorism Act of 2001, Pub. L. No.107–056, 115 Stat. 272 (2001); Enhanced Border Security and Visa Entry Reform Act of 2001, Pub. L. No. 107–173 (2001); Homeland Security Act of 2002, Pub. L. No. 107–296, 116 Stat. 2135 (2002).

29. Administration of George W. Bush, *Homeland Security Presidential Directive 2: Combating Terrorism through Immigration Policies,* October 29, 2001, fas.org.

30. U.S. Department of Homeland Security, "Creation of the Department of Homeland Security," September 24, 2015, dhs.gov.

31. Hagopian, ed., *Civil Rights in Peril*, 31.

32. Hagopian, ed., *Civil Rights in Peril*, 39.

33. See Nadine Naber, "Look, Muhammad the Terrorist Is Coming!" in Amaney Jamal and Nadine Naber, eds., *Race and Arab Americans Before and After 9/11: From Invisible Citizens to Visible Subjects,* Syracuse, NY: Syracuse University Press, 2008.

34. Nazia Hasan Kazi, *Islamophobia, Race, and Global Politics*, Oakland: University of California Press, 2019, 57.

35. Nadine Naber, "The Rules of Forced Engagement: Race, Gender, and the Culture of Fear among Arab Immigrants in San Francisco, Post-9/11," *Cultural Dynamics* 18: 3, 2006, 245.

36. Nancy Murray, "Arabs, Muslims and the Post-9/11 Hunt for the 'Enemy Within,'" in Elaine C. Hagopian, ed., *Civil Rights in Peril: The Targeting of Arabs and Muslims,* London: Pluto Press, 2004, 27–70, 44.

37. Salisbury, *Mohamed's Ghosts,* 125.

38. Cainkar, "Fluid Terror Threat," 58.

39. Nancy Murray, "Profiled," 36.

40. Murray, "Profiled," 37.

41. David Cole, "The New McCarthyism: Repeating History in the War on Terrorism," *Georgetown Law Faculty Publications and Other Works,* 2003, 74, scholarship.law.georgetown.edu.

42. Faiza Patel, *Rethinking Radicalization*, New York: New York University School of Law, 2011, 20.

43. For work on Muslims and the law, see the pioneering book by Kathleen M. Moore, *Al-Mughtaribun: American Law and the Transformation of Muslim Life in the United States*, Albany: State University of New York Press, 1995. And for a more recent book, see Cyra Akila Choudhury and Khaled A. Beydoun, eds., *Islamophobia and the Law*, Cambridge: Cambridge University Press, 2020.

44. Center for Human Rights and Global Justice, *Targeted and Entrapped: Manufacturing the "Homegrown Threat" in the United States*, New York: New York University School of Law, 2011, 10–11, chrgj.org/wp-content.

45. Leti Volpp, "The Citizen and the Terrorist," *UCLA Law Review* 49, 2002, 1575–1600.

46. Kundnani, *The Muslims Are Coming*, 97.

47. Associated Press, "Highlights of AP's Pulitzer-Prize Winning Probe into NYPD Intelligence Operations," ap.org, March 23, 2012.

48. David B. Caruso, "NYC Mayor, Yale Leader Spar over Muslim Spying," *USA Today*, February 22, 2012.

49. Alex Kane, "Newark Mayor and Yale President Slam NYPD Spying Program," Mondoweiss, February 24, 2012, http://mondoweiss.net/2012/02/newark-mayor-and-yale-university-head-slam-nypd-spying-program.html.

50. Glenn Greenwald and Murtaza Hussain, "Meet the Muslim-American Leaders the FBI and NSA Have Been Spying On," *Intercept*, July 9, 2014.

51. Jeremy Scahill and Ryan Devereaux, "Watch Commander: Barack Obama's Secret Terrorist-Tracking System, by the Numbers," *Intercept*, August 5, 2014.

52. Jeanne Theoharis, "Guantánamo at Home," *Nation*, April 2, 2009.

53. Center for Human Rights and Global Justice, Asian American Legal Defense and Education Fund, *Under the Radar: Muslims Deported, Detained, and Denied on Unsubstantiated Terrorism Allegations*, New York: New York University School of Law, 2011, chrgj.org.

54. Center for Human Rights and Global Justice, *Under the Radar*, 2.

55. Center for Human Rights and Global Justice, *Under the Radar*, 4.

56. Center for Human Rights and Global Justice, *Under the Radar*, 4–5.

57. Alia Malek, ed., *Patriot Acts: Narratives of Post–9/11 Injustice*, San Francisco: McSweeney's, 2011, 23, emphasis added.

58. Bayoumi, *How Does It Feel to Be a Problem?*, 26, emphasis added.

59. Stephen Downs and Kathy Manley, *Inventing Terrorists: The Lawfare of Preemptive Prosecution*, Albany, NY: Project SALAM and National Coalition to Protect Civil Freedoms, May 2014, 2, projectsalam.org.

60. Stephen Downs, *Victims of America's Dirty Wars: Tactics and Reasons*, Albany, NY: Project SALAM and National Coalition to Protect Civil Freedoms, February 2012, 17, projectsalam.org, emphasis in original.

61. For an analysis of Countering Violent Extremism programs involving the "suspect community," see Nicole Nguyen, *Suspect Communities: Anti-Muslim Racism and the Domestic War on Terror*, Minneapolis: University of Minnesota Press, 2019.

62. Kundnani, *The Muslims Are Coming*, 204–6, 220–22.

63. Kundnani, *The Muslims Are Coming.*

64. Clara Eroukhmanoff, *The Securitisation of Islam: Covert Racism and Affect in the United States Post-9/11*, Manchester: Manchester University Press, 2019, 57.

65. Michael Ratner, interview by Nicole Colson, "A New Stage in the War on Dissent," *Socialist Worker*, October 19, 2010.

66. Hamas effectively ruled only Gaza after the 2007 clashes when President Abbas dismissed the Hamas prime minister.

67. Downs, *Victims of America's Dirty Wars*, 22.

68. Downs, *Victims of America's Dirty Wars*, 14.

69. Jeanne Theoharis, "My Student, the 'Terrorist,'" *Chronicle of Higher Education*, April 3, 2011, http://chronicle.com/article/My-Student-the-Terrorist/126937/.

70. Theoharis, "My Student, the 'Terrorist.'"

71. Downs, *Victims of America's Dirty Wars*, 28.

72. Center for Human Rights and Global Justice, *Targeted and Entrapped*, 2.

73. Trevor Aaronson, *The Terror Factory: Inside the FBI's Manufactured War on Terrorism*, New York: Ig Publishing, 2013, 44.

74. Ed O'Keefe, "Transcript: Dianne Feinstein, Saxby Chambliss Explain, Defend NSA Phone Records Program," *Washington Post*, June 6, 2013.

75. Center for Human Rights and Global Justice, *Targeted and Entrapped*, 2

76. Center for Human Rights and Global Justice, *Targeted and Entrapped*, 2, emphasis in original.

77. Ted Conover, "The Pathetic Newburgh Four," *Slate*, November 23, 2010.

78. Conover, "The Pathetic Newburgh Four."

79. New American Foundation, "Terrorism in America after 9/11," newamerica.org.

80. Marc Sageman, *Misunderstanding Terrorism*, Philadelphia: University of Pennsylvania Press, 2016, 22.

81. John Mueller, *Overblown: How Politicians and the Terrorism Industry Inflate National Security Threats, and Why We Believe Them*, New York: Free Press, 2006; Charles Kurzman, *The Missing Martyrs: Why There Are so Few Muslim Terrorists*, Oxford: Oxford University Press, 2011.

82. Mitchell D. Silber and Arvin Bhatt, *Radicalization in the West: The Homegrown Threat*, New York: NYPD Intelligence Division, 2007, 5, nypdshield.org.

83. Quoted in Patel, *Rethinking Radicalization*, 15.

84. New American Foundation, "Terrorism in America after 9/11."

85. United States Department of Homeland Security, *Rightwing Extremism: Current*

Economic and Political Climate Fueling Resurgence in Radicalization and Recruitment, Washington, DC: Author, 2009, fas.org.

86. Associated Press, "Capitol Rioters Included Highly Trained Ex-Military and Cops," PBS NewsHour, Jan. 15, 2021, pbs.org.

87. Downs, *Victims of America's Dirty Wars*, 39.

88. Center for Human Rights and Global Justice, *Targeted and Entrapped*, 16.

89. Center for Human Rights and Global Justice, *Targeted and Entrapped*, 117.

90. Center for Human Rights and Global Justice, *Targeted and Entrapped*, 13.

91. Kundnani, *The Muslims Are Coming*, 186.

92. Arun Kundnani, "The FBI's 'Good' Muslims," *Nation*, September 19, 2011.

93. SourceWatch, "Taking the Fight to the Terrorists," sourcewatch.org, August 11, 2008.

94. The White House, "President Bush Delivers Graduation Speech at West Point," georgewbush-whitehouse.archives.org, June 1, 2002.

95. Deepa Kumar, "Jihad Jane: Constructing the New Muslim Enemy," *Fifth Estate Online*, April 2010, fifth-estate-online.co.uk (last accessed April 2011).

96. Anthony DiMaggio, "Fort Hood Fallout: Cultural Racism and Deteriorating Public Discourse on Islam," *Znet*, December 3, 2009.

97. Jerry Markon, "Pakistan Arrests Five Virginia Men at House with Jihadist Ties," *Washington Post*, December 10, 2009.

98. Tunku Varadarajan, "Going Muslim," *Forbes*, November 9, 2009.

99. Kundnani, *The Muslims*, 151–52.

100. Deepa Kumar and Arun Kundnani, "Imagining National Security: The CIA, Hollywood, and the War on Terror," *Democratic Communiqué* 26: 2, 2014, 72–83.

101. Jeremy Scahill, *Dirty Wars: The World Is a Battlefield*, New York: Nation Books, 2013, 519.

102. Amanda Simon, "President Obama Signs Indefinite Detention into Law," ACLU, December 1, 2011, aclu.org.

103. Naomi Wolf, "A Letter to Kathryn Bigelow on Zero Dark Thirty's Apology for Torture," *Guardian*, January 4, 2013.

104. "Ridge Says He Was Pressured to Raise Terror Alert," NBC News, August 20, 2009, nbcnews.com.

105. Deepa Kumar, "See Something, Say Something: Security Rituals, Affect, and US Nationalism from the Cold War to the War on Terror," *Public Culture* 30: 1, 2018, 143–71.

106. Kumar, "See Something, Say Something."

107. Barack Obama, "Empowering Local Partners to Prevent Violent Extremism in the United States," White House, August 2011, dhs.gov.

108. "NYPD Spied on Muslim Anti-Terror Partners," CBS News, October 6, 2011, cbsnews.com.

109. Eileen Sullivan, "White House Helps Pay for NYPD Muslim Surveillance," *Seattle Times,* February 27, 2012.

110. Ruth Wilson Gilmore has argued this case more generally about how Americans are deputized by the carceral state. "Ruth Wilson Gilmore Makes the Case for Abolition" (Part 1), interview with Jeremy Scahill, *Intercept,* June 10, 2020.

111. Sahar Aziz, "Policing Terrorists in the Community," *Harvard National Security Law Journal* 5: 147, 2014.

112. The New York Taxi Workers Alliance, "NYTWA Statement on Muslim Ban," n.d., nytwa.org.

113. Eli Blumenthal, "The Scene at JFK as Taxi Drivers Strike following Trump's Immigration Ban," *USA Today*, January 28, 2017.

114. Adam Chandler, "The Yemeni Bodega Strike," *Atlantic*, February 4, 2017.

115. Uri Friedman, "Where America's Terrorists Really Come From," *Atlantic*, January 30, 2017.

116. Rebecca Savransky, "'Giuliani: Trump Asked Me How to Do the Muslim Ban 'Legally'," *The Hill*, January 29, 2017.

117. Naber and Rana, "The 21st Century Problem of Anti-Muslim Racism."

118. Reuters Staff, "Trump Sets Record Low Limit for New US Refugees," reuters.com, October 28, 2020.

119. Associated Press, "Documents Show NYPD Infiltrated Liberal Groups," *New York Times*, March 23, 2012.

120. Rick Perlstein, "How FBI Entrapment Is Inventing 'Terrorists'—and Letting Bad Guys Off the Hook," *Rolling Stone*, May 15, 2012.

7. The New McCarthyites: The Right-wing Islamophobia Network and Their Liberal Enablers

1. The Council on American-Islamic Relations, "The Bias Brief: Trump's Impact on Anti-Muslim Bias," September 2019, islamophobia.org.

2. Bess Levin, "Surprise: Trump's Treasury Pick Said Obama Was a Muslim Who Took Orders from Terrorists," *Vanity Fair*, July 25, 2019.

3. Tina Nguyen, "Trump Suggests Obama Has a Secret Pro-Terrorist Agenda: 'There's Something Going On'," *Vanity Fair*, June 13, 2016.

4. Nathan Lean, *The Islamophobia Industry: How the Right Manufactures Fear of Muslims,* London: Pluto Press, 2012. See also Junaid Rana, "The Decade in American Islamophobia," *South Asian Magazine for Action and Reflection,* no. 37, 2011.

5. Wajahat Ali, Eli Clifton, Matthew Duss, Lee Fang, Scott Keyes, and Faiz Shakir, *Fear Inc.: The Roots of the Islamophobia Network in America*, Washington, DC: Center for American Progress, 2011, 22.

6. Wajahat Ali, Eli Clifton, Matthew Duss, Lee Fang, Scott Keyes, and Faiz Shakir, *Fear Inc.*, i.

7. Matthew Duss, Yasmine Taeb, Ken Gude, and Ken Sofer, *Fear, Inc. 2.0: The Islamophobia Network's Efforts to Manufacture Hate in America*, Washington, DC: Center for American Progress, 2015, 1.

8. David Caute, *The Great Fear: The Anti-Communist Purge under Truman and Eisenhower*, New York: Simon and Schuster, 1978.

9. Feisal Abdul Rauf, *What's Right with Islam: A New Vision for Muslims and the West*, New York: HarperCollins, 2005.

10. Ralph Blumenthal and Sharaf Mowjood, "Muslim Prayers and Renewal Near Ground Zero," *New York Times*, December 9, 2009.

11. Justin Elliot, "How the 'Ground Zero Mosque' Fear Mongering Began," *Salon*, August 16, 2010.

12. Laura Ingraham, interview with Daisy Khan, Fox News, December 21, 2009. Fox News Network filed copyright infringement notifications against sites that posted the video, and it no longer appears on the Fox News website.

13. Justin Lewis, *Constructing Public Opinion*, New York: Columbia University Press, 2001.

14. Pamela Geller, "Monster Mosque Pushes Ahead," *Atlas Shrugs*, May 6, 2010, pamelageller.com (last accessed May 2011).

15. Andrew Brown, "The Myth of Eurabia: How a Far-Right Conspiracy Theory Went Mainstream," *Guardian*, August 16, 2019.

16. Chris McGreal, "The US Blogger on a Mission to Halt 'Islamic Takeover'," *Guardian*, August 20, 2010.

17. Pamela Geller and Eliza Saxon, "Indomitable Israel," *Israel National News*, May 11, 2008.

18. Hilary Aked, Melissa Jones, and David Miller, "Islamophobia in Europe: How Governments Are Enabling the Far-Right 'Counter-Jihad' Movement," Public Interest Investigations, 2019.

19. See Aked et al., "Islamophobia in Europe," 7.

20. Ali et al., *Fear Inc.*, 1.

21. It is possible that on the twentieth anniversary of the events of 9/11, we might witness a similar spectacle.

22. Elliot, "How the 'Ground Zero Mosque' Fear Mongering Began."

23. Julie Shapiro, "Politicians Rally against Tea Party Bashing of World Trade Center Mosque," *DNAinfo*, May 20, 2010.

24. Oliver Willis, "Mark Williams Calls Allah a 'Monkey God,' Is He Still Welcome on CNN's Air?," *Media Matters for America*, May 18, 2010.

25. Ali et al., *Fear Inc*, 22.

26. Ali et al., *Fear Inc*, 30.

27. Edward Wyatt, "Three Republicans Criticize Obama's Endorsement of Mosque," *New York Times*, August 14, 2010.

28. Ali et al., *Fear Inc.*, 44.

29. Andy Barr, "Newt Compares Mosque to Nazis," *Politico*, August 16, 2010.

30. "The ADL Is Not an Ally," n.d., droptheadl.org.

31. Abraham Foxman, "The Mosque at Ground Zero," *Huffington Post*, August 2, 2010.

32. Elliot, "How the 'Ground Zero Mosque' Fear Mongering Began."

33. Adam Lisberg, "Mayor Bloomberg Stands Up for Mosque," *New York Daily News*, December 18, 2010.

34. David W. Dunlap, "When an Arab Enclave Thrived Downtown," *New York Times*, August 24, 2010.

35. Bobby Ghosh, "Islamophobia: Does America Have a Muslim Problem?" *Time*, August 30, 2010.

36. Moreover, *Time*'s cover just a few weeks prior to this issue featured an Afghan woman whose nose had been cut off, with the title "What Happens If We Leave Afghanistan"—both reinforcing the connection between Islam and violence against women and recycling the old "white man's burden" argument. See Aryn Baker, "Afghan Women and the Return of the Taliban," *Time*, August 9, 2010.

37. Rasmussen Reports, "20% Favor Mosque Near Ground Zero, 54% Oppose," *Rasmussen Reports*, July 22, 2010. See also Jordan Fabian, "Public Strongly Opposes Ground Zero Mosque," *The Hill*, August 11, 2010.

38. Brian Montopoli, "Nancy Pelosi Questions Funding of NYC Mosque Criticism," *CBS News Political Hotsheet*, August 18, 2010.

39. Chris Cillizza, "Democrats Divided over Proposed New York City Mosque," *Washington Post*, August 17, 2010.

40. Cillizza, "Democrats Divided over Proposed New York City Mosque."

41. Glenn Greenwald, "Howard Dean: 'Mosque' Should Move," *Salon*, August 18, 2010.

42. Tariq Ramadan, "Even Now, Muslims Must Have Faith in America," *Washington Post*, September 12, 2010.

43. Associated Press, "Obama Clarifies Statement in Mosque Debate," NBC New York, August 17, 2010.

44. David Jackson, "Obama: Quran Burning Is 'Stunt' that Threatens Troops," *USA Today*, September 9, 2010.

45. Mark Potok, "The 'Patriot' Movement Explodes," *Intelligence Reports*, no. 145, Spring 2012.

46. A few of us visited the mosque and saw that it was being used by Muslims in the area.

47. Andrea Elliot, "The Man Behind the Anti-Sharia Movement," *New York Times*, July 30, 2011.

48. Bob Smietana, "Anti-Muslim Crusaders Make Millions Selling Fear," *Tennessean*, October 24, 2010.

49. Max Blumenthal, "The Great Fear," *Tom Dispatch*, December 19, 2010.

50. Martin Kramer, *Ivory Towers on Sand: The Failures of Middle Eastern Studies in America*, Washington, DC: Washington Institute for Near East Policy, 2001.

51. Joel Beinin, "The New American McCarthyism: Policing Thought about the Middle East," *Race and Class* 46: 1, 2004, 109.

52. Beinin, "The New American McCarthyism," 110. Beinin quotes this assertion, and it was also cited on the media watchdog website SourceWatch. While the phrase has been taken down from the Campus Watch website, the site still links to articles that quote it; a campus-watch.org site search for the phrase "Middle East studies in the United States has become the preserve of Middle East Arabs" returned 123 articles on April 5, 2012.

53. David Horowitz, *The Professors: The 101 Most Dangerous Academics in America*, Washington, DC: Regnery, 2007.

54. Jeff Jacoby, "The Boston Mosque's Saudi Connection," *Boston Globe*, January 10, 2007.

55. Blumenthal, "The Great Fear."

56. Pamela Geller, "NYC Public School Madrassa a Failure," *Atlas Shrugs*, March 8, 2011, gellerreport.com.

57. Daniel Pipes, "A Madrassa Grows in Brooklyn," *New York Sun*, April 24, 2007.

58. Chuck Bennet and Jana Winter, "City Principal Is 'Revolting,'" *New York Post*, August 6, 2007.

59. Bennet and Winter, "City Principal Is 'Revolting.'"

60. Beinin, "The New American McCarthyism," 103.

61. The AVOT website has been taken down. This quote was taken from their website when it was still operational and was part of the first edition of this book. See also http://militarist-monitor.org/profile/Americans_for_Victory_over_Terrorism/

62. William Kristol and Robert Kagan, "Toward a Neo-Reaganite Foreign Policy," *Foreign Affairs*, July 1, 1996.

63. Maria Ryan, *Neoconservatism and the New American Century*, New York: Palgrave McMillan, 2010, 79.

64. Ryan, *Neoconservatism and the New American Century*, 79.

65. Danny Cooper, *Neoconservatism and American Foreign Policy: A Critical Analysis*, New York: Routledge, 2011, 12.

66. Cooper, *Neoconservatism and American Foreign Policy*, 12.

67. Gary Dorrien, *Imperial Designs: Neoconservatives and the New Pax Americana*, New York: Routledge, 2004, 2.

68. Andrea Elliot, "The Man Behind the Anti-Shariah Movement," *New York Times*, July 30, 2011.

69. For instance, Edward Luttwak, a fellow at the realist/liberal imperialist think tank Center for Strategic and International Studies, wrote an op-ed piece in the *New York Times* that was "anti-Muslim, and altogether Islamophobic to an unprecedented and scandalous degree," wrote Dabashi in *Brown Skin, White Masks* (London: Pluto Press, 2011, 121). The essence of Luttwak's argument was that Obama is a Muslim (because his father was Muslim) and that because he had adopted Christianity, Muslims were bound by their religion to execute him.

70. Thomas Friedman, "Green Shoots in Palestine," *New York Times*, August 4, 2009.

71. Emma Brockes, "Ayaan Hirsi Ali: 'Why Are Muslims so Hypersensitive?,'" *Guardian*, May 7, 2010.

72. Quoted in Sheehi, *Islamophobia*, 103.

73. David Horowitz, *Unholy Alliance: Radical Islam and the American Left*, Washington, DC: Regnery, 2004; Andrew McCarthy, *The Grand Jihad: How Islam and the Left Sabotage America*, New York: Encounter Books, 2010.

74. The origins of this argument go back to the 1980s and the influential conferences organized by the Zionist Jonathan Institute.

75. Ali et al., *Fear Inc.*, 3.

76. Steven Emerson, *American Jihad: The Terrorists Living among Us*, New York: Free Press, 2002; Steven Emerson, *Jihad Incorporated: A Guide to Militant Islam in the US*, Amherst, NY: Prometheus Books, 2006.

77. Ali et al., *Fear Inc.*, 51.

78. Debbie Schlussel, "HAMASGOP: Chris Christie Calls Opponents of Hamas "Crazies," Debbie Schlussel Blog, July 29, 2011, debbieschlussel.com.

79. Ali et al., *Fear Inc.*, 41.

80. Ali et al., *Fear Inc.*, 37.

81. Swathi Shanmugasundaram, "Anti-Sharia Law Bills in the United States," Southern Poverty Law Center, February 5, 2018, splcenter.org.

82. Shanmugasundaram, "Anti-Sharia Law Bills in the United States," 39.

83. P. David Gaubatz and Paul Sperry, *Muslim Mafia: Inside the Secret Underworld that's Conspiring to Islamize America*, Los Angeles: WND Books, 2009.

84. David Horowitz, "Muslim Liars: How the Muslim Students Association Deceives the Naïve," *FrontPage Magazine*, April 27, 2011.

85. See the list of interviewees at The Clarion Project, "The Third Jihad: Radical Islam's Vision for America," thethirdjihad.com.

86. Ali et al., *Fear Inc.*, 14.

87. Hilary Aked, Melissa Jones, and David Miller, "Islamophobia in Europe," 48.

88. Hilary Aked, Melissa Jones, and David Miller, "Islamophobia in Europe," 49.

89. Hilary Aked, Melissa Jones, and David Miller, "Islamophobia in Europe," 50.

90. Hilary Aked, Melissa Jones, and David Miller, "Islamophobia in Europe," 51.

91. Blumenthal, "The Great Fear."

92. Nicole Naurath, "Most Muslim Americans See No Justification for Violence," Abu Dhabi Gallup Center, August 2, 2011.

93. Samih Farsoun, "Roots of the American Antiterrorism Crusade," in Elaine C. Hagopian, ed., *Civil Rights in Peril: The Targeting of Arabs and Muslims*, London: Pluto Press, 2004, 150–52.

94. Elaine Hagopian, "The Interlocking of Right-Wing Politics and US Middle East Policy: Solidifying Arab/Muslim Demonization," in Hagopian, ed., *Civil Rights in Peril*, 194.

95. Quoted in Hagopian, "The Interlocking of Right-Wing Politics and US Middle East Policy," 152.

96. Ali et al., *Fear Inc.*, 75.

97. Ali et al., *Fear Inc.*, Chapter 3.

98. Ali et al., *Fear Inc.*, 64.

99. Ali et al., *Fear Inc.*, 66.

100. Brigitte Gabriel, *Because They Hate: A Survivor of Islamic Terror Warns America*, New York: St. Martin's Press, 2006.

101. Ali et al., *Fear Inc.*, 58.

102. Nonie Darwish, *Now They Call Me Infidel: Why I Renounced Jihad for America, Israel and the War on Terror*, New York: Penguin Random House, 2006; Nonie Darwish, *Cruel and Unusual Punishment: The Terrifying Global Implications of Islamic Law*, Nashville, TN: Thomas Nelson, 2008.

103. Thomas Cincotta, *Manufacturing the Muslim Menace: Private Firms, Public Servants, and the Threat to Rights and Security*, Somerville, MA: Political Research Associates, 2011.

104. Cincotta, *Manufacturing the Muslim Menace*, 15.

105. Walid Phares, *Future Jihad: Terrorist Strategies Against America*, New York: St. Martin's Press, 2005; Walid Phares, *The War of Ideas: Jihadism Against Democracy*, New York: St. Martin's Press, 2007; and *The Confrontation: Winning the War Against Future Jihad*, New York: Palgrave Macmillan, 2008.

106. Cincotta, *Manufacturing the Muslim Menace*, 31.

107. Cincotta, *Manufacturing the Muslim Menace*, 31.

108. Ali et al., *Fear Inc.*, 57, emphasis added.

109. Ali et al., *Fear Inc.*, 57.

110. Cincotta, *Manufacturing the Muslim Menace*, 23.

111. Spencer Ackerman, "FBI's '101 Guide' Depicted Muslims as 7th-Century Simpletons," *Wired*, July 27, 2011.

112. Spencer Ackerman, "Obama Orders Government to Clean Up Terror Training," *Wired*, November 29, 2011.

113. Anderson Cooper, interview with Walid Shoebat, *Anderson Cooper 360*, CNN, July 13, 2011.

114. Will Youmans, "The New Cold Warriors," in Hagopian, ed., *Civil Rights in Peril*, 111.

115. Youmans, "The New Cold Warriors," 112.

116. WND Staff, "Congressman: Muslims 'Enemy Amongst Us,'" WND, February 13, 2004.

117. Ali et al., *Fear Inc.*, 86.

118. Ali et al., *Fear Inc.*, 41.

119. Dabashi, *Brown Skin, White Masks*, 72–73.

120. Dabashi, *Brown Skin, White Masks*, 35.

121. Sheehi, *Islamophobia*, 97.

122. Ayaan Hirsi Ali, *Infidel*, New York: Simon and Schuster, 2007; *Nomad: From Islam to America: A Personal Journey through the Clash of Civilizations*, New York: Atria, 2010; *Heretic: Why Islam Needs a Reformation Now*, New York: HarperCollins, 2015.

123. Dabashi, *Brown Skin, White Masks*, 14.

124. Azar Nafisi, *Reading Lolita in Tehran*, New York: Random House, 2008.

125. Dabashi, *Brown Skin, White Masks*, 76.

126. Fatemeh Keshavarz, *Jasmine and Stars: Reading More than Lolita in Tehran*, Chapel Hill: University of North Carolina Press, 2007, 3.

127. Keshavarz, *Jasmine and Stars*, 29.

128. Josh Duboff, "Brooklyn College Required Reading Proves Controversial," *New York Magazine*, September 1, 2010.

129. Duboff, Brooklyn College Required Reading Proves Controversial," 35–36.

130. Arun Kundnani, "Islamism and the Roots of Liberal Rage," *Race and Class* 50: 2, 2008, 40–68.

131. Kundnani, "Islamism and the Roots of Liberal Rage," 42.

132. Christopher Hitchens, *God Is Not Great: How Religion Poisons Everything*, New York: Hatchette Book Group, 2007.

133. Richard Seymour, *The Liberal Defence of Murder*, London: Verso, 2008, 241–42.

134. Nathan Lear, "Dawkins, Harris, Hitchens: New Atheists Flirt with Islamophobia," *Salon*, March 20, 2013.

135. Sarah Wildman, "Geer Wilders, the Islamophobe Some Call the Dutch Donald Trump, Explained," *Vox*, March 15, 2017.

136. Lear, "Dawkins, Harris, Hitchens," 12.

137. Lear, "Dawkins, Harris, Hitchens," 12.

138. Kundnani, "Islamism and the Roots of Liberal Rage," 44.

139. See, for example, Norman Podhoretz, *World War IV: The Long Struggle Against Islamofascism*, New York: Doubleday, 2007.

140. Youmans, "The New Cold Warriors," 119.

141. "The ADL Is Not Our Ally," droptheadl.org, n.d.

142. "History of Targeting and Surveiling Progressive Movements," droptheadl.org, n.d.

143. W. E. B. Dubois, *The Souls of Black Folk,* CreateSpace Independent Publishing Platform, 2014.

144. Zareena Grewal, *Islam Is a Foreign Country: American Muslims and the Global Crisis of Authority*, New York: New York University Press, 2013, 302.

145. "Encouraging Cooperation with Law Enforcement," cair.org, n.d.

146. Stephen Sheehi, "Duplicity and Fear: Toward a Race and Class Critique of Islamophobia," in Sohail Daulatzai and Junaid Rana, eds., *With Stones in Our Hands: Writings on Muslims, Racism, and Empire,* Minneapolis: University of Minnesota Press, 2018, 35–55, 36–37.

147. Sheehi, "Duplicity and Fear," 48.

148. Sheehi, "Duplicity and Fear," 49–50.

149. Nazia Kazi, *Islamophobia, Race and Global Politics*, Lanham, MD: Rowman and Littlefield, 2019, 96.

150. Khizr Khan, *This Is Our Constitution: Discover America with a Gold Star Father*, New York: Knopf, 2017.

151. Mehdi Hasan, "Mike Pompeo Has Extreme Views on Islam—and Liberals Don't Seem to Care," *Intercept*, August 2019.

152. Dan Spinelli, "Meet the Iran Hawks Inside Trump's Administration," *Mother Jones*, January 3, 2020.

153. Pamela Geller with Robert Spencer, *The Post-American Presidency: The Obama Administration's War on America*, New York: Threshold Editions, 2010; Christopher Mathias, "John Bolton's Anti-Muslim Hate," *Huffington Post*, March 23, 2018.

154. Josh Harkinson, "The Dark History of the White House Aides Who Drafted Trump's Muslim Ban," *Mother Jones*, January 30, 2017.

155. James M. Lindsay, "The 2020 Election by the Numbers," Council on Foreign Relations, December 15, 2020, cfr.org.

156. Kevin Roose, "What Is QAnon, the Viral Pro-Trump Conspiracy Theory?" *New York Times*, January 17, 2021.

157. Sheren Khalel, "Masks to Sharia: QAnon Is Spreading Muslim Ideology Via Coronavirus Opposition," *Middle East Eye*, July 29, 2020.

Conclusion: Empire and the Matrix of Anti-Muslim Racism

1. Quoted in Thomas McCormick, *America's Half Century: United States Foreign Policy in the Cold War and After,* Baltimore, MD: Johns Hopkins University Press, 1995, 33. For more on US political strategy during World War II, see

Gabriel Kolko, *The Politics of War: The World and United States Foreign Policy, 1943–1945*, New York: Pantheon, 1990.

2. This was the famed advice that Senator Arthur Vandenberg offered to Harry Truman to sell support for aid to Greece and Turkey, a tactic that would be repeated with the Marshall Plan and the vast increases in military spending. McCormick, *America's Half Century*, 77ff.

3. McCormick, *America's Half Century*, 97–98.

4. Cited in Junaid Rana, "The Racial Infrastructure of the Terror-Industrial Complex," *Social Text* 34: 4, 2016, 111–38.

5. Department of Homeland Security, "Fusion Centers," September 19, 2019, dhs.gov.

6. See Alfred W. McCoy, *Policing America's Empire: The United States, the Philippines, and the Rise of the Surveillance State*, Madison: University of Wisconsin Press, 2009.

7. Charles Kurzman, *The Missing Martyrs: Why Are There So Few Muslim Terrorists?* New York: Oxford University Press, 2011.

8. "Calls to Suspend Syrian Refugee and Other Recent Anti-Muslim Statements by Government Officials," Institute for Public Accuracy, December 15, 2015, accuracy.org.

9. Lawrence Davidson, *Foreign Policy, Inc.: Privatizing America's National Interest*, Lexington: University Press of Kentucky, 2009.

10. William J. Boykin et al., *Shariah: The Threat to America*, Washington, DC: Center for Security Policy, 2010.

11. Boykin et al., *Shariah*.

12. Noah Schachtman and Spencer Ackerman, "US Military Officers Taught: 'Use Hiroshima,'" *Wired*, May 10, 2012.

13. Schachtman and Ackerman, "US Military Officers Taught."

14. Stuart Hall, Chas Critcher, Tony Jefferson, John Clarke, and Brian Roberts, *Policing the Crisis: Mugging, the State, and Law and Order*, 2d ed., London: Red Globe Press, 2013, 16.

15. See Jack Bratich, "Civil Society Must Be Defended: Misinformation, Moral Panics, and Wars of Restoration," *Communication, Culture and Critique* 13: 3, September 2020, 311–32.

16. See also my "dominance-resistance" model of the media in *Outside the Box: Corporate Media, Globalization and the UPS Strike*, Champaign: University of Illinois Press, 2007.

17. Deepa Kumar and Arun Kundnani, "Imagining National Security: The CIA, Hollywood, and the War on Terror," *Democratic Communiqué* 26: 2, 2014, 76.

18. Deepa Kumar and Arun Kundnani, "Imagining National Security", 76.

19. Michael Powell, "In Police Training, a Dark Film on US Muslims," *New York Times*, January 24, 2012.

20. Alex Kotch, "Exposed: Major Charities Are Helping Anonymous Donors Fund Anti-Muslim Films," *Sludge*, March 6, 2019, readsludge.com.

21. Elizabeth Poole, Eva Haifa Giraud, and Ed de Quincey, "Tactical Interventions in Online Hate Speech: The Case of #stopIslam," *New Media and Society*, March 3, 2020.

22. Hisham Aidi, *Rebel Music: Race, Empire, and the New Muslim Youth Cult*, New York: Vintage, 2019.

23. Nadine Naber, "So Our History Doesn't Become Your Future: The Local and Global Politics of Coalition Building After 9/11," *Journal of Asian American Studies* 5: 3, 2002, 217–18.

24. Nadine Naber and Junaid Rana, "The 21st Century Problem of Anti-Muslim Racism," nadinenaber.com, n.d.

25. Simret Aklilu, "Public Support for the Black Lives Matter Movement Has Dropped since June, Report Finds," CNN, September 22, 2020, cnn.com.

26. Jeremy Scahill, "Scholar Robin D. G. Kelley on How Today's Abolitionist Movement Can Fundamentally Change the Country," *Intercept*, June 27, 2020.

27. Naber and Rana, "The 21st Century Problem of Anti-Muslim Racism."

28. Jade Saab, ed., *A Region in Revolt: Mapping the Recent Uprisings in North Africa and West Asia*, Amsterdam, The Netherlands: Transnational Institute, 2020.

Index